WORLD FOOD RESOURCES
Actual and Potential

MICHAEL ALLABY

APPLIED SCIENCE PUBLISHERS LTD
LONDON

APPLIED SCIENCE PUBLISHERS LTD
RIPPLE ROAD, BARKING, ESSEX, ENGLAND

ISBN: 0 85334 731 X

WITH 87 TABLES AND 22 ILLUSTRATIONS

Printed in Great Britain by Galliard (Printers) Ltd, Great Yarmouth, Norfolk

WORLD FOOD RESOURCES
Actual and Potential

PREFACE

Is there a world food problem? The question must seem bizarre, yet the very complexity of the issues surrounding the production and distribution of food makes the doubt more reasonable than it may seem. Certainly any view which bases itself on a concept of a single unified world, in which there is a population and a kind of global farm, is so simplistic as to be meaningless. The real world is not unified; there is no global farm. Calculations of the theoretical limits of world food production, of the human carrying capacity of the planet, are at best academic, at worst dangerous, for they may lead us to suppose that the problem can be made to disappear if we attack it with an adequate armoury of computers.

In this book I have not tried to answer the questions. I do not know whether, in the years ahead, we will live in plenty or in want. All that I can try to do is to trace a sometimes tortuous path through the mountains and oceans of information that have accumulated.

I begin by outlining the present state of food production, paying particular attention to the major exporting regions and to the regions where shortages are most acute. I try to evaluate the arguments surrounding the 'population explosion'—another grossly simplified concept—and to relate population growth with the demand for food. I describe the theories underlying the 'Green Revolution' and the facts of its implementation, and I even go so far, in Chapter 4, as to attempt to compile a kind of inventory of the resources available to us for food production. I outline the history of agriculture and the nature of the changes that have taken place, during that history, in the ways in which we feed ourselves, continuing with this theme to explore the energy and genetic implications of modern farming. I consider some of the current theories of climate change, and then look at some of the research that may help farmers to grow more in the years to come. Farming, though, is such an old business, and farmers have acquired such a range of skills, that always there are dangers of rediscovering the wheel, of devising a cunning new technique that in some odd corner peasants have been practising for centuries. I suppose the most classic example of this is the scientific discovery that soya could be used to fortify the diets of Asian peoples who were short of protein, whereas the Chinese, with their traditional soy sauce, have been doing just that since the dawn of time. I also consider the contribution that is, or could be, made by the oceans—from conventional fishing and from aquaculture.

I think, though, that it is the final three chapters that are the most relevant, for as I wind my way through the data a pattern begins to emerge. I claim no originality for the discovery that if there is a world food problem it is not really susceptible to agricultural solutions. I know of no agricultural problems that cannot be solved using technologies—often well tried—that are available now or that will be available in the near future. The real problems are political, economic, social. Most of the people who are hungry are hungry because they lack the means to buy the food they need. Most of the farms that are underproductive are underproductive because the demand for food is too small or because they are trapped in a system of land tenure that makes it almost impossible for poor farmers to grow more, or both.

There are many general books on the world food situation. I have read some of them, and in this book I have tried to remedy their main deficiency for those who wish to pursue the subject a little further. I have included a great deal of data, in the form of tables of statistics, so that my interpretations of fact can at least be tested against the facts I have used.

The book is mine and I accept full responsibility for it, but many people have helped me, sometimes without even knowing it, simply by providing a new idea or a new interpretation. For space reasons I cannot acknowledge all of them, but I must thank a few: Fred Roberts who suggested the book in the first place and helped to prepare its initial outline; Kenneth Dahlberg of the University of Western Michigan; the Rev. Alain Blancy of the Ecumenical Institute, Bossey; Sam Smith of Manchester University; Stuart B. Hill of McGill University; Peter Stone, Editor of *Development Forum*; Brian Johnson of the University of Sussex; the staff of the Marine Biological Association in Plymouth; Lawrence D. Hills of the Henry Doubleday Research Association; Colin Hines of Earth Resources Research Limited; Domenico Schirone of FAO in Rome; and Roger F. Puterbaugh of the US Embassy in London.

MICHAEL ALLABY

CONTENTS

Chapter 1

WORLD FOOD—FEAST OR FAMINE?

In 1972 many people realised for the first time that the world was short of food. The poor of the world had known this, and at first hand, for some years and many informed and thoughtful citizens in the developed countries had known it too, although their knowledge was theoretical. It was in 1972 that, for the first time, the effects in the form of shortages of some food items and rapid rises in the prices of most foods were generally felt.

No country today is free entirely from world trade in food. As with any other commodity they are either net exporters or net importers. The USA, the world's largest producer and exporter of food, is also a major importer. When the world has surpluses, prices fall and unless steps are taken internally to protect them, American farmers suffer. When the world is short of food, prices rise and American livestock farmers may find themselves having to pay higher prices for feedingstuffs, because they are buying in competition with overseas buyers. Indeed, there have been occasions when US domestic production of feedingstuffs has been oversold abroad, leading to actual shortages at home.

At the other extreme among developed countries, the UK, which imports roughly half of its food, finds it very difficult to protect its own farmers from violent fluctuations in world prices. Table 1.1 shows that between 1971 and 1973 the price of wheat on world markets increased by 124 %, that of rice by 185 %, that of maize by 69 % and that of soybeans by 130 %. In each case the largest part of these rises occurred in the autumn of 1972. In 1974 prices continued to rise. In February, wheat reached a peak, 255 % above its 1971 level; rice reached a peak in April 1974 that was 388 % higher than the 1971 level; maize cost 125 % of its 1971 price in February. Soybeans peaked earlier. In June 1973 they cost 273 % more than they had cost in 1971.

Quite clearly the world had gone mad. In the words of an FAO (Food and Agriculture Organisation of the United Nations) official document, 'history records more acute shortages in individual countries, but it is doubtful whether such a critical food situation has ever been so worldwide'.[1]

Not only had the world gone mad but the world that went mad was one very different from the world that existed at any previous time. It was a world divided deeply between rich and poor nations, in which the rich had learned to export inflation in the interest of their own internal economies, just as, much earlier, they had learned to export unemployment by insisting that the processing of primary products be conducted on their own soil.

TABLE 1.1
Recent Changes in Export Prices of Selected Agricultural Commodities

	Wheat (US no. 2, hard winter, ordinary f.o.b. Gulf)	*Rice (Thai, white 5% f.o.b. Bangkok)*	*Maize (Yellow no. 2 f.o.b. Gulf)*	*Soybeans (US, c.i.f. Rotterdam)*
		(US $ per tonne)		
1971	62	129	58	126
1972	70	151	56	140
1973	139	368[a]	98	290
1972 January	60	131	51	125
June	60	136	53	138
December	104	186	69	174
1973 January	108	179	79	214
June	106	205[b]	102	470
December	199	521	113	254
1974 January	214	538	122	261
February	220	575	131	271
March	191	603	126	265
April	162	630	114	235
May	142	625	114	227[c]
June	156[d]	596	117[d]	—
July	169[d]	517[d]	135[d]	—

[a] Since Thai rice was not quoted regularly on the world market from the second week of March to November 1973, the annual average is an approximation based on the few quotations available.
[b] First week of March.
[c] First three weeks.
[d] Last three weeks of the month.
(Source: UN WFC E/Conf. 65/3).

The export of inflation is linked very closely with the export of hunger. This point needs emphasis, for the world food problem of the latter part of the twentieth century (there has usually been a food problem of some kind) is far less an agricultural problem than one of economics, politics and sociology.

Prior to this century, world trade in staple food items was minimal, although the UK became dependent on imported wheat in the eighteenth century. At that time a harvest failure in any country, or in any region of the world, would be followed by high prices and, perhaps, shortages in that country or region. While the wealthier classes paid higher prices for their food, the poorest might find themselves priced out of the market altogether. Acute shortages, leading to famine, could and did occur for several years at a time. They might develop slowly, as year after year supply failed to meet basic biological needs, the effect being masked by the fact that supply always met the effective economic demand. A point might be reached when the poor—then, as now, generally living in rural areas—were forced to eat their seed, leaving too little for sowing for the following year. That was when the famine took hold and it might take several years to pass. Famines were occasional, however. Were they to be repeated in the same area for more than a very few years in succession, the inhabitants of that area would migrate to a more hospitable environment.

Today the situation has changed. Food moves across the world in very large quantities. World trade in cereals in the period 1969–71 was valued at $6077 million.[2] In 1971 the world produced a total of 353·88 million tonnes of wheat, of which 16% entered world trade, and a total of 199·10 million tonnes of rice, of which 4·6% entered world trade. By 1973, 21·6% of the world's wheat was being traded and about 4·4%, but of an increased production, of rice.[3] Thus a country that can afford to do so may enter world markets as a buyer to make good what otherwise would be a shortfall in domestic supplies resulting from its own harvest failure. Temporarily, the importer buys a little land overseas. The result, inevitably, is felt as a pressure on supplies throughout the world and a consequent rise in prices. Any increase in prices is felt most acutely by the poor, and today the poor tend to be concentrated in the developing countries, so that it is those countries that are most likely to find themselves short of the foreign exchange they need to import food.

If the world's main producers of food were in the developing countries, all would be well. Shortages in the developed countries would lead to increased prices which the rich could afford to pay and which would benefit the poor. Unhappily, the reverse is true. The major food producers are in the rich countries where, by and large, they enjoy climates more favourable to farming. Because they are rich they are able to obtain more than their fair share of fertilisers, and they have easier access to the capital needed for investment in production machinery, better storage and distribution, and expensive projects such as irrigation schemes. Because they produce large surpluses of food they are able to ensure their own security of supply. If necessary, food can be diverted from export into the home markets and although export earnings are lost, internal prices are held down to levels that are acceptable to the public—the voters.

In this way, potential shortages are distributed throughout the world, where they are experienced by the poorer sections of the populations of the poor countries. Famine has been exported, along with the inflation that causes it.

The problem does not end there, for while famine in any particular region may be a rare phenomenon, famine somewhere in the world is rather common. Under the present economic order, no matter where the famine ought to be, it is transferred to the poor, even if basically they are living amid plenty, and it is repeated year after year. It is only with a thriving and probably protectionist economy that a country can isolate internal prices from those prevailing in the world at large.

This is bad enough, but even then the shortages are not distributed evenly. Some poor countries are affected more severely than others. The FAO has identified the countries that are affected most severely (and has labelled them the MSA—most seriously affected—countries): Bangladesh,

TABLE 1.2
Estimated Import Requirements of Cereals of the Most Seriously Affected (MSA) Countries[a] in 1974/75, Known Commercial Purchase and Contracts, and Food Aid Commitments as of mid-February 1975

	1973/74		1974/75				
	Total imports	*Food aid*	*Total import require-ments*	*Covered by commercial purchases or commitments*	*Food aid committed*	*Estimated to be not yet covered quantity*	*Estimated to be not yet covered est. value including freight (million US $)*
			(million tons)				
Wheat	8·5	1·6	13·7	8·6	2·3	2·3	534
Rice[b]	1·0	0·3	1·4	0·4	0·2	0·8	324
Coarse grains	2·9	0·3	1·9	0·7	0·2	1·0	195
Total	12·4	2·2	17·0	9·7	2·7	4·1	1053

[a] See text for the list of MSA countries.
[b] Calendar years 1974 and 1975.
(Source: UN WFC/11, 17 April, 1975).

Cameroon, Central African Republic, Chad, Dahomey, El Salvador, Ethiopia, Ghana, Guinea, Guyana, Haiti, Honduras, India, Ivory Coast, Kenya, Khmer Republic, Laos, Lesotho, Madagascar, Mali, Mauritania, Niger, Pakistan, Senegal, Sierra Leone, Somalia, Sri Lanka, Sudan, Tanzania, Upper Volta, Yemen Arab Republic and the People's Democratic Republic of Yemen. Table 1.2 shows that in 1974/75 these countries had a requirement of 2·3 million tons of wheat, 0·8 million tons of rice and 1 million tons of coarse grains that were not covered by imports of food aid. Their total cost amounted to more than 1 billion (thousand million) US dollars. According to a survey made in 1969/70[4] in Pakistan, 59% of all urban households and 64% of all rural households have an income of less than 200 rupees a month and this poorest section of the population has an average per caput daily food intake of less than 2000 kcal. In Bangladesh,[5] the situation is little better. There, 44 % of urban and 78 % of rural households have an income of less than 200 rupees and the daily food intake per person ranges from 1550 kcal to 2260 kcal. In Maharastra, India, in 1971, 83 % of the population earned 55 rupees per month per head or less, and food intake ranged from 940 kcal per day for 1 % of the population to 2590 for 15 %. Fifty percent had less than 2000 kcal per day. In 1962, in a survey of rural Madagascar, no one was eating as much as 2500 kcal per day.[6]

TABLE 1.3
Food Production Indexes—Total and per caput, 1972–74

	Total production			*Production per caput*		
	1972	1973	1974[a]	1972	1973	1974[a]
			(1961/65 = 100)			
Developing countries						
Developing market economies	125	128	130	99	99	98
Asian centrally planned economies	124	129	133	105	108	109
Total	116	122	121	101	102	101
Developed countries						
Developed market economies	122	126	128	112	114	115
Eastern Europe and USSR	133	148	145	122	135	131
Total	126	134	134	116	122	121
World	126	131	132	106	108	107

[a] Preliminary.
(Source: UN WFC/12, 20 May, 1975).

In the world as a whole it is estimated that at least 460 million people are suffering from hunger or malnutrition, and that of 97 developing countries, 61 had a deficit in food energy supplies in 1970.[1]

This situation is not new, of course. It has obtained for many years, although from time to time the list of MSA countries may change. Things reached crisis point in 1972 because of the interaction of a number of factors. For several years, although agricultural production had been increasing in almost all the developing countries it was being overtaken slowly by the growth of population. Table 1.3 shows that, for developing countries as a whole, production in 1974 was 30 % higher than the production averaged between 1961 and 1965 and that it was increasing by

2–3 % each year. This is a truly prodigious achievement, yet production per head of population was slightly lower than it had been in the earlier period. So the situation was deteriorating slowly. That was the first factor.

As we shall see later, world fishery catches began to level off by the late 1960s, and the failure of the Peruvian anchovy harvest increased pressure on the grain markets as developed countries sought alternative high protein feedingstuffs for their livestock, especially soya and wheat. This pressure was aggravated by a number of countries, most notably the USSR, where the national diet was changing to one that included a much higher proportion of meat derived from grain-fed animals. That was the second factor.

The third factor was the drought. For several years in succession the monsoon rains had failed, so reducing agricultural output throughout the monsoon belt, stretching right around the world. This caused acute problems in the Sahel Zone, along the southern edge of the Sahara Desert. Of the official list of MSA countries, six border the Sahara—Mauritania, Mali, Upper Volta, Niger, Chad and Sudan—while Ethiopia, Somalia, the Central African Republic, Cameroon, Dahomey, Ghana, Guinea, the Ivory Coast and Sierra Leone are also affected by the change in climate.

The final factor was the depletion of world reserves of food. They had been dwindling for several years as the countries with large stocks reduced what were becoming sources of economic embarrassment. It is at this aspect of the situation that we should look first, since it is the very small size of present food reserves that makes world trading in food unstable.

GRAIN RESERVES

World production of food had been out of balance with demand since at least the end of World War II. At that time Europe had been desperately short of food, with agriculture seriously disrupted over much of the region. North America, especially the United States, had large surpluses of grains and these were supplied at concessionary prices to relieve what was seen, correctly, as a temporary emergency.

As European agriculture recovered and the region approached self-sufficiency in food supplies, North American surpluses began to accumulate again. It was observed, however, that while the Europeans might have recovered sufficiently to be able to feed themselves, there were other parts of the world that seemed to face chronic shortages. Under Public Law 480, the US Agricultural Trade Development and Assistance Act, passed in 1954, and known later as 'Food for Peace', the disposal of food surpluses free, or at concessionary prices that might, for example, cover only shipping charges, was institutionalised. The other major producing countries, Canada, France and Australia, initiated similar schemes for the disposal of their surpluses.

The problem then, as now, was that food requirements exceeded effective demand. In other words, there were people in the world who were hungry not because no food was available for them, but because they could not afford to buy it. The problem was—and is—one of poverty. Thus the major producers were unable to supply them through normal economic mechanisms. There was food and there was hunger, but there was no commercial market for the food. This is a problem to which we will return later, and in more detail, for it is central to the present world situation.

A main aim of PL480 was to dispose of domestic surpluses that could not be released on to the market because the fall in prices that would result from such dumping would bankrupt the producers. Nor could it be released a little at a time without cutting back current production to compensate and this, too, would be socially and therefore politically disruptive. So it was a case of doing well by doing good. This is not to undervalue the genuinely humanitarian motives underlying PL480.

It would have seemed dangerous, in any case, to consider cutting back production. Over the years our attitudes to the world food situation have alternated between over-optimism and over-pessimism, and the 1950s and 1960s were decades of the deepest gloom. The FAO had compared rates of population growth with rates of growth in agricultural productivity and had reached predictably Malthusian conclusions. They were not alone, for those were the years of books with such titles as *Famine* 1975 and *The Hungry Planet: The Modern World at the Edge of Famine*.[7] Serious doubt existed as to whether famine on a global scale could be averted and the way in which the concept of famine was interpreted for popular consumption hinted strongly at starvation in Los Angeles and Paris, as well as in Lagos and Phnom Penh. So the US government, or the government of any other major food producer, could hardly reduce output if ways could be found of making their surplus food available to those in greatest need.

In the 16 years from the time the programmes were initiated until the end of June 1970, the US shipped abroad more than 177 million tonnes of grain, plus substantial quantities of dairy products and vegetable oils, and smaller amounts of other foods.[8]

The effects were not entirely those that had been predicted. If food surpluses cannot be dumped on to the market in a developed country without serious adverse effects on the agricultural sector of that country's economy, perhaps it was naive to suppose that the economies of developing countries were in some way immune. Perhaps, had the food been distributed only to the poorest and hungriest, those outside the normal market, then a special situation might have been created. Unhappily, the real world is rather more flexible than some planners would like it to be and the cheap American food found its way by various more or less devious routes into the normal market, where local farmers had to try to sell their produce against it. They could not compete—any more than American farmers could have done—and the indigenous industry was depressed just when what it needed most was stimulation.

This was reflected in the overall economy of the recipients. A necessary early step in economic development is the integration of all sections of the community into the money economy in order to provide sound domestic markets for industrial manufactures as well as for food. Since almost all countries aim to proceed from an agrarian to a partly industrial economic base, this means that the agricultural sector must develop economically in order to provide farmers, peasants and farmworkers, who form the majority of the population, with the money to buy manufactured goods. So an agricultural depression at such an early stage will delay the development of the industrial sector and of the entire economy. It may be, too, that some recipient governments believed that American food aid would always remain easily accessible to them, and so they placed less emphasis on the development of their own agriculture than was wise, in an attempt to short-cut the developmental process, by proceeding directly to industrialisation. Again, the availability of food aid may have shielded governments from the need to face the implications of the rate of growth of their populations. In conditions of rapid population growth, delays of two or three years in the institution of programmes to reduce family size can have serious consequences.

Even in the US the programmes had unpredicted results. According to Professor D. Gale Johnson:

'Food-aid, and the policies associated with it, has had some adverse effect upon American efforts to assist the developing nations. Congress was unwilling, at least until 1967, to permit United States technical assistance or economic aid to be used to assist a nation to increase its own output of a crop that would compete in world commercial markets with a crop exported by the United States. Thus when the United States was giving aid to Burma, technical assistance and other forms of aid could not be used to assist Burma to produce more rice because Burma was a major rice exporter. Agreements with countries receiving aid have often placed restrictions upon the exports of products similar to those received as aid. Thus the agreement with Pakistan in the mid-1960s required that country to limit its exports of rice unless it was willing to pay for some of the wheat received as aid.'[8]

It is at least possible that on any kind of long-term basis, food aid does more harm than good to the economy of the recipient.

As Americans became aware of the difficulties of implementing their aid programmes they were faced with a major switch in attitudes. Suddenly the world situation looked very hopeful. Scientists working in Mexico had developed new varieties of maize and wheat that promised to yield up to 10 times more than traditional varieties being grown in the sub-tropics. A little later, scientists at the International Rice Research Institute (IRRI), in the Philippines, developed parallel new varieties of rice. These new cereals provided the technological base for what came to be called the 'Green Revolution'. After years of anxiety the way ahead seemed clear and, not surprisingly, the world over-reacted. It began to look possible that by the latter part of the century the world food problem would be one of immense global surpluses, rather than shortages. In 1970 it was possible for Miss Mercedes Concepción, Chairman of the United Nations Population Commission, to warn a plenary session of the FAO's Second World Food Congress in The Hague that by the end of the decade the problems of developing countries would centre on employment rather than food. It was feared that a substantial increase in food supplies might stimulate an even more rapid growth of population, that could be fed if only it could be employed.

As the doom-laden air cleared and the world's leading agronomists began to eulogise about the 10 grains that would soon be growing where one had grown before, the governments of the major producers started looking for ways to reduce the size of their surpluses.

Table 1.4 shows the cost, in dollars, of the US programme to stabilise food production. The method chosen was to take land out of production and Table 1.5 shows the progress of this reduction in acreage. The figures require some slight qualification. To an extent they reflect the economic climate rather than deliberate government policy. If the price for a particular commodity is high, for example, and production costs are low, then it is likely that farmers will grow that crop either by diverting land previously set aside for grazing or for less profitable crops, or by bringing into production land that had been held in reserve. None the less, Table 1.5 shows that at its peak, in 1966, 63·3 million acres (25·6 million ha) was being held in reserve. At average US yields, this represented some 56 million tonnes of wheat a year, calculated on a three-year (1971/73) average wheat yield of 32·8 bushels per acre. By 1974 land had been brought back into production, so that only 2·7 million acres (1·1 million ha) remained out of production.

World food reserves are measured in terms of grains that are left over each year after trading has finished. It is a convenient way to measure food in store, but its significance does not end there. The principal grains are the staple foods for the populations of the world and they are the main source of traded feedingstuffs for livestock. Thus they underpin the cultures of nations—even sophisticated Europeans and Americans still refer to bread as 'the staff of life' and the British consume an average 48 oz (1·36 kg) of wheat and wheat products each week, rivalled only by 49 oz (1·39 kg) of potatoes[9]—and they also underpin agricultural systems where these seek to diversify diet by the introduction of animal products.

TABLE 1.4

Agricultural Stabilisation and Conservation Programmes: Payments to Producers, by Programme and Commodity, Programme Years 1968–73 (million dollars)

Programme and commodity	1968	1969	1970	1971	1972	1973[a]
Diversion						
Corn	651·3	780·3	645·0	—	—	—
Sorghum grain	89·2	114.2	107·6	—	—	—
Barley	—	22·1	18·3	—	—	—
Wheat	—	71·6	62·5	—	132·2	103·1
Cotton	144·7	26·4[b]	24·9[b]	—	—	—
Total	885·2	1 104·6	858·3	—	132·2	103·1
Price support						
Corn	514·4	584·9	583·1	893·1[c]	1 468·9[c]	909·7[c]
Sorghum grain	113·9	119·1	129·3	167·0[c]	289·3[c]	183·4[c]
Barley	—	23·9	26·5	—	107·2[c]	77·7[c]
Cotton	638·8	796·8	889·9	818·3[c]	807·3[c]	707·3[c]
Sugar (cane and beet)	92·0	90·4	82·6	86·2	89·8	86·5
Wool	54·4	50·4	64·0	102·3	68·0	—
Mohair	10·6	1·9	7·8	9·7	—	—
Total	1 424·1	1 667·4	1 783·2	2 076·6	2 830·5	1 964·6
Wheat marketing certificate	746·0	784·3	808·5	885·7	726·5	375·2
Total programmes						
Corn	1 165·7	1 365·2	1 228·1	893·1	1 468·9	909·7
Sorghum grain	203·1	233·3	236·9	167·0	289·3	183·4
Barley	—	46·0	44·8	—	107·2	77·7
Wheat	746·0	855·9	871·0	885·7	858·7	478·3
Cotton	783·5	823·2	914·8	818·3	807·3	707·3
Sugar (cane and beet)	92·0	90·4	82·6	86·2	89·8	86·5
Wool	54·4	50·4	64·0	102·3	68·0	—
Mohair	10·6	1·9	7·8	9·7	—	—
Grand total	3 055·3	3 466·3	3 450·0	2 962·3	3 689·2	2 442·9

[a] Preliminary.
[b] Programme in effect for small farms only.
[c] Set-aside programme payments.
Agricultural Stabilisation and Conservation Service.
(Source: USDA).

Grains also dominate world trade in food in terms both of bulk and value. In 1973 about 270 million tonnes of food items of all kinds was involved in world trade. Of this total, 165 million tonnes was of grains: 81·14 of wheat, 12·19 of barley, 49·68 of maize, 1·63 of oats, 1·92 of rye, 9·29 of sorghum and millet and 9·24 million tonnes of rice.[3] Of the grains it is wheat that is traded in the largest quantities. Although comparable quantities of rice are

TABLE 1.5
Cropland Acreage Withheld from Production under Specified Programmes, USA, 1959–74 (million acres)

Year	*Programme*										
	Conservation reserve	*Feed grain*					*Wheat*	*Cotton*	*Cropland conversion*	*Cropland adjustment*[a]	*Total*[b]
		Corn	*Sorghum grain*	*Barley*	*Oats*	*Total*					
1959	22·5	—	—	—	—	—	—	—	—	—	22·5
1960	28·7	—	—	—	—	—	—	—	—	—	28·7
1961	28·5	19·1	6·1	—	—	25·2	—	—	—	—	53·7
1962	25·8	20·3	5·5	2·4	—	28·2	10·7	—	—	—	64·7
1963	24·3	17·2	4·6	2·7	—	24·5	7·2	—	0·1	—	56·1
1964	17·4	22·2	6·5	3·7	—	32·4	5·1	0·5[c]	0·1	—	55·5
1965	14·0	24·0	7·0	3·7	0·1	34·8	7·2	1·0[c]	0·4	—	57·4
1966	13·3	23·7	7·3	3·7	[d]	34·7	8·3	4·6	0·4	2·0	63·3
1967	11·0	16·2	4·1	—	—	20·3	—	4·8	0·6	4·0	40·7
1968	9·2	25·4	7·0	—	—	32·4	—	3·3	0·5	4·0	49·4
1969	3·4	27·2	7·5	4·4	—	39·1	11·1	—	0·5	3·9	58·0
1970	0·1	26·1	7·4	3·9	—	37·4	15·7	—	[d]	3·9	57·1
1971	[d]	14·1	4·1	—	—	18·2	13·5	2·1	[d]	3·8	37·6
1972	[d]	24·4	7·3	4·9	—	36·6	20·1	2·0	[d]	3·3	62·1
1973	—	6·0	2·0	1·4	—	9·4	7·4	—	[d]	2·8	19·6
1974[e]	—	—	—	—	—	—	—	—	[d]	2·7	2·7

[a] State detail is available in *Agricultural Statistics*, 1968.
[b] Total cropland withheld, including acreage devoted to substitute crops.
[c] Not required to be put to conserving uses.
[d] Less than 50 000 acres.
[e] Projected estimates.
Agricultural Stabilisation and Conservation Service. Totals may not add due to rounding.
Data for 1956–58 in *Agricultural Statistics*, 1972, Table 755.
(Source: USDA).

TABLE 1.6
World Cereal Supplies, 1971/72 to 1973/74

Cereal	1971/72	1972/73 (*million tonnes*)	1973/74
Wheat			
Production[e]	353·6	346·2	377·9
Imports[a]	52·1	67·6	64·7
developed countries[g]	22·8	33·7	22·7
developing countries	29·3	33·9	42·0
Closing stocks of main exporting countries[b]	48·8	29·0	20·7
Coarse grains[c]			
Production[e]	651·4	633·5	674·9
Imports	47·4	55·4	62·7
developed countries[g]	40·9	45·4	48·4
developing countries	6·5	10·0	14·3
Closing stocks of main exporting countries[d]	55·6	39·6	31·8
Rice (milled equivalent)			
Production[e]	205·9	195·7	214·3
Imports[e]	7·7	7·6	7·4
developed countries	1·6	1·4	1·3
developing countries	6·1	6·2	6·1
Closing stocks of the main exporting countries[f]	9·1	6·3	3·7

[a] Including wheat flour in wheat equivalent.
[b] Argentina, Australia, Canada, EEC, USA.
[c] Rye, barley, oats, maize, sorghum and millets, mixed grains.
[d] Argentina, Australia, Canada, USA.
[e] Calendar years 1971, 1972, 1973.
[f] Japan, Pakistan, Thailand, USA.
[g] Excluding trade between EEC member countries.
FAO Commodity Review and Outlook, 1973–1974, Rome 1974.
(Source: UN WFC E/Conf. 65/3).

grown, most supplies are consumed in the countries that grew them. Most of the rice entering world trade was grown in the US, with smaller quantities originating from Japan, Pakistan and Thailand.

In 1972 several of the world's main grain producing areas were stricken by bad weather at the same time as the countries that had been importers suffered from the failure of the monsoons in some areas, floods in others and experienced reductions in their yields. As Table 1.6 shows, production of all grains fell back, in the case of wheat by a little over 2 %, of coarse grains by nearly 3 % and of rice by more than 5 %. The table records the final stages in the decline of the closing stocks of the main exporting countries. Table 1.7 summarises the main carry-over stocks of all countries, except for China and the USSR, and shows the decline in stocks of all cereals from 201

TABLE 1.7
Estimated Total Carry-over Stocks of Cereals (million tonnes)[a]

	Closing stocks					
	1969/70	1970/71	1971/72	1972/73	1973/74	1974/75[b]
Wheat						
Main exporting countries	65	50	49	29	26	20
Main importing countries	9	11	13	10	8	7
Others	13	11	12	11	10	9
Total	87	72	74	50	44	36
Rice						
Main exporting countries	10	9	6	4	4	4
Others	15	15	15	9	10	9
Total	25	24	21	13	14	13
Coarse grains						
Main exporting countries	54	39	54	39	28	19
Main importing countries	12	11	12	12	12	11
Others	23	21	22	20	18	18
Total	89	71	88	71	58	48
Total cereals	201	167	183	134	116	97
Proportion of total available supplies (%)	26	19	22	14	13	11

Note: Preliminary FAO estimates subject to revision. Compiled from official and unofficial sources.
[a] Excluding China and the USSR.
[b] Forecast.
(Source: UN/WFC/11, 17 April, 1975).

million tonnes in 1969/70 to an estimated 97 million tonnes in 1974/75. A significant factor in the present situation was the Soviet purchase of 20 million tonnes of wheat and 10 million tonnes of feed grains from the USA in 1972. There is little doubt that Soviet buyers used the secrecy inherent in the US cereal marketing system to obtain favourable prices, while at the time there were commentators who blamed the USSR for the pressure on world cereals supplies that led to the sharp price increases in that year. The global effect of Soviet intervention was probably exaggerated and, in any case, the wheat belt of the USSR was itself hit by that year's droughts.

The position in the summer of 1975 was that the world had become dependent on each year's harvests for the following year's food. This is not a novel situation, nor in itself an alarming one. For most of his history on this planet, man has depended on one year's harvest for the following year's food. In any case the carry-over stocks are not those on which we depend. They are what remains after the importing countries have made their purchases. So at present there is sufficient after each harvest to last until the next harvest. The novel element derives from the extent and structure of world trade in cereals, which arose from the existence of major surpluses in earlier years.

Today the demand for cereals from the importing countries requires them to buy in advance of the harvest. Orders must be placed early and consequently prices will be quoted from the spring of each year that will correspond to harvest forecasts and demand. If, later, the harvest figures appear to have been over-generous—and this happens frequently—then the quantity of the carry-over stocks becomes relevant. In times of surplus, cereals can be withdrawn from the market and added to the store, so strengthening prices, and in times of shortage stocks can be released into consumption in order to control the inflation of prices. If carry-over stocks are low they cannot be released in adequate quantities and prices may rise uncontrollably. They will remain high, at least for several years, because in any year that promises surpluses all the exporting nations and, increasingly, the importing nations as well will seek to divert quantities into reserve, so effectively increasing demand against increased supplies. Only when reserves have regained a satisfactory level can prices begin to fall. Table 1.8 summarises the structure of world trade in cereals.

We saw earlier that world trade in food is dominated by the wheat trade. Rice does play an important role, however, at least indirectly. Many peoples have a staple diet that can switch between wheat and rice. This is not difficult nutritionally, though it may create culinary problems, since the two grains are of comparable nutritive value and often are grown in adjacent regions. Historically surpluses of one have been used to make good deficiencies in supplies of the other. Over the past few years we have witnessed an increase in consumption of rice in Europe as an alternative to potatoes and bread, with the growing popularity of Asian cuisines. It is possible, then, to exploit the price differences between the two grains. The process is called 'caloric arbitrage' and it works to the benefit of net cereal importers that can grow both wheat and rice. In 1969, for example, the world price for rice was about 2·88 times the price of wheat. In that year China exported 712·5 thousand tonnes of rice. At the prevailing exchange rate this would have enabled her to import 2·052 million tonnes of wheat. This would have provided sufficient profit to feed six million people for a year. In fact, in 1969 China imported 3·2 million tonnes of wheat, so it is possible to say that some 1·4 million tonnes of this was free, paid for by the sale of rice.[10]

TABLE 1.8
Structure of World Trade in Cereals, Annual Average 1969–71

Exports to:	*Developed market economies*					*Centrally planned economies*			*Developing market economies*				*World total*
	EEC[a]	*Other Western Europe*	*North America*	*Others*	*Total*	*Eastern Europe*	*Asia*	*Total*	*Africa*	*Asia*	*Latin America and Caribbean*	*Total*	
Exports from:						(*US $ million f.o.b.*)							
Developed market economies													
EEC[a]	—	177	1	5	183	57	10	67	84	45	2	131	381
Other Western Europe	50	40	—	7	97	15	—	15	8	5	2	15	127
North America	527	343	155	616	1 641	129	140	269	128	674	255	1 057	2 967
Others[b]	33	104	4	131	272	10	80	90	71	273	30	374	736
Total	610	664	160	759	2 193	211	230	441	291	997	289	1 577	4 211
Centrally planned economies													
Eastern Europe	41	60	—	—	101	393	17	410	16	14	46	76	587
Asia	1	1	—	5	7	12	—	12	11	84	19	114	133
Total	42	61	—	5	108	405	17	422	27	98	65	190	720
Developing market economies													
Africa	14	18	—	1	33	50	—	50	35	25	2	62	145
Asia	3	6	—	48	57	6	26	32	31	232	1	264	353
Latin America and Caribbean[c]	252	129	9	77	467	15	2	17	12	18	134	164	648
Total	269	153	9	126	557	71	28	99	78	275	137	490	1 146
World total	921	878	169	890	2 858	687	275	962	396	1 370	491	2 257	6 077

[a] Original six members, excluding intra-trade.
[b] Chiefly Australia.
[c] Chiefly Argentina.
United Nations, *Monthly Bulletin of Statistics*, July 1973 and April 1974.
(Source: UN WFC E/Conf. 65/3).

LIVESTOCK AND INCOME ELASTICITIES OF DEMAND

The more people earn, the smaller the fraction of each increment they will spend on food. Indeed, it is a measure of the comparative wealth of a population to determine the proportion of household income that is spent on food items. In a developed economy it may amount to 25 % or less; in a very poor community it may be 70 %.

This relationship can be expressed mathematically according to a formula devised by Ernst Engel, a German civil servant, as long ago as 1857. If Y represents income and $\mathrm{d}Y$ the change in income, and E represents expenditure and $\mathrm{d}E$ the change in expenditure, then $\mathrm{d}EY/\mathrm{d}YE$ will give an index number, indicating the income elasticity of demand. Where this number is less than unity it indicates that an increase in incomes will not be reflected in a similar increase in expenditure on food.

This may be illustrated by an example. A particular household has, let us say, an income of £2000 and, since it is in a wealthy developed country, it spends £400 of this on food. The income increases to £2200. This means that a few luxury food items can now be purchased that were not purchased before, and so expenditure on food increases to £410: $\mathrm{d}EY/\mathrm{d}YE = 20\,000/80\,000 = 0{\cdot}25$.

This figure can be used to predict demand not just for food in general but for particular food items. Table 1.9 shows income elasticities of demand for

TABLE 1.9
Income Elasticities of Demand for Cereals

	All cereals	*Wheat*	*Rice*
World	−0·02	−0·24	0·23
Developed market economies	−0·24	−0·26	−0·21
Developing countries	0·13	0·23	0·20
Centrally planned economies	−0·10	−0·27	0·14

(Source: *Agricultural Commodity Projections*, 1970–1980, vol. II. FAO, Rome).

cereals in general and wheat and rice in particular, in developing, developed and centrally planned economies. It is based on data acquired from surveys.

It will be observed that while developing countries have positive income elasticities of demand for cereals that are less than unity, all other economies have negative values. This indicates that if incomes in those economies should rise, people will buy less of the particular food items, not more. Clearly, people who are poor do not eat less food as they become more prosperous. What happens is that patterns of consumption change. This phenomenon has been observed in every economic system and it should not surprise us, for it is what happened in Europe and America, although people alive today may not remember it. A poor family subsisting on a diet of bread and potatoes becomes more prosperous. It becomes possible to eat more interesting foods. Milk and eggs can be bought and, if prosperity continues to rise, meat products, proceeding eventually to the most expensive item of all, beef steaks. These items are not eaten in addition to similar increases in bread and potato consumption, but they replace a part of it. So instead of buying more bread and potatoes, first consumption of these items levels off—giving income elasticity of demand values of less than unity and approaching zero—then consumption of them begins to fall as they are replaced by other, more expensive foods. So the income elasticity of demand for bread and potatoes acquires a negative value and producers may know that should prosperity within the community continue to increase they should allow for a diminishing demand for bread and potatoes.

The more expensive food items that displace the staple foods include sugar, and then, invariably, animal products. This desire to eat animal products appears to transcend cultural barriers. The Japanese, whose culture is influenced strongly by Buddhist ethical values, which demand vegetarianism, began to eat meat as soon as they could afford to do so, despite the fact that only a generation earlier they had despised Europeans as barbarians because of their habit of eating flesh. Table 1.10 shows the

TABLE 1.10
Meat Consumption and Consumer Incomes in Japan, 1960–72

	Real per capita income (1963 US $)	*Meat consumption per caput (kg)*
1960	505	6·4
1963	631	11·0
1966	707	14·6
1969	1 054	17·5
1972	1 539	23·3

(Source: *Meat Balances in OECD Countries*, OECD; and *UN Annual Yearbook of Statistics*).

clear relationship between rising incomes and meat consumption in Japan during the years of the Japanese 'economic miracle'. Today it is said that in India one acquires prestige from being a vegetarian, imitating the dietary habits of the Brahmans. However, should India become a wealthy country we may expect, with some confidence, that the diet will change there, too, for it is difficult to imagine that the Indian taboo on meat-eating is stronger than the Japanese one.

This change in consumption occurred in Europe and America, it has been observed in Japan, and it is taking place now in the USSR and in other parts of eastern Europe. There is every reason to believe that the pattern is capable of extension into the rest of Asia, Africa, the Near East and Latin America. Thus we may expect demand for livestock products to increase

TABLE 1.11
Income Elasticities of Demand for Selected Food Products

	Cereals	*Sugar*	*Fats and oils*	*Dairy produce*	*Meat*	*Eggs*
North America	−0·5	0·0	0·0	0·08[a]	0·4	0·02
Oceania	−0·5	−0·05	0·1	0·1[a]	0·1	0·2
EEC[b]	−0·3	0·5	0·16	0·3	0·7	0·8
Denmark	−0·4	0·0	−0·05	0·06	0·4	0·3
Sweden	−0·4	0·0	−0·05	−0·02	0·5	0·3
UK	−0·4	0·0	0·02	0·09	0·4	0·3
Japan	−0·17	0·8	1·1	2·0	1·7	1·0
Near East and Africa	0·2	1·2	0·8	1·1	1·3	1·3
Asia and Far East	0·5	1·3	1·2	1·8	1·5	2·0
Latin America[c]	0·14	0·4	0·8	0·85	0·75	1·1

[a] Includes butter.
[b] The original 'Six'.
[c] Excluding Uruguay and Argentina.
(Source: *Agricultural Commodities: Projections for* 1970, FAO, Rome, 1962).

with growing prosperity, wherever it may occur. Table 1.11 gives us some idea of how close we may be to the 'take-off' point.

Based on surveys conducted some years ago the table shows that in all the developed countries there is a strong negative income elasticity of demand for cereals, sugar consumption has peaked or, in the case of Oceania, has acquired a small negative value (Oceania comprises Australia and New Zealand), and that demand for livestock products is less than unity. It is still very much larger than the negative values for cereals, however. Increases in the incomes of the citizens of the developed countries will still lead to an increase in consumption of animal products to replace cereals. Japan is just at the transition. Income elasticity of demand for cereals has a very small negative value but demand for animal products is strong, exceeding unity. This suggests that increases in incomes will encourage an even higher proportion of total income to be spent on these new introductions to the Japanese diet. An income elasticity of demand of 2·0 means that the whole of any increase in income will be spent on the item.

Consider now the values for developing regions. In each case there is still a small positive demand for cereals and, except in Latin America—which includes several major producers—a strong demand for sugar. Demand for livestock products is strong, but less so than in Japan, except in the case of eggs.

The point about these figures is, of course, that they are not immutable. They change with changing economic circumstances and reflect only the economic condition at a particular time. Allowing for the fact that the Japanese may have had some cultural aversion to animal produce and especially to the eating of red meat, is it possible that rather modest increases in income in developing regions will produce a rapid and very strong demand for livestock products, as in Japan, and that if incomes continue to rise they will proceed through the Japanese model until consumption stabilises again at a new level? If so, where is that level likely to be and how close are we to this surge in demand? The new level may be about that of Oceania. In other words, at the end of the process we will all eat—or we would like to eat, which is not quite the same thing!—as do Australians and New Zealanders today. In Oceania the income elasticity of demand is very close to zero for all items. How close are we? We may be very close indeed. In all the developing regions the demand for cereals is small and the demand for livestock products is large.

These figures are profoundly significant for the world as a whole. Livestock products are derived, almost exclusively, from poultry, pigs, cattle and sheep, with goats being used extensively in the Near East and on a minor scale elsewhere. In the temperate climates, where pasture is good, cattle are fed largely on grass. In the USA, however, and in harsher climates, they are usually fed on grain when the demand for dairy produce and meat exceeds the carrying capacity of the pasture. Fed on grain, in confined feedlots, animals gain weight more quickly and milk yields are higher in the dairying equivalent of the beef feedlot. Sheep are raised on grass invariably, but for some years research has been fairly intensive into ways of rearing them in intensive units. Pigs and poultry eat grain. Traditionally they were found on most European mixed farms, as marginal enterprises. They lived on wastes and surpluses, by scavenging spilled grain in the case of the hens that used to wander free in farmyards and barns, by grubbing up roots in the case of pigs. This diet was augmented by kitchen scraps from the farmhouse and by crop residues. The diet sustained a basic pig and poultry population that was permitted to increase in times of grain surpluses. In other words, surplus grains were 'stored' in livestock, which converted grain protein and fats into animal protein and fats and added variety to the human diet. The efficiency with which this conversion took place was not a major consideration. During the 1950s and 1960s, when the world had large surpluses of grains and prices were consequently low, pig and poultry populations were allowed to rise in the developed countries and people became accustomed to eating large quantities of eggs, poultrymeat and pigmeat.

Contrary to the view that was held for many years, goats constitute a much smaller problem. They browse on foliage and prefer not to eat grass or grains. It is not even certain that they contribute to soil erosion. At one time it was believed that over-grazing by goats was a major causal factor in the erosion of soils in the Mediterranean region and that they were contributing to the spread of deserts. This theory was based on the observation that goats, often in large numbers, were the most common form of livestock found in desert edge areas and in places where the soil was badly eroded. It is possible, however, that they have been accused unjustly.

An alternative theory holds that over-grazing first by cattle and then by sheep initiated the erosion, which proceeded to such a stage that these animals could not be grazed on the land. So they disappeared and their places were taken by goats, the only species of domesticated livestock that is able to subsist under such poor conditions. The theory is plausible. Sheep, in particular, can be harmful if stocking densities are too high, for they will nibble grass too close to the ground to permit it to recover easily. Cattle will cause soil compaction if they are stocked too densely, and this will lead to drainage problems and so to surface erosion. Goats will certainly exacerbate an existing erosion problem if their numbers are large and they are uncontrolled, since they will tend to kill bushes and even trees by eating off all the leaves. It is probable that they did not cause the erosion, however.

Any substantial increase in livestock production will be reflected in further pressure on supplies of cereals. This pressure will be disproportionate to any straightforward increase in human population or demand for food because of the large wastages that are involved. Hens convert vegetable protein into egg protein with an efficiency of about 24%. Other livestock enterprises are much less efficient. According to USDA figures revised by the New Zealand Ministry of Agriculture, milk is produced with conversion efficiencies of 19–22%, broiler chickens convert about 17% of the protein they are fed into protein edible for humans, pork is produced with an efficiency of about 13%, beef with an efficiency of 4·5% and lamb with an efficiency of 3·7%.

Tables 1.12(a) and (b) show the comparative yields per unit area of land for a range of farm products. It shows, quite clearly, that in terms of food energy and protein no livestock enterprise can compare in efficiency with vegetable crops. This means that for every kilogramme of egg protein the hen must consume more than 4 kg of grain protein; for each kilogramme of pork protein the pig must be fed 7·7 kg of grain protein; for every kilogramme of poultry meat protein the hen must receive 5·9 kg of grain protein; and, if we plan to produce beef in feedlots, fed on grain, then every kilogramme of beef protein represents an expenditure of 22 kg of grain protein.

TABLE 1.12(a)

The Yield of Product, Edible Protein and Edible Energy Which Can be Obtained from Breeding Populations Fed from the Produce of 1 ha

	Product (kg)			*Edible protein (kg)*	*Edible energy (MJ)*
	Carcass	*Eggs*	*Milk*		
Eggs	85	1 250		138	8 900
Broiler	1 225[a]			137	7 500
Turkey	1 000[b]			144	4 200
Rabbit	730			118	4 800
Bacon					
12 piglets/year	745			80	7 700
24 piglets/year	900			98	9 300
Sheep					
1·4 lambs/year	268			32	3 500
2·8 lambs/year	423			50	5 500
Suckler cow					
0·9 calves/year	255			35	2 800
1·8 calves/year	365			50	4 100
Milk with low concentrates[c]	60		3 940	138	11 500
Milk and 18 m beef[d]	166		2 800	116	9 500
Milk and 24 m beef[d]	162		2 600	110	9 400
Milk with high concentrates[e]	52		4 100	142	11 790
Milk and veal[d]	100		3 900	144	11 500
Milk and cereal beef[d]	1 355		3 100	120	9 700
Milk and 18 m beef	150		3 000	120	9 900

[a] Skin is included. If excluded, values are reduced to about 70 % of values shown.
[b] Skin is included. If excluded, values are reduced to about 80 % of values shown.
[c] Low concentrates, 900 kg/cow/year.
[d] The calves surplus to those needed to replace the milking herd are reared for veal, cereal beef, etc.
[e] High concentrates, 1650 kg/cow/year.

Sources:

Holmes, W. (1974). In *Meat* (edited by D. J. A. Cole and R. A. Lawrie), Butterworth, London, Ch. 28.

Holmes, W. (1975). The livestock of Great Britain as food producers, *Nutrition, Lond.* **29,** 331–6.

Holmes, W. (1977). Choosing between animals, *Proc. Roy. Soc. B.*

The possible effect on world supplies is obvious. During the period from 1961 to 1973, world production of milk increased by 21 %, of meat by 42 % and of eggs by 43 %. During the same period, wheat production increased by 64 %, barley by 106 % and maize by 51 %. Barley and maize are used mainly for the feeding of livestock. Between 1972 and 1973, while world food production increased by 5 %, much of this increase was lost through

TABLE 1.12(b)
Protein Yields from Conventional and Processed Crops

	Crop yield (kg/ha)	*Amount eaten (%)*	*Composition of edible portion*		*Yield/ha*	
			Protein (%)	*Energy[a] (Mcal/kg)*	*Protein (kg)*	*Energy (Mcal)*
Conventional crops						
Wheat	4 000	70	7·9	3·49	220	9 800
Potatoes	25 000	86	2·1	0·87	450	18 700
Field beans	3 300	100	27·0	2·70	890	8 900
Vining peas	4 500	100	5·8	0·64	260	2 900
Navy beans	2 000	100	21·4	2·58	430	5 200
Cabbage	40 000	60	2·2	0·25	530	6 000

	Crop yield (kg/ha)	*Protein (%)*	*Gross yield of protein (kg/ha)*	*Extraction of protein (%)*	*Net yield of extracted protein (kg/ha)*
Processed crops					
Soya bean	2 500	40	1 000	35	350
	Dry matter				
Lucerne	8 000	22	1 760	60	1 060
Cocksfoot	9 000	16	1 440	60	860

[a] For human nutrition (McCance and Widdowson, 1960).
1 Mcal = 4·18 MJ.
Sources:
Holmes, W. (1974). In *Meat* (edited by D. J. A. Cole and R. A. Lawrie), Butterworth, London, Ch. 28.
Holmes, W. (1975). The livestock of Great Britain as food producers, *Nutrition, Lond.* **29,** 331–6.
Holmes, W. (1977). Choosing between animals, *Proc. Roy. Soc. B.*

conversion from vegetable to animal products. Wheat production increased by 8 %, barley by 11 % and maize by 3 %. Milk production increased by 1·8 % and meat and egg production by 0·5 % each.[3] As we saw in Table 1.3, per caput food production increased by 2 % in the same period.

If rising prosperity in any of the developing regions in the world leads to a strongly positive demand for more livestock produce, it is doubtful whether the resultant demand for grains can be met at current levels of production without causing further steep rises in prices and so increasing the number of people at the bottom of the economic pyramid who cannot afford to import the food they need for survival. If this should happen it could lead to severe local famines and considerable political instability.

One should beware, though, of crude extrapolations of trends that make no allowance for governmental and consumer reactions to changing circumstances. While there is no evidence at present that this is happening generally, British consumers have reacted to increases in food prices, combined with a fall in real incomes, by buying less animal produce, especially fresh beef, pork and lamb.

A likelier possibility is that countries will seek to disengage somewhat from world trade in food. This has begun to occur as net importers and exporters alike plan to accumulate their own national reserves of grains. To some extent, of course, every grain growing country has its own carry-over stocks, held largely on farms by farmers who have not sold them, because they are being retained as feed for livestock on the farm itself, or for seed, or for some other reason, such as an improvement in prices. The developments in the years ahead may amount to much more of a global distribution of carry-over stocks, with less being held by the USA, Australia and France and more by every other nation. This may encourage nations to try to become much more self-sufficient. In the end, as we shall see later, the self-sufficiency of each region in the world is the only long-term solution to the food situation that has any real hope of success.

FISHERIES

In 1972 pressure on world grain supplies was increased by a marked fall in the world fish catch. Figure 1.1 shows how annual yields had risen steadily from 1955 or earlier, with a small drop in 1968, until 1971. Then, in 1972, the world catch was reduced by 4·7 million tonnes, just when an increase would have been helpful. The whole of this drop occurred in one area and to one country: the Peruvian anchovy harvest had failed and Peru's fish catch in 1972 was 5·8 million tonnes down on the 1971 figure. Figure 1.2 illustrates the history of the Peruvian industry, which grew very rapidly indeed throughout the late 1950s, experienced a brief reversal in 1963 and then encountered some instability in yields from 1964 onwards.

The trend continued sharply upward. From 1968 to 1971 Peru was the world's leading fishing nation, accounting for more than 16% of the entire world catch during those years. The relatively small falls in yield in 1963, 1965 and 1969 might have provided a warning of what was to come. The rather larger fall in 1971 was a similar, more urgent warning. In 1972, the fish simply were not there and in 1973 the situation was even worse. Reports since suggest that the anchovies have begun to return, but the history of the preceding years indicates that it is very unsafe to base predictions on the experiences of only one or two years.

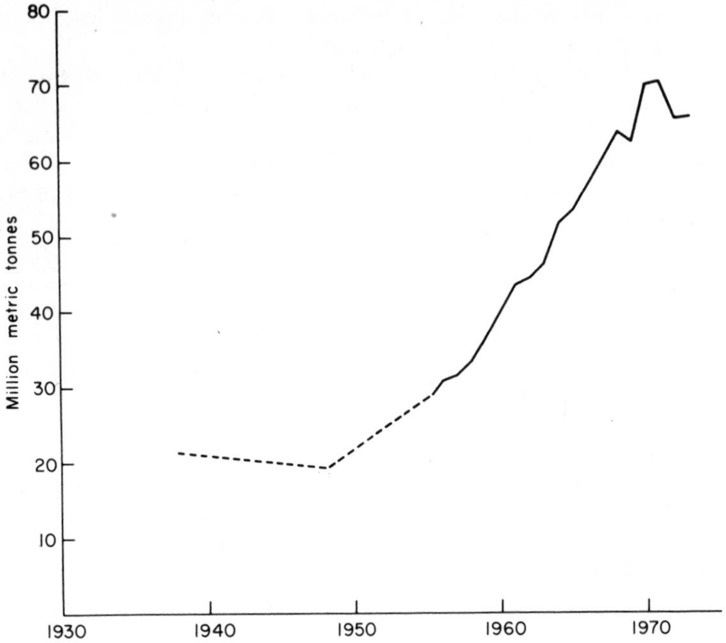

FIG. 1.1. Total world fish catch, 1938, 1948 and 1955–73 (Source: ref. 11).

No one knows precisely what happened. One school of thought holds that stocks had been over-fished. If this should happen, a point may be reached beyond which the population becomes non-viable biologically—there are too few breeding pairs to permit the population to recover. The statistics support this hypothesis. One would expect that before the final point is reached, stocks would be fished at a rate in excess of their natural capacity for regeneration. Thus there would be years in which the catch was low because recovery from earlier years was incomplete. The smaller catch would leave behind sufficient stocks to permit a recovery to higher levels in the following year. This would explain the falls in 1963, 1965, 1969 and 1971. Finally, though, the catch is so large that the drop in the following year is catastrophic. This accounts for the 1972 catch. Instead of leaving the fish alone in the hope that numbers would recover, however, so providing a regular, sustainable harvest in years to come, the fleets caught as many as they could in 1972 as well, so that by 1973 stocks were lower than ever.

This model ignores the basic biological fact that it takes longer than one year—it may take three or four depending on the species—for the fry to reach adult size, so that it is difficult to use the data to account for

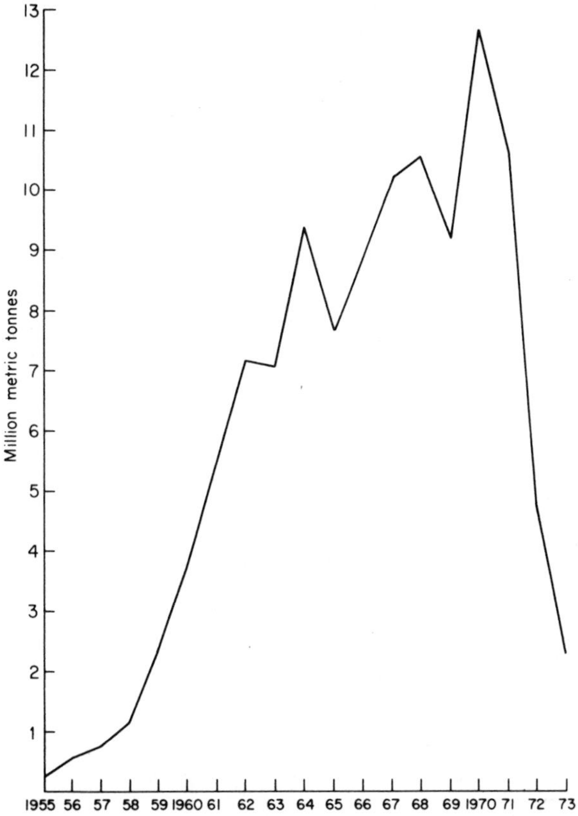

FIG. 1.2. Total annual fish catch, Peru, 1955–73 (Source: ref. 11).

substantial changes in catches in single years, if we must accept fish demography as the only cause.

However, the statistics also support alternative theories. One is that the cool Peru Current that sweeps along the Peruvian coastline shifted as a result of general climatic changes that were taking place all over the world at that time. There is no doubt that such a shift would explain the disappearance of the fish, which depend on the plankton fed by nutrients brought to the upper layers by numerous upwellings in the current and on the oxygen-rich water. One wonders, though, why the fishermen were unable to locate them again, since the new course of the current must have been known and the electronic equipment deployed in fish hunting is now very advanced. Nor does the theory account for the drops and recoveries of earlier years.

There is a theory that accounts for all the data and that borrows a little

TABLE 1.13
World Nominal Catch: by Countries, Arranged by Catch Size Groups (thousand tonnes)[a]

Code	Size group, country	1967	1968	1969	1970	1971	1972	1973	1973 − = + 1972	1972	1973
	World total	60 400·0	63 900·0	62 700·0	70 000·0	70 200·0	65 500·0	65 700·0			
1	5 000 000 tonnes and more	19 320·0	20 710·0	21 230·0	23 490·0	24 820·0	25 600·0	26 890·0			
	Japan	7 901·6	8 694·2	8 638·5	9 366·4	9 949·6	10 272·6	10 701·9	+	1	1
	USSR	5 777·2	6 082·1	6 498·4	7 252·2	7 337·0	7 756·9	8 618·7	+	2	2
	China	F/5 645·2	F/5 932·4	F/6 095·9	F/6 868·0	F/7 530·2	F/7 574·0	F/7 574·0	=	3	3
2	1 000 000 tonnes and more but less than 5 000 000 tonnes	27 260·0	29 010·0	27 310·0	31 540·0	29 770·0	24 070·0	22 460·0			
	Peru	10 198·6	10 555·5	9 243·6	12 612·9	10 606·1	4 768·3	2 299·3	−	4	6
	Norway	3 265·7	2 855·7	2 490·7	2 980·4	3 074·9	3 162·9	2 974·5	−	5	4
	USA	2 405·5	2 451·7	2 489·1	2 776·5	2 819·5	2 649·5	2 669·9	+	6	5
	Thailand	846·6	1 088·9	1 269·9	1 447·7	1 587·1	1 678·9	1 692·3	+	7	8
	India	1 400·4	1 525·6	1 606·8	1 756·1	1 851·6	1 637·3	1 958·0	+	8	7
	Spain	1 459·8	1 533·3	1 522·0	1 538·8	F/1 505·1	1 616·9	1 570·4	−	9	10

Denmark	1 070·4	1 466·8	1 275·5	1 266·5	1 400·9	1 442·9	1 464·7	+	10	11
Korea, Rep. of	760·7	841·1	879·1	933·6	1 073·7	1 338·6	1 654·6	+	11	9
Indonesia	1 180·4	1 159·0	1 214·4	1 228·5	1 244·5	1 267·8	1 300·0	+	12	13
Canada	1 295·7	1 498·7	1 404·8	1 389·0	1 289·8	1 169·1	1 151·6	−	13	15
Philippines	769·2	944·6	978·1	992·0	1 049·7	1 131·9	1 248·5	+	14	14
South Africa	1 583·2	2 045·3	1 849·6	1 562·2	1 164·6	1 123·3	1 331·7	+	15	12
UK	1 026·2	1 040·2	1 083·0	1 099·0	1 107·3	1 081·5	1 144·4	+	16	16
3 500 000 tonnes and more but less than 1 000 000 tonnes	5 150·0	5 320·0	5 250·0	5 900·0	6 310·0	6 160·0	6 180·0			
Korea, Dem. Pep. Rep. of	F/800·0	F/800·0	F/800·0	F/800·0	F/800·0	F/800·0	F/800·0	=	17	18
Chile	1 052·8	1 392·9	1 095·1	1 181·4	1 486·9	792·0	664·4	−	18	22
France	819·7	803·1	770·5	764·4	741·7	783·0	796·8	+	19	19
Iceland	897·6	600·6	689·5	733·8	684·9	726·5	906·2	+	20	17
Viet-Nam, Rep. of	410·7	410·0	463·8	517·4	587·5	677·7	713·5	+	21	20
Nigeria	119·3	F/120·0	115·1	542·9	592·7	645·6	664·8	+	22	21
Angola	292·1	293·4	417·5	368·2	316·3	599·1	470·2	−	23	27
Brazil	419·7	495·1	492·2	517·3	580·7	589·9	F/589·9	=	24	23
Poland	338·9	406·7	408·1	469·3	517·7	544·0	579·6	+	25	24

[a] For country footnotes see tables in Sections A1, A2, A3, A4, A5, A6 and A7 of the reference source below.
F/ signifies data estimated or calculated by FAO.
(Source: Yearbook of Fishery Statistics, Vol. 36, 1973. FAO, Rome).

from the other theories. The fish migrated to a different part of the current as a response to over-fishing, and the current moved as well. Fish do alter their behaviour. As we shall see later, in Chapter 10, in the mid-1960s large stocks of mackerel that had overwintered in the eastern Atlantic, close to the edge of the continental shelf, began to winter in the English Channel, giving rise to a huge local industry. Each year afterwards the fish returned, but each year they were a little further to the west. No one really knows why they took to wintering in the Channel, but they did. The Peruvian anchovies may have been numerous because of unusually heavy spawning in particular years—this, too, happened to the mackerel—then began to decline and move away, the final phase of the move being triggered by a change in the current.

The reasons for the collapse of the Peruvian industry are less important than the fact. As Table 1.13 shows, since 1971 Peru has slipped from first to sixth place among fishing nations. Table 1.13 also illustrates the structure of the world fishing industries, which are spread fairly evenly among regions, as one might expect, and among developing and developed countries. Of the 16 nations whose 1973 catches exceeded 1 million tonnes, seven are developing countries.

Their hierarchical order in terms of catch size is changed when we consider their relative contribution to one of the major uses of fish, as feedingstuff for livestock. Figures are not available for China, India, Spain, Indonesia and the Philippines, but of the remainder, expressed as a percentage of total world fishmeal production, the list runs: Japan (20), USSR (13), Peru (11), USA (10), Norway (9), South Africa (7), Denmark (6), UK (2), Canada (1), Thailand (0·6) and Republic of Korea (0·1). Together, these countries produce almost 80 % of the world's fishmeal.[11] In this reordering, the developing countries are low on the list, with the exception of Peru, which contributes a rather disproportionately large part of the world's fishmeal. This is—or was—a major source of income for Peru, but it means that high-grade animal protein is being directed into farm livestock production, where most of it is squandered in conversion. Peru's fishmeal production peaked in 1970, when she produced 41 % of the world's total output. Production in 1973 was only 18 % of that in 1970, and this loss was reflected in a drop in the world's production of 30 % between 1970 and 1973. In earlier years, then, Peru devoted an even higher proportion of her catch to fishmeal production than she did in 1973 and, indeed, Japan, her closest rival, produced in that year only 671 thousand tonnes against Peru's 2255·8 thousand tonnes.

Fishmeal had become important in the livestock industries of many developed countries and its sudden failure led farmers to switch to the only substitutes available, soya meal and grains. Thus, in 1972 and subsequent years, pressure on grain supplies was exerted by the reduction in world fish catches.

Climate

The size of an agricultural crop is determined by many factors: the nature and condition of the soil, the availability of water, the area planted, varieties of crop plants and breeds of animal, the availability of fertiliser and other 'inputs', the availability and quality of labour, implements and machines, and finally the weather. Most of these factors are subject to changes through time, but the weather is the only one that is quite outside human influence or control.

Although it is not possible to predict accurately the weather for a particular small area for very far ahead, it is possible to measure fluctuations in longer term weather patterns and to relate these to agricultural productivity. The result is called the 'instability index' and it is the percentage standard deviation of annual changes in production from the trend rate. In other words an instability index of 3 means that yields are likely to vary by 3% to either side of the trend. Indices of instability vary from less than 2 to as much as 37, covering the whole range of crops and of countries. In general, indices for cereal production are rather higher than those for other commodities, ranging from 4 in the Asian centrally planned economies to 6–8 in most other regions, to 10 in North America, 13 in Eastern Europe and the USSR and 42 in Oceania. The overall index for developed countries is 6 and for developing countries 3, and the overall index for cereals is 4. Variations either side of the trend of 4% mean that actual yields are liable to vary by 8%. On average this is the range of variation that occurs. The US Department of Agriculture defines 'drought' as that reduction in rainfall that causes a drop in yield of 10% or more.

In 1972 it was the prolonged drought in the Sahelian region of Africa that caught the attention of the world. Catastrophic though this was in the region itself, it had little effect on world food production, because it occurred in a region of low productivity.

Poor weather was not confined to the Sahel, however. In 1971 bad weather was widespread in developing countries and their annual increase in production was below normal. In 1972 bad weather was experienced again and, working from the low base of the previous year, the result was a slight fall in production.

In 1972, however, the weather was also bad in the major cereal growing areas of the developed world. Soviet wheat production declined by 13%, total world grain production was 7% lower than in 1971, and rice production was 5% lower.

In 1973 the weather improved. The USA brought back into production the land that had been held back. Table 1.5 shows how this area was reduced from 62.1 million acres (25·1 million ha) in 1972 to 2·7 million acres (1·1 million ha) in 1974. The USSR had a record grain harvest and in the Far East production increased by 9%, although in the Near East and in Africa production declined.

In the world as a whole, variations in all the factors that influence harvests tend to cancel one another. A fertiliser shortage in one area is compensated for by unusually good weather somewhere else; reduced sowings here coincide with increased sowings there. Thus the indices of instability are reasonably accurate and even during the unusually bad conditions of 1971/73, the shortfall fell within the predicted limits. It was made serious, as we saw earlier, by the run on grain reserves. The theories regarding changes in the world's climate are discussed in some detail in Chapter 8. For the moment it is enough to say that short term changes are well known and that they are associated with alterations in circulation patterns in the upper atmosphere, possibly connected with solar activity. The World Meteorological Association has concluded that the main overall trend appears to be a cooling in the northern hemisphere, bringing more frequent extreme weather conditions, such as droughts and floods—and even such apparently 'freak' conditions as the 1976 summer in northern Europe. Between the 1920s and the 1960s the rainy season in Africa extended well to the north; it appears to have retreated southward, probably as a result of the cooling to the north. For the future it is hoped that the relatively new science of agrometeorology may be able to contribute to agricultural forecasting and planning.

Water

As we shall see later, when we discuss in more detail the resources that are available in the world for food production, fresh water is not distributed evenly. In the areas of highest rainfall, the tropical rainforest areas, climatic and ecological constraints inhibit the development of agriculture. In more favourable areas, such as the sub-tropics, water is often in short supply.

The new cereal varieties on which much of the success of agricultural development plans for developing countries depend, require more water than do traditional varieties. Often the water is present, at least potentially. It is not used because of the high capital cost of installing appropriate irrigation equipment. Thus of the world's 740 million ha of arable land, only 93 million are irrigated, much of it in the Far East, where paddy rice growing has developed hydrological techniques as sophisticated as those of the great hydrological civilisations of the Fertile Crescent of Mesopotamia.

The lack of capital is not the only constraint, however. Large scale irrigation schemes often encounter other difficulties. Large dams in hot dry climates may lose more water from surface evaporation than they distribute. Large artificial lakes may contribute to the spread of such water-borne diseases as schistosomiasis, transmitted by an aquatic snail, and may necessitate new malaria control programmes to prevent the proliferation of the anopheles mosquitoes. The artificial raising of water tables may make more water available to farmers in the short term, but in the longer term it may lead to the waterlogging of the soil unless adequate drainage is also provided. Water must be removed from the soil as well as supplied to it. Water brought to the surface from a raised water table will carry with it a burden of dissolved salts acquired in the subsoil or even brought from the bed rock. If evaporation from the surface is rapid these salts may be left at the surface as evaporites, so raising the salinity of the soil until it becomes to all intents sterile. The remedy for this condition is simple but expensive. Large quantities of water must be applied to the surface to wash out the salts.

The lack of adequate irrigation systems has limited the increase in agricultural production in many regions, but the technical problems of remedying this deficiency increase the capital and running costs substantially and attempts to take 'short cuts' by providing water without adequate safeguards are likely to prove counter-productive in the long run.

SUMMARIES BY REGIONS

North America

Fears of long term world grain surpluses led the USA and Canada to reduce agricultural output during the 1960s and early 1970s by withdrawing land from production. The events of 1972 and 1973 have caused this land to be brought back into use, so that by 1974 only 1·1 million ha of land in the USA remained idle.

Table 1.14 gives details of the acreages sown to each major crop in the USA, the average yield per unit of cultivated land, total production and the farm value. The average yield for the principal grains, for 1973, are: wheat 2·14 tonnes per ha, barley 2·67 tonnes per ha and maize (corn) 5·74 tonnes per ha.

Tables 1.15 to 1.20 show stocks of principal grains held in the USA, on and off farms, foreign trade in barley and the supply and rate of disappearance of sorghum. The tables also show the decline in held stocks of all grains except oats between 1962 and 1973.

Official estimates of the 1976 US harvest promised high yields of wheat and maize but a reduced output of soybeans. Maize and soybeans were affected by yet another drought and there are fears that the mid-western states may be heading for a prolonged dry period that will make the yields of recent years difficult to sustain. There are fears, too, that the loss of farm land to urban expansion and through erosion may make it difficult to maintain the high levels of cereal production of the past, far less to increase them.

Western Europe

British livestock farmers, dairy farmers in particular, suffered from the rise in world cereal prices. The National Farmers' Union, principal spokesman

TABLE 1.14
Crops: Acreage, Production and Farm Value, USA, 1971–73[a]

Crop	Acreage harvested			Yield per harvested acre				Production			Farm value		
	1971	1972 (thousand acres)	1973[b]	Unit	1971	1972	1973[b]	1971	1972 (thousands)	1973[b]	1971	1972 (thousand dollars)	1973[b]
Corn for grain	64 047	57 421	61 760	bushel	88·1	97·1	91·4	5 641 112	5 573 320	5 643 256	6 095 027	8 732 714	13 357 361
Corn for forage	706	537	569										
Corn for silage	8 770	8 279	8 764	ton	12·4	13·1	12·5	108 667	108 520	109 848			
Wheat, all	47 674[c]	47 284[c]	53 875[c]	bushel	33·9	32·7	31·8	1 617 789	1 544 936	1 711 400	2 166 669	2 704 104	6 500 728
winter	32 359[d]	34 840[d]	38 407[d]	bushel	35·4	34·0	33·1	1 144 164	1 185 225	1 269 653	1 542 754	2 020 276	4 567 027
durum	2 864	2 550	2 974	bushel	32·1	28·6	28·5	91 805	72 912	84 860	120 479	141 049	491 665
other spring	12 451	9 894	12 494	bushel	30·7	29·0	28·6	381 820	286 799	356 887	503 436	542 788	1 442 036
Oats	15 772[c]	13 525[c]	14 110[c]	bushel	55·9	51·2	47·0	881 277	691 973	663 860	546 113	508 612	722 057
Barley	10 151[c]	9 707[c]	10 527[c]	bushel	45·7	43·6	40·3	463 601	423 461	424 483	458 737	507 190	853 462
Rye	1 754[d]	1 084[d]	1 038[d]	bushel	28·1	26·9	25·4	49 288	29 183	26 398	44 921	28 646	46 627
Flaxseed	1 545	1 151	1 725	bushel	11·8	12·1	9·5	18 198	13 909	16 437	43 228	43 092	126 692
Rice	1 817·9	1 817·9	2 170·2	cwt	4 718[e]	4 700[e]	4 277[e]	85 768	85 439	92 823	457 697	574 907	1 312 418
Popcorn	173·7	157·0	146·3	lb	3 246	3 339	3 217	563 850	524 111	470 768	18 321	16 109	17 664
Sorghum grain	16 301	13 368	15 940	bushel	53·7	60·5	58·8	875 752	809 264	936 587	904 748	1 107 704	1 995 854
Sorghum forage	2 717	2 510	2 137	ton									
Sorghum silage	1 008	850	842	ton	10·9	11·8	11·4	10 968	10 055	9 557			
Cotton lint	11 470·9	12 983·8	11 995·2	bale	438[e]	507[e]	519[e]	10 477·0	13 704·1	12 958·0	1 419 624	1 798 960	2 795 153
Cottonseed				ton	739[e]	831[e]	825[e]	4 239·8	5 393·0	4 947·4	240·874	267 136	495 915
Hay, all	61 405	59 821	62 190	ton	2·10	2·15	2·16	129 119	128 614	134 608	3 335 759	3 731 888	4 878 870
Beans, dry edible	1 316	1 402	1 390	cwt[f]	1 209[e]	1 292[e]	1 209[e]	15 917	18 118	16 803	173 718	199 638	438 185
Peas, dry field	202·7	135·1	136·4	cwt[f]	1 939[e]	1 557[e]	1 221[e]	3 930	2 103	1 665	13 632	11 494	32 613
Soybeans for beans	42 701	45 698	56 416	bushel	27·5	27·8	27·8	1 175 989	1 270 630	1 566 518	3 559 708	5 550 459	8 849 282
Peanuts harvested for nuts	1 454·5	1 486·4	1 495·7	lb	2 066	2 203	2 323	3 005 118	3 274 761	3 473 837	408 371	471 343	558 312
Potatoes	1 391·3	1 253·8	1 303·1	cwt	230	236	228	319 354	295 955	297 352	602 998	894 393	1 196 620
Sweetpotatoes	113·6	114·4	113·2	cwt	103	109	109	11 718	12 453	12 375	61 110	71 501	89 284
Tobacco	837·6	842·4	885·8	lb	2 035	2 076	1 962	1 704 884	1 749 085	1 737 569	1 339 644	1 451 275	1 565 309
Sugarcane for sugar and seed	648·1	701·8	748·3	ton	37·3	40·4	36·8	24 172	28 332	27 542	147 175[g]	212 375[g]	255 095[g]
Sugarbeets	1 341·9	1 328·7	1 222·2	ton	20·2	21·4	20·1	27 096[h]	28 410[h]	24 540[h]	416 279	454 250	441 720
Maple syrup				gallon				962	1 099	857	6 825	9 670	8 018
Broomcorn	71·0	51·0	19·3	ton	310[e]	290[e]	342[e]	11·0	7·4	3·3	4 844	3 228	1 634
Hops	28·9	29·7	31·4	lb	1 718	1 728	1 744	49 663	51 309	54 769	32 743	36 542	41 722
Seed crops:													
alfalfa	475	376	413	lb	246	280	248	116 679	105 355	102 263	40 669	45 763	91 978
red clover	375	261	322	lb	107	95	90	40 058	24 868	28 865	10 881	9 918	17 816
sweetclover	49			lb	227			11 226			884		
white clover	17			lb	276			4 800			1 866		

ladino clover	18	16	12	lb	275	250	260	4 950	3 875	3 120	3 168	2 422	3 120
lespedeza	122	77	81	lb	195	193	205	23 810	14 715	16 561	3 460	3 259	6 146
timothy	137	111	151	lb	206	189	156	28 286	20 938	23 408	2 270	3 258	7 427
orchardgrass	34	45	46	lb	256	436	457	8 573	19 630	21 156	1 650	4 566	7 150
tall fescue (Ky. 31 and Alta)	294	317	457	lb	310	282	292	91 158	89 405	133 270	8 298	11 055	22 876
crimson clover	17	11	8	lb	223	243	321	3 762	2 698	2 670	582	559	964
hairy vetch	45	42	33	lb	226	169	182	10 165	7 150	6 005	1 229	806	816
all ryegrass	174	173	180	lb	1 520	1 220	1 160	264 480	211 060	208 800	14 811	15 407	33 408
Apples, commercial crop				lb				6 080 600	5 870 000	6 205 000	299 121	377 670	544 333
Peaches				lb				2 862 900	2 408 500	2 604 900	166 568	159 487	202 839
Pears				ton				707	608	720	66 768	84 357	99 573
Grapes				ton				3 997	2 570	4 218	381 620	423 132	671 235
Cherries				ton				279	229	241	71 904	58 627	88 335
Apricots				ton				150	127	158	14 035	17 701	25 809
Plums (California)				ton				101	96	97	23 129	23 808	31 137
Prunes, dried (California)				ton				131	77	203	37 597	41 195	95 613
Prunes and plums, fresh basis (excluding California)				ton				65	42	65	5 770	7 228	9 796
Figs[i]				ton				45	36	42	3 959	5 132	8 982
Nectarines				ton				69	86	87	10 695	15 222	22 098
Olives				ton				55	24	73	8 140	10 043	26 062
Dates				ton				19	16	24	3 110	2 652	4 602
Avocados[j]				ton				45	89	67	31 218	44 371	46 519
Cranberries	22	22	23	barrel				1 640	1 976	2 014	24 405	26 035	27 616
Strawberries	48 580	43 810	40 860	cwt	107	105	117	5 209	4 583	4 773	117 005	109 765	131 592
Oranges[k]				box				189 560	191 450	224 660	465 109	549 369	603 305
Grapefruit[k]				box				60 560	64 140	65 640	145 287	185 586	180 116
Lemons[k]				box				16 450	16 680	22 200	82 226	80 266	102 230
Limes[k]				box				880	1 100	1 100	4 136	6 039	6 908
Pecans				lb				247 200	183 100	275 700	81 581	77 636	101 215
Walnuts				ton				136	117	174	57 106	65 854	100 890
Almonds				ton				134	125	134	87 100	98 125	192 960
Filberts				ton				11·4	10·2	12·3	4 708	5 157	7 720
Commercial vegetables:	*(acres)*	*(acres)*	*(acres)*										
artichokes	11 000	11 100	12 000	cwt	72	64	50	792	710	600	7 697	8 222	8 699
asparagus[l]	114 170	119 070	115 380	cwt	24	24	22	2 791	2 891	2 545	64 015	67 921	66 411
beans, green lima[m]	71 130	74 470	77 530	ton	1·13	1·22	1·27	80·7	90·7	98·1	14 960	18 829	20 714
beans, snap[n]	323 510	341 840	377 350	ton	2·32	2·25	2·36	751·2	769·6	892·2	99 691	107 904	130 404
beets[m]	13 690	12 670	16 400	ton	13·86	13·02	12·25	189·8	164·9	200·9	4 059	3 910	5 755
broccoli	42 520	47 300	53 590	cwt	74	77	63	3 159	3 644	3 398	35 417	39 451	41 990
brussel sprouts	5 400	6 100	5 900	cwt	115	115	115	621	702	679	7 835	10 112	9 506
cabbage[l]	108 140	104 630	110 350	cwt	219	214	218	23 728	22 393	24 026	78 164	78 235	124 098
cantaloups	99 000	96 550	93 100	cwt	124	134	121	12 255	12 944	11 270	80 168	93 957	90 925
carrots	70 780	74 350	82 500	cwt	260	257	260	18 398	19 139	21 475	93 565	99 828	106 872

TABLE 1.14—*continued*
Crops: Acreage, Production and Farm Value, USA, 1971–73[a]

Crop	Acreage harvested (thousand acres)			Unit	Yield per harvested acre			Production (thousands)			Farm value (thousand dollars)		
	1971	1972	1973[b]		1971	1972	1973[b]	1971	1972	1973[b]	1971	1972	1973[b]
cauliflower	24 960	28 080	30 480	cwt	98	106	87	2 456	2 989	2 655	25 107	31 537	32 183
celery	33 540	33 220	34 080	cwt	474	482	501	15 909	16 021	17 075	86 908	102 794	106 389
corn, sweet[l]	606 100	609 230	628 800	ton	4·41	4·55	4·54	2 674·4	2 772·6	2 853·0	122 840	137 218	157 836
cucumbers[l]	174 150	177 990	173 120	ton	4·48	4·53	4·76	779·4	806·2	824·2	85 203	91 925	99 556
eggplant	2 770	3 100	2 850	cwt	158	168	184	437	522	523	4 013	4 530	4 998
escarole	9 100	9 800	8 400	cwt	127	120	140	1 155	1 180	1 207	10 513	9 431	14 042
garlic	3 700	5 100	6 900	cwt	130	130	130	481	663	897	4 485	6 525	11 021
honeydew melons	12 300	13 200	14 100	cwt	166	175	174	2 039	2 307	2 448	12 712	14 390	18 331
lettuce	216 550	219 680	219 070	cwt	219	221	227	47 369	48 640	49 804	298 766	278 736	369 148
onions	98 800	94 470	104 390	cwt	302	300	280	29 803	28 355	29 188	105 330	167 715	193 395
peas, green[m]	382 910	377 670	413 390	ton	1·36	1·36	1·19	520·4	512·0	492·2	55 924	57 500	58 624
peppers, green	47 450	46 500	48 030	cwt	84	99	98	3 980	4 590	4 718	49 259	58 219	65 002
spinach[l]	36 420	36 540	37 620	ton	5·24	5·29	5·37	190·8	193·4	202·0	15 271	16 010	17 679
tomatoes[l]	391 040	406 530	431 400	ton	16·38	16·72	16·00	6 405·5	6 796·1	6 903·5	443 156	498 938	555 263
watermelons	252 400	268 000	241 300	cwt	105	94	109	27 094	25 320	26 260	67 892	63 266	77 465
peppermint	64 700	57 100	57 900	lb	58	53	55	3 746	3 004	3 205	15 377	15 765	22 400
spearmint	30 900	24 600	24 100	lb	65	61	53	2 008	1 511	1 274	8 403	7 766	9 442

[a] Hawaii is included in commercial vegetables and in acreage and production of sugarcane, but is excluded from other crops.
[b] Preliminary.
[c] Includes acreage seeded in preceding fall.
[d] Acreage seeded in preceding fall.
[e] Yield in pounds.
[f] Clean basis.
[g] Does not include Hawaii.
[h] Includes syrup later made into sugar. Does not include production in non-farmlands in Somerset County, Maine.
[i] Fresh basis.
[j] Year of bloom.
[k] Crop year begins with bloom in one year and ends with completion of harvest the following year. Citrus production is included with other crops on a harvested basis.
[l] For breakdown between fresh market and processing, see individual crop tables.
[m] Processing only.
Statistical Reporting Services.
(Source: USDA).

TABLE 1.15
Wheat: Stocks on and off Farms, USA, 1963–73

Year beginning October	On farms				Off farms[b]			
	October 1st	*January 1st*	*April 1st*	*July 1st*[a]	*October 1st*	*January 1st*	*April 1st*	*July 1st*[a]
				All wheat (1 000 *bushels*)				
1963	410 988	310 198	153 641	75 669	1 532 621	1 304 088	1 052 158	825 716
1964	503 656	389 672	263 450	132 515	1 305 655	1 059 621	881 757	684 740
1965	558 314	405 337	255 593	130 774	1 145 702	930 676	661 743	404 399
1966	537 841	406 879	237 852	144 890	896 351	640 577	461 370	279 525
1967	601 483	505 227	361 015	229 548	954 667	704 490	477 090	309 000
1968	727 772	576 932	460 476	325 906	951 545	764 418	648 980	490 754
1969	752 200	609 443	456 499	307 093	1 120 224	923 375	740 747	577 780
1970	663 673	526 092	381 098	240 276	1 124 797	883 878	679 337	491 202
1971	826 402	694 191	525 478	354 869	1 046 932	853 100	684 961	508 203
1972	729 492	509 808	315 926	133 876	1 140 699	888 801	611 253	304 578
1973[c]	614 037	368 032			835 349	566 423		
				Durum wheat (1 000 *bushels*)				
1963	52 648	46 968	10 846	1 791	35 649	32 360	50 614	39 178
1964	57 043	47 873	39 921	19 519	47 335	46 500	42 213	48 249
1965	75 997	57 608	48 993	24 029	48 387	42 402	34 294	30 388
1966	61 896	39 769	28 617	18 349	33 806	24 342	16 646	10 530
1967	58 269	49 015	32 891	18 181	19 475	14 338	13 386	6 143
1968	90 938	64 949	50 724	29 626	18 451	21 030	17 429	11 582
1969	107 938	92 460	81 498	63 140	23 187	20 285	16 441	17 584
1970	83 853	69 660	56 120	41 672	25 591	24 803	22 856	16 817
1971	105 737	94 340	75 345	48 086	27 070	24 928	24 959	21 165
1972	91 538	72 016	48 249	19 979	24 458	25 910	23 132	16 891
1973[c]	75 755	53 414			21 460	18 550		

[a] Old crop only.
[b] Stocks at mills, elevators, warehouses, terminals, processors, and those owned by Commodity Credit Corporation which are in bins and other storages under CCC control.
[c] Preliminary.
Statistical Reporting Service. Data for 1949–62 in *Agricultural Statistics*, 1972, table 13.
(Source: USDA).

TABLE 1.16
Corn: Stocks on and off Farms, USA, 1963–74

Year	On farms				Off farms[b]			
	January 1st	*April 1st* (*thousand bushels*)	*July 1st*	*October 1st*[a]	*January 1st*	*April 1st* (*thousand bushels*)	*July 1st*	*October 1st*[a]
1963	2 958 288	2 008 162	1 401 285	533 801	1 251 748	1 039 612	728 605	831 334
1964	3 209 565	2 269 686	1 513 667	681 101	1 135 189	1 008 777	862 813	855 421
1965	2 737 489	1 866 476	1 243 125	581 498	1 137 392	938 763	650 332	565 593
1966	3 096 601	2 129 392	1 327 409	531 157	956 475	740 542	459 284	310 538
1967	2 928 817	2 063 306	1 348 923	572 233	778 619	671 090	405 683	254 075
1968	3 453 956	2 433 095	1 670 424	788 195	866 061	809 946	530 578	380 493
1969	3 310 694	2 244 312	1 498 284	732 270	957 921	818 165	582 597	386 125
1970	3 390 099	2 263 432	1 425 733	575 630	993 137	767 827	519 562	429 593
1971	2 755 112	1 875 221	1 178 730	426 667	1 013 479	670 220	393 556	240 027
1972	3 551 121	2 482 580	1 588 713	751 298	1 149 084	898 109	584 022	374 980
1973	3 689 125	2 385 313	1 372 918	404 599	1 141 455	954 965	564 315	303 960
1974[c]	3 353 060				1 112 217			

[a] Old crop only.
[b] Stocks at mills, elevators, warehouses, terminals, processors, and those owned by Commodity Credit Corporation which are in bins and other storages under CCC control.
[c] Preliminary.

Statistical Reporting Service. Data for 1949–62 in *Agricultural Statistics*, 1972, table 42.
(Source: USDA).

TABLE 1.17
Oats: Stocks on and off Farms, USA, 1963–73

Year beginning October	*On farms*				*Off farms*[b]			
	October 1st	*January 1st* (*thousand bushels*)	*April 1st*	*July 1st*[a]	*October 1st*	*January 1st* (*thousand bushels*)	*April 1st*	*July 1st*[a]
1963	820 559	677 593	439 798	249 038	112 871	85 382	71 726	63 328
1964	728 807	604 469	389 534	213 738	120 316	87 774	71 050	62 770
1965	782 038	661 263	449 217	241 215	138 613	102 605	87 258	75 460
1966	678 804	557 581	355 033	199 294	156 250	105 110	87 895	71 346
1967	650 293	552 094	363 866	207 725	135 670	104 378	83 534	66 511
1968	791 680	668 396	448 085	278 688	154 655	123 227	109 377	99 949
1969	847 091	738 853	541 049	352 783	193 728	160 986	144 644	145 812
1970	859 136	711 572	509 833	316 235	246 292	210 771	199 540	200 822
1971	812 527	692 602	507 299	336 492	280 502	250 581	228 710	204 940
1972	679 205	556 083	377 191	228 974	249 036	220 117	206 575	180 974
1973[c]	606 322	472 767			198 719	161 409		

[a] Old crop only.
[b] Stocks at mills, elevators, warehouses, terminals, processors, and those owned by Commodity Credit Corporation which are in bins and other storages under CCC control.
[c] Preliminary.
Statistical Reporting Service. Data for 1949–62 in *Agricultural Statistics*, 1972, table 54.
(Source: USDA).

TABLE 1.18
Barley: Acreage, Yield, Production, Value and Foreign Trade, USA, 1959–73

Year	*Acreage seeded*[a] (1 000 acres)	*Acreage harvested for grain* (1 000 acres)	*Yield per harvested acre* (bushels)	*Production* (1 000 bushels)	*Season average price per bushel received by farmers*[b] (dollars)	*Farm value* (1 000 dollars)	*Price per bushel at Minneapolis, year beginning August*[c] (dollars)	*Foreign trade including barley, flour, and malt, year beginning July*[d]: *Domestic exports*[e] (1 000 bushels)	*Imports for consumption* (1 000 bushels)
1959	16 766	14 869	28·3	420 203	0·860	357 584	1·09	118 200	17 880
1960	15 527	13 856	31·0	429 005	·840	355 248	1·07	85 702	15 252
1961	15 623	12 806	30·6	392 441	·979	376 112	1·33	84 409	19 543
1962	14 380	12 214	35·0	427 726	·915	385 871	1·11	67 500	5 404
1963	13 452	11 236	35·0	392 833	·897	350 020	1·09	70 650	12 475
1964	11 652	10 277	37·6	386 059	·953	365 050	1·20	60 662	11 954
1965	10 123	9 166	42·9	393 055	1·02	399 575	1·32	77 029	7 573
1966	11 184	10 250	38·3	392 108	1·06	411 849	1·33	45 241	7 382
1967	10 077	9 230	40·5	373 745	1·01	374 412	1·23	31 288	8 305
1968	10 486	9 732	43·8	426 151	·921	390 241	1·16	13 181	9 967
1969	10 291	9 557	44·7	427 055	·885	377 878	1·08	17 016	13 015
1970	10 490	9 725	42·8	416 139	·973	400 368	1·22	78 220	9 338
1971	11 115	10 151	45·7	463 601	·993	458 737	1·16	50 723	15 256
1972	10 639	9 707	43·6	423 461	1·22	507 190	1·48	66 420	14 038
1973[f]	11 335	10 527	40·3	424 483	2·04	853 462	2·60		

[a] Barley sown for all purposes, including barley sown in the preceding fall.
[b] Obtained by weighting State prices by quantity sold. Includes allowance for unredeemed loans and purchases by the Government valued at the average loan and purchase rate, by States, where applicable.
[c] Price of No. 3 barley; average of daily prices weighted by carlot sales, as reported in the Minneapolis Daily Market Record.
[d] Compiled from reports of the US Department of Commerce. Barley flour and malt converted to grain equivalent.
[e] Includes shipments under the Army Civilian Supply Program.
[f] Preliminary.
Statistical Reporting Service and Economic Research Service. Data for 1909–58 in *Agricultural Statistics*, 1972, table 58.
(Source: USDA).

TABLE 1.19
Sorghum Grain: Stocks on and off Farms, USA, 1963–74

Year	*On farms*				*Off farms*[b]			
	January 1st	*April 1st* (*thousand bushels*)	*July 1st*	*October 1st*[a]	*January 1st*	*April 1st* (*thousand bushels*)	*July 1st*	*October 1st*[a]
1963	177 636	101 716	50 667	34 815	846 514	725 258	643 767	619 811
1964	189 625	110 128	63 091	42 347	833 074	730 349	651 776	606 453
1965	154 259	98 010	61 565	47 442	797 589	669 893	595 677	518 093
1966	212 919	133589	71 353	50 614	765 142	590 556	461 521	340 587
1967	234 170	133 178	81 981	44 414	586 872	393 312	253 553	199 486
1968	212 743	141 921	90 536	58 063	519 341	374 907	277 408	230 948
1969	217 904	127 380	81 996	51 913	523 364	413 366	302 491	235 040
1970	184 644	117 505	67 649	38 726	503 506	385 895	278 918	205 235
1971	151 672	87 885	35 576	13 334	459 066	268 081	141 300	77 140
1972	245 359	143 347	67 003	30 646	463 528	336 362	208 488	111 231
1973	219 295	95 161	45 585	13 791	401 830	267 714	153 996	59 003
1974[c]	221 318				426 777			

[a] Old crop only.
[b] Stocks at mills, elevators, warehouses, terminals, processors, and those owned by Commodity Credit Corporation, which are in bins and other storages under CCC control.
[c] Preliminary.
Statistical Reporting Service. Data for 1949–62 in *Agricultural Statistics*, 1972, table 74.
(Source: USDA).

TABLE 1.20
Sorghum Grain: Supply and Disappearance, USA, 1962–73

Year beginning October	Supply			Disappearance					
	Carry-over stocks	*Production* (million bushels)	*Total supply*	*Food and industrial uses*[a]	*Seed*	*Livestock feed*[b]	*Domestic dis-appearance* (million bushels)	*Exports*[c]	*Total dis-appearance*
1962	661	510	1 171	10	2	391	403	113	516
1963	655	585	1 240	11	2	471	484	107	591
1964	649	490	1 139	11	2	412	425	148	573
1965	566	673	1 239	11	2	569	582	266	848
1966	391	715	1 106	11	2	601	614	248	862
1967	244	755	999	11	2	532	545	166	711
1968	288	731	1 019	11	2	613	626	106	732
1969	287	730	1 017	7	2	638	647	126	773
1970	244	684	928	7	3	684	694	144	838
1971	90	876	966	7	2	692	701	123	824
1972[d]	142	809	951	4	2	660	666	212	878
1973[d]	73	937	1 010						

[a] Includes an allowance for wet-process products.
[b] Residual; includes small quantities of other uses and waste.
[c] Compiled from reports of the Bureau of the Census.
[d] Preliminary.
Economic Research Service. Data for 1949–61 in *Agricultural Statistics*, 1972, table 78.
(Source: USDA).

for farmers, and the Ministry of Agriculture, Fisheries and Food are united in urging a modest expansion in production over a five-year period. In fact, however, the combination of the 'green pound' exchange rate with the European Economic Community 'unit of account' in terms of which EEC common prices are fixed, and which does not take account of each devaluation of sterling, together with relatively low price guarantees, have led to a steady reduction in the size of the dairy herd and a slowing of production. Poor weather in 1974 and the first part of 1975 led to shortages of winter feed for livestock, and the dry summer of 1976 affected UK arable yield severely, although the effect in the rest of the EEC was less than had been feared.

The EEC is more than 90% self-sufficient in food but this level of production is based on very high outputs from certain countries, mainly The Netherlands, Denmark and France. Italy produces only about 20–30% of the meat it consumes and rising prices led to a situation in 1973 where meat imports accounted for about half the country's total trade deficit. Like British farmers earlier, Italian farmers have found themselves trapped between rising costs, which inflated meat prices, and falling consumption resulting from the high prices. In 1974 the Italian government introduced a five-year plan for agricultural expansion, with particular encouragement being given to cattle and sheep rearing and breeding programmes.

From June 1974 it has been illegal in Spain to slaughter cattle at carcass weights of less than 125 kg or sheep weighing less than 5 kg, while an additional payment is made for sheep weighing more than 13 kg at slaughter.

The Greek government is also encouraging the improvement of local breeds of beef cattle and is importing pedigree stock.

In 1973 and again in 1974, the Swedish government froze consumer prices for essential food items and paid subsidies to farmers. Farm prices are agreed between the government and producers and it has been decided that in future reviews shall take place twice a year instead of annually as before. Current arrangements allow for the compensation of farmers to cover increasing production costs.

Norway introduced a new general agreement on farm prices in the middle of 1974.

The EEC has suffered from shortages and surpluses. In 1972 and until the spring of 1973, beef was in short supply within the Community. The rising cost of imported feedingstuffs, especially of soybean meal, led to higher rates of slaughtering and this, combined with the seasonal increase in beef supplies, transformed the shortage into a surplus and the market began to deteriorate. France, Italy and the Benelux countries suspended the import of beef from third countries and Italy introduced unilateral import restrictions. Importers were obliged to buy, from the Community's national Intervention Boards, quantities of frozen meat equivalent to those they were importing, but intervention buying continued under the Common Agricultural Policy aim of stabilising markets, and a 'beef mountain' accumulated. This surplus is likely to be temporary, as the Community is still a net importer of beef.

The Common Agricultural Policy is under almost continual review at the request of several member states, including the UK and Germany.

Eastern Europe and the USSR

Throughout 1973, investment in agriculture continued in all the Eastern European countries, although it was spread less evenly than it had been in previous years. It increased considerably in Poland, to a lesser degree in Czechoslovakia, but decreased in the German Democratic Republic and in Romania.

Agricultural investment in the USSR increased by 7·9% in 1973 as compared with 1972. Much of this investment was in fixed plant and buildings, but an additional 980 000 ha of land were irrigated and 900 000 were drained. 6900 million roubles were allowed under the 1974 budget for further land reclamation, with emphasis being placed on the irrigated land used for vegetable production close to the cities. It was planned to reclaim 89 000 hectares of such land.

Table 1.21 shows the development of kolkhozes (collectives) and sovkhozes (state farms) from 1965 to 1973. The establishment of highly industrialised farm enterprises, allowing for the integration of industry and agriculture, together with other forms of association between kolkhozes, sovkhozes and other industries, is now a key element in Soviet agricultural planning.

TABLE 1.21
Evolution of Kolkhozes and Sovkhozes in the USSR

	Kolkhozes		*Sovkhozes*	
	1965	1973	1965	1973
Number[a] (thousands)	36·3	31·0	11·7	16·1[b]
Families associated (million)	15·4	13·9	—	—
Average number of workers (million)	18·6	16·0	8·2	9·4
Sown area (million ha)	105·1	98·6	89·1	99·6
Area under cereals (million ha)	62·6	57·0	59·7	63·0
Cattle (million)	38·3	44·9	24·5	32·5
Pigs (million)	24·6	32·1	12·6	19·3
Sheep and goats (millions)	54·6	53·4	46·4	60·2
Number of tractors (thousand)	772	1 049	681	894

[a] Excluding fishing kolkhozes.
[b] Excluding 1246 fattening sovkhozes.
(Source: *The State of Food and Agriculture* 1974. FAO, Rome, 1975).

A number of kolkhozes have disappeared by being merged together into larger units. Others have been converted into sovkhozes. Some 13 000 sovkhozes now use a cost accounting system and while the state finances major capital projects, they are expected to finance their own operations and to show a profit. By 1975 all state farms are expected to use this system.

The failure of the 1975 grain harvest led to fears of severe food shortages, perhaps even famine, but these fears were not realised and the 1976 harvest, although poor, showed a marked recovery. The current five-year plan, from 1976 to 1980, called for the production of 215–220 million tonnes of grain. The estimated 1976 harvest, of 190–195 million tonnes, is below the target but still much higher than the 135 million tonnes produced in 1975.

Oceania

Farm incomes in Australasia rose sharply from 1972, as world prices rose for the commodities these countries were exporting. Increases in production were confined to Australia, however. New Zealand suffered from severe drought. Export returns were reduced by the rising cost of ocean freight that followed the rise in oil prices. It would be natural to expect that the fall in livestock production in New Zealand, caused by drought several years in succession, would reduce investment in response to a fall in incomes, so leading to reductions in planned output. In fact, however, world shortages raised prices sufficiently to offset this effect and made it possible for both Australia and New Zealand to begin to plan more stable commodity and marketing schemes.

The Australian government encouraged almost unlimited wheat production in 1973. The area sown to wheat was increased by 18 %, to 9 million ha. Western Australia had a favourable season but the rest of the country suffered from wet weather and from rust, a fungal disease of cereals. The 1973 production was almost double that of the previous year, when Australia suffered acute and prolonged drought, but widespread crop disease meant that an unusually large part of the harvest was of poor quality. Exports were limited only by the availability of supplies and Australia ended the year with a carry-over stock of 0·5 million tonnes, which was exactly the same quantity it had in 1972.

The combined effects of drought and a high rate of slaughtering reduced the Australian sheep flock by 14 % between 31 March, 1972 and 31 March, 1973, bringing it to its lowest level since 1956. Wool yields were below average and lambing was poor. The rate of slaughter slowed later in 1973 and improved weather conditions permitted production of wool and meat to recover.

New Zealand wool production has declined for several years in succession. As in Australia, drought reduced the average clip and caused a low rate of lambing, while a high rate of slaughter reduced the size of the national flock by 4 %. The New Zealand Wool Marketing Corporation disposed of the whole of its carry-over stocks from the 1971/72 season and made no new purchases in 1972/73.

Latin America

New agricultural development plans were put into effect in Argentina, Barbados, Costa Rica, Ecuador, El Salvador, Honduras and Uruguay in 1973 and the early months of 1974. Plans are also being prepared in Brazil, Jamaica, Nicaragua and Venezuela. These plans all emphasise increased output but they aim, too, to ensure a more equitable distribution of work and incomes, to reduce regional differences and to develop and conserve natural resources.

Agricultural production in the region has increased steadily since 1969, by about 3·25% a year, marred only by the slow rates of increase in 1971 (1%) and 1972 (2%).

Near East

Countries in this region are also beginning to construct and implement development plans. These are aimed usually at nutritional objectives but employment also receives attention, as does the development of resources, especially water. In Egypt the 10-year plan (1973–1982) hopes to achieve a 3·9% annual increase in production during its first five years and a 39·4% increase by the end of the full period. Libya plans an even more ambitious expansion, of 16% a year, to bring the country close to self-sufficiency in major food items. 367 000 ha of new land are to be brought into production, of which 95 000 are to be irrigated. In the Yemen Arab Republic, where agriculture provides 90% of employment and contributes 70% of the gross domestic product, it is planned that agriculture shall provide the economic surplus used for industrial development. Crop and animal production are to increase and the irrigated area is to be extended by 100 000 ha.

Despite ambitious plans throughout the region, the annual increase in production between 1969 and 1973 has averaged only 2·25%. Production increased by 10% from 1971 to 1972, but actually fell by 7% in 1973. Per caput production is 2% lower than the 1961 to 1965 average.

Far East

Long range plans in the region are being revised regularly. The wars in Indochina and consequent political upheavals have delayed development. India's five-year plan, launched in 1974, was being revised in 1975 and Pakistan was planning on a year-by-year basis. Bangladesh aims to achieve self-sufficiency in food grains by 1978, with an annual agricultural growth rate of 4·6% and 24% of the total public investment in development. Burma plans to extend people's ownership to 48% and co-operative ownership to 26% by the mid-1990s as part of its plan to convert its agrarian economy into an economy in which agriculture provides a base for industrial development. Meanwhile, agriculture is planned to grow at an annual rate of 4 % and livestock and fisheries by 3·4 %.

The aim of India's plan is to eliminate poverty and make the country economically self-reliant. In pursuit of this latter aim the importance of agriculture within the economy is to be reduced, although food production is planned to grow at an annual 5·5 % in order to raise the consumption levels of the poorest 30 % of the rural population, amounting to 25 million households. India hopes to become independent of imports of crude oils, metals, machinery and equipment and fertilisers. The plan had to be revised because of the general world inflation and the rise in prices for imported oil and food.

Indonesia plans an agricultural growth of 5 % per year and an industrial growth of 13 % per year, in order to halve the country's dependence on foreign aid. The Philippines, too, plans an agricultural growth rate of 5 % per year and a faster rate of industrial growth and investment. Malaysia plans for an agricultural growth rate of 8·3 % per year but admits that it is likely to achieve only about 7 %.

Chinese agricultural production continues to expand, both to provide more food and to provide raw materials for industry This has led to problems in some provinces, such as Hunan and Fukien, where communes that should have increased their output both of grains and of cotton in fact grew cotton at the expense of grains because it was more profitable, and found themselves short of food. The central government has now provided directives to guide communes in deciding how to allot their land. The country is also short of labour for the many major capital products that are needed and for which machinery is not available. Senior schoolchildren and students are drafted into the countryside to assist but China is aiming at a much higher degree of mechanisation and electrification in order to release labour. Some of the mass-labour projects completed during the 1973/74 season were the bringing of 1·6 million ha of land into cultivation, the levelling of 2·6 million ha of hilly land, the terracing of 460 000 ha and the bringing into cultivation of 800 000 ha of former wasteland. Communes in Hunan alone built 50 000 new power wells and completed some 110 000 small and medium water conservation projects in 1973/74.

Chinese statistics are difficult to obtain but agriculture probably provides employment for about 80 % of the population and provides about 60 % of the national income. Fertiliser manufacture in the first half of 1976 was 14·5 % higher than in the same period a year earlier, although this rate of increase was likely to fall as coal had to be diverted to industry from fertiliser production following the Tangshan earthquake. China has no centralised national plan, but in mid-1975 some provinces were aiming to expand agricultural production by 16–17 % a year. During the early 1970s agricultural output grew at about 3·6 % a year, which is excellent by international standards.

Japan aims to increase home production because of the probability of further rises in world food prices, which could place an economic strain on a country heavily dependent on imports. Overall, Japan's level of self-sufficiency declined from 93 % in 1960 to 78 % in 1972. This decline was not spread evenly and it reflects the increase in the consumption of meat and other livestock products. Self-sufficiency in wheat during the period declined from 39 % to 5 %, in concentrated feedingstuffs for livestock from 67 % to 36 %, in soybeans from 28 % to 4 %, in meat from 91 to 81 %, and there was also a decline in respect of fruit, from 100 % to 82 %.

Japan's agricultural land area is limited and land is lost continually for urban and industrial development. The high degree of security provided by law for farm tenants makes landlords unwilling to rent land and the fact that land prices doubled between 1969 and 1972 encourages them to hold on to their land in the hope of speculative profits. A large part of Japan's increased security of food supply is to be achieved by stockpiling both home-grown and imported food commodities.

In the Far East as a whole, production increased steadily between 1969 and 1973, by a total of 12 % in the developing market economies, although per caput production declined a little. In the centrally planned Asian economies there was an overall increase of 12 %, but this occurred mainly in two leaps, in 1969/70 and 1972/73. In 1971/72 there was a small fall in output. Per caput production increased by 3 % over the period.

Africa

Per caput food production has fallen sharply since 1971, so that now it is 5 % below the 1961–1965 level, although good harvests were reported for 1976. Total production has increased, however, and is about 22 % above the base year level, although in 1973 it fell 4 % below the output achieved the year before.

Several African countries, including those of the Sahelian Zone, are recovering slowly from prolonged drought. For some of them the only way to increase production may be through very large and very expensive irrigation schemes that may be ecologically hazardous even if they can be financed.

Algeria plans to increase cereal production by 50 %, pulse production by 90 % and vegetable production by 70 % by 1980, although this will still not make the country self-sufficient in food. Morocco plans for an annual agricultural growth rate of 4 % and Tunisia plans to increase cereal production by 6·4 % a year, vegetable production by 7·5 % and livestock by 6 %. Details are not available of Ghana's plans, but so far as agriculture is concerned they will be included in a programme called 'Operation Feed Yourself'.

In Guinea the aim is to make each region self-sufficient in staple foods, especially in rice, which at present is imported at a high cost. Nigeria is in serious difficulties. Rising oil prices have drawn people from agriculture into the cities and oil-producing areas, while agricultural productivity has achieved less than half the target set for it. For the moment this is not serious, because oil revenues enable the country to import such food as it needs. Since the oil boom is expected to last no longer than 25 years, however, it is essential that agriculture develops both to feed and provide employment for the population and to provide a firm long term base for industrial development. The Central African Republic plans to direct 24 % of its total investment to agriculture. Ethiopia's plans are in disarray because of world inflation, especially the rise in the prices of oil and food, the country's own severe and prolonged drought and because of the political changes that have taken place. Kenya has achieved a steady average rate of growth of 5 % per year in agriculture but the country still faces acute unemployment problems.

The Sahel countries have set up an inter-state committee for combating the drought and its aftermath, with headquarters in Ouagadougou, and it is possible that regional food reserves will be established throughout Africa. This has been urged for several years by the Organisation for African Unity. The majority of African countries now have links with the EEC through the Yaoundé Convention, which sets out the bases of trade links between the EEC and signatory African nations. More recently, the Lomé Convention has been created to safeguard the trading interests of developing countries in all the world's developing regions.

Table 1.22 gives indices of total and per caput food production by regions between 1969 and 1973.

During 1975/76 world production increased and the estimates for 1976 suggested that total cereal production was likely to increase by a further 6 % over the 1975 figure, to 1324 million tonnes (an increase of 77 million tonnes). Wheat production was expected to increase by 11 %, to 393 million tonnes, coarse grains by 6 % to 703 million tonnes and rice, which is more difficult to forecast because it is harvested later in the year, was estimated to fall a little to 340 million tonnes. This is less than was produced in 1974 but it is still the second highest yield ever recorded. In the Far East the monsoon rains were erratic once again, leaving some areas short of water and others flooded, and in some countries pest infestations reduced yields. The country most seriously affected was Sri Lanka, which experienced a prolonged drought.

The generally good 1976 harvest was expected to permit some accumulation of reserves. After the 1975 harvest US grain stocks stood at about 230 000 tonnes. The 1976 harvest was expected to increase this to over 1 million tonnes, and India was also expected to accumulate some reserves. World rice stocks were expected to increase also, from the perilously low 13 million tonnes of 1975 to about 16 million tonnes (excluding China and the USSR). The FAO anticipated some reduction in

TABLE 1.22
Index Numbers of Total and per caput Food Production, World and Major Regions, 1969–73

	Total food production					*Per caput food production*				
	1969	1970	1971	1972	1973	1969	1970	1971	1972	1973
	(*index numbers* 1961–65, *average* = 100)									
Developed market economies[a]	116	116	123	122	126	109	108	114	112	114
Western Europe	115	117	122	122	125	110	111	115	113	116
North America	115	113	124	122	125	107	104	113	110	112
Oceania	123	121	127	127	139	108	107	109	108	116
Eastern Europe and USSR	123	130	132	133	148	116	121	123	122	134
Total developed countries	118	121	127	126	134	1·11	112	117	116	121
Developing market economies[a]	119	124	125	125	130	102	103	102	99	100
Africa	118	121	124	126	122	102	102	102	100	95
Far East	118	124	124	120	130	102	104	102	96	101
Latin America	120	125	126	128	133	102	103	100	99	100
Near East	122	124	128	138	131	104	103	102	107	98
Asian centrally planned economies	116	122	125	123	128	104	107	108	105	107
Total developing countries	118	123	125	125	129	103	105	104	101	102
World total	118	122	126	126	131	105	106	108	106	108

[a] Including countries in other regions not specified.
(Source: FAO index numbers of agricultural production, United Nations population estimates. UN WFC C/Conf. 65/3).

world trade in food as many regions achieved a higher level of self-sufficiency, and a corresponding easing of prices.[12]

THE OUTLOOK

At the UN World Food Conference, held in Rome in November 1974, 22 complex resolutions were passed, the most important being:

(1) That objectives and strategies for food production should be devised with the help of all the relevant international institutions.
(2) That priorities should be devised and implemented for rural development.
(3) That fertilisers should be made more easily available in developing countries.
(4) That there should be an intensification of research, especially into the impact of different ecological conditions on agricultural production in various climatic zones and most of all in tropical and marginal land and in agrometeorology, while agricultural training and extension services should be improved.
(5) That food and nutritional plans should be prepared to provide basic requirements, especially for pregnant women, nursing mothers and small children, the groups at greatest risk, that deficiencies of vitamins be reduced and that possibilities be studied of increasing the production and consumption of vegetable crops other than cereals.
(6) That there be a global inventory made of land that could be brought into agricultural production, taking account of ecological constraints and the likely availability of input resources, and that a World Soil Charter be prepared as a basis for international cooperation towards the most rational use of the world's land resources.
(7) That work be intensified in water management.
(10) That the global distribution, use and environmental impact of pesticides be studied with a view to improving crop protection and safety.
(11) That a programme be devised for the control of African animal trypanosomiasis.
(12) That the seed industry be developed.
(13) That an international fund be established for agricultural development.
(15) That more food aid be provided for the victims of wars in Africa.
(16) That a global information and early warning system be established.

(17) That there be an international undertaking on world food security, whereby food stock policies are developed and implemented in developing countries.
(18) That food aid be increased.
(19) That the terms of world trade in food commodities be adjusted in favour of developing countries.
(22) That a committee on World Food Security be established as a standing committee of the FAO Council and that other steps be taken to ensure effective follow-up of the conference resolutions.

By mid-April 1975, only a few months after the conference ended, the FAO was able to report that progress had been made toward implementing all the resolutions listed above.

Even so the need to rebuild stocks is urgent. Table 1.23 shows that the developing countries are still likely to be experiencing net shortages of wheat, rice and coarse grains by 1985. The centrally planned Asian economies will be in balance overall, but only because of their surpluses of coarse grains, which are not used (generally) for human consumption. The developed countries will have a surplus of wheat by 1985, out of which the deficiencies of the developing countries must be met.

Table 1.24 compares actual consumption in 1970 with projected demand for 1985 and 1990.

Harvest forecasts have never before been publicised so widely, nor have they had such ominous significance. The reason, as we have seen, is more commercial than nutritional. Table 1.25 shows the rate at which world trade in food has been growing. The low level of carry-over stocks encourages forward buying against crops that have not yet been harvested. Prices follow a fairly predictable pattern, subject to short term distortion. Early in the season, harvests are estimated simply by multiplying the areas sown to each crop by the average yields per hectare in those areas. This produces an estimate. As the growing season progresses, so the yield estimates change with the changing weather and the effect of diseases and pests. Generally prices start low early in the season and then rise.

In 1975, for example, July estimates of US harvests were high: 6046 million bushels of maize (153·57 million tonnes) and 2187 million bushels of wheat (59·52 million tonnes). This led to low prices but US estimates of the Soviet harvest suggested that the USSR could be short of 50 million tonnes of grains, of which some 20 million tonnes might be purchased on the US market. This raised prices. In fact, however, it turned out to be an unduly pessimistic view of the Soviet prospects and the USSR imported only 13·5 million tonnes, not all of that from the USA. Then there were doubts about the size of the US harvest, following reports of prolonged drought and a heat wave in Nebraska and Iowa. By September the USSR had concluded a regular agreement with the USA for the purchase of grain every year. This

TABLE 1.23
All Cereals: Balances for 1969–71 and 1985

	All cereals		*Wheat*		*Rice paddy*		*Coarse grains*	
	1969–71	1985	1969–71	1985 (*million tonnes*)	1969–71	1985	1969–71	1985
World								
Total demand	1 207	1 725	331	447	310	447	566	831
of which: feed	422	650	69	108	5	10	348	532
production	1 239	n.s.	329	570	302	n.s.	608	n.s.
balance	32	n.s.	−2	123	−8	n.s.	42	n.s.
Developing countries								
Total demand	590	929	127	208	288	422	175	299
of which: feed	51	128	8	—	3	—	39	—
production	585	853	98	172	278	378	209	303
balance	−5	−76	−29	−36	−10	−44	34	4
Developing market economies								
Total demand	386	629	87	140	171	275	128	214
of which: feed	36	79	3	6	1	3	31	70
production	370	544	67	121	168	236	135	187
balance	−16	−85	−20	−19	−3	−39	7	−27
Asian centrally planned economies countries								
Total demand	204	300	40	68	117	147	47	85
of which: feed	15	49	5	14	2	6	8	29
production	215	309	31	51	110	142	74	116
balance	11	9	−9	−17	−7	−5	27	31
Developed countries								
Total demand	617	796	204	239	22	25	391	532
of which: feed	372	523	61	88	2	2	309	433
production	654	n.s.	231	398	24	n.s.	399	n.s.
balance	37	n.s.	27	159	2	n.s.	8	n.s.

n.s. = not shown.
(Source: UN WFC E/Conf. 65/3).

TABLE 1.24

Cereals: Actual Consumption and Projected Trend Demand by Main Types of Utilisation, 1970–1990. 'Trend' Growth Assumption

	Actual cons. 1970	1980	*Projected demand* 1985 *(million tonnes)*	1990	1980/70	*Percentage increase* 1985/70 (%)	1990/70	1970–80	*Rates of growth* 1970–85 (*% p.a. compound*)	1970–90
Developed countries										
food	160·9	163·1	164·1	164·6	1·3	2·0	2·0	0·1	0·1	0·1
feed	371·5	467·9	522·7	565·7	25·9	40·7	52·3	2·3	2·3	2·1
other uses	84·9	100·6	109·5	116·4	18·5	29·0	37·1	1·7	1·7	1·6
Total	617·3	731·6	796·3	846·7	18·5	29·0	37·2	1·7	1·7	1·6
Per caput (kg)	576	623	649	663	8·2	12·7	15·1	0·8	0·8	0·7
Developing market economies										
food	303·7	409·3	474·5	547·2	34·8	56·3	80·2	3·0	3·0	3·0
feed	35·6	60·9	78·6	101·9	71·1	120·8	186·2	5·5	5·4	5·4
other uses	46·4	64·1	75·4	88·5	38·1	62·5	90·7	3·3	3·3	3·3
Total	385·7	534·3	628·5	737·6	38·5	63·0	91·2	3·3	3·3	3·3
Per caput (kg)	220	233	240	246	5·9	9·1	11·8	0·6	0·6	0·6
Asian centrally planned economies										
food	164·1	200·5	215·2	225·3	22·2	31·1	37·3	2·0	1·8	1·6
feed	15·3	38·7	48·7	61·4	152·9	218·3	301·3	9·7	8·0	7·2
other uses	24·6	32·6	36·0	39·1	32·5	46·3	58·9	2·9	2·6	2·3
Total	204·0	271·8	299·9	325·8	33·2	47·0	59·7	2·9	2·6	2·4
Per caput (kg)	257	290	298	304	12·8	16·0	18·3	1·2	1·0	0·8
World										
food	628·7	772·9	853·8	937·1	22·9	35·8	49·1	2·1	2·1	2·0
feed	422·4	567·5	650·0	729·0	34·4	53·9	72·6	3·0	2·9	2·8
other uses	155·9	197·3	220·9	244·0	26·6	41·7	56·5	2·4	2·4	2·3
Total	1 207·0	1 537·7	1 724·7	1 910·1	27·4	42·9	58·3	2·5	2·4	2·3
Per caput (kg)	333	349	355	357	4·8	6·6	7·2	0·5	0·4	0·3

(Source: FAO estimates, UN WFC E/Conf. 65/3).

TABLE 1.25

Index Numbers of the Volume of Gross Food Imports and Their Rates of Growth, World and Main Regions, 1961–63 to 1972

	Volume of gross food imports[a]			*Annual rate of growth (% per year)*	
	1961–63	1969–71	1972	1961–63 *to* 1969–71	1961–63 *to* 1972
Developed market economies[b]	96	128	140	3·6	3·8
Western Europe	96	125	133	3·4	3·7
North America	102	116	123	1·7	1·9
Oceania	97	114	123	2·0	2·4
Eastern Europe and USSR	86	113	154	3·5	6·0
Total developed countries	95	126	142	3·6	4·1
Developing market economies[b]	96	127	138	3·4	3·5
Africa	100	123	135	2·6	3·1
Far East	93	120	125	3·2	3·0
Latin America	96	127	154	3·5	4·8
Near East	94	135	135	4·5	3·6
Asian centrally planned economies	96	106	120	1·2	2·2
Total developing countries	96	123	134	3·2	3·4
World total	95	125	139	3·4	3·9

[a] Index numbers 1961–65, average = 100.
[b] Including countries in other regions not specified.
(Source: UN WFC E/Conf. 65/3).

TABLE 1.26
Food Aid in Cereals from all Sources (thousand tons)

Country	1969/70[a]	1970/71[a]	1971/72[a]	1972/73[a]	1973/74[a]	1974/75[a]	1975/76[a]	1976/77[a]	1977/78[a]
USA	9 030	8 321	8 463	6 211	2 936	5 430[b]	5 800[c]		
Argentina	23	23	23	23	23	23	23[d]		
Australia	212	226	240	225	225	320	400[b]		
Canada	663	1 608	605	712	499	516[b]	1 000	1 000	1 000
EEC	1 287	1 287	1 035	1 161	1 287	1 287	1 287[d]		
Finland	14	14	14	14	14	14	14[d]		
Japan	395	729	603	442	298	225	225[d]		
Norway	14	14	—	—	—	10[e]	—		
Sweden	54	54	35	35	35	35	75[f]	75[f]	75[f]
Switzerland	32	32	32	32	32	32	32[d]		
Iraq	—	—	—	—	—	283[g]	—		
Saudi Arabia	—	—	—	—	—	—	100[h]	100[g]	
UA Emirates	—	—	—	—	—	83[g]	4[i]	6[h]	
Algeria[j]	—	—	—	—	—	18[g]	—		
Others	78	364	615	103	51	350	—		
Total	11 802	12 672	11 665	8 958	5 400[k]	8 626	8 960		

[a] Represents for each aid-giving country its budgetary period for which food aid is programmed; for countries which programme their food aid on a calendar year basis, the year refers to the first year of the split year indicated, i.e. 1974 programme is shown under 1974/75, and so on.
[b] Estimated.
[c] Indicative figure, subject to change.
[d] Assuming that the obligations under FAC, which expired on 30 June, 1975, will be continued.
[e] Subject to Parliamentary approval.
[f] FAC obligations of 35 000 tons per year (which it is assumed will be continued) plus additional pledge of 40 000 tons wheat per year for three years from 1975/76 which is subject to Parliamentary approval.
[g] Incomplete; quantity estimated in wheat equivalent on the basis of $180 per ton of wheat, from known cash contributions during January–October, 1974.
[h] Represents commodity content at two-thirds of $50 million pledged to WFP for two years, 1975 and 1976, notionally estimated in wheat equivalent on the basis of $180 per ton of wheat.
[i] Represents commodity content at two-thirds of $3 million pledged to WFP for two years, 1975 and 1976, notionally estimated in wheat equivalent on the basis of $180 per ton of wheat.
[j] Including triangular transactions, occasional aid from various countries, and food aid provided under UNEO in 1974/75 up to 31 March, 1975.
[k] Does not include USSR food loan of 2 million tons to India repayable in kind.
(Source: UN WFC/6, 2 May, 1975).

means that Soviet demands can be predicted and the USSR will not have to enter the US market each time it predicts a shortfall.

It was Soviet intervention that played a major part in the disruption of the market in 1972, and though this was probably exaggerated it produced a considerable effect inside the USA. Japan has agreed to buy 14 million tonnes or more of US grain and soybeans annually for three years up to 1977.

So the need is to rebuild stocks and to provide short term aid. Table 1.26 shows the food aid in cereals that had been pledged by 2 May, 1975. Thirty governments had by that date adopted the objectives and policies needed to implement the recommendations of the World Food Conference: Australia, Belgium, Bolivia, Burundi, Canada, Chad, Chile, Cyprus, Denmark, Ecuador, Egypt, Finland, France, Federal Republic of Germany, India, Indonesia, Ireland, Japan, Kuwait, Luxembourg, Malta, Mexico, Netherlands, Niger, Portugal, Sri Lanka, Sweden, UK, USA and Upper Volta.

The FAO estimated that unless stocks were rebuilt within a few years the rate of population growth in the developing countries would ensure that increases in annual demand accounted for the whole of any increases in production, leaving no surpluses.

Was this an over-reaction to a population problem that, even then, was showing signs of solving itself? The underlying assumption to all the fears of global famine is the Malthusian one—that population is pressing hard against an absolute limit. We should look now at the rate of world population growth to try to determine why and how this growth is occurring, whether it may ease off naturally and if not what steps can be taken to stabilise it, and the extent to which it may represent a genuine threat on a global scale.

REFERENCES

1. FAO (1974). *Assessment of the World Food Situation*. UN WFC E/Conf. 65/4, Rome.
2. UN (1973 and 1974). *Monthly Bulletin of Statistics*. July 1973, April 1974.
3. FAO (1975). *The State of Food and Agriculture*, 1974. Rome.
4. *The Pakistan Development Review*, **XII**(4).
5. *East Pakistan Nutrition Survey* 1962–63: *Preliminary Report*. Directorate of Nutrition and Research, Pakistan, 1965.
6. *Budgets et alimentation des ménages ruraux en* 1962. Ministère des Finances et du Commerce, Madagascar.
7. Borgstrom, G. (1965). *The Hungry Planet: The Modern World at the Edge of Famine*. Collier-Macmillan, New York.
8. Johnson, D. G. (1973). *World Agriculture in Disarray*. Macmillan, London.

9. MAFF (1975). *National Food Survey. Household Consumption in the First Quarter of* 1975. Ministry of Agriculture, Fisheries and Food, London, June.
10. Griffin, K. (1972). *The Green Revolution: An Economic Analysis*. UNRISD, Geneva.
11. FAO (1974). *Yearbook of Fishery Statistics*, 1973. Rome.
12. FAO (1976). Press release 76/48, 1 September; and 76/50, 13 September.

Chapter 2

POPULATION AND FOOD DEMAND: THE MALTHUSIAN EQUATION

Knowledge that the population of the world has been increasing at a rate of 2 % each year has become almost a part of our folk lore. Since this growth is held to be exponential, each increment being a fixed percentage of the last year's total plus earlier increments, it can be predicted with some certainty that the population will double every 34·655 years or, in more convenient round figures, every 35 years.

At least, it could be so predicted were we to accept the assumption that rates of change continue in a constant fashion over long periods of time. In fact, such an assumption is, to say the least, unreliable. Today, all over the world—as we shall see—populations are showing signs of stabilising. It is what we would expect: a graph that shows a rapid growth proceeds to flatten, perhaps eventually to fall a little, as that which grew reaches a new, stable level. However, this is not to dismiss entirely the 'population problem'.

Most popular debates about the future of the world food situation mainly concern the relationship between population and food production, basing themselves on some approximation of the Malthusian relationship between the growth of population and of the resources needed to sustain that population. In 1798 the Rev. Thomas Robert Malthus argued that since populations grow geometrically, or as we would say exponentially, while the availability of resources increases only arithmetically, or in a linear fashion, population growth must always be curbed by physical limits, causing inevitable poverty and hunger among a section of the population. More recently, neo-Malthusians have argued that while this model undoubtedly reflects accurately the relationship between population and resources, the effects can be averted by the voluntary limitation of population, especially through the control of human fertility. Thus they use Malthusian reasoning to urge family planning.

Critics of Malthus point out that the predictions made by Malthus himself proved entirely wrong. Prosperity actually increased during the nineteenth century, when the population of Western Europe was increasing most rapidly, and the 'population collapse' that he believed inevitable did not occur. The rate of population growth slowed. In the 1920s and 1930s it appeared to be actually declining, and governments became seriously worried about the economic implications of a diminishing, ageing population and began to introduce 'pro-natalist' policies. Today, over most of Europe, populations are stabilising again. If this can happen in Europe, may it not happen in other parts of the world?

Increasingly, both views hold that population will stabilise. The argument concerns only the level at which that stabilisation will occur and the form it will take. Anti-Malthusians hold that it will occur naturally and smoothly, while neo-Malthusians hold that unless positive steps are taken to bring it about, it will occur through catastrophe.

As is often the case in such debates conducted in very general terms, the public finds itself confused by equally plausible arguments. No one can doubt that Europeans became more prosperous as they became more numerous and that famines disappeared from their continent. Nor can anyone doubt that European rates of population growth slackened markedly long before the introduction of modern contraception techniques such as the oral pill or the IUD (intra-uterine device). On the other hand it is also true that during the period of expansion, European colonies in North America, Australasia and elsewhere were being established and that they were exporting large food surpluses to their home countries, so that Europe became rather like a large, densely populated conurbation, whose farmlands extended most of the way around the world. This may have been true then, but today, when Europe's population is larger than ever before, the nine countries of the European Economic Community produce 91 % of the food they eat. In terms of yield per unit area of land, Europe is roughly twice as productive as North America.

Yet the logic of the Malthusian argument remains. If, say, each set of parents produces four offspring, then the issue from two parents will be 2:4:16:64:256:1024, and so on, increasing fourfold with each generation. If an additional hectare of farmland is brought into production to increase food supply, however, this makes it no easier to develop more virgin land later and, indeed, it may make it more difficult. So, undeniably, population tends to increase geometrically, while the resources to sustain it increase only arithmetically. In this situation, actual numbers matter little. Any sustained growth of population must end in catastrophe. The difficulty arises, of course, because of the level at which the debate is conducted. The world is far more complex than such crude models would make it appear.

To begin with, there is no simple, direct relationship between population size and demand for food. Obviously people need food, so that the more people there are the more food will be needed, but demand for food is related not to population size only but also to levels of prosperity. Most of the people who are hungry in the world today are hungry not because there is too little food but because they cannot afford to buy what food they need. We saw earlier (Table 1.9) that the income elasticity of demand for cereals remains positive in developing countries, but that in developed countries it has a negative value. In Table 1.11 we saw that income elasticities of demand for meat and eggs remain positive everywhere, and we considered the implications of changing patterns of food consumption as people become more affluent.

The highest rate of population growth in the world is found probably in Bangladesh, where the figure is 3·5 %. This means that unless the rate of growth changes, the population of Bangladesh will double in a little less than 20 years. It does not mean that 20 years from now the people of Bangladesh will be buying twice as much food as they buy now. To calculate that figure we need to know what level of prosperity will have been attained during the 20-year period, and the income elasticity of demand for various products. Such a calculation shows, in fact, that the demand for food in Bangladesh is increasing at a rate of 1·6 % per year, so that while population may double in 20 years, it will take 43 years for food demand to double. This tells us either that Bangladesh will become much poorer and starvation will be widespread or that most people in Bangladesh have almost enough food, so that a modest increase in incomes will not be reflected in a similar increase in food purchases. This complicates the Malthusian argument by introducing economic criteria, but it does not refute it entirely. It is still possible that a situation might arise in which insufficient food could be produced to feed an increasing population, and it is equally true that before that point were reached, increasing pressure on available supplies might cause sharp price rises, so causing suffering among people too poor to pay the new, high prices. Indeed, this may be what is happening in the world today. We simply do not know how much more food we could produce if we tried: we cannot know unless we do try.

The pure Malthusian argument also holds that should the availability of resources increase, then a growth in population will be triggered to take advantage of that increase in a somewhat Parkinsonian fashion. It implies, clearly, that improvements will be made only with the greatest difficulty, if at all, and that there must always be a minority living close to subsistence levels who will starve in times of shortage: 'The poor will always be with us'. It may well be that poverty as we define the term cannot be eliminated from our societies, but the notion that increases in food production will stimulate increases in population is quite untrue. The factors that govern population size are certainly much more complex than this, and farmers do not produce food in an economic vacuum if they can help it. They grow what they believe they will be able to sell and they try to avoid creating surpluses that would reduce their returns.

The final over-simplification results from our fascination with numbers that leads us to extrapolate too eagerly. Malthus was British and confined his observations to the Europe of the late eighteenth century. His conclusions, however, have universal relevance since he postulated a very general kind of ecological relationship. It is tempting, therefore, to 'globalise' the situation. It is also simpler. If we think of the world as a single set of interlocking systems, or 'Spaceship Earth' as it has been called, then we need do no more than balance global population against global food production. By extrapolating global trends into the future we can predict the state of that balance at least for a few years ahead. Then, proceeding from the general to the particular, we can issue warnings to those countries or regions whose local trends depart from the global trends.

When we do this, we see that the world is too complex. The initial extreme aggregation involves gross distortion. Ghana is very different from Germany, and Denmark cannot be lumped together with Paraguay or even with Ireland. Each small region of each continent must be seen separately. When we examine each area we tend to find that populations adjust themselves approximately to the conditions in which they find themselves.

At this stage, perhaps, we need to question the whole thesis. It is plausible but is it good ecology? In natural plant and animal communities we find that populations are seldom limited by Malthusian constraints unless the entire system of which they are part is unbalanced by disturbance from outside. Self-regulating mechanisms operate to control fertility so that absolute limits are rarely encountered. Is man the exception? There seems to be no good reason to suppose that he is.

Does it make sense, then, to talk of global problems at all? Certainly it does, for global problems do exist, but they may not be so simple as popular conceptions of them suggest. The global food problem, for example, has two main aspects. On one hand it relates to patterns of trade, especially between developed and developing nations. At present these work to the disadvantage of the poor. On the other hand it is necessary to increase the production and availability of food in many developing countries—but by no means in all—so that nutritional standards can be improved now, so that future demands can be met and so that a secure base can be established for a balanced economic development. The global population problem is more tenuous. It is concerned with the need to inform everyone of all the implications of continued population growth—good and bad—and to bring every possible assistance to those countries whose rate of growth is so high that the task of increasing individual prosperity becomes impossibly difficult as the mounting cost of providing housing, schools, hospitals and other services diverts scarce capital that otherwise might be invested in industries that would provide employment.

The rather simple globalisation of the population question led to misunderstanding and considerable ill feeling in the early 1970s. Still smarting from their struggles to free themselves from colonial rule and striving to achieve political stability and economic advancement, the developing countries were already deeply suspicious of the motives of the rich. The suggestion that because they were poor they should therefore limit the size of their populations was rejected almost out of hand by the majority of them. It appeared to them that the rich were unwilling either to accept the likelihood of real competition for the resources on which wealth is based, or to take steps to reduce the poverty that was their legacy from years or centuries of colonialism.

The popular movement in America and Europe to stabilise population at a global level was directed primarily at the developing countries because they had the highest rates of growth but, as they were quick to point out, the economic impact of an American, British or French baby was much greater than that of a Brazilian or Nigerian one. The argument became acrimonious and the rich were frequently charged with attempted genocide, especially when it was suggested that programmes to reduce rates of population growth should be a condition of economic aid.

Since the people who supported the population movement in the developed countries were nearly all supporters of a whole range of liberalising reforms it is likely that they were inspired by humanitarian motives and it is very doubtful whether racialism could have played any part in their motivation. All the same, the Caucasian races found themselves urging limitations in the numbers of the coloured races and the term 'eco-fascist' was coined. By 1970, at the FAO's Second World Food Conference in The Hague, discussion of the population issue was heated and, in 1972, at the UN Human Environment Conference in Stockholm, it had to be excluded from the agenda, although it was mentioned in the final Declaration on the Human Environment.

The year 1974 was designated World Population Year by the UN and its climax was the conference held in Bucharest, Romania. The divisions were carried through into the conference and little of any substance was achieved. Indonesia, with the fifth highest population in the world, pressed for world recognition of the population crisis, as did Tunisia, Mexico, Iran, Jamaica and Bangladesh. The majority rejected their plea, however, and the World Population Plan that had been drawn up by the secretariat was dismembered.

Clauses that were removed entirely would have committed all countries to provide their citizens with access to family planning services and would have invited all countries to establish population goals for themselves and to try to achieve those goals by 1985. Curious alliances were born. China, the USSR and the Holy See joined forces to attack the concept of a world population crisis. China's attitude was particularly paradoxical. As we shall see later, it has the largest and most successful programme in the world to reduce the rate of growth of its own population, yet in international conferences it opposes any concerted action on population and at Bucharest it demanded the suppression of two UN reports on its population policy and the deletion from conference documents of all statistics on its own population.

An aspect of population growth that is often overlooked and that was ignored at Bucharest is coming to be known as 'demographic aggression'. Many European countries, including Britain after World War I, Italy under

Mussolini and France since Napoleonic times, have aimed at high rates of population growth in order to ensure that they would have large armies available to resist potential aggressors and, when all else failed, to persuade neighbours to accept their foreign policies. Countries that have determinedly pro-natalist policies may make it very difficult for their neighbours to take a different view. It is said that the demographic policies of Brazil, which believes itself to be under-populated, have stimulated similar attitudes in Peru and Argentina.

The attitude of China can be explained by its determination to secure the political support of the majority of developing countries, which would effectively increase its political influence. This leadership cannot be achieved if China opposes publicly the majority view, regardless of what it does within its own territory.

How is it, though, that so many countries refuse to recognise demographic arguments and the facts on which they are based? This question has puzzled many reformers but perhaps it is not so difficult to understand.

We have seen already that the Malthusian relationship between populations and resources is questionable and by no means is it accepted universally. Then there are real doubts about the facts themselves. We use UN data on populations because they are the best that are available, but they may be subject to large errors. On a global scale this may not be important, because what matters is rate of change and this can be estimated. On a local scale, however, errors can make a great difference.

Population censuses in most developed countries are well established and can provide accurate records of the size, age structure and distribution of populations. In most developing countries this is not so. Censuses must take account of scattered populations, sometimes nomadic, often living in remote areas where access is difficult and people are suspicious of governmental interference in their lives. In many countries as few as 3% of the population participates in censuses, and the rest is estimate.

We must remember, too, that our own concern about population growth is of very recent origin. Similar fears have been expressed by members of ancient civilisations and by individual members of our own throughout history, but more often we have feared a decline in population, often with good reason.

In any case, who says that an increasing population creates problems? It is all a matter of priorities. Present high levels of population growth are the result of declining death rates, while birth rates have remained fairly constant. A declining death rate reflects improved public health and, therefore, a rising standard of living. No country is willing to risk measures that might increase death rates and in many developing countries it seems more important to maintain this trend than to take action over birth rates. There was an unofficial slogan at Bucharest that sums up this attitude:

'Take care of the people and the population will take care of itself'. In other words, maintain rising standards of public health, attack poverty and the population problem will disappear.

To understand this attitude better, indeed to understand the whole debate surrounding population growth, we need to look a little more closely at the history of human population growth and at some of the key demographic concepts.

THE HISTORY OF POPULATION GROWTH

Although human numbers have grown throughout our history, this growth has not occurred as a steady progression. There have been periods of rapid growth followed by declines and there have always been wide regional disparities both in total population density (the number of persons per unit of land surface) and in rates of growth.

It is estimated[1] that around the year 10 000 BC the total world population amounted to some 5 million persons. The year is significant because, as we shall see later, it is associated with the beginnings of agriculture. Population increased fiftyfold, to 250 million, by AD 1, at an average rate of 0·04 % per year. The same growth rate was maintained until 1650, by which date population is estimated to have been 545 million. Then the rate of growth began to increase to 0·29 % per year, to bring the population to 728 million by 1750; to 0·45 % per year, to bring it to 906 million by 1800; to 0·53 % per year, to bring it to 1171 million by 1850; to 0·65 % per year, to bring it to 1608 million by 1900; to 0·91 % per year, to bring it to 2486 million by 1950; to 2·09 % per year, to bring it to 3632 million by 1970; and to 2·10 % per year, to bring it to 3900 million by 1974.

Late in October 1976, a report from the Worldwatch Institute in Washington suggested that the growth rate fell to 1·9 % a year between 1970 and 1975 due to the success of the Chinese programme to reduce birth rates, to deaths among the very poor in some developing countries due to malnutrition and starvation, and to rising death rates in India and Bangladesh.

We may say that population has been growing ever since man first appeared on the planet. No extraordinary historical event need be adduced to account for this fact; in ecological terms man is an opportunist species adapted to no particular niche and his expansion is entirely natural. Since around 1700, however, it seems that the rate of increase has accelerated. This phenomenon does require explanation.

Figure 2.1 illustrates population growth through history. The phase of the graph after 1950 shows clearly why so many people have become concerned at the rate of growth, since the curve exhibits all the characteristics of exponential growth or, when applied to certain chemical

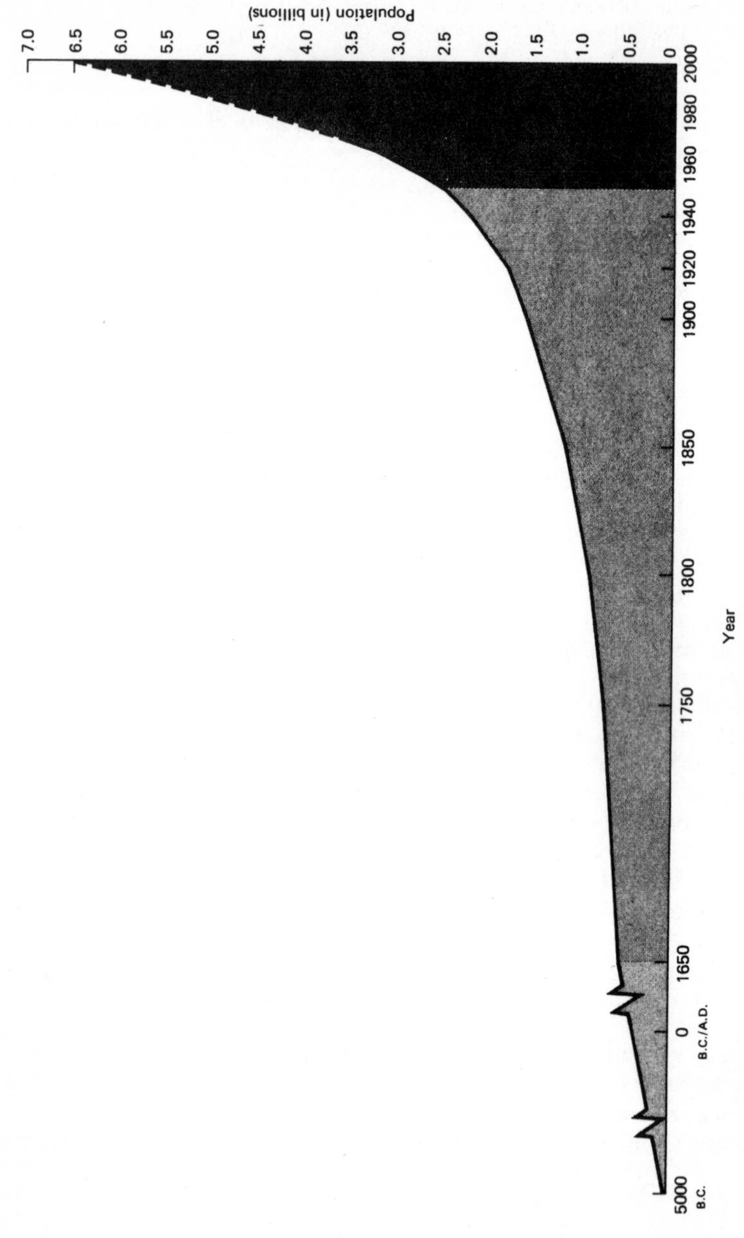

FIG. 2.1. World population through history (Source: ref. 10).

TABLE 2.1
World Population: 1970 and Projections[a] for 1985 and 1990

	Actual	*Projected*		*Rates of growth*		
	1970	1985	1990	1960–70	1970–85	1970–90
	(*millions*)			(% *per year compound*)		
Developed market economies	724	828	861	1·1	0·9	0·9
Northern America	226	262	271	1·3	1·0	1·0
Western Europe	354	386	396	0·8	0·6	0·6
Oceania	15	20	21	1·9	1·8	1·7
Others	129	160	169	1·4	1·4	1·4
Eastern Europe and USSR	348	399	416	1·0	0·9	0·9
Total developed countries	1 072	1 227	1 277	1·1	0·9	0·9
Developing market economies	1 755	2 623	2 997	2·6	2·7	2·7
Africa	279	427	498	2·5	2·9	2·9
Latin America	284	428	489	2·8	2·8	2·7
Near East	171	262	303	2·7	2·9	2·9
Far East	1 021	1 506	1 707	2·5	2·6	2·6
Asian centrally planned economies	794	1 008	1 072	1·8	1·6	1·5
Total developing countries	2 549	3 631	4 069	2·3	2·4	2·4
World totals	3 621	4 858	5 346	1·9	2·0	2·0

[a] UN 'medium' assumption, provisional, 1974.
(Source: *Assessment of the World Food Situation*, E/Conf. 65/3. FAO, Rome, 1974).

reactions, of an explosion—hence talk of the 'population explosion'. Table 2.1 gives rates of growth and projected 1985 and 1990 populations compared with those of 1970 for the major regions of the world and Fig. 2.2 interprets these figures graphically.

Already we have begun to break down, or dis-aggregate, the world data. While Fig. 2.1 gives global figures, Fig. 2.2 shows that these rates of growth occur in particular areas. While the growth rates for developed countries average 0·97 % per year, those for developing countries average 2·67 %. The actual size of populations in each region is not significant, since regions vary greatly in land area and in resources.

Throughout history, populations have been held in check by natural and man-made calamities. Where populations were small, famine, disease epidemics and wars might have a significant effect not only in reducing actual population levels but in inhibiting rates of increase. In the fourteenth century, for example, bubonic plague epidemics are estimated to have reduced the population of Europe by 25 %,[2] and in the early seventeenth century further outbreaks accounted for a 9 % decrease in a European population that by then was much larger.

Epidemic diseases have been known and recorded throughout history, although we have no way of estimating with any accuracy the effect they may have had on the size of populations. Smallpox was known in China in 1122 BC and smallpox, cholera and leprosy were known in India before 200 BC. Epidemics are recorded in the Bible. Samuel 2, Chapter 24, Verse 15,

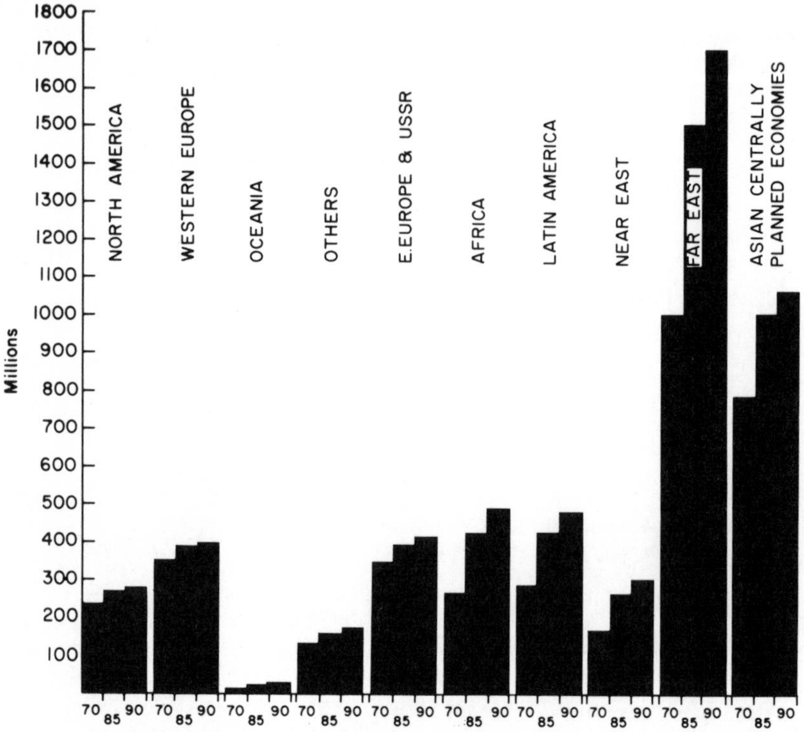

FIG. 2.2. World population, 1970 (actual), 1985 and 1990 (forecast); UN medium assumption, provisional, 1974 (Source: ref. 11).

records that: 'So the Lord sent a pestilence upon Israel from the morning even to the time appointed; and there died of the people from Dan even to Beersheba seventy thousand men.'

In 1527 the French army outside Naples was struck by typhus and within a month more than half the soldiers had died. Some accounts claim that of an army of 25 000 men only 4000 survived. The Christian armies on the First Crusade were reduced from 300 000 to 60 000, mainly by epidemics, by the time they reached Jerusalem.[3] As late as the Crimean War (1854–56) deaths from disease amounted to 104 494 men, compared to 63 261 men killed in action.[3] In the three years from 1816 to 1819, 700 000 people died from typhus in Ireland and 3 million people are believed to have died from this disease in Russia between 1917 and 1923. The list is endless and even today there are fears of an outbreak of plague in parts of the USA, as the population of flea-infested rats increases.

Epidemic diseases that strike civilian populations tend to kill the weaker members in larger number than those who are more robust or who have acquired some resistance to the disease through exposure to and recovery from earlier outbreaks. There may be a social effect, since some diseases affect the poor more than the rich. Plague, for example, was always a disease of poverty and so produced little political effect, the ruling classes often escaping. Smallpox, on the other hand, might attack anyone. In Britain, for example, Queen Elizabeth I nearly died from it.[4]

The first effect of an epidemic, then, is to reduce the total population, perhaps affecting some classes more than others. However, since more children, pregnant women and nursing mothers die in all classes than adult males or females who are not pregnant or nursing, a secondary effect is to reduce the size of the following generation. It is understandable, therefore, that any measures aimed at reducing the impact of epidemics favour the survival of children and may actually be directed quite specifically to that end. It is not a matter of sentimentality—though it explains the distress most of us feel at the idea of small children dying—but of survival.

In the UK the infant mortality rate, which is the number of infants under 1 year of age who die in each year for every 1000 live births, has been reduced from 142 in 1900–1902 to 17·2 in 1973.[5] Since 1950 the average expectation of life at birth (i.e. the number of years a newborn baby may expect to live) has increased from 66·2 to 68·7 years for males and from 71·2 to 75·0 years for females. During the same period the average life expectancy of persons aged 45 has increased from 26·4 to 27·2 years for males and from 30·6 to 32·6 years for females.[5] In other words, while life expectancy at birth has increased during the period by an average of 3·15 years, only 1·4 of those years have been added in later life. The chances of surviving to the age of 45 are greater than they were, while chances of surviving into old age after 45 are much the same.

Life expectancy at birth has increased by 40 % between 1950 and 1975 in the developing world, by 12 % in the developed world and by 35 % in the world as a whole.[1] Thus the gains made in the UK and other industrialised countries during the nineteenth and early twentieth centuries are now being made in developing countries.

Wars, too, once took a measurable toll of the human populations, although until this century disease killed more soldiers than did the weapons wielded by their opponents. Yet modern man has no monopoly of cruelty. It is said that the Persian King Darius I had 3000 Babylonian prisoners of war crucified. In AD 60 the Romans crucified 3600 Jews following a rebellion, and Samuel 1, Chapter 4, records a battle between the Israelites and the Philistines in which the Philistines slew some 4000 Israelites in the first encounter and then returned to slay a further 30 000, only to succumb themselves to an epidemic shortly afterwards.

The most devastating war in history, of course, was World War II, in which 22 060 000 people died. In AD 1, this would have amounted to 8·8 % of the population of the world; In 1965 it would have amounted to 0·7 % and if the UN projection for a world population of 5346 million in 1990 is correct, by that year it will amount to 0·4 %.

The rather obvious point is that the larger the population the greater must be the war that will make a serious impression on its numbers. Shattock[3] has estimated that in AD 1 it would have taken 220 years to replace the number of people who died in World War II, but that by the end of this century it will take only 3·1 months. If we turn the statement round we see that if they are to be regarded as a check on the size of populations, wars must occur on a scale appropriate to the size of the populations they are to check. In the present world it is difficult to see how anything short of full thermonuclear war could have much effect. Our revulsion at the thought of war on this scale is a measure of our changing attitudes more than of anything else. Such a war, or at least a large-scale but still limited nuclear war, would create no more devastation today than did large wars in earlier times among much smaller populations with much smaller towns and areas of settled, worked land. Perhaps we may allow ourselves to hope that it is against war itself that we revolt, not merely against the scale of modern warfare.

Wars devastate landscapes, partly by being fought across them but much more, historically at least, by taking farmers and agricultural workers away from the land. So wars are often followed by famine. In 1975 the Khmer Rouge forces that gained control of Cambodia found it necessary to move the urban populations into the countryside as a matter of great urgency. Town dwellers, whose numbers had swollen during the prolonged war, had become dependent on economic subsidies that could not be continued. The country had to feed itself, yet the drift of population away from the countryside had left the farms seriously undermanned and run down. If serious food shortages were to be avoided the new rulers felt they had no alternative but to draft labour, however ruthlessly, into the fields.

Famines have occurred throughout history and war is only one of their causes. Some famines have taken colossal numbers of lives. It is said[3] that the Bengal famine of 1769, in which 10 million people died, reduced the population of India by one-third. Three million people died in Bengal in 1669, a century earlier. In 10 famines between 1860 and 1890, 15 million Indians died, while 9·5 million Chinese died in a famine in 1876. The Irish Potato Famine killed about 25 % of the population of Ireland in 1845 and 1846, and caused a further 25 % to emigrate. In 1878 Cornelius Walford compiled a chronicle of 350 famines, going back as far as a famine in Rome in 436 BC.[2]

Again, it is clear that famines would have to occur on a scale that is barely credible if they were to produce any significant effect on the size of today's world population.

All figures for mortalities taken from historical records are open to doubt, yet taken together, epidemic disease, wars and famine did provide a substantial check on the increase of populations. Although the incidence of wars has shown no sign of diminishing, improved standards of public hygiene have almost eliminated epidemic disease in the developed countries and have made inroads into them in the tropics. It is almost certain that smallpox has now been eradicated, its virus extinct. Improved medical care, including immunisation, has improved greatly the chances of survival of those who do contract a disease that once would have been almost certainly fatal.

Improved agricultural techniques have made food more plentiful and supplies of it more reliable, so reducing the risk of famine, again mainly in the developed countries. So, as powerful checks were removed, populations were enabled to rise. This does not account for the whole of what has happened, however. Populations were encouraged to rise. We saw earlier that 'demographic aggression' can produce an effect. What we did not consider, nor apparently did the World Population Conference, was the persuasive arguments that have been advanced in favour of large populations.

We must consider the demographic history of Europe if we are to understand what is called the 'demographic transition'—the growth and then stabilisation of populations that occurred throughout Europe in the nineteenth and twentieth centuries and on which many developing countries pin their own hopes. First, though, we must understand some of the key demographic concepts.

The first official population census in Britain was taken in 1801. Censuses then followed at 10-yearly intervals until 1941, when they were interrupted by World War II. Before 1801 all data are based on estimates, but between 1801 and 1841 the collection of census figures was largely in the hands of local poor law overseers, who visited every house and entered their findings on tally sheets. The census takers were often poorly educated and they worked without supervision at a task they probably regarded as of little real importance. They asked their questions at the doorstep, which is recognised now as being notoriously limited and liable to produce inaccuracies. So, although the early censuses provided some useful information, their figures for total populations are not reliable.

In 1837 the registration of births, marriages and deaths became obligatory and the information from the registrars was sent regularly to the General Register Office at Somerset House, in London. In 1841 the method for the collection of census data was changed for the better. From that year, then, demographic data for the UK became reliable. Data for developing countries today may be no more reliable than were UK data in the early years of the nineteenth century.

If the figures are based on guesses, however, they are highly educated guesses, for masses of records exist locally and there were many amateur census takers, including Malthus, before censuses were introduced officially. The least satisfactory figures are those for migrations.

In the nineteenth century, ships' masters were required to keep lists of passengers, but only of those travelling to destinations outside Europe, and until 1912 they were not required to record whether passengers were changing their places of permanent residence. The passenger lists were collected and aggregated into returns but only for the very short period between 1773 and 1776, and then they state only the weekly number of people moving into or from the UK. They were suspended at the time of the American War of Independence and resumed briefly in 1803, but a continuous series goes back only as far as 1815. It was 1853 before masters were required to state the nationalities of their passengers. In practice, migration figures are reasonably complete and accurate only as far back as about 1876.[6]

Increases in population can be measured at census times but census results are used to check mid-census estimates and to provide base figures for future estimates. From year to year the critical figures are those for births, deaths, immigration and emigration. Birth and death figures are measured as the number per thousand of the population and sometimes they are called the crude birth and death rates. By deducting deaths from births a figure is produced for the net gain or loss to the population. Expressed as a percentage, this is called the rate of natural increase or decrease. When the effects of migration are included the result is called the rate of population increase or decrease.

The other main group of figures relates to fertility. Total fertility is the number of children a woman would have were she to bear the average number of babies for a woman of her age each year from the age of 15 to 50, the average being calculated for seven age groups. The fertility for each of those groups is called the age-specific fertility rate. The gross reproduction rate is the number of daughters a woman would bear were she to have children at the age-specific fertility rate from the age of 15 to 50. The figure is calculated by adjusting the total fertility by the ratio of females to males being born.

Most women do not bear children through the whole of their reproductive life. When this fact is taken into account, fertility rates are adjusted downward to give the net reproduction rate. The number of daughters each woman bears affects the rate at which the population grows or declines. If the net reproduction rate is 1, then the population will replace itself but will neither increase nor decrease in size. In actual fact, when allowance is made for deaths the replacement fertility level is about 1·2.

When the size of populations is changing, people often become concerned about changes in the dependency ratio. This is a rough measure of the ratio of workers to dependents—children and old people. It is calculated by adding together the number of persons under 14 years of age and those over 65 and dividing by the number aged between 15 and 64.

If the net reproduction rate is much higher than 1 the population will increase. Thus the number of children will exceed that of the parents. If the population size is to fall again, the second generation of mothers must have a net reproduction rate of less than 1. If they have the same net reproduction rate as their own mothers the third generation will be larger than the second.

It is possible, then, to tell whether or not a population is growing by examining its age structure. The age structure will also indicate the kind of problems that could arise over dependency ratios, and the time it might take to stabilise the size of the population at a new level. If the number of persons in each age group is drawn, either as a number or as a percentage of the total, as a horizontal block, with the number in the next older age group above it and so on, an overall shape will emerge that is characteristic for that population. Figure 2.3 shows the structure of the UK population in 1975,

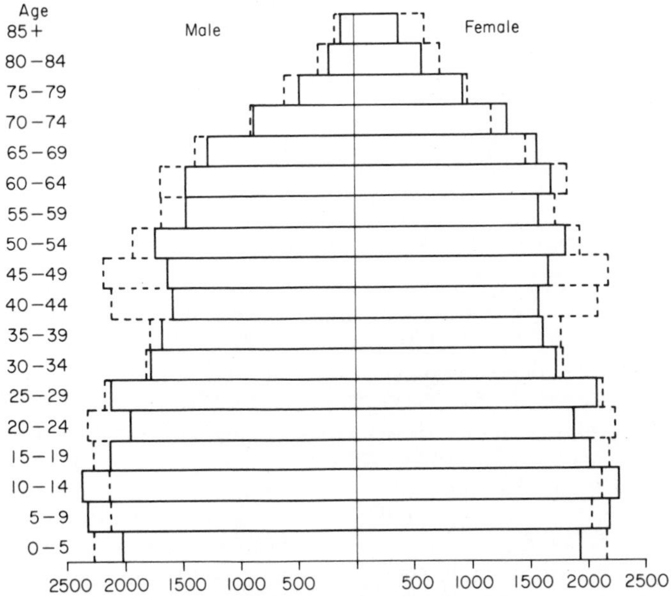

FIG. 2.3. Structure of UK population, 1975 (——) and 2011 (– – –), in thousands; estimates from the Government Actuaries Department (Source: ref. 5).

with the projected population for 2011 (which has since been revised downwards). The 1975 dependency ratio for the UK is 0·59.

The UK population structure exhibits a roughly rectangular shape, suggesting that numbers will remain very nearly stable. As one moves higher up the diagram, the centre line appears to move to the left, showing that among older persons females outnumber males. This reflects the fact that for some years increases in life expectancy have favoured females.

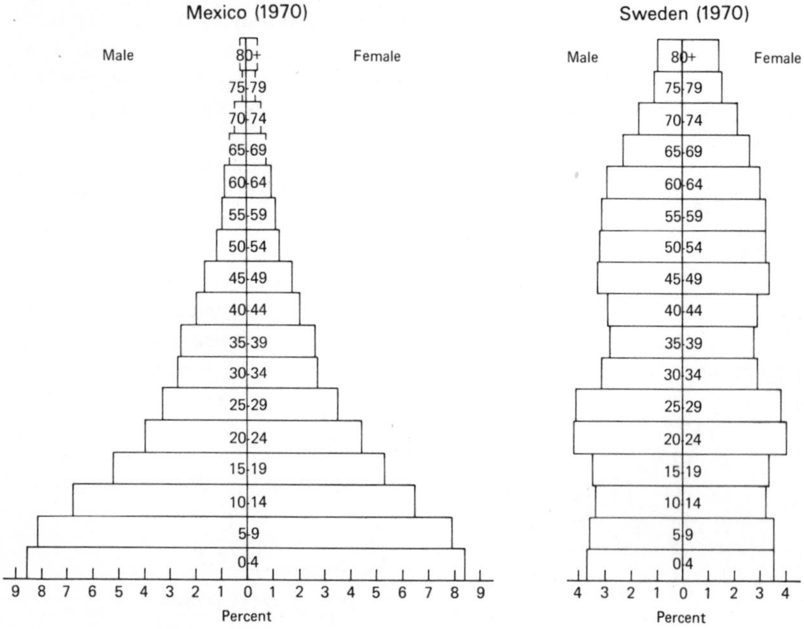

FIG. 2.4. Age structure (1970) in Mexico and Sweden (Source: ref. 12).

Consider now Fig. 2.4, which compares the age structures of a typical developed country and of a typical developing country, in this case Sweden and Mexico. While the Swedish diagram is roughly rectangular, that for Mexico is pyramid shaped. For each age group in the reproductive range the number of children exceeds the number of parents. This indicates a high level of fertility and therefore a high reproduction rate. This population is growing, in fact at 3·4 % per year, which means that unless the rate of growth changes (which it is almost bound to do) the population will double every 20 years or so. Of course, fertility may be reduced, but even if it is, a population whose age structure exhibits such a distinct pyramid shape will continue to grow for some time under its own inertia. This is because a large proportion of the present population has yet to enter the reproductive stage of its life.

In Mexico about 46% of the female population is below 15 years of age, whereas in Sweden only about 20% of the female population is below reproductive age. In the UK about 23% of the population is below 15 years of age. Thus a very large block of females—the largest in the pyramid—have yet to become mothers themselves. If one shifts the lowest three blocks in the Mexican pyramid upward, to account for ageing, and reduces them a little to allow for intervening mortality, then even if the replacement fertility rate were achieved immediately, the rectangle produced by the time those about to enter their reproductive lives reached the age of 50 would be very wide. In such a population the achievement of replacement fertility rates must be followed by an increase in total numbers of at least 70% before the size stabilises at a new, high level.

Populations with such a pyramid-shaped age structure must be either very rich or very poor. The ratio of workers to dependents is high and therefore a large part of the country's earnings must be devoted to supporting non-productive members of the community. If the country is extremely wealthy it may choose to spend its wealth in this way. There are worse ways, and as we shall see when we discuss the demographic transition, it is possible that beyond a certain economic level this indeed is the way wealth may be spent. If the country is poor, however, then any increase in its earnings must be swallowed up at once in providing services.

It is argued that a similar situation would obtain were a population to decline in size. The smaller number of children would produce a short term improvement in the dependency ratio, but as the population aged, a smaller number of workers would have to support a proportionately larger number of retired people—their own parents. It is probable that this danger has been over-emphasised. A declining population is likely to have a more favourable dependency ratio than a growing one, since mortality will ensure that the actual number of dependents in the upper age groups is smaller than that in the lower, and old people place less strain on communal resources than do children. They require no education and they can make some measurable economic contribution.

It is also feared that a declining population would become an older one as the smaller number of children led to an increase in the average age. This, it is felt, would tend to produce a rather conservative outlook in the community as a whole, a reluctance to accept necessary change or radical reforms. The fear is understandable but there is no evidence to suggest that in practice this result would ensue. Indeed, periods of declining population and consequent overall ageing have often been periods of major reform. Old people are not necessarily reactionary!

It is probable that rates of population increase are beginning to slacken in many countries. If this is so, then eventually the pyramid-shaped age structure of most developing countries may come to resemble that of the developed countries. It is an interesting fact that a sharp distinction of this

Crude birth rate	Country
55	Nigeria
50	Ethiopia, Kenya, Morocco, Sudan, Afghanistan, Iraq
	Algeria, Uganda
	Tanzania, Bangladesh, Iran, Pakistan
45	Colombia, Nepal, Philippines
	Zaire, Peru
	Mexico, South Vietnam
	Indonesia
	Brazil, Venezuela, Thailand
40	South Africa, Burma
	India, North Korea
	Egypt, North Vietnam, Turkey
35	
	China, West Malaysia
30	Chile, Sri Lanka
	South Korea
25	
	Taiwan
	Argentina
20	Romania, Australia
	Japan, Spain
	Soviet Union, Yugoslavia
	France, Poland
	Canada, Czechoslovakia, Italy, Netherlands
15	United States, Hungary, United Kingdom
	East Germany
	West Germany
10	

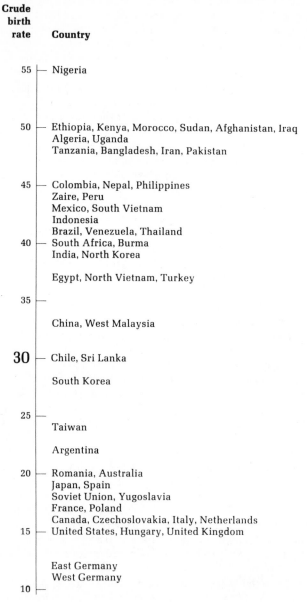

FIG. 2.5. Crude birth rates, per thousand population (Source: ref. 13).

kind can be made between developed and developing countries, simply on the basis of the structure of their populations. Very approximately, countries whose crude birth rate is below 30 per thousand population are developed, those whose crude birth rate is higher than 30 are developing.

Figure 2.5 illustrates this by grouping countries according to their crude birth rates. With Chile and Sri Lanka just on the 30 mark, only South Korea, Taiwan and Argentina—which may be a developed country in terms of its per capita GNP—have crude birth rates that place them among the developed countries, while South Africa and Turkey are the only developed countries to find themselves among the developing nations. Turkey has large areas that are essentially agrarian and developing, while South Africa's political and economic structure is such as to confine full economic development to one section of the population.

How does the pyramid become a rectangle? Does the transition occur naturally and smoothly? Too little is known about the causes underlying demographic trends for there to be a clear answer, but interest in them has stimulated detailed investigations of the demographic transition as it occurred in Europe.

THE DEMOGRAPHIC TRANSITION

During the late eighteenth century the population of most European countries began to rise more rapidly than it had done in the past. This rate of growth reached its peak between 1800 and 1850 in England, Wales, Scotland, France, Denmark and Norway, rather earlier in Ireland and Finland, and rather later in Holland and Belgium. Table 2.2 shows the rates

TABLE 2.2
The Rate of Population Growth in Western European Countries: Annual Average Percentage Increases

	1700–1750	1750–1800	1800–1850	1850–1910	1910–1940
England/Wales	0·2	0·7	1·8	1·6	0·5
France	0·1	0·6	0·7	0·2	0·1
Holland	0·7	0·8	0·8	1·5	1·7
Belgium	0·8	0·7	0·9	1·2	0·4
Sweden	—	0·6	1·0	1·0	0·5
Scotland	0·6	0·5	1·6	0·9	0·4
Ireland	0·6	1·1	0·6	0·6	0·1
Denmark	—	0·3	1·6	1·4	1·0
Finland	—	3·0	1·2	1·6	0·6
Norway	0·4	1·0	1·3	1·0	0·8

(Source: ref. 6).

of growth for these countries between 1700 and 1940. Then the rate of growth began to decline until it reached its present low levels of 0·5% for the UK (a UN figure but the actual rate of growth is now believed to be about zero or possibly very slightly negative), 1% for France (whose population is growing again), 1·3% for Holland, 0·6% for Belgium/Luxembourg, 0·7% for Sweden, 0·1% for Ireland, 0·7% for Denmark, 0·8% for Finland and 0·9% for Norway.

The theory of the demographic transition, as applied to countries whose rates of growth are very high at present, is that populations increase rapidly as economies begin to develop an industrial base, then, as affluence

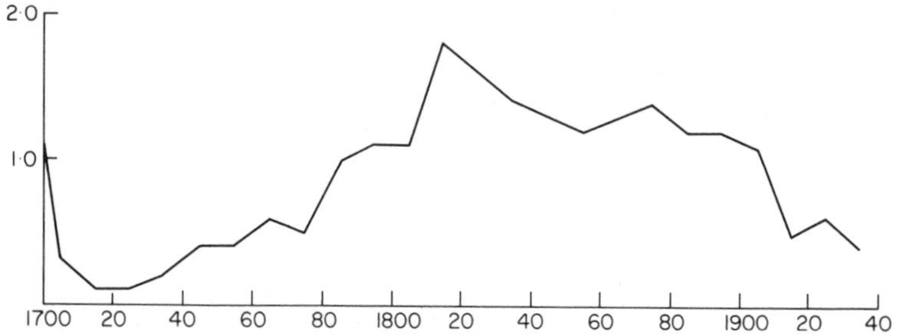

FIG. 2.6. The demographic transition; rates of population growth (%), England and Wales, 1700–1940 (Source: ref. 6).

increases, they stabilise. Thus, it is maintained, the population problem—if such exists—in developing countries can be dealt with best by encouraging a rapid rate of industrialisation to increase per capita incomes. Again the Bucharest slogan, mentioned earlier: 'Take care of the people and the population will take care of itself'. Figure 2.6, which traces the change in rates of population growth for England and Wales between 1700 and 1940, represents graphically the kind of transition for which people hope.

Opponents of this view hold that extrapolations cannot be made so easily from one culture to another and that more significant than crude population size is the per caput demand for resources—a point that has been made in developing countries themselves. While such a transition might possibly occur throughout the world, if growth rates must be reduced by means that require large increases in per capita consumption of resources, then the problems are simply transferred. The population problem becomes a resource depletion problem. Also, they point out, while growth rates in developed countries have certainly slackened, and populations are stabilising in some of these countries, in others they are still growing, albeit at a slower rate. Figure 2.7 shows this quite clearly. So the shift from population growth to increased depletion of resources may represent no gain and perhaps even a loss to the world as a whole.

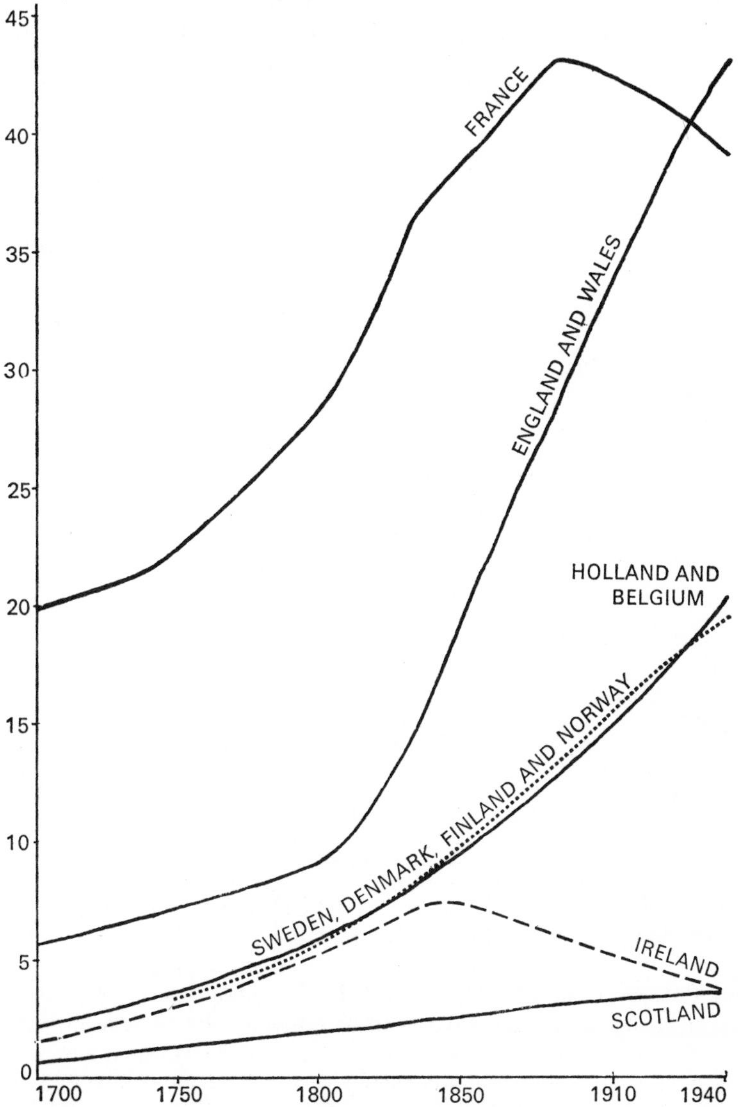

FIG. 2.7. The growth of population in various Western European countries, in millions (Source: ref. 6).

This is the pattern that may be followed in developing countries. Or may it? It is argued that the rapid growth in population in Europe might have had adverse effects were it not for the fact that large land areas overseas were populated very sparsely. This meant that surplus population was able to emigrate and that agricultural land overseas could be developed to provide food for the European homelands, while colonial populations provided markets for manufactured goods.

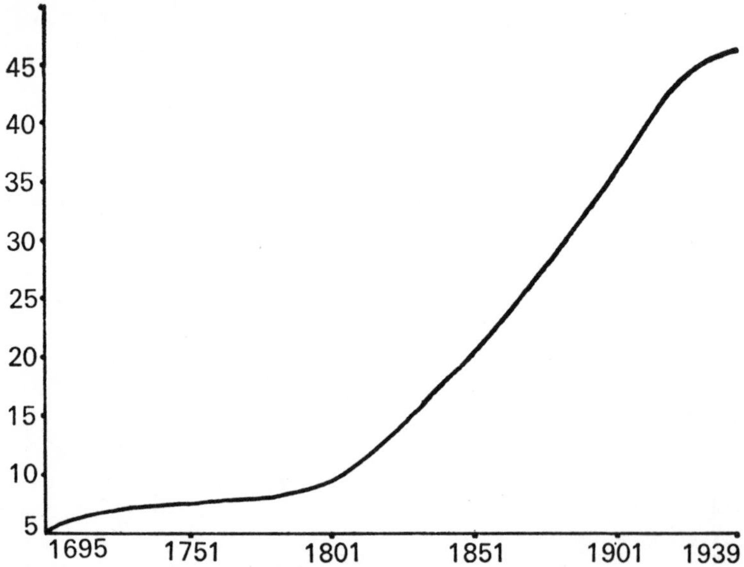

FIG. 2.8. The population of England and Wales, 1695–1939, in millions (Source: ref. 6).

Figure 2.8 shows how the population grew in England and Wales during the whole of this period—from 1695 to 1939. Figure 2.9 shows the net effect of migration on the size of the population. The sharp loss in 1911–15 was caused by World War I, when troops were moved overseas; were the graph to continue beyond 1936–38, it would show a similar loss in 1939–46. It is quite clear, however, that emigration had an effect on population size. It had another effect on marriages, since the large majority of emigrants were single men, so leading to a greater surplus of women to men than might have been the case otherwise.

It is very unlikely that the European history of the demographic transition will be repeated in developing countries, at least in any form that is closely similar. Lack of capital for investment leads to slow rates of economic development, so that the increasing population of working age

FIG. 2.9. Net gain or loss by overseas migration in England and Wales by sub-periods (Source: ref. 6).

cannot be absorbed into employment. Without employment and wages, they do not constitute a home market for manufactured goods sufficiently large to permit expansion at the rate needed. In some countries, as we saw in the previous chapter, food is in short supply, while everywhere food prices are high. Thus a large proportion of earned income must be spent on necessities, imposing a further restriction on the growth of demand for industrial products. Table 2.3 shows the per caput gross domestic product for developed and developing countries, together with the projections for the years until 1990.

In an increasing number of developing countries there are clear indications that fertility rates are falling. Almost certainly this is due to the voluntary control of fertility by couples. We must consider now the policies that are being pursued to reduce the rate of population growth. Table 2.4 lists the 15 countries that together account for some 70% of the world's population. It would be sensible to deal with these in descending order of importance.

China (People's Republic)

Despite its denials in international meetings, China has shown great determination to stabilise the size of its population. The 1975 population

TABLE 2.3
Per caput Gross Domestic Product: 1970 and Assumptions for 1985 and 1990

	'Trend' assumption						'High' assumption	
	Actual	*Projected*		*Rates of growth*			*Projected*	*Rates of growth*
	1970	1985	1990	1960–70	1970–85	1970–90	1985	1970–85
	(*US $ at* 1970 *prices*)			(*% per year, compound*)			(*US $ thousand million, at* 1970 *prices*)	(*% per year, compound*)
Developed market economies	2 916	4 903	5 923	3·8	3·5	3·6		
Northern America	4 736	7 338	8 551	2·8	3·0	3·0		
Western Europe	2 201	3 851	4 753	4·1	3·8	3·9		
Oceania	2 666	4 363	5 386	3·1	3·3	3·6		
Others	1 711	3 514	4 451	9·0	4·9	4·9		
Eastern Europe and USSR	1 723	3 695	4 833	5·4	5·2	5·3		
Total developed countries	2 529	4 510	5 568	4·2	3·9	4·0		
Developing market economies	221	371	451	2·6	3·5	3·6	414	4·3
(excluding oil exporters)	(217)	(330)	(390)	(2·5)	(2·8)	(3·0)	(374)	(3·7)
Africa	158	243	286	1·5	2·9	3·0	268	3·6
Latin America	536	868	1 042	2·6	3·3	3·4	972	4·1
Near East	321	786	1 036	4·2	6·2	6·0	838	6·6
Far East	134	194	226	2·2	2·5	2·6	223	3·4
Asian centrally planned economies	163	232	266	0·9	2·4	2·5	256	3·1
Total developing countries	203	333	402	2·2	3·3	3·5	370	4·1
World totals	892	1 388	1 637	3·2	3·0	3·1		

(Source: *Assessment of the World Food Situation*, E/Conf. 65/3. FAO, Rome, 1974).

TABLE 2.4
The Fifteen Largest Countries in the World

Country	*Latest available data or estimate* (*c.* 1973)				
	Population (millions)	*Crude birth rate*	*Crude death rate*	*Rate of natural increase* (%)	*Urbanised* (%)
China	800(?)	32–37	15–17	1·9–2·2	15
India	580	37–39	15–17	2·2	20
USSR	250	17·8	8·2	1	57
USA	210	15·3	9·3	0·6	74
Indonesia	130	40–45	18–21	2–2·5	17
Japan	105	19·2	6·6	1·3	53
Brazil	100	40–42	10–12	3	57
Bangladesh	80	45–50	15–20	2·5–3	5
Pakistan	65	45–50	14–18	2·5–3	20
Nigeria	60	50+	25–27	2·5+	20–25
West Germany	60	11·4	11·8	−0·04	81
UK	56	14·9	12·1	0·3	81
Italy	55	16·8	9·6	0·7	53
Mexico	55	43–45	10–12	3·2–3·5	57
France	52	17·2	10·8	0·6	70

(Sources: Based on United Nations, *Population and Vital Statistics*, Report 25, No. 2 (Series A), 1973; and *Demographic Yearbook*, 1971).

was estimated to be 800 million, plus or minus 20 or 30 million, and the population age structure is typical of that for a developing country. The mortality rate, which was at least 40 per thousand persons before the revolution, has been reduced to 13 per thousand, an average figure that allows for a much lower (5 or 6) death rate in cities, a rather lower (9–12) rate in towns and a rather higher (14–18) rate among the great mass of the rural population.[7]

The Chinese intend to reduce the death rate to 8 per thousand as soon as possible. Birth rates have been reduced from about 43 in 1953 to 29, and the objective is to reduce it to 18, which will reduce the rate of population growth from 1·6 to 1% per year. It is possible that this was achieved by 1976. At present the population projected for 1985 is between 880 and 930 million. At least 40% of the present population is under 15 years of age, so that further growth in total numbers is inevitable. The infant mortality rate is still rather high, at 20–30, but much lower than the figures for, say, India or Pakistan.

Per caput GNP is still that of a developing country, at $185 per annum, so China experiences all the difficulties of any other developing country in raising the standard of living of its people. Current thinking on the demographic transition holds that an annual per capita GNP of $500 is needed before parents will begin to limit voluntarily the size of their families. China's approach to economic development does not fit well into patterns devised in the developed countries, however, and its success in reducing its rate of population growth is one result of this approach.

Despite the monolithic appearance the country may present to outsiders, in fact it is highly decentralised, combining this with a high degree of organisation down to the lowest hierarchical level. Thus, while a high degree of political uniformity may reduce individual liberty, there is every opportunity for the individual to participate in the making of decisions that affect his or her life within that political framework.

In the cities, Dr Norman Myers[7] found that about 70 % of women at risk employ some method of fertility control, if one includes abortion and sterilisation as well as more conventional methods, and oral contraceptives are popular. In rural areas, between 20 and 40 % of women practise fertility control. This level may be expected to rise steeply in the near future with the dissemination of the 'paper pill'. This is progesterone-impregnated rice paper, perforated into 22 squares for each month's supply. It is easy to produce, can be transported easily and is simple to use. It will be distributed among the 80 million married women in the Chinese countryside. For political reasons, China is committed to the provision of contraceptive information and materials to all who want them. Its population policy is clearly anti-natalist.

This is only the technological aspect of the country's approach, however. Ninety percent of women of reproductive age are now literate and working and they are encouraged to marry relatively late in life. In the towns, marriage is acceptable socially only when a man is 28 and a woman 25. In rural areas the ages are 25 and 23, and within marriage it is usual to have a five-year interval between children.

In some cities, particularly Peking and Shanghai, the desire to stabilise the population size has been much keener than in the country as a whole. Peking's annual rate of natural growth is 1·24 % per year but owing to the policy of encouraging workers to leave the cities and go into the countryside, the capital actually loses more people than it gains by immigration and the population is falling. In parts of Shanghai, city communes have introduced a form of rationing, by deciding for themselves how many babies it would be desirable to produce and then permitting 'deserving' couples to have a child. The predictable result is a very low birth rate.

It is not China's aim to end population growth altogether, but only to strike a balance between the size of the population and the resources available to sustain it. This balance will be different for different regions and for different ethnic groups. Minority groups are not urged to practise birth control at all unless they wish to do so.

The Chinese approach to population planning is very much a part of the overall approach to development. Parts of this approach may be appropriate elsewhere. The 'barefoot doctors', for example, are able to provide basic health care over wide areas very much more cheaply than fully-trained doctors could, and they have played a central role in reducing mortality, which is an early step in reducing rates of population growth. These paramedical workers now have counterparts in many other developing countries. Beyond such specific measures, however, it is probable that the Chinese demographic transition can be achieved only by countries that adopt a total political structure rather similar to that in China, although this means adaptation to local conditions rather than slavish imitation. While some countries can and will do this, there are others that would find it more difficult.

India

Family planning has been encouraged in India at least since the 1920s, yet its achievements have been modest. The population still increases by between 2·1 and 2·2% a year, a rate of growth that inhibits economic development seriously.

India has suffered spectacular failures of programmes whose concept was little short of heroic. Probably the most widely publicised was the plan to provide a free transistor radio to each male who accepted a vasectomy. In order to be able to supply radios on the scale needed, the government had to encourage the manufacture of vast numbers of radios at a very low price. The result was that the radios leaked on to the open market, where men who wanted them could afford to buy them without the inconvenience of being vasectomised.

This incident was comic, but the difficulties are very real. Although liberal Hindus favour birth control provided it does not afford opportunities for promiscuity, the religion is pronatalist. The 'lingam' or phallus, and the 'yoni', the female sex organ, are objects of worship in countless Indian villages. The blessings and good wishes at a Hindu wedding all concern procreation and couples wishing to practise contraception must first overcome a great weight of cultural tradition. Housing conditions make matters worse. It is common for poor people to sleep 10 or 12 to a room, which means there is little opportunity either to hide contraceptive materials—they will be disapproved of by parents if they are found—or to use them. Indeed, sexual intercourse usually takes place in the fields, which is far more private, but contraception is almost impossible because of the high degree of spontaneity, which makes no allowance for preparation.

There have been strenuous efforts to promote vasectomy programmes. In 1976 it was even reported that the government was beginning to introduce a degree of coercion, although this was denied. Vasectomy offers a practical and cheap solution to the difficulties involved in any other form of birth control. There have been vasectomy camps—more than 60 000 operations were performed in one camp in Kerala in 1971—operations on railway stations and in clinics. There have been public exhibitions of contraceptive techniques and stalls giving away condoms.[10]

The current aim is to reduce the crude birth rate from its present level of between 37 and 39 per thousand, to 25 by 1980–81.

USSR

The country's birth rate is declining, although it is higher in the Central Asian regions than in the Slavic regions. Mortality is tending to level out. The urban population is increasing and it is becoming common to find one-child families in the towns. Women are educated and economically active, and abortion is legal and used widely. There is no formal population policy, although some Soviet demographers believe the population should increase slightly.

USA

Since 1972 the fertility rate has been around the replacement level. In 1972 the Commission on Population Growth and the American Future recommended that the government should provide family planning facilities and sex education in schools. This recommendation is supported by the majority of the public. Since the late 1960s there has been some federal support for family planning facilities for low income groups, and in 1973 the Supreme Court ruled that abortion is legal. The 'Zero Population Growth' movement (ZPG) attracted wide publicity and, together with the movement for women's liberation and the environmental movement, probably influenced the trend toward smaller families. Immigration is controlled but the USA still accepts more immigrants than any other country in the world.

Indonesia

The government is committed firmly to a policy to reduce fertility and it spoke out strongly at the 1974 UN Conference in Bucharest. The government has invested heavily, with the help of foreign aid, in family planning programmes. The number of acceptors of contraceptive materials has risen from 53 000 in 1969–70 to 800 000 in 1972–73. The rate of growth is still very high, however, at 2·5% per year.

Japan

Japan is often cited as the prime example of the demographic transition in practice. The country may not be typical, however. At the end of the war it was faced with an acute problem of physical survival and to deal with it was equipped with a highly organised population distributed in a small land area with good communications. What appears to have happened is that during the 1920s and early 1930s the population was fairly stable, with mortality beginning to decline, so introducing modest growth. Later in the 1930s there were signs that the birth rate was declining with the introduction of contraception. The birth rate fell further when Japan attacked China and large numbers of young men were stationed overseas. The family planning movement came under pressure as preparations for war continued, and the need was felt for a larger population. The family planning movement was disbanded altogether in 1935. At the end of the war the birth rate rose very rapidly. Probably this was due to the return to Japan of some 6·6 million soldiers and many migrants. At the same time, the introduction of more advanced medical techniques and improved public health reduced the death rate, so that in 1947 the population was increasing at a rate of 1·97% per year, and in 1948 by 2·16%.

At that time the Japanese were threatened by famine, and in May 1949 the government recognised officially that the country was over-populated. The Population Problem Council was formed in November 1949, two years later the government began to promote contraception and by 1952 this had evolved into a detailed plan. One of the most prominent aspects in the Japanese programme—and one of the most publicised—was the liberalisation of the abortion laws as early as 1948. By 1954 only some 30% of women were using contraceptives, yet the birth rate was falling fast. The abortion laws had to be liberalised because of the health risks of inevitable high rates of illegal abortions and because of the very urgent nature of the population problem. The 1948 Eugenic Protection Law revised the existing laws, which had been modelled on those of Nazi Germany, and permitted abortion for a wide range of medical reasons and for the one that, in fact, was used almost exclusively: a pregnancy might be terminated if a mother's health might be affected seriously by its continuation or by delivery, from the physical or economic standpoint.[9]

Today, abortion is still used widely but the morality of the operation arouses controversy. The oral contraceptives and IUDs are not approved for general use; the government is probably mildly pronatalist, although the deliberate regulation of population size is a delicate political issue. The population may be increasing again: the present growth rate is 1·1–1·3% per year.

Thus, although Japan may have experienced a demographic transition of a kind, it is certainly not the purely economically triggered transition described earlier and it is unlikely that any other country could reproduce the conditions that led to it sufficiently accurately for it to be repeated.

Brazil

The official international view is that Brazil is strongly pronatalist. The country is large, the population density is low, natural resources are immense and there are areas in need of development that are under-populated. There is no national policy but family planning does have official support in one state and the national family planning association is recognised by the government as a public utility. It is possible that Brazilian attitudes are changing as some economists and government officials begin to recognise the desirability of demographic policies.

Bangladesh

With an annual rate of population increase of 3·5%, Bangladesh could double its population in 20 years. The problem is urgent and is recognised and a policy may emerge in the years ahead, although at present such programmes as there are have little effect.

Pakistan

Islam is, on the whole, pronatalist and Pakistan is still a very male-dominated society, with many women in purdah. There is a plan to reduce the rate of population growth, but it lacks staff and support among the people and it has changed direction several times. 'Dais', or indigenous midwives, are used as paramedical personnel to distribute contraceptive pills and IUDs, but organisation is poor. There has been a vasectomy programme, somewhat similar to that in India, but political changes have made it very difficult to maintain a constant policy. Census data are far from reliable. At present it is estimated that the population is increasing at 3% a year.

Nigeria

Family planning is permitted, but there is no sense of urgency in programmes and in the Islamic regions views are strongly pronatalist. Even if programmes could be introduced it would be difficult to find staff to implement them. The population is growing at about 2·4 to 3% a year, although census data are not very reliable.

West Germany

The debate over population policies rages, as it does in most west European countries and in America, with political and religious divisions running deep. West Germany has accepted very large numbers of immigrant workers—more than 3 million in recent years—and this movement of population has affected demographic figures. For a time it appeared that an excess of deaths over births was causing a slight decline in population size. More recent estimates than those in Table 2.4 suggest that the population is now growing again, at about 1% a year.

UK

Latest figures show that the population is very close to stability and deaths may exceed births very slightly to give a negative growth rate. Abortion laws were liberalised but came under review again in 1975, with campaigns both to liberalise them further and to impose more restrictions. Some of the suggested amendments to existing legislation would lead to a more repressive situation. Contraceptive materials are distributed through the National Health Service at a purely nominal cost to the user. Several government inquiries and committees have recommended that the country adopt a population policy, but this has not been done, at least formally.

Italy

The position of the Roman Catholic Church with regard to population questions encourages individuals to make their own decisions, although abortion and sterilisation are opposed. In 1975 the use of the contraceptive pill became legal. In practice, Roman Catholics use the whole range of techniques for the control of their fertility. The country has no formal population policy as such, but family allowance schemes, health care programmes and other measures have a generally pronatalist effect. The population is growing at 0·7 % a year, which suggests that contraception is practised widely.

Mexico

Family planning is supported officially but the multiplicity of ethnic and language groups and wide regional disparities make it difficult to implement a policy. The high rate of growth, by migration, of Mexico City poses problems of its own. The population is increasing at about 3·4 % a year, one of the highest rates of growth in the world.

France

The population is growing at 1 % a year or less but much of this growth is caused by immigration and the birth rate has been falling. The sale of contraceptives is permitted and there have been campaigns to liberalise the abortion laws, though the controversy in France rages as it does in most countries. Birth control is advocated primarily for women's liberation rather than demographic reasons.

IMPLICATIONS FOR FOOD DEMAND

As we saw earlier, the demographic transition, if it occurs, must be related to economic development and rising prosperity. The same is true of the impact of population size on food demand. Table 2.5 projects the rate of growth of the gross domestic product up to 1990. The figures show that national prosperity is expected to increase faster than population in all developing regions from the 1970s.

Table 2.6 interprets both population growth and economic development in terms of demand for food, and compares population growth with

TABLE 2.5
Gross Domestic Product: 1970 and Assumptions for 1985 and 1990

	'Trend' assumption						'High' assumption	
	Actual	*Projected*		*Rates of growth*			*Projected*	*Rates of growth*
	1970	1985	1990	1960–70	1970–85	1970–90	1985	1970–85
	(*US $ thousand million, at* 1970 *prices*)			(*% per year, compound*)			(*US $ thousand million, at* 1970 *prices*)	(*% per year, compound*)
Developed market economies	2 112	4 058	5 100	5·0	4·5	4·5		
Northern America	1 072	1 924	2 352	4·1	4·0	4·0		
Western Europe	779	1 485	1 880	4·9	4·4	4·5		
Oceania	41	87	116	5·1	5·2	5·3		
Others	220	562	752	10·5	6·4	6·3		
Eastern Europe and USSR[a]	599	1 475	2 012	6·5	6·2	6·2		
Total developed countries	2 711	5 533	7 112	5·3	4·9	4·9		
Developing market economies	388	974	1 352	5·2	6·3	6·4	1 087	7·1
(excluding oil exporters)	(318)	(721)	(970)	(5·1)	(5·6)	(5·7)	(816)	6·5
Africa	44	104	142	4·0	5·9	6·0	114	6·6
Latin America	152	372	510	5·5	6·1	6·2	416	6·9
Near East	55	206	314	7·0	9·3	9·1	220	9·7
Far East	137	292	386	4·8	5·2	5·3	337	6·2
Asian centrally planned economies[a]	130	234	285	2·8	4·0	4·0	258	4·7
Total developing countries	518	1 208	1 637	4·6	5·8	5·9	1 345	6·6
World totals	3 229	6 741	8 749	5·2	5·0	5·1		

[a] For centrally planned economies based on net material product. See FAO, *Agricultural Commodity Projections* 1970–80, vol. II, pp. XXIV–XXV.
(Sources: *Assessment of the World Food Situation*, E/Conf. 65/3. FAO, Rome, 1974).

TABLE 2.6
Population, Food Supply and Demand for Food in Individual Countries

	Population	*Food production*[a]	*Domestic demand for food*[b, c]	*Dietary energy supply*[c, d]		*Protein supply*[c, d]
	(% rate of growth per year[e]*)*			*(kcal per caput per day)*	*(% of requirements*[f]*)*	*(g per caput per day)*
	(1)	(2)	(3)	(4)	(5)	(6)
Developed countries						
Albania	2·8	3·6	4·6	2 390	99	74
Australia	2·1	3·7	2·4	3 280	123	108
Austria	0·4	2·5	1·1	3 310	126	90
Belgium/Luxembourg	0·6	2·1	1·2	3 380	128	95
Bulgaria	0·8	4·3	2·8	3 290	132	100
Canada	2·2	2·2	2·5	3 180	129	101
Czechoslovakia	0·9	1·8	1·9	3 180	129	94
Denmark	0·7	1·6	1·3	3 240	120	93
Finland	0·8	2·4	1·1	3 050	113	93
France	1·0	3·0	2·0	3 210	127	105
German, Dem. Rep.	−0·3	1·6	0·8	3 290	126	87
Germany, Fed. Rep.	1·0	2·5	1·9	3 220	121	89
Greece	0·8	4·0	2·3	3 190	128	113
Hungary	0·5	3·0	1·9	3 280	125	100
Ireland	0·1	1·7	0·3	3 410	136	103
Israel	3·4	7·7	4·9	2 960	115	93
Italy	0·7	2·9	2·3	3 180	126	100
Japan	1·1	4·3	3·7	2 510	107	79
Malta	0·1	3·2	1·2	2 820	114	89
Netherlands	1·3	3·0	1·7	3 320	123	87

TABLE 2.6—*continued*

	Population	*Food production*[a]	*Domestic demand for food*[b, c]	*Dietary energy supply*[c, d]		*Protein supply*[c, d]
	(% *rate of growth per year*[e])			(*kcal per caput per day*)	(% *of requirements*[f])	(*g per caput per day*)
	(1)	(2)	(3)	(4)	(5)	(6)
Developed countries—*contd.*						
New Zealand	2·1	2·7	2·0	3 200	121	109
Norway	0·9	1·3	1·3	2 960	110	90
Poland	1·4	3·0	2·3	3 280	125	101
Portugal	0·6	1·7	2·3	2 900	118	85
Romania	1·1	3·2	2·7	3 140	118	90
South Africa	2·4	3·9	3·2	2 740	112	78
Spain	0·9	3·4	3·0	2 600	106	81
Sweden	0·7	0·9	1·0	2 810	104	86
Switzerland	1·5	1·7	1·9	3 190	119	91
USA	1·5	2·0	1·6	3 330	126	106
USSR	1·5	3·9	3·0	3 280	131	101
UK	0·5	2·8	0·7	3 190	126	92
Yugoslavia	1·2	4·5	2·4	3 190	125	94
Developing countries						
Afghanistan	1·9	1·7	2·2	1 970	81	58
Algeria	2·4	−0·8	3·4	1 730	72	46
Angola	1·8	2·7	3·0	2 000	85	42
Argentina	1·7	1·8	2·0	3 060	115	100
Bangladesh	3·5[g]	1·6[g]	—	1 840	80	40
Barbados	0·6	−0·1	—	—	—	—
Bolivia	2·3	5·0	2·7	1 900	79	46
Botswana	2·0	2·3	—	2 040	87	65

Brazil	3·0	4·4	4·0	2 620	110	65
Burma	2·2	2·4	3·3	2 210	102	50
Burundi	2·0	2·4	2·4	2 040	88	62
Cameroon	1·8	3·3	2·5	2 410	104	64
Central African Rep.	1·8	2·8	1·1	2 200	98	49
Chad	2·1	0·9	1·2	2 110	89	75
Chile	2·5	2·2	3·3	2 670	109	77
China	1·7	2·3	—	2 170	91	60
Colombia	3·3	3·1	3·9	2 200	95	51
Congo	1·9	2·2	3·7	2 260	102	44
Costa Rica	3·8	5·4	4·8	2 610	116	66
Cuba	2·2	1·1	2·0	2 700	117	63
Cyprus	1·1	5·4	2·3	2 670	108	60
Dahomey	2·3	1·5	0·1	2 260	98	56
Dominican Rep.	3·3	2·2	3·6	2 120	94	48
Ecuador	3·3	5·4	4·0	2 010	88	47
Egypt	2·6	3·4	3·8	2 500	100	69
El Salvador	3·0	3·6	4·1	1 930	84	52
Ethiopia	1·8	2·3	3·0	2 160	93	72
Gabon	0·6	3·6	2·4	2 220	95	57
Gambia	1·8	4·4	—	2 490	104	64
Ghana	2·9	3·9	3·2	2 320	101	49
Guatemala	3·0	4·1	4·2	2 130	97	59
Guinea	2·0	2·0	3·4	2 020	88	45
Guyana	3·0	2·5	3·6	2 390	105	58
Haiti	2·3	1·0	2·2	1 730	77	39
Honduras	3·3	4·0	4·2	2 140	94	56
India	2·1	2·4	3·0	2 070	94	52
Indonesia .	2·5	2·0	2·6	1 790	83	38
Iran	2·8	3·3	5·4	2 300	96	60
Iraq	3·3	2·8	5·2	2 160	90	60
Ivory Coast	2·2	4·9	2·6	2 430	105	56

TABLE 2.6—*continued*

	Population	*Food production*[a]	*Domestic demand for food*[b, c]	*Dietary energy supply*[c, d]		*Protein supply*[c, d]
	(*% rate of growth per year*[e])			(*kcal per caput per day*)	(*% of requirements*[f])	(*g per caput per day*)
	(1)	(2)	(3)	(4)	(5)	(6)
Developing countries—*contd.*						
Jamaica	1·9	1·9	3·3	2 360	105	63
Jordan	3·2	1·8	6·6	2 430	99	65
Kenya	3·0	2·6	4·7	2 360	102	67
Khmer Rep.	2·8	3·5	4·3	2 430	109	55
Korea, Dem. Rep.	2·7	—	—	2 240	89	73
Korea, Rep.	2·7	4·8	4·7	2 520	107	68
Laos	2·4	3·7	3·7	2 110	95	49
Lebanon	2·8	5·0	3·1	2 280	92	63
Lesotho	1·6	0·5	—	—	—	—
Liberia	1·5	1·1	1·8	2 170	94	39
Libyan Arab Rep.	3·6	5·3	—	2 570	109	62
Madagascar	2·4	2·8	2·1	2 530	111	58
Malawi	2·5	4·7	3·7	2 210	95	63
Malaysia (West)	3·0	5·2	4·3	2 460	110	54
Mali	2·1	1·6	4·3	2 060	88	64
Mauritania	2·0	2·4	3·0	1 970	85	68

Mauritius	2·6	1·3	3·0	2 360	104	48
Mexico	3·4	5·3	4·3	2 580	111	62
Mongolia	2·9	—	—	2 380	106	106
Morocco	3·0	2·8	3·3	2 220	92	62
Mozambique	1·7	2·7	3·2	2 050	88	41
Nepal	1·8	0·1	2·1	2 080	95	49
Nicaragua	3·0	4·9	3·9	2 450	109	71
Niger	2·8	4·1	2·2	2 080	89	74
Nigeria	2·4	2·0	3·1	2 270	96	63
Pakistan	3·0	3·0	4·2	2 160	93	56
Panama	3·2	4·3	4·8	2 580	112	61
Paraguay	3·1	2·6	3·4	2 740	119	73
Peru	2·9	2·9	3·9	2 320	99	60
Philippines	3·2	3·2	4·2	1 940	86	47
Rhodesia	3·4	3·9	4·1	2 660	111	76
Rwanda	2·6	1·8	1·9	1 960	84	58
Saudi Arabia	2·4	2·9	5·0	2 270	94	62
Senegal	2·2	3·3	1·2	2 370	100	65
Sierra Leone	2·0	2·4	3·9	2 280	99	51
Somalia	2·2	1·1	1·5	1 830	79	56
Sri Lanka	2·5	3·6	3·1	2 170	98	48
Sudan	2·9	4·3	3·9	2 160	92	63
Surinam	3·1	—	4·0	2 450	109	59
Syrian Arab Rep.	3·0	1·8	4·6	2 650	107	75
Tanzania	2·4	3·1	3·0	2 260	98	63
Thailand	3·1	5·3	4·6	2 560	115	56
Togo	2·3	5·4	2·4	2 330	101	56
Trinidad and Tobago	2·5	1·9	4·8	2 380	98	64
Tunisia	2·9	0·8	4·3	2 250	94	67

TABLE 2.6—*continued*

	Population	*Food production*[a]	*Domestic demand for food*[b, c]	*Dietary energy supply*[c, d]		*Protein supply*[c, d]
	(*% rate of growth per year*[e])			(*kcal per caput per day*)	(*% of requirements*[f])	(*g per caput per day*)
	(1)	(2)	(3)	(4)	(5)	(6)
Developing countries—*contd.*						
Turkey	2·7	3·0	3·8	3 250	129	91
Uganda	2·4	1·8	3·2	2 130	91	61
Upper Volta	1·8	4·7	1·2	1 710	72	59
Uruguay	1·3	0·8	1·2	2 880	108	100
Venezuela	3·5	6·1	4·0	2 430	98	63
Vietnam Dem. Rep.	2·7	—	—	2 350	114	53
Vietnam, Rep.	2·5	4·3	3·2	2 320	107	53
Yemen Arab Rep.	2·4	−0·2	3·9	2 040	84	61
Yemen, Dem. Rep.	2·4	1·6	−1·0	2 070	86	57
Zaire	2·0	0·2	2·3	2 060	93	33
Zambia	2·9	4·3	4·8	2 590	112	68

[a] Food component of crop and livestock production only (i.e. excluding fish production).
[b] Calculated on basis of growth of population and per caput income, and estimates of income elasticity of farm value of demand in *FAO Commodity Projections* 1970–1980, Rome, 1971.
[c] Total food, including fish.
[d] 1969–71 average.
[e] Exponential trend 1952–72.
[f] Revised standards of average requirements (physiological requirements plus 10 per cent for waste at household level).
[g] 1962–72.
(Source: *Assessment of the World Food Situation*, E/Conf. 65/3, FAO, Rome, 1974).

TABLE 2.7
Rate of Growth of Food Production in Relation to Population, World and Main Regions, 1952–62 and 1962–72

	1952–62			1962–72		
		Food production			*Food production*	
	Population	*Total*	*Per caput*	*Population*	*Total*	*Per caput*
			(*% per year*[a])			
Developed market economies[b]	1·2	2·5	1·3	1·0	2·4	1·4
Western Europe	0·8	2·9	2·1	0·8	2·2	1·4
North America	1·8	1·9	0·1	1·2	2·4	1·2
Oceania	2·2	3·1	0·9	2·0	2·7	0·7
Eastern Europe and USSR	1·5	4·5	3·0	1·0	3·5	2·5
Total developed countries	1·3	3·1	1·8	1·0	2·7	1·7
Developing market economies[b]	2·4	3·1	0·7	2·5	2·7	0·2
Africa	2·2	2·2	—	2·5	2·7	0·2
Far East	2·3	3·1	0·8	2·5	2·7	0·2
Latin America	2·8	3·2	0·4	2·9	3·1	0·2
Near East	2·6	3·4	0·8	2·8	3·0	0·2
Asian centrally planned economies	1·8	3·2	1·4	1·9	2·6	0·7
Total developing countries	2·4	3·1	0·7	2·4	2·7	0·3
World totals	2·0	3·1	1·1	1·9	2·7	0·8

[a] Trend rate of growth of food production, compound interest.
[b] Including countries in other regions not specified.
(Source: *Assessment of the World Food Situation* E/Conf. 65/3. FAO, Rome, 1974).

increase in food output. On these projections it is clear that the demand for food is not being met from indigenous production in many developing countries.

Table 2.7 shows how this situation developed from 1952 to 1972 by comparing population growth with the growth of total and per caput food output. In each case the increase in per caput production has been positive but very small.

Table 2.8 projects the growth of populations and food production to 1985. In general it is anticipated that food production will increase faster than population by 0·2% per year in the developing countries, but this

TABLE 2.8
Extrapolated Growth Rates of Food Production and Projected Population Growth, 1969–71 to 1985

	Food production (*% per annum*)	*Population*
Developed countries	2·8	0·9
Market economies	2·4	0·9
USSR & Eastern Europe	3·5	0·9
Developing countries	2·6	2·4
Developing market economy countries	2·6	2·7
Africa	2·5	2·9
Far East	2·4	2·6
Latin America	2·9	3·1
Near East	3·1	2·9
Asian centrally planned countries	2·6	1·6
World	2·7	2·0

(Source: *Assessment of the World Food Situation*, E/Conf. 65/3. FAO, Rome, 1974).

TABLE 2.9
Projections of Food Demand: 1969–71 to 1985 (medium population variant)

	Compound growth rates with:			*Total volume of demand with:*		
	'Zero' income (*% per annum*)	*'Trend' income*	*'High' income*	*'Zero' income* (1969–71 = 100)	*'Trend' income*	*'High' income*
Developed countries	0·9	1·5	—	115	126	—
Market economies	0·9	1·4	—	114	124	—
Eastern Europe & USSR	0·9	1·7	—	115	130	—
Developing market economies	2·7	3·6	4·0	150	170	180
Africa	2·9	3·8	4·1	153	176	183
Far East	2·6	3·4	4·0	148	166	180
Latin America	2·8	3·6	3·8	151	170	175
Near East	2·9	4·0	4·2	154	180	186
Asian centrally planned economies	1·6	3·1	3·5	127	158	168
All developing countries	2·4	3·4	3·8	143	166	176
World	2·0	2·4	(2·7)	134	144	(148)

(Source: FAO estimates).

rather optimistic figure is produced mainly by the very large growth foreseen for the Asian centrally planned economies. In Africa it is forecast that food production will lag behind population growth by 0·4% a year, in the Far East by 0·2% a year, in Latin America by 0·2% a year and that in the Near East it will exceed population growth by 0·2% a year.

Table 2.9 projects the demand for food, by regions, to 1985, both as annual growth rates and as indices compared with the 1969–71 average. If incomes continue to rise according to the recent trend, then by 1985 the developing countries as a whole will demand 66% more food than they did during the base period, only 15 years earlier.

Table 2.10 gives the actual balances of meat and fish foods in stock in the

TABLE 2.10
Meat and Fish Balances for 1970 and 1985

		Beef and veal		*Mutton and lamb*		*Fish*	
		1969/71	1985	1969/71	1985	1969/71	1985
				(*million tonnes*)			
Developing countries							
Total demand		11·7	21·4	3·2	6·6	33·2	51·3
of which:	Feed	—	—	—	—	13·6	13·6
	Production	12·7	20·0	3·2	4·1	35·2	51·1
	Balance	1·0	−1·4	—	2·5	2·0	−0·2
Developing market economies							
Total demand		9·6	17·3	2·6	5·5	25·9	37·9
of which:	Feed	—	—	—	—	13·6	13·6
	Production	10·6	17·0	2·6	3·4	27·2	38·3
	Balance	1·0	−0·3	—	2·1	1·3	0·4
Asian centrally planned economies							
Total demand		2·0	4·1	0·6	1·1	7·3	13·3
of which:	Feed	—	—	—	—	—	—
	Production	2·1	2·9	0·7	0·8	8·0	12·8
	Balance	0·1	−1·2	0·1	−0·3	0·7	−0·5
Developed countries							
Total demand		27·0	38·4	3·7	5·2	34·5	43·2
of which:	Feed	—	—	—	—	12·6	12·6
	Production	26·6	39·0	3·9	4·9	34·5	45·5
	Balance	−0·4	0·6	0·2	−0·3	—	2·3
World							
Total demand		38·7	59·8	7·0	11·8	67·7	94·4
of which:	Feed	—	—	—	—	26·2	26·2
	Production	39·3	58·8	7·1	9·1	69·7	96·6
	Balance	0·6	−1·0	0·1	−2·7	2·0	2·2

(Source: UN WFC E/Conf. 65/3).

TABLE 2.11
Vulnerable Population Groups, 1970 and 1985[a]

	Children, age 0–4		*Pregnant and lactating women*[b]		*Old aged, 65 and over*		*Totals*		*Total population*	
	1970	1985	1970	1985 (*millions*)	1970	1985	1970	1985	1970 (*percent*)	1985
World, total	506	652	246	301	189	266	941	1 218	26·0	25·1
Developed countries	95	114	40	48	103	127	238	289	22·1	23·6
Developing countries	412	537	206	253	86	138	703	929	27·6	25·6
Developing market economies	305	423	154	201	54	89	513	714	29·2	27·2
Africa	50	79	26	39	8	12	84	130	30·0	30·3
Far East	178	233	90	111	30	51	299	394	29·3	26·2
Latin America	47	68	22	30	11	18	79	116	27·9	27·0
Near East	30	44	15	21	6	9	51	74	29·7	28·3
Asian centrally planned economies	107	114	52	52	32	49	191	215	24·0	21·4

[a] FAO estimates based on UN ‘medium’ population projections.
[b] Estimated on the basis of crude birth rates (number of births times 2).
(Source: *Assessment of the World Food Situation*, E/Conf. 65/3. FAO, Rome, 1974).

base period 1969–71 and compares this with the stocks anticipated in 1985, comparing supplies with demand in each case.

In estimating the supply of and demand for food in years ahead we must take account not simply of the total size of populations and the rate at which they are growing, but of the groups within them that are particularly at risk. Small children, pregnant women and nursing mothers have special requirements and both they and old people may be particularly weak economically. It is they, therefore, whose circumstances must be watched carefully. The numbers of infants and mothers is a function of the birth rate, of course, but Table 2.11 uses the UN 'medium' population projections to indicate both the total number of people involved and their significance as a dependent percentage of total populations. In the world as a whole, the relative size of the dependent population is expected to decline by 0·9 % between 1970 and 1985. In the developed countries it is expected to increase by 1·5 % but in developing countries it should decline by 2 %. This suggests that more satisfactory dependency ratios will be achieved but not everywhere. In Africa the number of dependents may increase by 0·3 %. Thus it is in Africa that problems of food supply may become more acute. On the whole, though, the population situation shows what may be the beginning of a sign of a long term improvement. World population may be starting to stabilise.

REFERENCES

1. *Reports on Population/Family Planning, January* 1974, No. 15. Population Council, New York.
2. Ehrlich, P. R. and Anne H. (1972). *Population, Resources, Environment.* W. H. Freeman, San Francisco.
3. Shattock, F. M. (1973). The effect of wars, natural disasters and disease on population control, *The Ecologist*, **3**(12), 456.
4. Howe, B. M. (1972). *Man, Environment and Disease in Britain.* Pelican, Harmondsworth, UK.
5. *Annual Abstract of Statistics*, 1974. HMSO, London.
6. Tranter, N. (1973). *Population Since the Industrial Revolution: The Case of England and Wales.* Croom Helm, London.
7. Myers, N. (1975). Of all things people are the most precious, *New Scientist*, **65**(931), 56.
8. Moraes, D. (1974). *A Matter of People.* Andre Deutsch, London.
9. Johnson, S. (1970). *Life Without Birth.* Heinemann, London.
10. Keyfitz, N. (1966). How many people have lived on earth? *Demography*, **3**(2), 581; Carr-Saunders in Thompson, W. S. and Lewis, D. T. (1965). *Population Problems*, 5th ed., p. 384. McGraw-Hill, New York; United Nations, *Demographic Yearbook* for 1961 and 1971; and Population Division (1970). Working Paper, No. 37, 17 December. Mimeo.

11. FAO (1974). World Food Conference, E/Conf. 65/3. Rome.
12. United Nations, *Demographic Yearbook* for 1970 and 1971.
13. UN (1973). *Monthly Bulletin of Statistics*, **27**(11), Table 2; Nortman, D. (1973). Population and family planning: A factbook, *Reports on Population/Family Planning*, 5th ed., No. 2. September.

Chapter 3

THE GREEN REVOLUTION

We may never know with any certainty how the term 'Green Revolution' began, who first used it or where. It has been absorbed into our vocabulary so rapidly and so completely that today it is an expression used all over the world. It may well have been an official of the FAO who used it first, although the FAO would probably prefer to attribute it to a journalist seeking a convenient slogan that would conjure a simple picture of the aims and hopes contained in long, technical and very complex plans, forecasts and programmes.

The origin of the term is not really important but its meaning is, and although the two magic words are used daily by the FAO in its official publications and speeches, the organisation deplores them. They are too potent. They conjure an image that is too simple. At worst they engender a dangerous complacency.

As public opinion began to awaken to the existence of widespread hunger in the world, in the late 1940s and 1950s, it was possible that the governments of the wealthy industrial nations might be compelled by their own electorates to provide assistance to the poor nations in quantities and forms that would be appropriate to their needs. When technologies were developed through which this assistance could be channelled, hopes rose further and the possibility began to emerge of a major agricultural expansion that would transform the world food situation and the economies of the developing regions. It might be, in truth, a Green Revolution. The term itself, however, based as it was on technological advances, might have suggested to many people that the problem was solved, so allowing them to lapse into an apathy based on the comfortable assurance that their interest and support was no longer needed. They could believe that the world food problem was solved. As we know only too well, it was not.

So the term is not really apt. What it described is not some clever, convenient, technological fix whereby overnight the deserts can be made to bloom, but a very complex mixture of technologies and strategies. In the sense that these have led to a major expansion in food production in most regions, they have succeeded, although as we shall see in later chapters they have encountered formidable difficulties and often created as many problems as they have solved. In the sense that they have provided a clear once-and-for-all solution to the problem of supplying food to the poor people of the world, they have failed. This is not necessarily a criticism of them but only a statement of the rather obvious fact that international institutions are no better at performing miracles than any other human agency, and that there is more to feeding people than inventing slogans. It was never possible that the Green Revolution could achieve as much as many people wanted it to achieve. It over-sold itself among the guilty, concerned, frightened citizens of the rich countries.

Let us, then, abandon the Green Revolution and consider instead the FAO strategies, especially those outlined in the document that provided the bases for the Green Revolution but that has a less romantic title—the *Indicative World Plan for Agricultural Development* or IWP for short. The full version is a long document, consisting of two main volumes, comprising 15 chapters with a total of 672 pages, together with supporting charts, graphs and tables of statistics, and a third volume, of 72 pages, summarising the main conclusions.

The IWP was suggested originally at the First World Food Congress, called by the FAO and held in Washington DC in June 1963. The final declaration from that congress called for further congresses to be held from time to time:

'to review a world survey, presented by the Director-General of FAO, of the world food situation in relation to population and overall development, together with a proposed programme for future action'. Commission II of the congress called for 'the formulation of a world plan in quantitative terms which would be based on nutritional and economic development need, and would indicate the type and magnitude of external assistance needed', while Commission IV wanted 'a balance sheet ... to list and make known the needs and the resources available for the war on hunger'.

The IWP was completed by 1969 and was presented, as a provisional plan, to the Second World Food Congress, held in The Hague in June 1970. In his speech at the opening session of the congress, the then Secretary-General of the United Nations, U Thant, recalled that the UN had been in existence for a quarter of a century. He described the changes that had taken place during that period, the divisions that led nations to arm for what would be, were the weapons ever to be used, the most destructive and expensive war the world had ever known, or probably would ever know. He summed up very clearly the view of the world that prevailed as the congress met, the view that provided the context within which the food situation was considered.

'No other quarter of a century has been so profoundly marked by new scientific and technical advances as the period just past. During this period, man has advanced dramatically into the infinitely large and the infinitely small. Instruments, linked by instant communication to our planet, have been sent farther and farther into the universe. Humans have set foot on the moon and have returned safely to earth. Outer space is being used for unprecedented systems of worldwide communication and observation of the earth's resources and physical conditions. World transportation has expanded dramatically from the limitations of land and sea to the atmosphere with ever-larger and faster planes. Man has reached with his tools the abyss of the seas. We have witnessed the birth of electronics, of cybernetics, the harnessing of atomic energy, and we are about to experience an equally exhilarating and frightening phase of scientific advance in microbiology marked a few days ago by the first complete synthesis of a gene.

'These advances have led to immense improvements of life on earth. Yet they have also engendered new preoccupations. The number of humans on earth has increased from 2485 million in 1950, when the first meaningful postwar statistics were available in the United Nations, to 3632 million today. The earth's population will reach 6 billion before the end of the century. The world death rate has been reduced from 17 per thousand of the population in 1950 to 14 per thousand in 1970. Thirty-seven percent of the world's people live today in urban areas compared with 28 % in 1950. World industrial production has tripled since 1950. The volume of world exports has quadrupled. Agricultural production has increased by 1·7 times. The phenomenal growth in the production of certain commodities can be illustrated by the petroleum output which increased 5 times since 1950, plastics which increased 15 times, aluminium 5 times, cement 4 times, crude steel 2·8 times, motor vehicles 2·7 times, and so forth. The statistics published by the United Nations and its specialised agencies show a doubling or tripling of most world aggregates during the past 20 years. Transformations in the physical and biological conditions of the earth are thus taking place accompanied by mass phenomena of unprecedented proportions. Projections for the future indicate further accelerated changes in practically every direction. Even food production, which was lagging behind, may be on the threshold of a breakthrough thanks to the recent discoveries of high-yielding varieties of cereals due to advances in genetic research.

'While in the midst of progress and wealth in the more advanced countries humans begin to be concerned with the price they have to pay for their blessings, two-thirds of humanity have not yet been reached by these blessings. Progress toward justice and human solidarity has seriously lagged behind scientific and technical progress. Your congress has evidence before it of the enormous disparities in nutrition of the people of the world. In this very same world, in some of the most advanced countries, man has a life expectancy of more than 70 years, while in some of the poorer countries he has a life expectancy of only 25 years! One wonders how human communities can live side by side in such disparity of conditions. It is not necessary to go to the moon, to reach into the universe to find new challenges for human creativity and progress.'[1]

THE PROBLEM

The IWP study began with a survey of the world food situation. For this purpose the world was divided into three zones, A, B and C, as shown in Table 3.1.

TABLE 3.1
The Three Zones of the IWP Study

Zone	1962 *population (thousands)*	*World population* (%)
World	3 159 978	100·0
Zone A: developed market economies—	698 964	22·1
region A1 N. America	205 261	
A2 Europe	364 761	
A3 Other	128 942	
Zone B: centrally planned economies—	1 066 833	33·8
region B1 Western	321 217	
B2 Eastern	745 616	
Zone C: developing countries	1 394 181	44·1

Zone C countries were broken down into regions. Latin America, with a population of 225 309 thousand (1962), included Argentina, Bolivia, Brazil, Chile, Colombia, Costa Rica, Ecuador, El Salvador, Guatemala, Honduras (now Belize), Mexico, Nicaragua, Panama, Paraguay, Peru, Uruguay and Venezuela. Africa south of the Sahara, the second region, with a population of 201 173 thousand, included Cameroon, Central African Republic, Chad, Congo, Democratic Republic of the Congo, Dahomey, Ethiopia, Gabon, the Gambia, Ghana, Ivory Coast, Kenya, Madagascar, Malawi, Mali, Mauritania, Niger, Nigeria, Senegal, Tanzania, Togo, Uganda, Upper Volta and Zambia. The Near East and north west Africa (population 135 115 thousand) included Afghanistan, Algeria, Iran, Iraq, Jordan, Kuwait, Lebanon, Morocco, Saudi Arabia, Southern Yemen, The Sudan, Syria, Tunisia, United Arab Republic and Yemen. Asia and the Far East (population 832 584 thousand) included Ceylon (Sri Lanka), China (Taiwan), Republic of Korea, India, Malaysia (West), Pakistan, the Philippines and Thailand.

It is important to note that the People's Republic of China was not a member of the United Nations or, therefore, of the FAO at that time and so was not included, and that the list of countries studied, although it is far from complete, does account for 90% of the population of Latin America, 84·2% of the population of Africa south of the Sahara, 96·1% of the population of the Near East and north west Africa and 80·5% of the population of Asia and the Far East.

A calculation of the UN medium population growth forecast, coupled with the anticipated rate of economic growth in terms of gross domestic product and the income elasticities of demand for major foodstuffs, led the FAO to estimate that in the period from 1961 to 1963, which provided the base data, and 1985, food demand in the developing countries would increase by nearly $2\frac{1}{2}$ times. About two-thirds of the increase would arise simply from natural increase in population sizes, the balance would be caused by rising prosperity.

It was assumed that the major shortages that existed in 1962 were of protein foods and that the main aim of any programme for improvement must be to increase the supply of protein, and at the same time to improve its quality by increasing the proportion of dietary protein derived from animal sources.

Most of the clinical symptoms of malnutrition seen in developing countries were those of protein deficiency. It was understandable, therefore, that a 'protein gap' should be assumed to exist. It was observed that the foods poor people did manage to obtain were those generally thought of as 'energy' foods—those eaten, at least in Europe and North America, primarily for their calorific value in diets much of whose protein was supplied by meat, fish, cheese, eggs and milk. Today that view is largely discounted by nutritionists, at least in its simple form.

The view was that children were especially susceptible to protein malnutrition because during the early years of life growth is characterised by the multiplication of cells. Later in life growth is based on the enlargement of existing cells but no new cells are added. Although both processes require protein it is the manufacture of DNA for new cells that exerts the heavier demand. If new cells are not formed during the appropriate stage of life, they cannot be formed later and so the body will be short of them throughout life. This may lead to stunted growth and to the overloading of certain organs of the body that develop insufficiently to cope with the normal demands made on them by an adult body. Calorie deprivation, on the other hand, can be made up at any time in life, when an increase in the energy available will permit cells to increase in size.

Experiments have shown, however, that not only protein deprivation causes reduction in the rate of cell proliferation, but so also does calorie deprivation.[2] Both DNA synthesis and protein formation in cells require energy to transform dietary protein into reserves of various kinds. Thus a protein deprivation will reduce the quantity of the reserves themselves but a calorie deprivation will reduce the amount of energy needed for the chemical reactions that provide the reserves. In other words a shortage of protein will deprive the body of raw materials, while a shortage of calories will deprive the body of the energy it needs to digest the protein. So even in terms of the formation of brain tissue, which is almost entirely protein, malnutrition is caused by deficiencies and imbalances more complicated than simple protein deprivation.

More generally, the body's demands for both calorie energy and for protein are not equal. Energy is the first and more urgent need. If the body is deprived of energy, not only will the digestion of protein be inhibited but protein will be metabolised to supply energy. This process is very inefficient but it is a natural response to calorie deprivation.

It is believed today that food shortages are shortages of both calories and of protein. Since the energy demand takes precedence, however, the first clinical symptoms to appear are often those of protein deficiency. The obvious remedy, then, of feeding the victim a diet rich in protein, will prove counter-productive. The protein will simply be burnt to provide energy and the symptoms will continue until a point is reached where the body's energy needs are satisfied and proper metabolism of proteins can begin. At this stage a nutritionally satisfactory diet may be achieved, but at a very high cost since by and large protein foods—certainly those that are thought of as protein foods in the developed countries—are more expensive than energy foods, especially when they are derived from animal produce.

Later studies revealed a possible further cause of malnutrition among children that had nothing to do with diet at all. It was found that where the relationship between a small child and its mother was disturbed, so that the child became very insecure, a number of inhibitions may result. The child is likely to become less adventurous physically and mentally, and excretory and digestive functions may be disturbed. So an unhappy, insecure, inhibited child may be unable to digest properly the food available to it and if its diet approximates closely to the minimum requirement for its age and body size, then symptoms of malnutrition may occur.[2] In stable rural populations and affluent urban populations such problems seldom occur, but they are likely to be much more common among the urban and rural poor during periods of rapid and stressful change such as may characterise the early stages of the development process.

It is thus very possible that the IWP began with an incorrect assessment of the nature of the world food problem and that its emphasis on increasing the supply and availability of protein foods was inappropriate and unnecessarily costly.

Figure 3.1 shows the balance of animal and vegetable protein in the diet of various developed and developing countries. This provides a fairly accurate guide of relative prosperity but nutritionally it is of little significance. Table 3.2 and Fig. 3.2 which compare regions against a balanced protein–calorie diet requirement, are more informative. Where

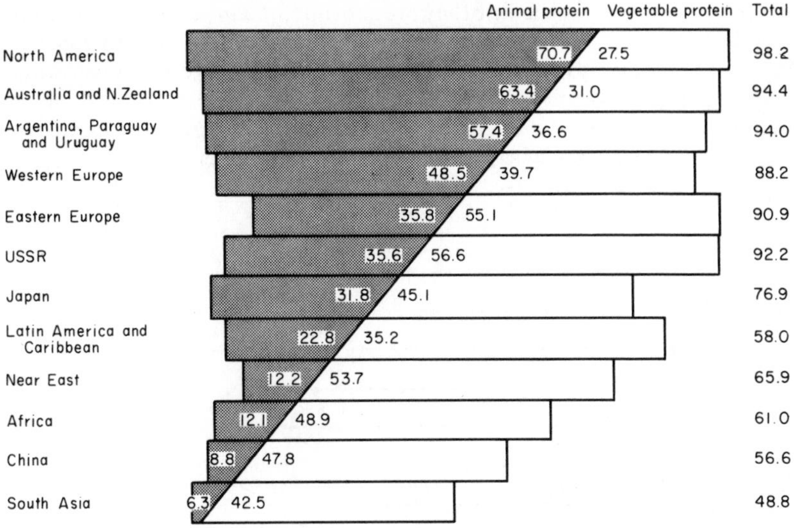

FIG. 3.1 The balance of animal and vegetable protein (average gram consumption per caput per day) in various countries (Source: FAO (1975), *Ceres*, May/June).

TABLE 3.2
Estimated Number and Percentage of People with Insufficient Protein/Energy Supply by Regions (1970)

	Population	*Percentage below lower limit*	*Number below lower limit*
	(*thousand million*)	(%)	(*million*)
Developed regions	1·07	3	28
Developing regions[a]	1·75	25	434
Latin America	0·28	13	36
Far East	1·02	30	301
Near East	0·17	18	30
Africa	0·28	25	67
Total	2·83	16	462

[a] Excluding Asian centrally planned economies.
(Source: *The State of Food and Agriculture*, 1974. FAO, Rome)

people are hungry it is because they are short of food in general, not because of a deficiency of protein in particular. The only exception to this rule may be found among peoples whose staple foods are based on cassava, which contains much less protein than either wheat or rice. For people who eat mainly wheat or rice, if they receive sufficient food to provide them with the energy they need they will automatically receive sufficient protein.

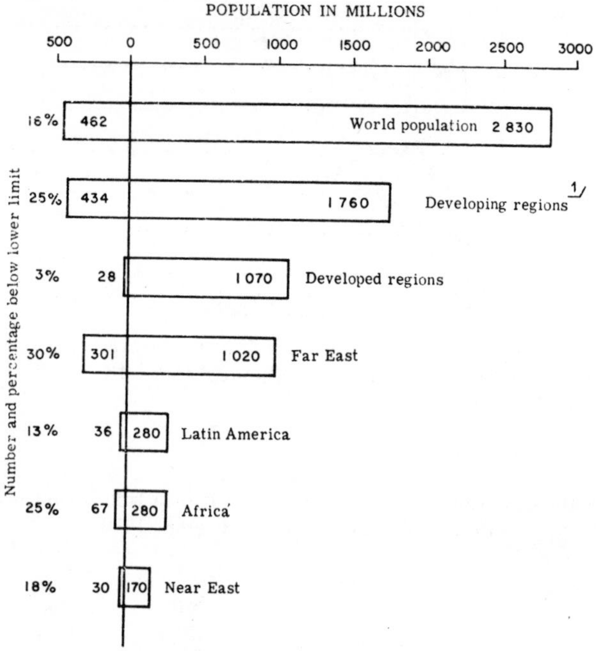

FIG. 3.2 Estimated number of people with insufficient protein/energy supply, world and regions, 1970 (Source: ref. 14).
[1]Excluding Asian centrally planned economies.

It was argued by the FAO that the additional food required in developing regions could not be supplied from the developed regions. Quite apart from the internal effect on the economies of primarily agrarian countries of dumping large quantities of food, it was calculated that by 1985 the food import bill for those countries would amount to some $40 000 million at constant 1962 prices, if they attempted simply to import all the additional food they needed.

In 1962 their food import bill was about $3000 million and the FAO believed it was quite unrealistic to allow for an increase in their prosperity on so dramatic a scale. The food had to be produced in the regions and, so far as possible, in the countries where it was to be consumed. Nor can this increase in production be based to any great extent on the expansion of agriculture into new lands. As we shall see in a later chapter, the uncultivated land still available to agriculture, though it amounts to a considerable area, is strictly limited and would soon realise the whole of its potential. The cost of cultivating this new land would be high and would divert capital that might be invested more profitably in other forms of agricultural expansion. The IWP concluded, then, that the aim must be to intensify production in existing farmed areas.

Because of its concern over the 'protein gap', the plan suggests an expansion in livestock production as the first step. Thus poultry and pork production would increase at an annual rate of 4·1 %, compared with 3·8 % for fisheries, 3·6 % for crops and 3·5 % for forestry.

'If poultry and pig production are not stepped up immediately, production of all foods of animal origin is almost certain to fall below effective demand, prices are likely to rise sharply and protein malnutrition could grow worse in those groups where it is now most serious.'[3]

If it is essential to increase livestock production at any cost, then pigs and poultry are the obvious choice, because their breeding cycles are much shorter than those of cattle and sheep. The price of such a rapid increase may be high, however, and the attractiveness of non-ruminant livestock species may be based on the recent experience of the developed countries rather than on their longer experience.

Traditionally, pigs and poultry were kept as marginal enterprises on most farms. They consumed wastes and surpluses, especially surpluses of grains. Most pictures of European farmyards at any time up to the 1960s will show a pig or two in a sty and hens ranging free, scratching for grain spilled on its way to or from the barns. When they lived in this way the non-ruminants afforded a useful method of converting food that otherwise would be lost into highly palatable proteins and fats. Their populations were allowed to float. In years when the grain harvests were good, more grain would be available for them and their populations would be allowed to increase. In poor years they would be killed. In a sense they filled a dual function as scavengers and as 'biological storehouses'.

During the postwar years, when large surpluses of grain were available to those countries able to buy them, the populations of non-ruminants in the developed countries increased more rapidly than at any time in the past and their products came to assume much greater importance in the diet of Europeans and Americans than ever before. Their number grew to such an extent that new systems of management were needed and the development of intensive systems of rearing non-ruminants made it possible to absorb even larger quantities of surplus grain, and although prices for pork, bacon, ham and other pigmeat products were regulated by the price of other red meats, poultry and egg prices fell so that the roast chicken that had been an occasional luxury not many years earlier became the cheapest form of meat.

The whole enterprise depended on the availability of grain surpluses. Today, as we saw earlier, those surpluses no longer exist and so some agronomists are advising the developed countries to permit their non-ruminant livestock populations to float downwards again to new, more realistic levels. The alternative is to support them very expensively indeed, as they consume food that can be eaten directly by humans, that is required for human consumption and that therefore can be sold at the higher prices paid for human foodstuffs.

In developing countries, therefore, increases in the non-ruminant populations must be paid for in grain, and even though the resultant animal protein may be of higher quality that the initial cereal protein—itself a controversial view in terms of modern nutritional knowledge—it is converted at efficiencies of no more than about 20 %. If the equation is to balance, the animal protein must be five times more nutritious, weight for weight, than vegetable protein in order to supply the same amount of food in a more concentrated form.

At the same time as the non-ruminant population was to increase, steps were to be taken to increase ruminant production:

'Increasing production of milk, beef, veal and other meat is urged, but is inevitably slow because the biological cycle of cattle and other ruminants is so long.'[3]

The basis of all the increases has to be cereal production, and as prosperity increased these would be required more and more to sustain livestock populations. As the programmes to expand cereal production by increasing yields from each unit area of land succeed, the stabilisation of demand for cereals will permit land to be taken out of cereal production and devoted to growing other necessary crops, such as pulses, oilseeds, fruit, vegetables, fodder and raw material crops, of which new high-yielding varieties will be needed.

High-yielding varieties

Table 3.3 shows the extent to which, even as late as 1969–71, cereal yields in developing countries lagged behind those in developed countries. In 1962 the gap was even wider, although in some regions yields had increased.

The IWP proposed that in order to satisfy the demand anticipated by 1985, rice yields in Asia needed to increase by 2·7 % annually, compared with the 0·8 % annual increase actually achieved during the decade from 1954 to 1964; in the Near East, where for a decade yields of wheat had been falling by 0·8 % annually, they should increase by 2·8 % a year; in north west Africa, where they had been increasing at 0·2 % per year, the rate of increase should accelerate to 3·2 %.

It was clear that increases of this magnitude could not be sustained without considerable technological improvement of existing agricultural systems. In all developing countries the majority of the population depends upon agriculture directly for its living—indeed, this is one definition used to identify developing economies. So agriculture was likely to be highly labour-intensive, ensuring that each unit of production received very great care.

TABLE 3.3
Average Yields of Selected Crops in Selected Countries 1969–71

Wheat		*Rice* (*tonnes per ha*)		*Maize*	
Germany, Fed. Rep.	4·14	Japan	5·48	USA	5·15
Mexico	2·94	Thailand	1·97	Kenya	1·32
Pakistan	1·11	Brazil	1·44	India	1·05

(Source: *Assessment of the World Food Situation*, E/Conf. 65/3. FAO, Rome)

Farmers and peasants usually inherit with their land the accumulated experience of many generations of their forebears, who, across the centuries, have achieved a fine and subtle adaptation to their local environment. They know very well the conditions under which they must work, the capabilities of their land, their crops and their climate. Small improvements are often possible. An outside adviser might see that a minor change in the timing of cultivations, for example, could affect dramatically the ease with which weeds and pests were controlled.

Often no more than a modest injection of capital was needed to improve irrigation and drainage. Such small changes could add up to significant improvements but they could not be repeated year after year. The Malthusian argument appeared to hold, in that each increase in food output was achieved by a development that could not be repeated. Yet the IWP targets, if sustained for long, implied a doubling of Asian rice production in about 25 years, a doubling of Asian wheat yields in 16 years, a doubling of Near Eastern wheat yields in 25 years and a doubling of north western African wheat yields in 21 years. What was needed was a single major leap ahead, to buy more time.

It was impossible not to look at the disparities in yields between developed and developing countries and to consider the possibility of translating to tropical and sub-tropical environments the agricultural technologies that had achieved such dramatic increases in Europe, North America and Japan.

Essentially these improvements were based upon increasing the capital invested in agriculture, a task that might be undertaken by aid programmes. The capital was invested in machinery and equipment. No one can say precisely whether or by how much this increased yields, since a main aim was to economise on labour, and so agricultural efficiency tended to be measured as much in terms of productivity per worker as productivity per unit of production. Credit was also provided to enable farmers to buy better seed, fertiliser and other input commodities. Though doubt might exist regarding the appropriateness of heavy investment in fixed plant, buildings and machinery in developing countries, where social problems were more likely to be caused by unemployment and under-employment in rural areas than by labour shortage, there was much less doubt about the efficiency of fertiliser use.

Even so, for a period of several years developing countries were encouraged to accept farm machinery as part of their aid. Perhaps the motives of the donors were genuine and they were anxious to do no more than offer farmers in poor regions the tools whereby their own farmers had grown prosperous. In that case it must be coincidence that large farm machines, labelled clearly to show their country of origin, demonstrated to the peoples of the recipient countries the extent to which they should be grateful to the citizens of the USA, the USSR, of Europe and, later, of China. It is difficult to believe that aid in this form was politically motiveless.

Increases in fertiliser use were encouraged but immediately a biological problem appeared, especially with cereal crops. Traditional varieties of cereals tended to respond to increased nutrient inputs by growing larger. This of course is what they were meant to do, but they grew larger in every part of the plant. The effect was to produce much taller plants that were physically unstable and that had difficulty in supporting the weight of the (also heavier) seed. They tended to fall. Once 'lodged' the crop is much more difficult to harvest. A modern combine harvester can cut fairly low, but it must leave a stubble a few inches high. If it tries to cut lower than this, the cutting blades will be damaged by stones and the grain will be contaminated by lumps of earth. If a lodged crop of ripe grain becomes damp the grain may germinate. Lodging, even in developed countries, leads to serious crop losses but in those countries the problem was largely solved by developing short-stemmed varieties that allowed additional nutrient to accumulate in the seed, which acts as a 'nutrient sink'. Such varieties were adapted to day length, light intensity, temperature and moisture conditions found in temperate climates and they would not grow well in the very different conditions of the tropics and sub-tropics.

There was a need to develop varieties of cereals that would respond to increases in their supply of nutrient without lodging. Much more of the growth had to be concentrated in larger numbers of heavier seeds, rather than in the stem. Work to develop new varieties of wheat began in 1943, in

Mexico, where a team led by Dr Norman E. Borlaug was working on a programme sponsored jointly by the Mexican government and the Rockefeller Foundation. At that time Mexico was dependent on large imports of wheat. In 1943 the country imported more than 275 000 tons, at a cost of about $21 million. Dr Borlaug described the situation in Mexico when the programme began:

'Wheat was grown primarily as a winter irrigated crop. It was planted from September through December and harvested from April through June, depending upon the elevation. The varieties were all of spring habit and, with the exception of two Sonora varieties introduced from California, were of unknown origin. Varieties in the ordinary sense of the word did not exist, but were mixtures of many different types. All varieties were susceptible to stem rust caused by *Puccinia graminis tritici*, the most serious disease of this crop. In years when ecologic conditions were favourable to the pathogen, as was the case in Sonora in 1939, 1940 and 1941 and in the Bajio region in 1948, devastating epidemics brought economic ruin to the wheat producer. Cultural practices were very primitive in every area except Sonora, where mechanisation and improved methods were well advanced. The Egyptian plough was the only implement used in land preparation and planting operations in most areas, and harvesting was done largely by the use of a hand sickle.

'An analysis of the causes of low yields and lack of interest in wheat production indicated that through research it would be necessary to develop: (1) improved disease-resistant, high-yielding, good quality varieties that would also possess the agronomic characteristics making them well adapted to improved agricultural methods and practices; (2) basic information on the soil fertility levels of the different principal soil types where wheat was grown and, with this information, suitable fertilisation and rotation practices as a stride toward attaining higher yields; (3) improved economical methods for land preparation, planting and harvesting, which are all-important considerations in reducing costs and increasing yields; (4) the proper irrigation practices necessary for efficient utilisation of the benefits expected from the use of improved varieties and fertiliser practices; and (5) basic pathological and entomological information on the important diseases and insect pests, and also to make this information available to the breeding programme so that resistance could be incorporated into the new varieties, wherever feasible, or direct biological or chemical control measures devised.'[4]

By 1954, after 10 years of work, an absolute limit seemed to have been reached. Yields could not be increased beyond 3 tons an acre because of lodging. Then work began to alter the architecture of the wheat plant.

After World War II a Japanese variety of wheat, called Norin 10, was taken to Washington State University in the USA, where over the succeeding years a USDA wheat breeder, Dr O. A. Vogel, used it to develop several new varieties, including Norin 10 × Baart and Norin 10 × Brevor. Norin 10 was a dwarf wheat, its dwarfing characteristic being carried by one gene that was transferred to the new hybrids. In 1954 the Mexican team imported these varieties and crossed them again with the best of their own varieties. The effect was to shorten the stem but to increase tillering, which is the production of multiple shoots from a single seed. So shorter but much denser stands were produced and yields increased to 6–8 tons an acre (15–20 tonnes per ha), since the dwarfing gene had no inhibitory effect on the size of the ear.

The new wheats were highly responsive to inputs of fertiliser, provided adequate water was present. Unfortunately, just like the IWP itself they were misnamed almost at once and announced to the world as 'high-yielding varieties', later shortened to HYVs. In a sense this is what they are. They make it possible to increase yields but only if their essential requirements for fertiliser and water are met. In the absence of these inputs they may yield no more heavily, or even less heavily, than traditional varieties. They are adapted to an environment that contains large quantities of nutrient. Once again, the world was able to relax with the idea of new wheat varieties that, by themselves and with no further help, would transform agriculture in the tropical and sub-tropical wheat-growing regions.

A few years later, similar developments occurred in rice breeding at the International Rice Research Institute (IRRI) in the Philippines. The most famous of the new rices developed there was called, popularly, IR8. Its full title was IR8-288-3.

In 1962 a short-stemmed Indica rice, imported from Taiwan, called Dee-geo-woo-gen, was crossed with a tall Indica from Indonesia, called Peta. The resulting hybrid was called IR8. To produce the first generation (F1) 130 seeds from this plant were grown in greenhouses. Seeds from the best F1 specimens were collected and sown in fields, where they produced about 10 000 F2 plants. Any undesirable specimens, those that were too tall or that matured late, were removed and seeds from the remainder were planted in a nursery where they were exposed to a whole range of fungal diseases. Of some 10 000 F3 plants exposed, 298 were selected as the most resistant to diseases, and seed from them was sown to provide 298 rows of F4 plants. From these plants just one was selected, from row 288, to provide the seed for the F5 generation and this supplied the basic seed stock for the plant that became known as IR8-288-3. The process took four years.

IR8 stands 36–42 in (91–107 cm) high and matures in 120–130 days. It does not lodge readily and it yields up to 6·5 tonnes per ha, compared to the 2·2 tonnes per ha from Dee-geo-woo-gen, 2·4 tonnes per ha from Peta and 1·4–2 tonnes per ha from most local varieties being grown in the Philippines at that time.

It is not only their heavier yields and resistance to lodging that is significant. The new cereal varieties mature more rapidly, which makes it possible to grow more than one crop a year on the same land in some areas. In places it is even feasible to grow three crops a year. Traditional varieties of rice are double-cropped on about 5% of all rice-growing land in South and South-East Asia. It is likely that the total area suitable for double-cropping with HYVs is about twice this area.

The public reaction to news of the development of high-yielding varieties of rices was understandably jubilant. They were hailed as 'miracle rices' and they added to the image of imminent agricultural prosperity throughout Asia, of a 'Green Revolution'. Although widely publicised, IR8 was not the success it seemed. It produced grain of inferior quality and although it was highly resistant to some pests and diseases it was highly susceptible to bacterial leaf blight. It was only the first of a long list of new rices, however. Like the Mexican wheat it represented a genuine technological breakthrough.

While the short stem provided resistance against lodging, other characteristics are involved in the uptake of nutrients. Experiments in the Philippines[5] have shown that the angle of incidence of the leaves is important. The new varieties have rather erect leaves, which permit light to penetrate more deeply into the plant. This, in turn, allows light to be distributed more evenly over the whole leaf canopy and gives rise to greater total photosynthesis and so more sugars for storage in the grain. Tillering is also important. Tillers are sub-stems that emerge from the roots around the main stem. They may be considered as the cereal equivalent of branches. The tillers produce panicles and the panicles produce seeds, while the leaves produced by the tillers increase overall photosynthesis. In general, then, a high tillering rate is desirable. However there are disadvantages. There is greater mechanical strain on the main stem of the plant and the mutual shading by leaves may inhibit photosynthesis, especially if the leaves produce a large horizontal area. The vertical leaves of IR8 are doubly advantageous.

The degree of response to nutrients supplied by fertilisers depends on the climate and on the soil, and thus varies quite widely from place to place. In general, HYVs respond to between 60 and 120 kg of nitrogen fertiliser per ha. Some improved traditional Indica rices respond to fertiliser at 120 kg per ha, but others began to decline erratically at levels above 60 kg. In these varieties, yields are much lower than with the HYVs, and some HYVs continue to respond to increasing fertiliser applications up to 150 kg of nitrogen per ha. We will consider soils in more detail in a later chapter, but soil type and condition affect responsiveness to nitrogen and also determine the requirement for phosphatic and potassium fertiliser.

Water is essential, not only because plants themselves require water and the quantity they require is related to their physical size, but also because nutrients are taken up by plants from the aqueous soil solution. If water drains from the soil rapidly and horizontally, into water courses, then fertiliser will be lost by leaching in quantities that may be unacceptable economically as well as environmentally. Again, we will consider fertilisers in more detail later, but it is nitrogenous fertilisers that are used in the largest amounts and it is they that are most soluble in water and so most likely to be leached from the soil.

This increase in fertiliser use represented a considerable demand in developing countries where in the late 1960s arable farmers were using an average of 12–13 kg per ha.[6] In the areas suitable for double- or even triple-cropping the demand was even greater. Similarly, improved irrigation systems were required and, unless they were to lead to waterlogging or salinisation, adequate systems of drainage. Clearly, substantial financial aid would be required before the HYVs could be introduced on any scale.

The demand did not end there. In the field the new varieties often proved susceptible to local diseases and pests and the increase in the land area covered by uniform stands of crops that were genetically similar necessitated an increase in the use of chemical insecticides and herbicides. Genetic vulnerability may prove to be one of the major dangers in the new agricultural technology, but for the time being it can be controlled only chemically in many instances. Again an economic strain was placed upon the agrarian societies.

In some ways the technology was quite inappropriate for the economic situations into which it was planned to be introduced. The 'industrialisation' of temperate climate agriculture, on which it was based, was a complex process that took place in distinct phases.

THE COSTS OF 'MODERNISATION'

Modern agricultural technology as developed in Europe and North America requires a degree of sophistication in its application and it would be unrealistic to expect peasant farmers experienced in methods hallowed by centuries of tradition to adopt the new methods overnight and without appropriate training. Accordingly an important aspect of agricultural development is concerned with education and especially with extension education. Peasants the world over are extremely practical people, unlikely to be impressed by theories no matter how impressive the scientific literature that supports them, so most extension systems work by example. An agricultural adviser will live in a village for a time and as soon as he has persuaded one prominent local farmer to allow him to demonstrate new crops or new techniques on his farm he will set up his demonstration. This will arouse comment and discussion locally and the adviser will help by explaining what he has done, how he did it and how all local farmers might do the same.

The discussions may range far beyond cultivation of the land and crop varieties. New roads may be needed to bring in seed and other inputs and to carry produce to the best market, credit will probably need to be arranged, there may have to be new buildings for storage and administration and electricity may have to brought to the village. These and many other requirements will be discussed with the agricultural adviser and he will be expected to help in providing them. So the modernisation of agricultural technology extends quickly into a very radical change of entire lifestyles.

The role and activities of extension services in many developing countries can probably be summed up by the experience of one village in India and of one villager, a man called Ramji Pawar.[7] Ramji farmed 4 hectacres of land, which made him quite an important farmer, and half of the land was irrigated by a well. His living was precarious and his farming methods based on the use of farmyard manure, cattle urine and ash as an insecticide, and seed that he had grown himself year after year. In 1952 an adviser from the community development agency came to live in the village and he persuaded Ramji to allow him to cultivate and sow demonstration plots on his land.

'The land was prepared, it was fertilised, the seeds and sugarcane sets were planted, and all was properly irrigated. The demonstration plot began to flourish, but then there was an outbreak of insect pests. Insecticides were sprayed on the crop, and the plague passed. Ramji got twice the yield he had ever had before, but more than the yields he valued the new technical know-how he had acquired from the *gramsevak* (literally "servant of the village").

'The demonstration plot was a success. Many farmers from the village and from neighbouring villages came to see and learn. Even the agricultural-extension officer and the block-development officer, who were stationed at block headquarters, came to see the plots.

'Because of his frequent association with the *gramsevak*, Ramji started learning many new things. He began to formulate his own opinions about such things as the improvement of agriculture, livestock, health and education. The village people began to recognise Ramji as a leader; others came to him for advice. Gradually, a group of like-minded persons associated with Ramji and they became recognised as leaders by the village people.'[7]

A co-operative was formed, in which most farmers brought shares and which was registered with the government, which entitled it to loans for agricultural development. A road was built and, eventually, a school building, a community centre, a primary health centre, a store and now the village has electricity as well. Their whole way of life had been transformed.

This transformation was 'progress', but in this final quarter of the twentieth century 'progress' has become a loaded word. Let us call it, more accurately, rapid change, and admit that rapid change brings costs as well as benefits. In a later chapter we will consider some of the implications of the social change wrought by the introduction of new agricultural technology, and in the light of European and American experience we may find we are asking whether Ramji's village can survive for long at all, now that the first large steps have been taken toward a structure that encourages urbanisation and rural unemployment. Economically this village found itself integrated into a wider system over which it could exert no influence. Ramji and his colleagues had become dependent on seed that was imported to the village and that they were unable to grow themselves. They were dependent on fertiliser and pesticides, which also had to be imported, possibly imported to India let alone to their corner of that country. They were dependent on capital, borrowed from elsewhere, on which they must pay interest and which eventually must be repaid in full. Never again can that village be independent or self-sufficient. This may be inevitable, the benefits of improved prosperity may outweigh the costs, but the change in status of the villagers should be noted.

Thus those who introduce the new HYVs bear a very heavy responsibility. Before this change occurred, the village was poor but it continued to survive. Should the HYVs fail now it is very doubtful whether the village can return to its former way of life, whether their official and commercial creditors will waive their bills. The ticket to progress is a one-way ticket. There can be no return. The failure of HYVs in regions where they have been introduced must reduce the inhabitants of those regions to a poverty much more dire than that which they knew before.

The size of the problem is illustrated by Table 3.4, which shows the input costs for the new technology in a group of Zone C countries that includes India. During the IWP period, from 1961 to 1963 (in this and some other tables called 1962 and having an asterisk) to 1985, agricultural output is planned to increase annually by 3·5%, measured in monetary terms. Fertiliser costs are estimated to rise by 11·6% and pesticide costs by 11·2% a year, while more than $112 000 million are required for investment during the period. In the end these input costs and this investment capital must be paid for out of increased production by Ramji and his fellow villagers.

Just as Ramji's village finds itself integrated into a regional and national economic system, so the national economy finds itself bound ever more tightly into an international economic system. As we shall see in more detail later, the application to agrarian societies of agricultural technologies devised in and for industrial societies must make the agrarian societies dependent on them for capital. The technology itself cannot be transferred easily across economic and cultural barriers. Industrial societies are able to support more universities, more research programmes backed by the universities, by industry and by government. It is no coincidence that new pesticides are developed in the industrial world. It is there that the industries

TABLE 3.4
Identified Current Inputs and Investment Requirements[a] of Zone C Study Countries

	Value 1962*	*Value* 1985	*Change* 1962* *to* 1985 (%)	*Growth rates* 1962* *to* 1985 (% *per year*)
	(*million dollars at* 1962* *prices*)			
Identified Current Inputs				
seed	1 673·1	2 473·6	+48	1·7
feed	3 028·8	6 993·8	+131	3·7
fertilisers	671·4	8 362·4	+1 146	11·6
crop protection[b]	180·0	2 076·9	+1 054	11·2
mechanisation	797·1	2 610·2	+227	5·3
irrigation	1 494·7	2 433·7	+63	2·1
total crops and livestock	7 845·1	24 950·6	+218	5·2
fishery	358·9	983·7	+174	4·5
forestry	183·9	413·0	+125	3·6
Total identified inputs	8 387·9	26 347·3	+214	5·1
Total output (gross value)	54 900·1	121 640·4	+122	3·5
Ratio input/output	15·3	21·7		

	Cumulative 1962 *to* 1985 (*million dollars at* 1962* *prices*)	*Distribution* (%)
Identified investment requirements		
land improvement and development	47 100	42
equipment, machines, etc.[c]	39 064	35
livestock inventory and buildings	18 229	16
fisheries: vessels, etc.	4 329	4
forestry and logging	3 743	3
Total identified investments	112 465	100

[a] As taken from regional studies.
[b] Excluding Central America.
[c] Excluding Africa south of the Sahara.
(Source: FAO/IWP).

exist that can support the necessary research and development, and it is there that the pools of trained scientists and technologists are found to perform that research and development.

The present industrial countries were not able to industrialise until their agrarian economic base was sufficiently secure to provide capital and labour. The development of manufacturing industry then made it possible to industrialise agriculture in a kind of second industrial revolution. The experience of some developing countries that have attempted to take short cuts to full industrialisation appears to confirm this sequence as having general applicability. Such industrialisation must be based on capital borrowed abroad, so it begins with a heavy debt. It then tends to divert capital and labour away from the agricultural sector, so bringing about an agricultural decline rather than an expansion, and making the country more heavily dependent on imported food. In order to redress its probable balance of payments deficit at this stage, the expansion of agriculture will divert capital that is now essential to sustain the level of industrial development and so probably it will lead to a general economic stagnation.

Thus the expansion of agriculture is a necessary first step whereby the full economic development of agrarian societies is made possible. Can it be, though, that 'industrialisation' of agriculture, based on imported high technology, is an attempt to short-cut this development process and that it, too, can be sustained only at a very high cost? As more and more questions come to be asked about the role of aid and about the true nature of economic development, this question becomes increasingly pertinent. If there are alternative paths to development, based on the exploitation of indigenous resources and technologies, then it may be wiser to explore them than to accept too readily technologies that must continue to be imported for a long period until, indeed, the expansion of the industrial base has made it possible to supply the inputs of research and of materials that are required by a highly technological agriculture.

The Chinese model is often quoted as one such alternative path, although it may be so much the product of Chinese society that it cannot be applied very generally. Before the Revolution, Chinese agriculture was characterised by rich landlords who owned the best land but maintained it at less than its optimium level of productivity, and peasants generally occupying the poorer land, which was divided into very small strips. The Revolution led fairly quickly to the redistribution of land in what may have been the most important single reform. Since then the aim has been not to integrate rural communities into a national cash-based economy but to begin by ensuring that each village can supply itself with its essential needs.

The country's largest resource was its labour force and the industrial base was weak. Thus people were encouraged to adapt and develop existing agricultural techniques based on the use of resources that could be obtained easily. The amalgamation of strip farms made it possible to terrace hillsides, so helping to halt soil erosion. Irrigation channels and dykes helped to control rivers and prevent flooding. All human and livestock wastes were recycled, so that the organic matter content of soils increased. On occasions the high degree of labour-intensity made it possible to perform tasks that would be unthinkable in an industrialised capital-intensive agricultural system, because in no way could they be performed economically. Entire cereal crops have been planted out as seedlings and watered by hand during times of drought.

As the food supply became more secure it was possible to increase the forested area, which controlled soil erosion further and also contributed a valuable timber crop for future years. There is no ideological objection to 'modern' agriculture or to the use of agrochemicals, provided these can be produced inside China. Consequently, between 1970 and 1973 the average annual increase in chemical fertiliser production was nearly five times what it had been in the preceding 10 years.[8] Much of this production takes place within rural communes themselves, in factories owned by the communes. Similarly, Chinese production of machinery and implements has increased, based mainly on small machines that are cheap to make, simple to maintain and that are most subtly adapted to the immediate needs of farm workers.

'In the past four years, the numbers of tractors, diesel engines, chemical fertiliser, plastic sheets and electric power supplied to agriculture by industrial departments surpassed the total figure in the previous 20 years. In 1972 the number of tractors for farm use was 2·6 times that of 1965, walking tractors over 50 times, installation capacity in small power stations 8 times; mechanised farming area expanded 40 % and rural electric power increased 250 %. Compared with 1972, in 1973 production of tractor and internal combustion engine parts, rubber-tyred push carts, walking tractors and combine harvesters increased 30–60 %, and chemical fertiliser, internal combustion engines and pumps more than 20 %.'[8]

While overall statistics are difficult to obtain and interpret, it is claimed that on the Tachai brigade (village) area, in the Taihang Mountains, 1000 m above sea level on soil and with a climate that is not especially favourable to agriculture, grain yields have risen from 700 kg per ha shortly after the Revolution to more than 8 tonnes per ha in 1971 and, following the severe drought in 1972 and another drought lasting several months in 1973, the 1973 grain harvest was 385 tonnes, 16 % more than in 1972.

This is a tiny amount of grain on which to base statistical claims, but in Hsiyang County, where the Tachai brigade lives, total grain output in 1971 was 2·8 times that in 1966, and despite the droughts the 1973 harvest was about 1·2 % higher than that of 1971. In 1973 total production of grains amounted to 119 500 tonnes, which from 27 000 ha of cultivated land gives an average yield of 4·4 tonnes per ha. If this level of production is, or could be, typical, then it is impressive. Table 3·3 compares the average yields of typical staple crops in various countries and shows that 4 tonnes per ha is an average yield for a developed country employing capital-intensive methods based on western high technology. In 1972/73, the year to which the Chinese figures refer, the average yield of wheat in the nine Member States of the EEC was 3·73 tonnes per ha, and of rice 3·15 tonnes (EEC/MAFF figures).

Predictably the introduction of the HYVs encountered a series of obstacles. The IWP proposed the expansion of the area sown to these varieties so that by 1985 they would occupy about one-third of the total area planted to cereals, compared with about 5% sown to them in 1968.

In some countries the necessary infrastructure required for this kind of industrialisation of agriculture did not exist. Roads and railways were inadequate for the movement of bulky items, such as seed and fertiliser, into regions or for the efficient movement of produce from farms to their urban markets. Credit was not always available and there was a tendency for the new technology to be adopted only by farmers who were rich already. Land values rose, tenants lost their holdings and either left agriculture altogether or became labourers, and the moneylenders grew wealthy.

In some places water was not available in the quantities required. In the temperate climates to which this technology is best adapted, rainfall tends to be adequate and spread fairly evenly through the year. A cool or cold winter checks plant growth and so assists in the control of weeds and pests. In the sub-tropics where the winter is not cold, plant growth is checked by a pronounced dry season and a climate whose rainfall is seasonal. For much of the year, however, the land is semi-arid and water is likely to be in short supply. The drilling of new wells, the installation of irrigation systems and their associated drainage systems requires capital expenditure but capital was not always available. Its availability in the form of direct aid or loans from the industrial nations has not been improved by the recession in world trade, although to some extent the gap has been filled by the emergence of the Arab oil-producing states as major donors.

Fertilisers and pesticides are manufactured mainly within the industrial nations and must be bought by developing countries out of their foreign exchange. The prices of these commodities has been affected by the rise in the prices of oil and of phosphates, and fertiliser and pesticide use has not increased in developing countries so rapidly as the IWP hoped it would.

Lack of adequate storage facilities exacerbated problems of crop wastage that were serious before the HYVs were introduced.

In areas growing IR8 there was consumer resistance to the new rice because of its inferior quality, while in general increased production led to falls in price. So the HYVs were sometimes less profitable than had been anticipated. Dana G. Dalrymple of the International Development Foreign Agriculture Service of USDA, reported in April 1969 that:

'The returns on rice have not been uniform either seasonally or by market. Farm management studies on rice in the Philippines in 1967 suggested that net returns per hectare for IR8 were two-thirds higher than traditional varieties during the wet season but only slightly higher during the dry season. The situation in Burma varies by market: as of late 1968 it was (a) profitable to raise IR8 for sale to the government, because the purchase price was the same as for other types of rice but (b) not profitable to grow it for the free or black markets because of a lack of demand brought on by quality problems.

'Returns can also be viewed on a macro or micro basis. The gross value of the increased wheat production in Turkey during the 1967/68 season was estimated at \$23·6 million, while total additional costs to farmers were placed at \$18·0 million, giving very roughly a net return of more than \$5 million. A linear programming study of foodgrain production in the Punjab in India in the mid-1969s, however, suggested that net income levels per acre would not be significantly increased until fertiliser levels were increased substantially and capital was not a constraint.'[9]

The Punjab is the most productive wheat growing area in India and the new varieties have been accepted and have succeeded there more than anywhere else. However, wheat accounts for only 15 % of India's total area sown to food grains, whereas rice accounts for 31 %, and the new rices have proceeded much more slowly. This has been due partly to their later development, partly to technological problems and partly to the structure of rice farming, which is based on a much larger proportion of very small, comparatively poor holdings than is wheat production.

By far the largest changes and problems have arisen socially and politically, as traditional peasant societies have been exposed suddenly and with little protection to the full force of a free market economy that aims to develop as rapidly as it can. The effects have been so profound that observers have commented that 'the Green Revolution is turning red'.

AIMS AND ACHIEVEMENTS

Although the introduction of HYVs is the keystone of the IWP, it is not the whole of it. The plan has five main points:

'Reduction of waste. As much as 30 % of the produce in some countries is lost after harvest[6] (perhaps a conservative figure—wastage can amount to more than 40 % of the harvest): on the farm, in transit to market, in merchants' stores and through lack of processing facilities. Much fish, one of the most valuable sources of protein, is lost for want of adequate and efficient fishing fleets and freezing plants; good timber, which would earn or save foreign exchange needed for industrial imports, is lost through inefficient felling and sawmilling. These are only some of the symptoms of what amounts to a running sore affecting the economy of food and agricultural production throughout the world.

'Closing the protein gap. The shortfall between adequate and insufficient diets involves the study and development of new kinds of foods, some of them derived from traditional resources of agriculture and fishing, some from entirely new sources (discussed in more detail in Chapter 9). Of equally pressing importance is the introduction of food education, preservation processing, packaging and modern marketing into countries where these are at present largely unknown.

'Promotion of high-yielding cereal varieties. Rice, wheat, maize, sorghum and millet at present supply about half of the world's protein. In developing countries, where the need is greatest, the proportion is higher but crop yields are lower. By raising yields it should be possible to reduce the protein gap measurably as well as to provide more food for tens of millions of people who simply do not get enough.

'Earning and saving foreign exchange. What has this to do with production? The answer in the case of all developing countries is: everything. Thus the success of high-yielding varieties of cereals depends on extensive irrigation schemes and the heavy use of imported fertilisers. Expensive pesticides are also essential and the mechanisation of farming and fishing will become increasingly necessary as the population expands. Efficient storage, processing and freezing plants, as already indicated, will be needed. All this requires foreign exchange, which is thus a key factor in the process of development.

'Utilisation of human resources. Manpower in the developing countries is abundant to a degree that threatens widespread unemployment. Skilled, well-trained and educated manpower is, by comparison, rare. Yet it is difficult to see how any significant agricultural projects can be successful without adequate supplies of these human resources trained to a good technical level. There will also be, for a very long time, many labour-intensive projects of a kind (dam-building, for example) made familiar by the United Nations/FAO World Food Programme. The constructive work potentialities of the coming superabundance of humanity could be, therefore, the positive side of the population problem. Given training and organisation it can effectively underpin the four other priorities.'[10]

The success of agricultural programmes cannot therefore be measured simply in acreages planted to the HYVs, although the IWP does set targets for such acreages. It estimated that in eight Asian countries it studied, the area sown to HYVs could be expanded from about 10 million ha in 1967/68 to about 75 million by 1985, which would represent almost half the area required for cereal growing by that date. It anticipates, too, that a number of countries not included in the study, such as Indonesia, Laos, Nepal and the Republic of Vietnam, will also be growing significant quantities of HYV rice by 1975.

The IWP estimates that there are about 7·5 million ha in Afghanistan, Iran, Iraq, Saudi Arabia, the Sudan and the United Arab Republic that could be growing HYVs by 1985, compared with about 1 million ha sown to them in 1968. About 55% of this would be wheat. The plan calls for 5 million ha to be irrigated and the remainder of the land would be rain-fed, being in areas where the annual rainfall exceeds 350–400 mm. By 1985 about one-quarter of the total cereal growing land in the Near East should be growing HYVs.

The introduction of the HYVs is not planned on any great scale in Africa south of the Sahara. Conditions are not generally favourable and there is still uncultivated land into which agriculture may expand using traditional crop varieties. HYV rice could be introduced in about 800 000 ha of irrigated land in Madagascar, however, and in about 520 000 ha elsewhere, mainly in West Africa.

Despite the fact that the high-yielding varieties of wheat were developed in Mexico, the introduction of HYVs in Latin America is beset by problems. Some of these have been economic and some what the IWP calls 'structural', by which it refers particularly to Latin American systems of land tenure. The minifundia in some areas and the latifundia in others provide too little incentive for farmers to increase production, although for different reasons. Because there is so much uncertainty the IWP makes no predictions and sets no targets for HYV acreages in Latin America. Instead it lists the conditions that must be fulfilled before any major expansion can occur:[11]

(1) A suitable physical environment with freedom from drought and deep flooding and an assured and adequate supply of water to the crop.

(2) A continued flow of suitable new varieties, resistant to the major pests and diseases and capable of high yields in response to the application of modern farming technology. This implies both a multidisciplinary breeding and research programme to produce and test the varieties and a well-organised multiplication and distribution programme to ensure that quality seed is available to farmers in adequate quantity.

(3) The availability of a carefully planned package of supplies of fertiliser, pesticides and machinery to complement an assured water supply and the production of responsive varieties. They must be supported by adequate institutional credit and advice as to their use.

(4) An adequate and properly organised marketing structure, including satisfactory facilities for drying, milling, storage, transport, and a mechanism for price regulation.

Progress has been made in Latin America. The Centro Internacional de Agricultura Tropical released two new varieties suitable for the region in 1971, and Cuba has reported that more than three-quarters of its rice land is sown to the new varieties, mostly IR8. The big advances have been in the Philippines, Pakistan and India, and programmes are advancing well in Indonesia, Thailand, Sri Lanka, Malaysia, Burma and the Republic of Vietnam.[12]

One would expect the rapid spread of the new rices in the Philippines, since it is there that they were developed and so they are likely to be better adapted to environmental conditions there than anywhere else, while local farmers are in a better position to observe their success. Table 3.5 shows that in 1970 more than 90 % of the rice growing area on irrigated two-crop farms in the area around the city of Gapan, in the province of Nueva Ecija in the Philippines, was planted to HYVs. Neuva Ecija is the main rice growing region of the country and it is interesting to note that here HYVs have been accepted more readily by small farmers than by large ones. The small farmers therefore use more fertiliser per hectare, but because small farms

TABLE 3.5
Yields and Technology Employed on Irrigated Two-Crop Farms in Gapan, Neuva Gapan, Neuva Ecija, Philippines, 1970

	Less than 2 ha	*2–4 ha*	*More than 4 ha*
1. Yield per ha, in tons, 1965 (pre-HYV)	2·4	1·7	1·8
2. Yield per ha in 1970	2·9	2·6	2·2
3. Percent of area planted to HYVs, 1970	97·0	96·9	93·0
4. Percent of farmers using tractors	20·0	37·0	43·0
5. Percent of farmers using herbicides	48·2	53·4	52·4
6. Percent of farmers using insecticides	85·5	91·8	95·2
7. Nitrogen per ha (kg)	51·4	45·1	42·5

(Source: IRRI, Los Baños, Philippines)

are much more labour-intensive they use rather less herbicides, insecticides or tractors than do large farmers. Their yields per hectare are markedly higher than those of the larger farmers and were so before the introduction of HYVs. It appears that the large farmers have substituted machines and chemicals for labour and, as a result, produced lower yields per hectare and provided less employment than do smaller farmers. This is a typical effect of 'industrialising' agriculture if the process encourages the amalgamation of farms into larger units.

Table 3.6 compares farms in the same region that are irrigated with those that are partially irrigated or wholly rainfed. It shows that the adoption of HYVs has been more widespread on farms that are fully irrigated and that these farms use 72 % more nitrogen fertiliser than the partially irrigated farms and 143 % more than the rainfed farms; 15 % more insecticides than partially irrigated farms and 59 % more than rainfed farms; 138 % more herbicides than partially irrigated farms and 356 % more than rainfed farms; and 60 % more tractors than partially irrigated farms and 45 % more

TABLE 3.6
Water Supply and Adoption of High Yielding Varieties of Rice on 513 Farms in Gapan, Neuva Ecija, Philippines, 1970

	Irrigated 2 crops	*Partially irrigated*	*Rainfed*
1. Percent of area planted to HYVs	96·5	62·5	31·6
2. Yield per ha (tons)	2·7	2·1	1·8
3. Nitrogen per ha (kg)	49·8	28·9	20·5
4. Percent of farmers using insecticides	90·5	78·2	56·8
5. Percent of farmers using herbicides	52·0	21·8	11·4
6. Percent of farmers using tractors for ploughing	32·0	20·0	22·0

(Source: IRRI, Los Baños, Philippines)

than rainfed farms. For these inputs they achieve yields that are 28% higher than those of partially irrigated farms and 50% higher than those of rain-fed farms.

There is some disagreement over the total areas planted to HYVs of wheat and rice. Tables 3.7 and 3.8 give the Poleman, Thomas and Freebairn[12] estimates for wheat and rice, respectively, which they calculated in a project for Cornell University. Table 3.9, however, gives rather different figures calculated by the USDA and accepted by the FAO. It is notoriously difficult to obtain accurate data from regions that are often remote and inadequately served by networks of communications, among tens of thousands of small farmers. It is no longer easy even to define a 'high-yielding variety', since many countries have their own breeding programmes producing improved strains quite independently of those produced under direct FAO auspices. Thus there will always be statistical disagreement.

Table 3.10 avoids some of these difficulties by measuring agricultural output and comparing it with the IWP objectives. In Africa south of the Sahara, actual production has consistently fallen short of IWP targets, by 0·8% a year up to 1967 and by 0·6% a year since. After a disastrously bad start, up to 1967, the Far East improved until it came within 0·7% of its target in the period 1967–73, since when the rate of increase has slowed again and the gap has widened.

Following a special study of Latin America the FAO introduced two targets for the increase of production in that region, a high figure of 5% a year and a low figure of 3·6%, both figures for the decade 1970–80. Up to 1967, production was increasing at 3·8% a year, thus slightly exceeding the

TABLE 3.7
Land Area Devoted to the High-Yielding Varieties of Wheat in 1970

Country	*Area (thousand ha)*
India	6 100
Pakistan	3 200
Turkey	800
Afghanistan	150
Nepal	75
Other countries	400[a]
Total	10 725

[a] This is a rough estimate but it is considered to be conservative and would include Tunisia, Morocco, Algeria, Lebanon, Iran, Syria, UAR, the Sudan, Tanzania, Kenya, Rhodesia and South Africa, where it is known that the new wheats are already being grown by farmers.
(Source: Ref. 12)

TABLE 3.8
Area Planted to High-Yielding Rice Varieties in the Developing Countries (Estimates for 1970)

Country	*Area (thousand ha)*
India	4 860
Philippines	1 200
Indonesia	1 000
Pakistan	1 000
South Vietnam	250
Burma	180
Ceylon	150
All others	1 500
World total	10 140

(Source: Ref. 12)

TABLE 3.9

Far East: Area under High-Yielding Varieties of Wheat and Rice in Selected Countries, 1967/68 to 1970/71

	1967/68	1968/69	1969/70	1970/71[(a)] *Area under high-yielding varieties*	*Total area*	*Area under high-yielding varieties as percentage of total*
	(thousand hectares)					(%)
Wheat						
India	2 942	4 793	4 910	5 892	17 891	32·9
Nepal	25	54	76	98	388[b]	25·3
Pakistan	957	2 396	2 960	2 959	6 186	47·8
Total	3 924	7 243	7 676	8 949	24 465	36·6
Rice						
Burma[c]	3	167	144	201	4 976	4·0
Ceylon[d]	—	7	26	30	651[b]	4·5
India[c]	1 784	2 681	4 341	5 501	37 431	14·7
Indonesia[c]	—	198	750	932	8 237	11·3
Laos	1	2	2	54	769[b]	7·0
Malaysia (West)	64	91	96	132	541	24·5
Nepal	—	43	50	68	1 174[b]	5·8
Pakistan	71	462	765	1 087	11 416	9·5
Philippines[c]	701	1 012	1 354	1 565	3 113	50·3
Thailand[c]	—	—	—	162[e]	7 600	2·1
Vietnam, Rep. of	—	40	201	502	2 599	19·3
Total	2 624	4 703	7 729	10 234	78 507	13·0

[a] Preliminary.
[b] 1969/70 area.
[c] Includes improved local varieties.
[d] Excludes improved local varieties (averaging over 400 000 ha).
[e] Rough estimate.
(Source: *Imports and Plantings of HYV of wheat and rice in the less developed nations*, Foreign Economic Development Service, 1972, Report No. 14. USDA, Washington DC.

low target for the following decade, but since then it has fallen to under 3 % a year, so falling well below even the low target. Production increases in the Near East and north-west Africa began well, exceeding the target by 0·1 % a year, but fell badly short between 1967 and 1973. Since then they have recovered somewhat but they are still below the IWP target.

In general, agricultural production has not increased in developing

TABLE 3.10
Average Annual Rate of Growth of Agricultural Production in Developing Regions in Comparison with IWP Objectives

	Actual growth of production			*IWP objectives*[b]	
	1961–63 *to* 1967	1967 *to* 1973	1961–63 *to* 1973	1961–63 *to* 1975	1975 *to* 1985
Africa south of the Sahara	2·4	2·6	2·6	3·2	3·3
Far East	1·5	2·9	2·6	3·6	4·0
Latin America	3·8	2·4	2·9	[c]	[c]
Near East and north-west Africa[a]	3·5	2·6	3·2	3·4	3·5
Average	2·5	2·7	2·6	3·4	3·7

[a] IWP objectives for north-west Africa based on 1965.
[b] These figures are those derived from the four IWP regional studies; the final IWP objectives in the world study, based on faster growth rates for pig and poultry production, raised these rates of growth to 3·6 and 3·9 % respectively (3·7 % over the whole period).
[c] The original IWP objectives for Latin America were superseded by a study covering South America and giving for the decade 1970–80 two target growth rates, a high of 5·0 % and a low of 3·6 %.
Note: The regional groupings cover the 65 countries studied in the IWP: 24 in Africa south of the Sahara (84 % of regional population), 8 in the Far East (80 %), 17 in Latin America (90 %), and 15 in the Near East and north-west Africa (96 %). Thus, although they cover most of the population of the developing regions, the data in this table are not fully comparable with those in other tables.
(Source: *Assessment of the World Food Situation*, E/Conf. 65/3. FAO, Rome)

countries as fast as the IWP planned that it should and, as Table 3.11 shows, the nutritional situation is still serious, although it has improved since 1961. In Latin America 5 countries have moved into a surplus in their caloric supply; in the Far East 4 countries have moved into surplus; in the Near East 2 countries and in Africa 6 countries have a caloric surplus. However, there remain 11 Latin American, 8 Far Eastern, 10 Near Eastern, 26 African and 2 Asian communist countries that have insufficient food for their needs, and 1 East European country that is slightly deficient.

OUTLOOK

As we shall see in later chapters, while the picture of the world food situation is grim when the expansion of production is measured against IWP targets, it is far from hopeless. As we saw earlier, it may be that some aspects of the

TABLE 3.11
Countries with Surplus and Deficit Energy Supply by Region

	1961				1969–71 *average*			
	Surplus		*Deficit*		*Surplus*		*Deficit*	
	more than 10%	*less than* 10%	*more than* 10%	*less than* 10%	*more than* 10%	*less than* 10%	*more than* 10%	*less than* 10%
Western Europe	14	5	—	—	17	2	—	—
North America	2	—	—	—	2	—	—	—
Oceania	2	—	—	—	2	—	—	—
Eastern Europe and USSR	4	3	—	1	7	—	—	1
Other developed countries	1	2	—	—	2	1	—	—
Total developed regions	23	10	—	1	30	3	—	1
Latin America	5	4	8	8	8	6	4	7
Far East	—	4	7	5	4	4	3	5
Near East	1	1	10	2	1	3	4	6
Africa	—	5	18	14	3	8	12	14
Asian centrally planned economies	—	2	2	—	1	1	1	1
Total developing regions	6	16	45	29	18	22	24	33
World	29	26	45	30	48	25	24	34

(Source: *Food and Nutrition*, **1**(1), 1975. FAO, Rome)

Green Revolution were ill-conceived. The emphasis on the protein gap may have been based on false nutritional concepts.

More seriously, the attempt to transplant agricultural high technology from developed into developing countries was certain to prove extremely difficult and the chance of failure was inevitably high. Similarities between the agricultural sector of developed economies and agrarian undeveloped economies are very superficial. European history since the seventeenth century was one of agricultural improvement, permitting the accumulation of capital for investment and the liberation of population, coupled with the natural explosion of population, to provide a labour force. A period of gradually accelerating industrialisation followed and when the economy was securely established as being based on manufacturing industry, then agriculture was developed into its present capital-intensive high-technology form. If the direct transplantation of a manufacturing economy into an agrarian country is impossible, it is no more likely that the transplantation of agricultural high technology will succeed. It might even have been more appropriate to transplant the attitudes to agriculture and the techniques that raised husbandry to the high standard it reached in the eighteenth century, when yields were high, the fertility of the land was improving, but each farming region and often each farm was entirely independent of imported inputs.

Even so the IWP has not been abandoned and while it cannot be said to have succeeded, neither has it failed altogether. Targets have not been met but agricultural output has expanded. The HYVs may not have produced the spectacular results some people expected of them but the concentration on agricultural development has led to a general global awareness of the need for developing countries to produce much more of their own food. So, to a very large extent, developing countries themselves, and regions within those countries, have been stimulated to examine their own resources of land, soils, water, climate, capital and people, as their own traditional knowledge of food production within their environment, to see what may be achieved.

The situation remains critical. In November 1976, FAO's new Director-General, Edouard Saouma, reported that although the 1976 world cereal harvest of more than 1300 million tons was expected to be 7% higher than the 1975 harvest, so that carry-over stocks could be increased, food aid to developing countries remained an urgent need. 'Until they have aquired the capacity to produce the food they need or to buy it on world markets', he said, 'food aid is to be seen basically as an interim measure, helping to fill the gap.'[13]

It is easy to be wise after the event, to argue that some of the unanticipated effects of agricultural development should have been foreseen, that the FAO's schemes were too ambitious. Yet if we ever imagined that so complex a set of problems could be resolved in a purely technological fashion we betray our own naivety. It is unlikely that human problems will respond to purely technological solutions and we may not abdicate our responsibility for the welfare of other human beings by the simple expedient of passing on to them our machines.

We must continue to care, not just about fertilisers and seed but about the most difficult issues of the exploitation of the poor by the rich, and of the rights of people to determine their own futures within the context of their own environments and cultures. In the end the world food problem has a great deal to do with the relationships among regions, among nations and among men.

REFERENCES

1. FAO (1970). *Proceedings of the Second World Food Congress*, Vol. 1. Rome.
2. Palmer, I. (1972). *Food and the New Agricultural Technology*. UNRISD, Geneva.

3. FAO (1970). *A Strategy for Plenty*, p. 9. Rome.
4. Borlaug, E. (1958). The impact of agricultural research on Mexican wheat production. *Trans. New York Acad. Sci.*, Vol. 20, No. 3. New York, January.
5. IRRI (1971). *Rice Policy Conference: Current Papers on Rice Technology, May* 1971. Physiological basis. Manila.
6. Allaby, M. (1972). *Who Will Eat?* Tom Stacey. London.
7. Axinn, G. H. and Thorat, S. (1973). *Modernizing World Agriculture: A Comparative Study of Agricultural Extension Systems*, Ch. 2. Praeger, New York.
8. Cheng Shih (1974). *A Glance at China's Economy*. Foreign Languages Press, Peking.
9. Dalrymple, D. G. (1969). *Technological Change in Agriculture: Effects and Implications for the Developing Nations*. USDA, Washington.
10. FAO (1970). *Five Keys to Development*. Rome.
11. FAO (1970). *Indicative World Plan for Agricultural Development*. Rome.
12. Poleman, T. T. and Freebairn, D. K. (1973). *Food, Population and Employment: The Impact of the Green Revolution*, Ch. 2. Praeger, New York.
13. FAO (1976). Press release 76/66, November 15. Rome.

Chapter 4

AN INVENTORY OF THE WORLD

In this world, as the old saying goes, nothing comes free. Everything must be made from something and so the capacity of any living species to utilise the constituent parts of its environment is limited by the availability of certain key resources.

In this respect man is different from other species, in that he has developed great skill for 'improving' his environment. The inverted commas are necessary, because 'improvement' in this context is an entirely anthropomorphic concept. What we really mean by it is that man has modified his environment in such a way as to enable larger numbers of his own species to subsist, or for stable populations to increase their security or level of physical comfort.

So agricultural expansion is limited by the availability of the resources on which it depends. There are not many of these, since agriculture of all kinds, be it forestry, the growing of fibres or other cash crops, arable or grassland farming or livestock production, is based on primary plant production. Thus the requirements for plant growth determine the limits for every kind of agriculture. They do not necessarily define the limits of food production, since today, as we shall see later, the production of food is not confined entirely to agriculture.

Plants require space, in the sense of a sufficient area of territory for them to extend their foliage. They need soil or some other medium to provide them with anchorage. They need light, warmth, air, water—usually fresh—and a range of nutrients. In considering the actual and potential production of food on the earth's surface it is at these resources that we should look.

Certain of them may be eliminated at once since they are so freely available as to be virtually limitless or, if not limitless, at least available on a scale large enough to permit of their continued exploitation until the limit of another resource is reached. There is no effective limitation of space, for example, because long before such a limit could be reached the limits of available light and heat would be encountered. Agriculture cannot expand into the arctic or antarctic, although these regions offer large surface areas. Similarly there is no effective limit to air, or to soil for anchorage.

There are limits of light, heat and fresh water, which we may call the climatic limits, and there are limits to the availability of certain nutrients.

Chemically plants consist of a range of elements. Carbon, hydrogen and oxygen account for most of the weight of any plant, but these three elements are not usually regarded as nutrients in the agricultural sense, since carbon is derived from atmospheric carbon dioxide, and hydrogen and oxygen from water. The remaining nutrients are divided into two groups, the major and minor, or macro and micro, nutrients. Table 4.1, which is based on the analysis of crop plants grown in the UK and interpreted as quantities of

TABLE 4.1
Approximate Average Amounts of Major and Minor Nutrients in British Crop Yields

Major nutrients	*kg/ha*	*Minor nutrients*	*g/ha*
Nitrogen (N)	100	Iron (Fe)	600
Potassium (K)	100	Manganese (Mn)	600
Calcium (Ca)	50	Zinc (Zn)	200
Phosphorus (P)	15	Boron (B)	200
Magnesium (Mg)	15	Copper (Cu)	100
Sulphur (S)	30	Molybdenum (Mo)	10
		Cobalt (Co)	1

(Source: ref. 9).

nutrient per hectare of land on which they were grown, shows clearly the differences in the amounts of nutrients that are required, differences of several orders of magnitude, ranging from 100 kg per ha for nitrogen to 1 g per ha for cobalt.

In nature, plants derive all of their nutrients from their immediate surroundings, from the soil and from the air. A gross inherent deficiency of one or more of the major nutrients will therefore render a soil naturally infertile, although it is very unusual for a soil to be so deficient in nutrients as to make all plant growth impossible. Modern man has the ability to modify the natural fertility of soils by moving nutrients from one place to another, in the form of fertilisers.

Chemical fertilisers contain phosphorus (P) or potassium (K), the most localised of the major nutrients in their global distribution, or nitrogen (N), which is the nutrient required in the largest quantity, or some combination of two or all three of them. Minor nutrients may be added but fertilisers are usually evaluated by their content of N, P or K. As we shall see in Chapter 7, P and K fertilisers are not usually supplied in the form in which they occur in nature and so an energy cost is incurred in their processing and transport.

In nature, plants derive their nitrogen from the bacterial fixation of atmospheric nitrogen, from nitrogen released by the decay of organic material in the soil and from nitrogen fixed by lightning and washed to the ground in rain. Since nitrogen constitutes about four-fifths of our atmosphere, there can be no theoretical shortage of it. The limit is imposed by the capacity of soil micropopulations, and to overcome it man has devised a number of strategies and is certain to devise more in the future. Our present use of nitrogenous fertiliser represents one such strategy, based on the industrial fixation of atmospheric nitrogen. This process, too, requires the expenditure of energy and in this case energy that must be derived from fossil fuels, since in addition to supplying the primary energy for the process they also supply the feedstock, as hydrocarbon compounds (at present most commonly natural gas or naphtha derived from petroleum) are broken down to release hydrogen that unites with the nitrogen to form ammonium (NH_4) compounds.

Thus the capacity of soils to sustain plant growth can be extended by the use of fertilisers. In this chapter we should consider the world production and consumption of fertilisers, but in Chapter 7 we may explore in more detail the energy implications of their use.

Even with the use of chemical fertilisers, plants obtain most of their nutrients from substances available naturally in soils. Fertilisers merely add to the natural reservoir, although it is possible that industrial fixation of nitrogen now approaches, in terms of sheer quantity, quite close to the amount fixed naturally, globally, each year. It has been calculated[1] that each year about 30 million tonnes of nitrogen are fixed bacterially on land, 14 million tonnes by bacteria associated with leguminous plants, 10 million tonnes by marine organisms, 7·6 million tonnes by atmospheric processes and 0·2 million tonnes by geochemical processes. In 1972/73 total world production of nitrogenous fertiliser amounted to about 38 million nutrient tonnes (the measure of the actual nutrient content of the fertiliser, rather than the gross weight that includes the inert carrier). Thus of a total of 99·8 million tonnes being fixed each year, 38 % is being fixed by man. Since it is also estimated that about 83 million tonnes are being denitrified annually and returned to the biological cycle or to the atmosphere, it is possible that the difference between the two totals, 16·8 million tonnes, may be accumulating in the biosphere. This could have profound implications for the ecology of certain parts of the world, which may or may not be beneficial to man.

We should begin to examine the resources for agricultural production by looking at the world's soils. It would seem logical to proceed from soils to water and thence to a general look at climate. It is believed by many climatologists that the climate of the world today may be changing. In Chapter 8 we consider this in much more detail, for as we shall see, comparatively small changes in light intensity, in the length of the day and in average temperatures and rainfall can have disproportionately large effects on agricultural output. Then we should look at world production, distribution and consumption of fertilisers. Finally we will look at the world geographically, rather than as a whole, by considering its main continents and regions in turn.

The extent to which soils, water and climate impose actual limits on agricultural production is shown in Table 4.2. Of the entire land surface of the earth only 24 % is even potentially cultivable as arable land, and in 1965 only 10·5 % was being so cultivated. Furthermore, the term 'arable' is being used rather more loosely in this context than is usual. It covers crop land in the very widest sense, including temporary grassland, horticulture, fruit growing and such cash crops as rubber plantations. In any one year the actual land harvested amounts to one-half to two-thirds of the land nominally under cultivation. There is no doubt about the need to expand agricultural production in all the developing regions and the table suggests that there is room to expand the cultivated area in Africa and South America. As we shall see, this impression must be qualified rather heavily.

SOILS

Soil is the loose, more or less friable substance that covers much of the surface of the earth. It is composed of rock that has weathered, by chemical, biological and physical alteration, into small particles, to which have been added the decay products of once-living organisms and the populations sustained by them. The creation of soil that will sustain plant life is a process that may occupy many thousands of years.

A vertical section cut through an undisturbed soil reveals that it is stratified into clear layers, called 'horizons', and conventionally labelled first with a letter and then, for subdivisions within a capital horizon, with one or more small letters. At the bottom of the profile lies the parent material. It is this parent material that gives most soils—the exceptions being soils whose upper horizons have been moved into a position different from the one in which they started—many of their particular characteristics and so the classification of soils into types depends on the study of profiles. Until quite recent times, soils were classified on the basis of their superficial appearance as 'clay' or 'sand' or 'loam', but for an understanding of their true characteristics and potential much more information is needed.

The topmost layer of the earth, called the A_0 or O horizon, is composed of fresh organic litter (A_0L) overlying partly decomposed litter (A_0F) overlying dark-coloured humus (A_0H).

Beneath the A_0 horizon lies the A horizon, of mixed organic and mineral matter, overlying a layer of leached, acid or basic matter (A_e or E_a).

The next set of horizons is given the prefix B. The uppermost part of the B horizons, B_h, may be enriched with humus or, B_{ir}, it may be an iron cemented pan or hard, impermeable layer. Below this layer the soil may be enriched with different elements, depending on the nature and composition of the parent material. A B_f horizon is enriched with oxidised iron, a B_{fh} horizon with iron and humus, a B_s horizon with translocated sesquioxides

TABLE 4.2
Farmland per Person, 1970 and 1990[a]

Continent	*Area*	*Potentially arable*	*Cultivated,* 1965	*Population,* 1970 (*m*)	*Cult. ha/caput* 1970	*Population,* 1990 (*m*)	*Cult. ha/caput* 1990
	(*million hectares*)						
Africa	3 019	732·5	157·8	279	0·57	498	0·32
Asia[b]	2 736	627·3	518·0	1 986	0·26	3 082	0·17
Oceania	822	153·8	16·2	15	1·08	21	0·77
Europe and USSR	2 711	530·2	380·4	702	0·54	812	0·47
N. America	2 108	465·4	238·8	226	1·06	271	0·88
S. America[c]	1 752	679·9	76·9	284	0·27	489	0·16
Total	13 148	3 189·1	1 388·1	3 621[d]	0·38	5 346[e]	0·26

[a] 1970 population figures taken from actual UN figures; 1990 figures from UN medium assumption, as at 1974.
[b] Includes the Near East, Far East and Asian centrally planned economies.
[c] Includes Central America.
[d] Disparity in total of 129 million is accounted for by 'other' developed market economy populations counted but not specified by UN.
[e] By 1990 this figure accounts for 173 million persons.
(Sources: (1) *Assessment of the World Food Situation*. FAO, Rome, 1974. (2) Ehrlich, P. R. and Ehrlich A. H., 1972. *Population, Resources, Environment*, W. H. Freeman, San Francisco. (3) The World Food Problem. US President's Science Advisory Committee, 1967).

of iron and aluminium. The B_s horizon, or if there is a B_f or B_{fh} horizon that with the B_s horizon below it, then extends all the way down to the C horizon, which is the parent material.

These horizon labels provide more detailed information about soils than those that preceded them, which used only letters and numbers, A_1, A_2 and so forth.

A particular soil may vary considerably from the standard and may lack all horizons, or may have horizons that are poorly defined. Like any other feature of the earth's surface, soils age and so may be young or old, and the age of a soil will affect its composition and structure. Soils may be disturbed, either naturally by weather or by earth movements, or as a result of man's agricultural or other activities, and this too will alter their characteristics. Much of the early work on the classification of soils was performed in Russia and so many of the older names for soil types are derived from Russian words, such as 'podsol', 'solonchak' and 'rendzina'. Such names are still used but gradually they are being superseded by a new system of classification, known as the US 7th Approximation, that is simpler. The 7th Approximation divides soils into 10 main types:

(1) Entisols, which are very young embryonic soils with no profile development.

(2) Inceptisols, which are young soils—either because they are still forming or because their development has been arrested—with horizons that are weakly developed.

(3) Alfisols, which are leached soils, from which elements have been removed, slightly basic or acidic, and with a clay-enriched (B_t) horizon, the name Alfisol being taken from aluminium (Al) and iron (Fe), in which they are often rich.

(4) Spodosols, which are leached, acid soils.

(5) Ultisols, which are leached, acid, deeply weathered, old soils.

(6) Oxisols, which are also old, deeply weathered, leached, acid soils, but with an axic horizon.

(7) Mollisols, which have a thick, dark ('mollic') surface layer rich in humus and in calcium and magnesium bivalent ions.

(8) Aridisols, which are typical of desert environments and are saline and alkaline mineral soils.

(9) Vertisols, which are clay soils that have been disturbed and inverted.

(10) Histosols, which are organic soils.

Finally soils are classified as zonal, intrazonal and azonal. Zonal soils are well developed and characteristic of a particular climate and vegetation pattern. Intrazonal soils are also well developed but their characteristics are dominated by local variations in parent material or vegetation that differ from those of the region as a whole. Azonal soils have poorly developed characteristics.

The soils of the greatest value to agriculture are the brown earths (inceptisols), which are not necessarily brown in colour. They have been cultivated for a long time and occur especially in the eastern part of North America. They vary somewhat in their base status and at their extreme become very calcareous, becoming rendzinas and red earth ('terra rosa') which may be inceptisols or mollisols. As brown earths weather they may become more acid in a process that leads to podsolisation. Podsols (spodosols) are the final result. As they begin to weather, inceptisols become alfisols, which are also of value to agriculture.

All the spodosols, a group that includes every stage in podsolisation, are much poorer. They may support coniferous forest or, in wetter climates, heaths. They may develop an impermeable pan of concentrated ferric oxide in the B horizon that can be up to 1 cm thick, leading to the accumulation of water above the pan, a process known as 'gleying'. This accentuates the leaching of salts from the A horizons in a soil that easily becomes waterlogged. This is an extreme condition but one to which spodosols are prone at all stages of podsolisation.

Large areas of the USA are covered by lithosols and other desert soils and, in the south east, by bog and semi-bog soils, all of which are unsuitable for cultivation. Alluvial soils are often waterlogged. Other areas are mountainous. Mountain ranges tend to produce entisols on their steeper slopes, where soil development is inhibited by constant erosion. Soils are thus thin and highly mineral, often with outcrops of rock projecting above the surface.

In the USA the entisols are found in the northern part of the Rocky Mountains range and become much more pronounced in the Canadian Rockies.

If there is no room for further agricultural expansion in the USA, Canada's large land area is even more restricted. The grain belt runs in a comparatively narrow band eastward from the Rockies, through Alberta, Saskatchewan and Manitoba. To its north and in northern Ontario and Quebec, soils are largely podsolised, with extensive bogs. Further north still, the soils of the tundra are mainly inceptisols and entisols, young, poorly developed soils. Soil development does not occur beneath ice and snow and the arctic regions have been covered with ice and snow for most of the period since the last glaciation. Around the North Pole the climate is that of dry desert and such land as there is is permanently frozen. To the south, from a line running around the world and passing rather to the north of Central Alaska, the permafrost is discontinuous, which means there is a short summer period during which plant growth can take place.

It will be clear that in no way can the soils of the tundra and arctic regions be brought into agricultural production, for even were the climate to change, or were ways to be found of thawing them to provide what could be a long and intensive growing season in terms of the hours of daylight available, the soils themselves are unsuitable and very poor in nutrients.

The tundra extends right across northern Europe and Asia, also with a very wide belt of spodosols to the south of it. In the USSR the growing of grain is confined mainly to the alfisols, mollisols and, to the east, the inceptisols, bounded on the north by the spodosols and to the south by desert aridisols. Figure 4.1 shows the generalised world distribution according to the 7th Approximation, and indicates very clearly that the inceptisols and alfisols that favour arable farming extend westward across all of Europe, with the exception of Ireland and the western part of Great Britain, where the soils are in a process of podsolisation and so are generally inferior. The agricultural limitations of this area are due more to topography and climate than to the inherent fertility of their soils, however.

We may conclude, then, that there exists a broad belt of soils that are eminently suitable for arable agriculture, extending from the eastern side of the Rocky Mountains, across southern Canada and northern USA, extending southwards to the east of the American desert, then continuing across Europe and into the USSR, where it is bounded to the north by spodosols and tundra and to the south by desert. There is some room for expansion but not a great deal, although more recent soil surveys suggest that estimates of potential agricultural land may have been too low;[2] this argument, however, centres more on the possibilities of extending cultivation in the tropics than on the soils of higher latitudes.

As we saw in Table 4.2, more than 71 % of the European–Russian land area is cultivated already. The remaining 30 % is to the north of the Soviet grain belt, into what Figure 4.1 shows to be mollisols and then alfisols. Soviet attempts to expand its farmed area into virgin lands have proved unsuccessful on the whole, for reasons we shall consider later, and they are always very costly. The large area in North America that Table 4.2 shows was uncultivated in 1965 is now in production and there is little room for expansion in that continent.

Since the distribution of soils is a product partly of climate, we might expect to find a similar belt of good agricultural land in the southern hemisphere in latitudes corresponding to those of the North American and Eurasian arable lands. In the southern hemisphere, however, there is much less land of any kind and little that extends south as far as the northern farmlands extends north. This is shown by the location of the aridisols in Figure 4.1, which correspond to the Saharan, American and Asian deserts of the northern hemisphere. In South America, Africa and Australia the deserts border the southern coasts, although the Patagonian Desert of South America does extend further, to a latitude corresponding to that of southern England, The Netherlands and north Germany or, in North America, to that of Lake Winnipeg or Edmonton, Alberta. The South American desert that is more truly comparable to the deserts of southern Africa and Australia lies to the north, along the Pacific coast, where it is

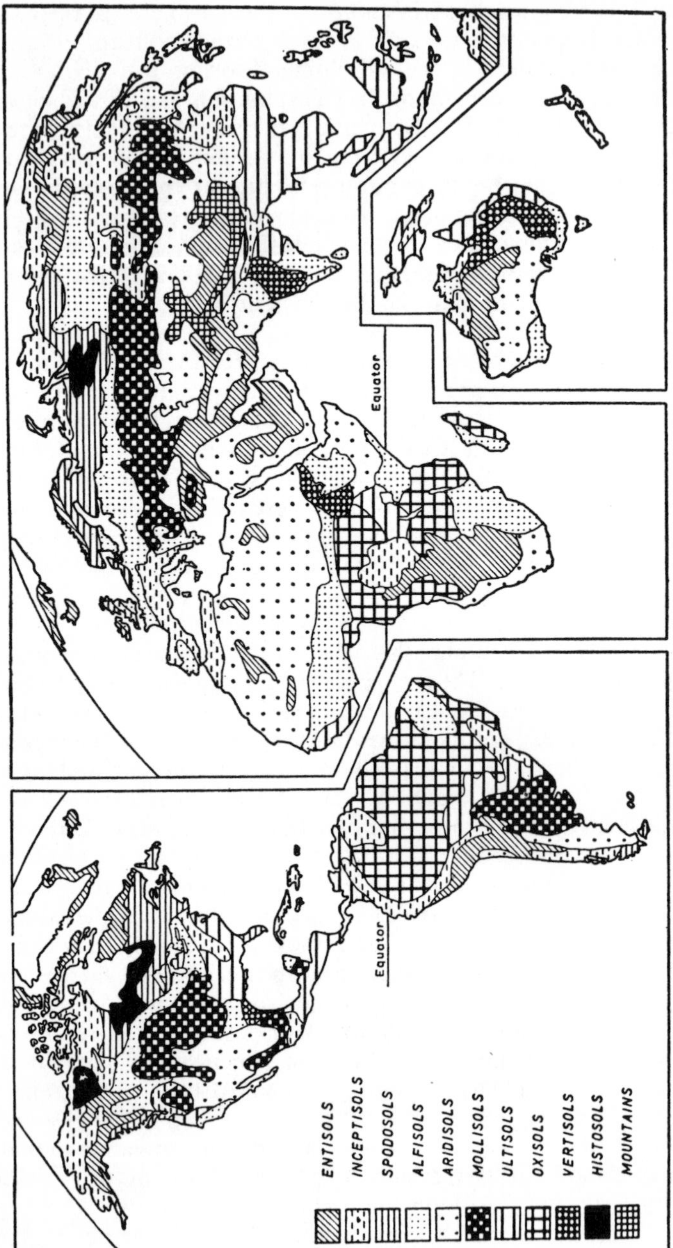

FIG. 4.1. Generalised world distribution of the soil orders of the 7th Approximation—adapted from publications of the US Department of Agriculture, Soil Conservation Service. (Source: ref. 12).

called the Atacama Desert and is shown on Figure 4.1 as a small area of aridisol. The Patagonian Desert is more like northern steppe.

To the east of the aridisol zone of the Iranian Plateau, another steppe-like region, lies the dry Thar Desert of Pakistan and, surrounding it and extending across the northern part of the Indian sub-continent, lies a more fertile region in the Indus and Ganges Valleys. To the east of the high Tibetan Plateau, extensive areas of inceptisols and alfisols provide good farmland in China. Most farmland in Asia is utilised, although much of it might be used more intensively. There is little room for physical expansion, however, and to the south of the temperate zones the climate is dominated by the seasonal monsoon rains, which impose further constraints.

Of the potentially cultivable land in Africa in 1965, only about 21% was in agricultural use. Some grain is grown in the inceptisol belt inland from the north west coast and in the inland alfisol belt near the west coast, at about latitude 10°, as far as the limit imposed by the desert in the east. Grain is also grown in the alfisol area of southern Africa. The main wheat growing area is confined, however, to the extreme south western tip of the continent. Elsewhere grain crops are combined with the pasturing of cattle. In the area surrounding the great tropical rainforest of the Congo Basin, such tropical food crops as sorghum, millet and manioc are grown, as well as some maize. Elsewhere there is more or less cash cropping, using such crops as cotton, coffee, tea and tobacco. The expansion of African agriculture must be based on the arable cropping of lands that are used mainly for grazing. It cannot occur through expansion into tropical rainforest.

In South America, too, there is room for considerable expansion by extending the cropped area into grazing land. The area of mollisol is in use, growing wheat and other grains, as is the alfisol area in the north east of the continent. Surrounding and linking these cropped areas there lies an extensive zone, from the Patagonian steppe in the south all the way to the north east coast, that is used for the ranching of cattle. Much of this land is poor but there is little doubt that parts of it might be cropped and that its overall productivity could be increased considerably. The problem here is one of land tenure that maintains large estates at a productive level far below their potential.

As in the case of Africa, however, the figure for potentially cultivable land given in Table 4.2 may include parts of the rainforest area, which is very much larger than that in Africa. Some governments are planning to expand farming into land from which rainforest has been cleared. It is rather doubtful whether such schemes can succeed in the long term.

Where temperate soils are subject to podsolisation, an aging process, tropical soils are subject to oxidation once they are exposed to high temperatures and humidity from which dense forest cover protects them. Ultisols and oxisols are typical tropical soils and they merge into alfisol or inceptisol brown earths on their sub-tropical dry borders, soils which support grassland vegetation, and into alfisols and inceptisols on their cooler, moister margins.

Ultisols are often very deep, 2 m or more, and though they are very weathered they still contain considerable reserves of minerals. They are less acid than spodosols and often they make excellent agricultural soils. They are found mainly in the Gran Chaco region of South America, where they are grazed, in south central Africa, where they extend to the east of the rainforest and are used to grow tropical food and cash crops, very widely in south-east Asia, where they support fertile and intensively exploited rice growing areas, and along the east coast of Australia, where they support tropical farming.

However, where they are rich in sesquioxides of iron, ultisols are prone to laterisation, as are oxisols. Oxisols are found extensively in the tropical rainforest areas of both South America and Africa and they have little agricultural potential. They can be quite deep but if they have an A horizon at all it is very deficient in organic matter and nutrients. The B horizons may be red in colour and this, together with the fact that they support the most productive ecosystems on the earth's surface, sometimes deceives would-be farmers into believing the soils themselves are fertile. They are not.

The paradox occurs because of the very high rate of production within wet tropical climax ecosystems. Nutrients are recycled very quickly and the processes of decay and regeneration are highly accelerated. In any ecosystem the soil holds a reserve of nutrients, a kind of food store that can be exploited by species. It is possible to determine whether or not a system has reached its climax by measuring the extent of these nutrient reserves. If they are extensive, offering nourishment to plants that may enter and establish themselves, then the system cannot have reached its climax. When it does reach its climax, and no more species can be supported except by reducing the population of competitors to make room for them, then the reserves of nutrients in the soil will be at a minimum. As leaves fall, as plants and animals deposit wastes and, on death, their own tissues, upon the surface, the decomposing organisms consume them and so reduce them to ever simpler chemical compounds, eventually to simple salts that can be taken up again by plants. In a climax system they are taken up again quickly; in a system that has not yet reached its climax they may accumulate, along with the nutrients that are being added constantly by inward leaching from surrounding areas and by weathering of the parent material.

This knowledge is not new although it is sometimes forgotten, especially when virgin soils appear to offer rich agricultural rewards. The Russian experiences are typical. Virgin forest or grassland is cleared and crops are sown. Immediately, the farm crops take the place of the vegetation that was removed and they exploit the nutrients that otherwise would have supported the natural climax. The harvesting of the crops deprives the soil of these nutrients and because the nutrient status of the soil is inherently low, normal dressings of fertiliser or organic manure are insufficient to replace them. The soil loses its fertility and after a few years it may have to be abandoned unless there is considerable investment of capital and effort made to improve it. Eventually, of course, it may be possible to make of it good farmland. After all, farm soils were all wild once. What we forget is that soils can be 'wild', just as animals can, and that just as livestock has to be domesticated before it can achieve its potential of commercial production, soils must be domesticated as well.

In the case of tropical soils the problem is more serious and it is doubtful whether those in rainforest areas can ever be domesticated at all on any large scale. Because of the high temperature and high humidity, conditions for both growth and decay are optimal. When the natural vegetative cover is removed, most of the nutrients in the system are removed with it. The nutrients remaining in the soil are then exposed to even higher temperatures and humidity because of the loss of the leaf canopy that sheltered them. The organic residues in the soil oxidise rather quickly. The increased weathering effect of heavy rain directly on the surface accelerates the leaching and erosion of soil from which have been removed the plant roots that gave it cohesion. The result is rapid and complete podsolisation to a barren, infertile, acid oxisol. The addition of fertiliser or organic manure does little to remedy the situation, for these are oxidised or leached away very quickly. If the soil is prone to laterisation, a hard impermeable pan will form just beneath the surface and the combination of drenching and baking will reduce the soil on the surface to a rock-like solidity.

From the point of view of the ecology of their soils, farmers aim to remove climax ecosystems, with small nutrient reserves, and replace them with successional systems that, because they are managed, are never able to reach their climax. Thus with careful farming the nutrient status may improve steadily over the years. The system works well in temperate climates, in sub-tropical climates where the soil is suitable but only occasionally in the wet tropics. The exceptions are found where large deposits of volcanic ash permit andosols to develop. Andosols are inceptisols with an AC profile and they contain large reserves of weatherable minerals and more clays with a lattice structure suitable for cropping than have oxisols. Such soils are found in Indonesia and Hawaii, along with the ultisols shown in Figure 4.1.

We can summarise the possibilities for agricultural expansion into new lands, then, by qualifying the figures in Table 4.2. In Africa there are areas of alfisols in the north east, south east and in parts of the west, at present used mainly for stock rearing, that might be cropped, but it is difficult to see how this area could amount to the whole of the 575 million ha the table suggests, and this figure probably includes areas of oxisol and ultisol in the

Congo Basin and the savannah regions to its south. It is doubtful whether these soils can be brought into agricultural production and any attempt to do so might result, within a very few years, in their yielding less food than they do at present, which at least is sufficient to meet the needs of the hunting and gathering peoples that inhabit them.

In Asia most land capable of producing crops is in use. In Oceania some increase in the cropped area might be achieved by improving the mollisols in eastern Australia, but while Table 4.2 suggests that in 1965 only 10·5% of potential arable land was being cultivated, the total potential land is still rather small—only one-third of that in North America, for example. In Europe changes in agricultural policies could encourage the expansion of arable farming into some marginal lands, but hopes of expansion in the USSR must be regarded with caution. In North America virtually all the land held out of production in 1965 is now back in use and so there is no room for further expansion. In South America considerable expansion could take place if economic, political and social measures were taken to alter systems of land tenure.

It is not realistic to consider world totals of potential land, since these are not distributed at all evenly. We should look, rather, at the land that is available in those regions of the world where food demands exceed, or are likely to exceed, production. Then we see that the acute problems are to be found in Asia, so far as land is concerned. It is important to emphasise that this is an examination only of land and soils, for agriculture has other requirements, and much hunger in Africa and Asia results from a shortage of water not of land. However, the FAO has estimated[3] that in 1970, 737 million ha were being cultivated in the developing regions and that by 1985 it should be possible to increase this to 900 million ha. If this land were to produce grain with yields of, say, 1·6 tonnes per ha—the average yield for wheat, rice and maize grown in different parts of Africa, Latin America and Asia—some 261 million tonnes of food would be added to the annual combined production of those regions.

WATER

About four-fifths of the surface of the earth is covered by water and all terrestrial life forms have evolved from aquatic species. Without water no life is possible. Our own bodies are composed largely of water by weight.

All but a very few land species require fresh water, however. There are a few euryhaline species that are able to regulate the concentration of salts in their tissues and so can survive in either a fresh water or salt water environment, and there are xerophilous species that have evolved in such a way that they utilise water with very great economy and so can survive in comparatively arid environments. The vast majority of species requires

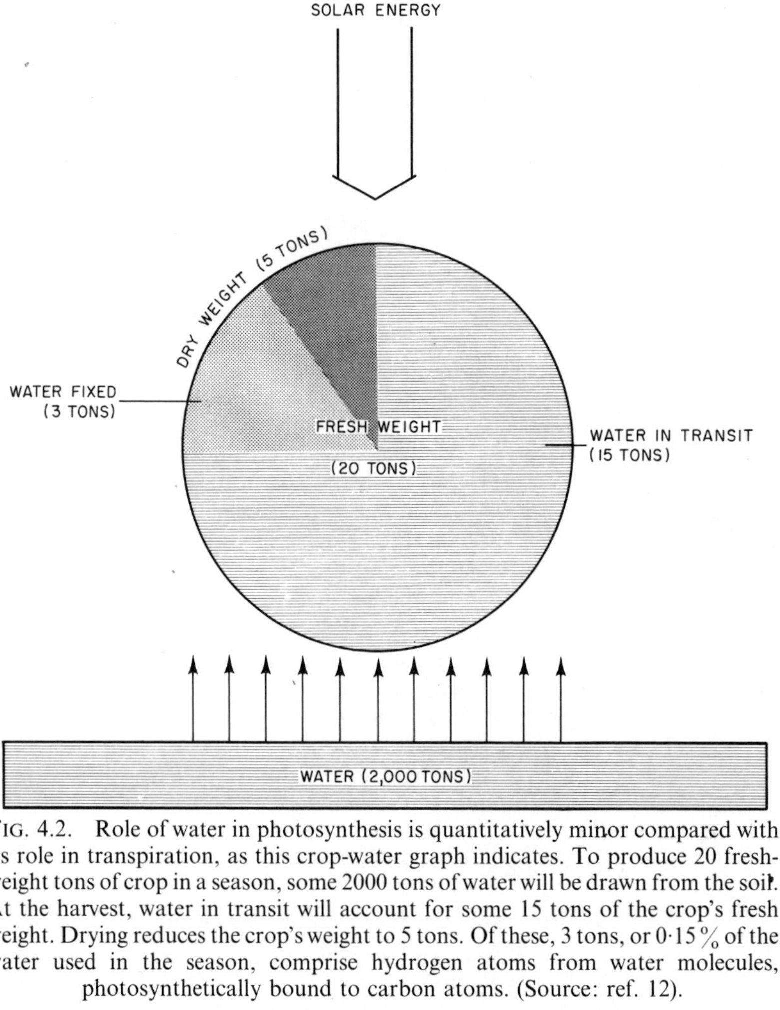

FIG. 4.2. Role of water in photosynthesis is quantitatively minor compared with its role in transpiration, as this crop-water graph indicates. To produce 20 fresh-weight tons of crop in a season, some 2000 tons of water will be drawn from the soil. At the harvest, water in transit will account for some 15 tons of the crop's fresh weight. Drying reduces the crop's weight to 5 tons. Of these, 3 tons, or 0·15 % of the water used in the season, comprise hydrogen atoms from water molecules, photosynthetically bound to carbon atoms. (Source: ref. 12).

fresh water, and in large amounts. About 1500 tonnes of water are needed to grow 1 tonne of wheat, about 4000 to grow 1 tonne of rice and about 10 000 tonnes to grow 1 tonne of cotton fibre.[4] As Figure 4.2 shows, most of this water is required for transpiration.

The presence of salt water rather than fresh water leads to dehydration, owing to osmosis. When two solutions of mineral salts are separated by a semi-permeable membrane such as a cell wall, pure water will pass from the weaker solution to the stronger until the concentration of salts in the two solutions equalises. The difference in the initial concentrations of the two solutions exerts an osmotic pressure and liquids in this situation obey laws similar to the physical laws that relate the temperature, pressure and volume of gases. In order to maintain a constant level of tissue fluid, therefore, the concentration of salts within cells must approximate very closely to the concentration outside. Thus if a salt water species of plant or animal is placed in fresh water, its tissues will be invaded by water until the internal pressure ruptures cell walls, causing swift but unpleasant death. If a fresh water species is placed in salt water, water will flow out of its tissues, the concentration of salts will increase and it will dehydrate, because the water that is lost cannot be replaced.

When water evaporates, it does so as pure water, and dissolved salts are left behind. So rain water and snow are always fresh and before living species could survive on land they had to adapt to environments containing only fresh water. The price they paid for so doing was the loss of their ability to survive in salt water.

For agricultural purposes, then, we are concerned only with fresh water and because fresh water is produced only by evaporation and precipitation, we must consider the way water moves about the planet.

Almost all the water on the earth is engaged in a cycle of evaporation, precipitation and run-off from the land masses back into the sea. Ninety-seven percent of all water is contained in the oceans and seas as salt water, and all the requirements of terrestrial species must be met from the remaining 3 %. In fact much less than that is available, because 98 % of the world's fresh water is held in the polar icecaps. If these were to melt, the sea level would rise by about 51 m, inundating many lowland areas and reducing the salinity of the seas, a condition to which marine species might or might not be able to adapt. The amount of water held in the icecaps is almost static, however, because both polar environments are very arid. We need consider only the 'current account' part of the hydrological cycle—the quantity of water that changes from salt to fresh and back to salt again each year.

Obviously the cycle must balance, otherwise water would accumulate or be lost. Juvenile water is being released constantly from the earth's magma as a result of volcanic activity, but in very small amounts; perhaps 0·1 cubic kilometres (km^3) per year.[5] An infinitesimal amount is lost into space as atoms of dissociated hydrogen. The main part of the cycle works in much larger quantities. Each day about 875 km^3 evaporates from the surface of the seas and about 775 km^3 falls on the seas as precipitation; 100 km^3 is carried over the land and 160 km^3 evaporates from the land surface; 260 km^3 falls as precipitation over land, and the cycle is completed by the return of 100 km^3 to the seas by rivers. In human terms these are very large quantities of water and it might seem that modern man should find little difficulty in increasing the amounts available to agriculture where this would increase yields.

Unhappily, fresh water is distributed far from evenly over the earth's land masses and much of the precipitation falls on regions in quantities larger than can be used, while other regions are chronically short. Theoretically, fresh water can be distilled from salt water industrially, by the process of desalination, but this is restricted to coastal regions—unless heavy costs are to be incurred in transporting water inland—and the energy cost is very high. The technique of reverse osmosis works well in some areas and is much cheaper than distillation, but constraints exist even so. If sea water is to be treated then sites are restricted and the large arid areas inland cannot benefit to any great extent, and if brackish ground water is treated there are possible limits to the resources contained in the aquifers. In parts of the Near East, for example, including the Gaza Strip, there are large reserves of brackish ground water and schemes have been suggested for treating them. However, it is probable that at one time the brackish water lay below fresh water or that the depletion of earlier fresh water reserves has permitted salt water to enter the aquifers from the sea. If this is so then the exploitation of the brackish water, at rates greater than those by which it is being replenished by fresh water delivered by precipitation from above, is likely to lower water tables and so permit the entry of even larger quantities of sea water, so that the ground water will become increasingly saline and the cost and complexity of treatment will increase.

A further constraint on the desalination of sea water or brackish water concerns the disposal of the resultant effluent, a liquor with a very high saline concentration. To some extent it can be used—and is being used in some places—as a source of minerals which are extracted from it. It cannot be discharged into the sea from whence it came because of its effect on local salinity and the consequent ecological effect, which might well be to damage thriving local fisheries.

In the main, regions where water is in short supply may improve the situation only by making better use of the water that is available to them.

Of the 737 million ha of farmland the FAO estimates to be under cultivation in the developing countries, only 93 million ha are irrigated. Most of this irrigated land is in Asia, where the arts of skilful irrigation have been developed to a high degree. Even there almost half the irrigation systems require improvement and renovation and the water delivered by irrigation is not generally used efficiently because too little attention has been paid to the levelling of land, the distribution of fields, drainage and regulation of the flow of water.

There is much scope, then, for the improved use of water. If they are to succeed, irrigation schemes must take account of the whole of the local water economy of that particular section of the hydrological cycle. There is much more to it than simply digging channels from the nearest river to the fields, and the dangers of adopting too simple an approach are great.

When water is diverted into fields two things happen. The first is that the water table, the level of the ground water beneath the surface, is raised as water drains downward from the irrigation channels. The second is that the quantity of water evaporating from the surface increases, for the simple reason that the total water surface area has increased. Either tendency can cause trouble and in extreme, but regrettably common, cases they may combine. The rising water table can lead to the waterlogging of the top soil, so reducing the amount of air that is held within a fertile soil and that is essential for the survival of necessary aerobic organisms. Processes of decomposition are interrupted and altered, and most crop plants will fail in this radically changed environment. At the same time, soluble nutrient salts will all be dissolved very quickly, so that the water in the soil becomes saline, the salts dissolved out of the top soil being joined by those dissolved out of the lower horizons. Water that evaporates from the surface will leave behind any salts that were dissolved in it, so increasing the salinity of the water that remains. If the water table should reach the surface, surface salinity can increase in quite a short period to levels at which most crop plants suffer severe dehydration by osmosis. Effectively the land is sterilised.

Irrigation cannot succeed, then, unless it is associated with proper drainage to ensure that the ground is flushed constantly to remove surplus salts. Unless the drainage system is constructed with care, it may simply lead to the physical erosion of the top soil, and in any case it may accentuate the natural leaching of soluble nutrients from the soil, so increasing the need to replace them with fertilisers.

The failure of ancient irrigation systems has often been spectacular. The hydrological civilisations of the Fertile Crescent of Mesopotamia and of the Indus Valley succeeded eventually in leaving behind them sterile, saline soils that were sometimes dry, sometimes waterlogged. In modern times the Aswan Dam in Egypt has increased the area of cultivable land but the lake behind the dam loses very large amounts of water by evaporation; thus farmers downstream now need to use fertilisers in large amounts not to increase their yields but to replace nutrients that are leached out by the irrigation–drainage system and to compensate for the loss of the fertile silt that the annual floods used to deposit across the surface.

The salinity of the Nile Delta has altered, causing the failure of the previously prosperous and productive sardine fishing industry in that part of the eastern Mediterranean, and the effective abolition of the annual dry season has allowed a large increase in the population of the water snails that are vectors for several diseases, including schistosomiasis. As if that were not enough, there is some reason for associating large dams with earthquakes. Like all dams, Aswan is silting up, as the rich alluvial soil from the upper reaches of the river accumulate behind it. It is likely that the era of large dams has ended, partly because of their adverse side effects, partly because of their high capital cost.

Although farmland has been irrigated for several millenia, surprisingly little is known about the behaviour of water in the ground at particular sites. Hydrology, the science of water on the earth's surface, is derived from several disciplines—those of the geographer, the climatologist, the physicist, the geologist and the engineer in particular. The hydrologist usually studies a complete catchment area as his basic unit, measuring the water that enters and tracing its flow within and out of the area. This may not be constant through time, for apart from changes in climate that vary the amount and timing of annual precipitation, the use to which the land is put may alter drainage patterns considerably. The construction of any system for the management of water, for irrigation or in some areas for flood control, depends critically on the accuracy with which water flows can be predicted. This in turn requires either educated guesses about past flows, or detailed and accurate records. As Dr J. S. G. McCulloch, Director of the British Natural Environment Research Council's Institute of Hydrology points out:

'... given a sufficient sequence of yield records, such as the flow of a river at a given site over a long period of years, statistical techniques may be applied to calculate probable return periods of given floods, all on the assumption that no physical change of hydrological significance has occured in the catchment area over the period of the records. This assumption is seldom justified. In developing countries, overgrazing and consequent deterioration of the vegetative cover of the water catchment areas may cause a more erratic flow regime; in developed countries urbanisation or the mechanisation of agricultural and forestry practices can accelerate the run-off after heavy rainfall in a rather similar fashion.'[6]

So water management schemes cannot be devised hastily. They must be founded on accurate, detailed and, above all, recent research in the area concerned, bearing in mind that it is shortage of water as much as anything that may lead to pasture deterioration, overgrazing and so further deterioration that itself may alter water flows. The International Hydrological Programme aims to improve our understanding of the details of the hydrological cycle to compile data and to study certain major river basins.

In some areas ground water can be tapped more cheaply and conveniently than rivers can be dammed or diverted. The technology to obtain the water is simple and well known but caution is still required. Ground water may be moving slowly so that the water abstracted from it depletes it and the resource becomes, to all intents and purposes, finite.

Peoples who live in arid environments have often developed highly ingenious methods for conserving water and for using it with optimum efficiency. The *foggara* of the Sahara provide an example. There is ground water beneath some parts of the Sahara Desert. In places the water table reaches the surface to make an oasis. Elsewhere the ancient Jews and

Berbers made artificial oases by finding the points where the water table rose closest to the surface, digging wells and then joining up these wells by channels in such a way as to drain water into depressions, where it could provide irrigation. In other places the planting of trees may tap ground water, while at the same time halting the wind-borne spread of sand, and binding soil together until in time it becomes possible to provide grazing for livestock.

Even so, water can be managed efficiently only if the water is there in the first place. Less than about 250 mm of precipitation a year will produce desert conditions almost anywhere on the earth's surface, but beyond that the amount of precipitation needed to support plant life depends also on the rate of evaporation from the surface. In North Dakota about 500 mm a year is needed to prevent extreme aridity, but further south, in Texas, about 750 mm is required. The average annual rainfall in the Sahara is about 100 mm.

There is no way in which extremely dry regions can be made to support agriculture, but in the very long term climates do change. Only a very small percentage of the world's water is carried in the atmosphere at any particular moment and quite small changes, of one or two per cent, may produce startling alterations in climates. The day may come when the dry deserts of the world become green and fertile, as they have been at various times in the past, but they are unlikely to do so in the foreseeable future.

The FAO considers that the present irrigated area of farmland could be increased by about 50%, from 93 million ha to about 140 million ha. The cost of renovating existing irrigation systems, developing new ones and of bringing new land into cultivation is estimated to be about $90 thousand million, calling for a total annual investment of $8–8·5 thousand million, at least, until 1985.

CLIMATE

The seeding of clouds with silver iodide smoke from aircraft to cool them and so to supply nuclei on which water vapour may crystallise into snow flakes, is one of the many ways in which man has tried to make rain. Most societies in the dry regions of the world have attempted to use magic to control the weather at one time or another. It is extremely doubtful whether any of the techniques developed, magical or technological, are very reliable. Even if they should succeed in causing precipitation it is precipitation that otherwise would fall somewhere else. It is not difficult to see that success in such short term manipulation of local weather conditions, in regions where such manipulation was important (and where else would anyone do it?), could lead quickly to hostility and possibly to a new weapon of war.

Yet man can and does modify climate in other ways, as we shall see in

Chapter 8. The Soviet government is building a system of dams and canals that will link the Ob and Yenisei rivers and form an inland sea five-sixths the size of Italy, to the east of the Ural Mountains and to the north of the Altai Mountains in the Western Siberian lowlands. The cities of Omsk, Novosibirsk, Krasnoyarsk and Irkutsk will lie on its shores. By preventing 12·5 % of the water that flows naturally into the Arctic Ocean from these two rivers from reaching the sea, the government plans to irrigate very large areas in the central steppe. A secondary effect may be a major alteration of the climate of the region. The possible effects of such a change can be guessed, but there is no way in which they can be known in advance with any precision and the Soviet authorities are proceeding with very great caution, monitoring the effect of each step in the scheme and assuring themselves that it is safe to proceed to the next.

If it is possible to alter slightly the precipitation, at least locally, much less can be done to influence temperatures, except as this is itself controlled by cloud cover. A clear sky will allow more heat to radiate to the surface in summer, and from it in winter, but there is no way in which average temperatures can be raised or lowered deliberately other than by constructing glasshouses. Yet little plant growth is possible below about 5 °C, so the average temperature of an area may make it quite unsuitable for agriculture, regardless of the annual precipitation.

Since the development of soils is conditioned by climate and by plant growth, most regions that are too cold for farming also have soils that are too poor. Thus the southern limit for cereal growing lies at about 45 °S. Only the southernmost tip of South America lies south of this latitude. The northern limit is much more variable, lying between about 50 and 60 °N, in both cases following the 10 °C July isotherm. Table 4.3 gives the minimum, optimum and maximum temperatures required for the germination of a number of important farm crops, and by relating these temperatures to the January and July isotherms it is possible to obtain a rough guide to the geographical limits of the crops.

Plants are also more or less sensitive to day length and the intensity of daylight. In a general kind of way the seasonal changes in the angle of incidence of sunlight and its length determine the length of the growing season. Once again it is unlikely that plants whose range is restricted by ambient temperatures and soils will not also be restricted by the length of duration and intensity of light. Plants adapt to a whole environment not just to particular parts of one, and climate and soil must be seen as a single entity. It does show, however, that a problem of poor soil may not be solved simply by moving soil from one place to another if the journey carries that soil across the boundary into a different climatic zone, nor may a problem of temperature be solved simply by covering the land with glass and installing heating. In the end the would-be grower may find himself having to cover areas with glass, import soil, install heating and lighting, and

TABLE 4.3
Cardinal Temperatures for the Germination of some Important Agricultural Crops

Crop	*Cardinal temp. (°C)*			*No. of days necessary for germination at different temps (°C)*			
	min.	*opt.*	*max.*	4·3	10·2	15·7	19·0
Wheat	3–4·5	25	30–32	6	3·0	2·0	1·7
Rye	1–2	25	30	4	2·5	1·0	1·0
Barley	3–4·5	20	28–30	6	3·0	2·0	1·7
Oats	4–5	25	30	7	3·7	2·7	2·0
Maize	8–10	32–35	40–44	—	11·2	3·2	3·0
Rice	10–12	30–32	36–38	—	—	—	—
Grass	3–4	26	30	—	6·5	3·2	3·0
Flax	2–3	25	30	8	4·5	2·0	2·0
Tobacco	13–14	28	35	—	—	9·0	6·2
Hemp	1–2	35	45	3	2·0	1·0	1·0
Sugar beet	4–5	25	28–30	22	9·0	3·7	3·7
Red clover	1	30	37	7·5	3·0	1·7	1·0
Lucerne	1	30	37	6	3·7	2·7	2·0
Peas	1–2	30	35	5	3·0	1·7	1·7
Lentil	4–5	30	36	6	4·0	2·0	1·7
Vetch	1–2	30	35	6	5·0	2·0	2·0

(Source: ref. 10).

monitor the flow of water by providing irrigation and drainage. In other words he must create an environment appropriate to his crop at a cost that is clearly very high. For most crops, under most economic circumstances, it is quite uneconomic.

Having said this it is only fair to point out that it does not tell the whole story. While it may not be possible to alter climates to suit plants, to some extent it is possible to modify plants to suit particular environments, and this is a subject for intense research and development. The very concept of the HYVs is based on the developing within cereal varieties a tolerance to extreme environments.

PLANTS AND ANIMALS

In compiling any kind of balance sheet of resources available for food production, we must not overlook the species of crop plants and domestic animals on which this production must be based. They are not immutable; indeed they have already been changed, in some cases almost beyond recognition, since man first began to tame and husband them. This is such an important subject that it will be discussed in much more detail in

Chapters 7 and 9. For the moment it is sufficient to bear it in mind and to remember that the FAO's suggested increase of 20 % in the cropped area of the developing countries may produce more than a 20 % increase in food, if it is farmed carefully with crops that are well adapted to the conditions that prevail in the areas concerned.

Fertilisers

As we saw in Table 4.1, plants require six nutrients in fairly large quantities, the major nutrients, and a further seven in much smaller quantities, the minor nutrients. All of these elements can be, and are, supplied in fertilisers when and where they are needed. The minor nutrients are used to remedy known deficiencies in soils and no problem exists regarding their supply. Magnesium is used in the same way. Calcium, used as lime, is not usually considered as a fertiliser and it is applied to soils separately from fertilisers, as required, to neutralise excessive acidity.

The remaining four major nutrients, nitrogen, phosphorus, potassium and sulphur, are used in the manufacture of fertilisers, but of these four only three, nitrogen, phosphorus and potassium, are usually considered as the principal constituents of fertiliser. Known generically as 'N, P and K', in fact they may be supplied in a variety of compounds. Fertiliser quantities are measured either in 'units' or, for our purposes, in nutrient tonnes. A nutrient tonne is the weight of the nutrient in a fertiliser, regardless of the weight of the material used as a carrier. In the case of nitrogen, the weight of elemental N is given, in the case of phosphorus it is measured as phosphorus pentoxide (P_2O_5) and in the case of potassium it is measured as K_2O.

The raw material for nitrogen fertiliser production is, of course, atmospheric nitrogen. As we saw earlier, atmospheric nitrogen is fixed chemically to yield ammonium (NH_4) compounds and simple amides (NH_2) such as urea ($CO(NH_2)_2$). Alternatively nitrogen can be supplied as a nitrate, such as calcium or sodium nitrate, directly as ammonia (NH_3) or ammonium nitrate, or as calcium cyanamide ($CaCN_2$), which is hydrolysed in the soil to form urea. The hydrogen is supplied by methanol (natural gas) but it is possible to use naphtha, a petroleum derivative, instead. Ammonium sulphate and ammonium nitrate-sulphate also supply sulphur.

Phosphorus fertiliser is produced from rock phosphate (mainly calcium phosphate) in the mineral apatite ($Ca_5(PO_4)_3ON$) that is mined at a limited number of sites throughout the world. It can be crushed and used directly as ground rock phosphate, from which nutrients are released very slowly, or it can be treated with sulphuric acid to produce 'superphosphate', or with phosphoric acid to produce 'triple superphosphate', or by reacting ammonia and phosphoric acid to produce ammonium phosphate (which also supplies nitrogen). Whereas the raw material for nitrogen fertiliser is in practice natural gas or petroleum, but in theory any source of hydrogen that can be reacted to fix atmospheric nitrogen, the raw material for phosphate fertiliser is a mineral resource limited in quantity and in distribution.

No one knows precisely how much rock phosphate there is in the world. The total has been estimated at between 100 and 150 thousand million tonnes but this is little more than an educated guess, for many areas have not been surveyed. Those that have been surveyed most thoroughly are in countries which already mine phosphate and which therefore have an immediate interest in knowing how much lies within their territory. Although phosphate may seem virtually inexhaustible, however, most of the known deposits are of poor quality and whether or not they can be mined is an economic matter, not a mining one.

Comparatively little work has been done to devise methods for extracting and processing low-grade phosphate ores, for the simple reason that most of those being mined are of high quality and until they begin to deplete there is little economic incentive to invest in the development of new technologies. In some North African countries, in Florida and in Spain, the poorer deposits are now being worked to some extent and as the better deposits are used we may expect prices to rise, so financing the exploitation of the inferior deposits.

Since almost all rock phosphate is processed before use, figures for annual phosphate fertiliser production are misleading, since they take no account of the source of the raw material. All continents—though by no means all countries—produce some rock phosphate but the major producers are North America (USA), East Europe (USSR) and Africa.

TABLE 4.4
World Production and Consumption of Rock Phosphate, 1973

	Production (*thousand tonnes*)	*Consumption* (*thousand tonnes*)
West Europe	113	22 937
East Europe	21 580	23 787
Africa	27 304	4 344
North America	38 226	31 459
Central America	129	1 490
South America	268	1 459
Asia	7 216	11 170
Oceania	3 066	4 262

(Source: ref. 7).

As Table 4.4 shows, most North American production is consumed within North America, East European farmers import rock phosphate despite the large Soviet output, and the rock phosphate that enters world trade comes mainly from Africa. If North American and East European output is deducted from the total for 1973, Africa supplied 71·7 % of the remainder.[7]

Within Africa the main suppliers were Morocco (16 564 thousand tonnes), Tunisia (3 473 thousand tonnes), Togo (2 272 thousand tonnes), Senegal (1 752 thousand tonnes) and South Africa (1 300 thousand tonnes—all of it consumed within South Africa so that none enters world trade from this source). The Spanish Sahara, which contains rich reserves, yielded only 696 thousand tonnes in 1973, but its potential is certainly much higher and exploitation awaits only a rise in price that will justify the mining of its rather more expensive, because rather lower grade, ores.

The bulk of the supply, then, came from a group of countries in North and West Africa. If we add the lesser quantities supplied by Algeria and Egypt (608 and 500 thousand tonnes, respectively) we see that of the total African output of 27 304 thousand tonnes, 25 965 thousand tonnes, or 95 %, came from a group of seven countries, all of them African, all developing and all sharing many historical and cultural attributes.

At present this group of countries controls a sufficiently large share of the world trade to enable it to form a producer cartel, though whether it will maintain this position is not certain. Large reserves may be discovered in Brazil and too steep a rise in prices could make economical the mining of lower grade ores elsewhere in the world; the OPEC cartel managed to adjust its price levels with sufficient skill to avoid this problem, so perhaps the phosphate producers could do the same. The very large rise in phosphate prices in the early 1970s can be explained by the extremely low prices that had prevailed for many years. Instead of prices rising steadily, year by year, they were held for a prolonged period and then jumped abruptly to a new level, which represents much more accurately their real value.

Potassium ('potash') fertilisers are also mined from a limited mineral resource, most commonly potassium chloride (KCl) which is sold for direct use as 'muriate of potash'. KCl is also processed into a number of forms for fertiliser use, including potassium sulphate, potassium magnesium sulphate, potassium nitrate and potassium metaphosphate. Potash acquired its name because if was first derived from wood ash, which may contain from 2–5 % K. Seaweeds also supply useful amounts of potassium in areas where they are abundant.

World reserves of potassium chloride are large but they are not distributed evenly. The largest reserves, covering an area of about 62 000 km^2, are in Germany. Canada has the world's second largest known deposits, and the USSR, Israel, USA, France, Spain, Poland, Italy and the UK also have significant quantities, not all of them being mined at present. There are also reserves in Japan, Australia, South Africa and India. Production of potash fertilisers occurs mainly in West and East Europe and in North America. In 1973/74, Africa and Asia produced 74 and 44%, respectively, of the quantities they consumed, but the only producing country in Africa is Egypt, and Israel and China are the only Asian producers. The only producing country in South America is Chile which supplies very small quantities that do not satisfy even its own demand; none is produced in Oceania or in Central America.

Thus while potash reserves are more than adequate for any foreseeable world demand and will last a long time into the future, by and large the developing countries will remain dependent on the industrial nations for their supply, since it is in the industrial countries that the major deposits are located.

Although fertiliser production and consumption is measured conventionally in terms of N, P and K, sulphur is also an essential nutrient. In most of the industrial countries the need for it to be supplied by fertilisers is small at present because of the quantities delivered to plants from atmospheric sulphuric acid, dissolved sulphur dioxide, an industrial and domestic pollutant. The world's leading deposits of elemental sulphur are in Louisiana and Texas in the USA, in Mexico, Poland, Italy, Japan and China. Sulphide ores (pyrite) are found in Spain, Canada, France, the USA, the USSR, Norway, the German Democratic Republic, the Federal Republic of Germany, China and Finland. In 1973 the world's leading producers of sulphur in all forms were the USA (24% of the world total), Canada (16%), Poland (8%), France (4%), Spain (2%), Mexico (3%) and the Federal Republic of Germany (2%).

Table 4.5 breaks down world production of N, P and K to show the percentage contribution made by developing and developed countries. It shows that in 1972/73, 56·2% of the world's N, 65·2% of the P and 57·9% of the K were produced in the developed regions. This proportion had been declining over the preceding decade as production in developing countries increased, but it still shows a considerable imbalance when it is related to population or to area of cropped land.

Table 4.6 compares fertiliser consumption on a similar basis, showing that, again in 1972/73, the developed countries consumed 46·5% of the world's N fertiliser, 59·2% of the P and 55·3% of the K. Again these figures have declined as consumption of fertilisers in developing countries has increased.

These changes are illustrated more clearly in Tables 4.7, 4.8 and 4.9, which show production, consumption and trade in N, P and K, respectively, together with the percentage changes over the period from 1967/68 to 1972/73. The developing countries have been increasing their annual production of N fertiliser very much faster than have the developed countries, although the quantities involved are still a great deal smaller. However, from about 1969 they began to export N fertiliser and from 1970 their own imports began to increase. Similarly they began to export P fertiliser in about 1970 and their imports, which had been declining, rose rapidly. The same pattern is repeated in the case of K fertilisers.

The figures are a little less paradoxical than they seem. The quantities being exported were very small, so that a small increase in the amounts shows as a considerable percentage change, while the quantities imported were very much larger and the percentage increase in imports consequently less significant.

Table 4.10 summarises these figures as world production, consumption and trade in fertilisers. It shows that from 1967/68 to 1972/73 world production of N increased annually by an average of 8·2%, of P by an average of 5·8% and of K by an average of 5·8%. World trade in fertilisers of all kinds has increased by an average of 7% each year.

It is not until we study Table 4.11, however, that these highly aggregated totals for the world or for large regions can be seen in relation to farming practice. This table considers well over 100 countries, by continents, and compares their consumption of N, P and K per hectare of arable land, per hectare of cultivated land of all kinds and per caput of population.

In the USA, for example, an average of 84·6 kg of fertiliser is used on each hectare of arable land. In India, also a country with considerable areas sown to wheat and rice, the average is 16·2 kg per ha, while in China it is 38·4. In Japan, which grows rice, the average per hectare of arable land is 387 kg. The world's heaviest user of fertiliser is the Netherlands, with 716·9 kg per ha of arable land, 285·2 kg per ha of agricultural land of all kinds and 45·2 kg per caput each year. In Europe generally, an average of 190·3 kg of fertiliser is used on each hectare of arable land, 116·8 kg on each hectare of farmland of all kinds and 58·8 kg for every member of the population. In Laos, in contrast, 0·2 kg is used on each hectare of arable land, 0·2 kg on each hectare of agricultural land of all kinds—the two categories being, presumably, identical—and 0·1 kg for each member of the population.

Clearly there is room for change. In Chapter 7 we look in more detail at the role of fertilisers, pesticides and machinery as energy-related inputs to agriculture and we look, too, at some of the economic and environmental consequences of the industrialisation of agriculture. It is very probable that the industrial countries have reached optimum levels of total fertiliser consumption and that increases on certain crops might best be bought by decreasing levels of application elsewhere.

It is in the developing regions that substantial increases are needed. Are they possible? As we have seen, the raw materials required for the production of nitrogen fertilisers, while theoretically unlimited, are in fact subject to economic constraints and the price of N fertiliser is linked directly to energy prices. The world's reserves of rock phosphate are large but at present are being exploited only in certain areas in ways that could work to the advantage of developing countries if the African states, in which they are being mined, adopt an attitude to developing countries similar to the

TABLE 4.5
Contribution of Economic Classes and Regions to World Production

Classes and regions	1961/62–1965/66	1966/67	1967/68	1968/69	1969/70	1970/71	1971/72	1972/73
				N (%)				
Developed	70·7	67·3	66·7	64·5	62·2	59·9	57·1	56·2
N. America	27·5	26·9	27·8	27·1	27·4	27·0	25·4	24·3
W. Europe	34·2	31·8	30·3	29·1	26·5	25·4	24·4	24·2
Oceania	0·2	0·2	0·2	0·3	0·5	0·4	0·5	0·5
Other	8·8	8·4	8·4	8·0	7·8	7·1	6·8	7·2
Developing	6·2	5·7	5·9	7·0	8·0	8·3	9·3	10·1
Africa	—	—	—	—	0·1	0·3	0·4	0·4
Lat. America	2·9	2·2	2·0	2·2	2·5	2·3	2·3	2·2
Near East	1·0	1·1	1·1	1·0	0·9	1·1	1·5	2·1
Far East	2·3	2·4	2·8	3·8	4·5	4·6	5·1	5·4
Other	—	—	—	—	—	—	—	—
Centr. Plann.	23·1	27·0	27·4	28·5	29·8	31·8	33·6	33·7
Asia	4·1	4·8	4·5	4·5	4·6	5·0	5·9	6·5
Europe (USSR)	19·0	22·2	22·9	24·0	25·2	26·8	27·7	27·2
				P_2O_5(%)				
Developed	76·4	73·9	73·1	71·0	69·8	67·9	66·2	65·2
N. America	28·6	30·4	30·4	27·4	28·3	28·5	28·2	26·8
W. Europe	34·6	31·0	30·3	31·5	30·1	29·7	28·5	28·5
Oceania	7·8	7·4	6·9	6·4	5·9	4·9	4·9	5·3
Other	5·4	5·1	5·5	5·7	5·5	4·8	4·6	4·6

Developing	3·7	4·6	5·3	6·3	6·2	6·3	7·3	8·4
Africa	1·1	1·7	1·9	2·1	1·9	1·8	1·9	2·2
Lat. America	1·3	1·2	1·4	1·5	1·5	1·7	2·1	2·4
Near East	0·5	0·6	0·5	0·7	0·7	0·8	1·1	1·5
Far East	0·8	1·1	1·5	2·0	2·1	2·0	2·2	2·3
Other	—	—	—	—	—	—	—	—
Centr. Plann.	19·8	21·5	21·6	22·7	24·0	25·8	26·5	26·4
Asia	3·4	3·7	3·7	3·8	4·1	4·5	5·0	5·0
Europe (USSR)	16·4	17·8	17·9	18·9	19·9	21·3	21·5	21·4
K_2O(%)								
Developed	68·5	67·0	65·7	64·8	65·1	61·2	59·9	57·9
N. America	28·7	33·0	33·6	33·1	34·2	30·4	31·5	31·0
W. Europe	38·4	32·0	30·0	29·6	28·3	27·6	25·6	23·9
Oceania	—	—	—	—	—	—	—	—
Other	1·5	2·0	2·1	2·1	2·6	3·2	2·8	3·0
Developing	0·2	0·2	0·1	0·1	0·5	1·0	1·5	1·5
Africa	—	—	—	—	0·4	0·9	1·4	1·4
Lat. America	0·2	0·2	0·1	0·1	0·1	0·1	0·1	0·1
Near East	—	—	—	—	—	—	—	—
Far East	—	—	—	—	—	—	—	—
Other	—	—	—	—	—	—	—	—
Centr. Plann.	31·3	32·8	34·2	35·1	34·4	37·8	38·6	40·6
Asia	0·7	1·2	1·1	1·2	1·4	1·4	1·4	1·5
Europe (USSR)	30·6	31·6	33·1	33·9	33·0	36·4	37·2	39·1

(Source: ref. 8).

TABLE 4.6
Contribution of Economic Classes and Regions to World Consumption

Classes and regions	1961/62–1965/66	1966/67	1967/68	1968/69	1969/70	1970/71	1971/72	1972/73
				N (%)				
Developed	61·1	55·4	56·0	51·9	50·8	49·4	47·5	46·5
N. America	27·2	26·4	27·1	24·7	24·6	24·2	22·9	22·2
W. Europe	27·9	24·0	23·9	22·4	21·9	21·3	21·4	20·9
Oceania	0·4	0·5	0·6	0·7	0·6	0·5	0·4	0·6
Other	5·6	4·5	4·4	4·1	3·7	3·4	2·8	2·8
Developing	13·7	13·9	14·0	15·7	16·4	16·3	17·5	18·4
Africa	0·8	0·8	0·8	0·8	0·8	0·9	1·2	1·1
Lat. America	4·0	3·7	3·9	4·2	4·1	4·3	4·3	4·6
Near East	2·4	2·0	2·2	2·4	2·5	2·4	2·6	2·8
Far East	6·5	7·4	7·1	8·3	9·0	8·7	9·4	9·9
Other	—	—	—	—	—	—	—	—
Centr. Plann.	25·2	30·7	30·0	32·4	32·8	34·3	35·0	35·1
Asia	7·3	9·8	8·1	9·6	9·9	10·6	10·2	10·3
Europe (USSR)	17·9	20·9	21·9	22·8	22·9	23·7	24·8	24·8
				P_2O_5(%)				
Developed	71·8	68·6	67·7	64·9	63·6	62·2	60·3	59·2
N. America	25·6	26·5	26·2	25·0	23·5	23·6	22·5	22·4
W. Europe	33·0	28·9	29·2	27·8	28·5	28·4	27·9	26·8
Oceania	7·9	8·0	6·8	6·7	6·4	5·4	5·3	5·4
Other	5·3	5·2	5·5	5·4	5·2	4·8	4·6	4·6

Developing	7·4	8·5	9·1	10·9	11·4	11·5	12·6	13·7
Africa	0·8	0·8	0·9	1·0	1·1	1·2	1·3	1·3
Lat. America	3·1	3·3	3·9	4·2	4·1	4·7	4·7	5·6
Near East	0·9	1·1	1·3	1·5	1·7	1·5	1·7	2·0
Far East	2·5	3·3	3·0	4·2	4·5	4·1	4·9	4·8
Other	—	—	—	—	—	—	—	—
Centr. Plann.	20·8	22·9	23·2	24·2	25·0	26·3	27·1	27·1
Asia	4·1	3·9	3·7	3·9	4·4	4·7	5·3	5·3
Europe (USSR)	16·7	19·0	19·5	20·3	20·6	21·6	21·8	21·8
				K_2O(%)				
Developed	70·2	64·6	63·2	61·2	60·2	59·3	57·6	55·3
N. America	25·1	26·5	25·6	25·1	24·6	24·1	23·4	22·3
W. Europe	37·7	31·4	31·2	29·7	29·5	29·7	29·2	28·0
Oceania	1·3	1·3	1·1	1·2	1·2	1·2	1·1	1·1
Other	6·1	5·4	5·3	5·2	4·9	4·3	3·9	3·9
Developing	4·8	5·6	5·9	7·0	7·6	8·0	8·2	9·4
Africa	0·7	0·7	0·7	0·7	0·8	0·8	0·9	1·1
Lat. America	2·4	2·5	2·6	3·5	3·7	4·0	3·8	4·4
Near East	0·1	0·1	0·1	0·2	0·2	0·2	0·2	0·2
Far East	1·6	2·3	2·5	2·6	2·9	3·0	3·3	3·7
Other	—	—	—	—	—	—	—	—
Centr. Plann.	25·0	29·8	30·9	31·8	32·2	32·7	34·2	35·3
Asia	1·1	1·7	1·8	2·2	2·2	2·2	2·2	2·2
Europe (USSR)	23·9	28·1	29·1	29·6	30·0	30·5	32·0	33·1

(Source: ref. 8).

TABLE 4.7
Nitrogen Fertilisers: Production, Consumption, Trade and percent Change by Economic Classes

Economic classes	1967/8	1968/9	1969/70	1970/1	1971/2	1972/3	1967/8 *to* 1968/9	1968/9 *to* 1969/70	1969/70 *to* 1970/1	1970/1 *to* 1971/2	1971/2 *to* 1972/3
	(*thousand tonnes*)						(% *change*)				
					Production						
Developed	17 008	18 309	18 746	19 726	19 995	21 380	8	2	5	1	7
Developing	1 504	1 995	2 420	2 736	3 268	3 830	33	21	13	19	17
Centr. Plann.	6 986	8 080	8 968	10 458	11 736	12 818	16	11	17	12	9
World total	25 498	28 384	30 134	32 920	34 999	38 028	11	6	9	6	9
					Consumption						
Developed	13 379	13 804	14 560	15 682	15 777	16 758	3	6	8	1	6
Developing	3 356	4 163	4 716	5 201	5 826	6 648	24	13	10	12	14
Centr. Plann.	7 165	8 621	9 422	10 880	11 651	12 646	20	9	16	7	9
World total	23 901	26 588	28 699	31 763	33 254	36 052	11	8	11	5	8
					Exports						
Developed	4 887	5 660	5 507	5 544	5 396	6 158	16	−3	1	−3	14
Developing	272	331	333	466	550	744	22	1	40	18	35
Centr. Plann.	398	591	690	800	1 211	1 241	49	17	16	51	3
World total	5 557	6 582	6 530	6 810	7 157	8 143	18	−1	4	5	14
					Imports						
Developed	1 693	1 781	1 875	2 072	2 183	2 368	5	5	11	5	9
Developing	2 827	2 785	2 766	2 588	2 896	3 659	−1	−1	−6	12	26
Centr. Plann.	1 079	1 714	1 837	2 113	1 696	1 680	59	7	15	−10	−1
World total	5 600	6 280	6 478	6 773	6 776	7 707	12	3	5	0	14

(Source: ref. 8).

TABLE 4.8
Phosphate Fertilisers: Production, Consumption, Trade and percent Change by Economic Classes

Economic classes	1967/8	1968/9	1969/70	1970/1	1971/2	1972/3	1967/8 *to* 1968/9	1968/9 *to* 1969/70	1969/70 *to* 1970/1	1970/1 *to* 1971/2	1971/2 *to* 1972/3
	(*thousand tonnes*)						(*% change*)				
				Production							
Developed	13 171	13 204	13 448	14 107	14 831	15 450	0	2	5	5	4
Developing	952	1 166	1 193	1 317	1 641	1 979	23	2	10	25	21
Centr. Plann.	3 890	4 217	4 632	5 352	5 915	6 258	8	10	16	11	6
World total	18 012	18 587	19 274	20 775	22 388	23 686	3	4	8	8	6
				Consumption							
Developed	11 478	11 797	11 965	12 327	12 740	13 371	3	1	3	3	5
Developing	1 549	1 989	2 144	2 285	2 663	3 105	28	8	7	17	17
Centr. Plann.	3 930	4 391	4 694	5 212	5 731	6 119	12	7	11	10	7
World total	16 958	18 177	18 804	19 824	21 134	22 595	7	3	5	7	7
				Exports							
Developed	2 469	2 486	2 312	2 416	2 804	3 295	1	−7	5	16	18
Developing	258	296	296	286	395	458	15	0	−3	38	16
Centr. Plann.	119	117	105	167	146	182	−2	−10	59	−13	25
World total	2 847	2 898	2 713	2 869	3 345	3 935	2	−6	6	17	18
				Imports							
Developed	1 048	1 079	1 308	1 281	1 467	1 542	3	21	−2	15	5
Developing	1 311	1 188	1 114	1 104	1 317	1 606	−9	−6	−1	19	22
Centr. Plann.	284	297	224	260	280	428	5	−25	16	8	53
World total	2 643	2 563	2 647	2 645	3 064	3 576	−3	3	0	16	17

(Source: ref. 8).

TABLE 4.9
Potash Fertilisers: Production, Consumption, Trade and percent Change by Economic Classes

Economic classes	1967/8	1968/9	1969/70	1970/1	1971/2	1972/3	1967/8 *to* 1968/9	1968/9 *to* 1969/70	1969/70 *to* 1970/1	1970/1 *to* 1971/2	1971/2 *to* 1972/3
			(*thousand tonnes*)						(*% change*)		
					Production						
Developed	10 089	10 347	10 994	10 937	11 658	11 704	3	6	0	7	0
Developing	18	16	85	188	298	303	−11	431	121	59	2
Centr. Plann.	5 240	5 605	5 820	6 747	7 513	8 191	7	4	16	11	9
World total	15 347	15 969	16 898	17 872	19 469	20 198	4	6	6	9	4
					Consumption						
Developed	8 926	9 025	9 387	9 894	10 140	10 363	1	4	5	3	2
Developing	834	1 022	1 193	1 329	1 442	1 770	23	17	11	9	23
Centr. Plann.	4 356	4 692	5 015	5 459	6 018	6 617	8	7	9	10	10
World total	14 116	14 739	15 595	16 682	17 600	18 750	4	6	7	6	7
					Exports						
Developed	5 665	5 977	6 695	6 414	7 030	7 701	6	12	−4	10	10
Developing	15	10	10	11	11	15	−33	0	10	0	36
Centr. Plann.	2 108	2 337	2 354	3 048	3 369	3 526	11	1	30	11	5
World total	7 787	8 324	9 060	9 473	10 410	11 241	7	9	5	10	8
					Imports						
Developed	5 248	5 343	5 946	5 955	6 446	6 770	2	11	0	8	5
Developing	1 034	1 049	1 118	1 227	1 429	1 745	2	7	10	17	22
Centr. Plann.	1 444	1 619	1 790	2 086	2 220	2 349	12	11	17	6	6
World total	7 726	8 011	8 855	9 268	10 096	10 865	4	11	5	9	8

(Source: ref. 8).

TABLE 4.10

World Production, Consumption and Trade of Nitrogen, Phosphate and Potash and percent Changes, 1967/68 to 1972/73

Type of fertiliser	1967/8	1968/9	1969/70	1970/1	1971/2	1972/3	1967/8 *to* 1968/9	1968/9 *to* 1969/70	1969/70 *to* 1970/1	1970/1 *to* 1971/2	1971/2 *to* 1972/3
	(*thousand tonnes*)						(*% change*)				
Production											
Nitrogen (N)	25 498	28 384	30 134	32 920	34 999	38 028	11	6	9	6	9
Phosphate (P_2O_5)	18 012	18 587	19 274	20 775	22 388	23 686	3	4	8	8	6
Potash (K_2O)	15 347	15 969	16 898	17 872	19 469	20 198	4	6	6	9	4
All fertilisers (N, P_2O_5, K_2O)	58 857	62 940	66 306	71 567	76 856	81 912	7	5	8	7	7
Consumption											
Nitrogen (N)	23 901	26 588	28 699	31 763	33 254	36 052	11	8	11	5	8
Phosphate (P_2O_5)	16 958	18 177	18 804	19 824	21 134	22 595	7	3	5	7	7
Potash (K_2O)	14 116	14 739	15 595	16 682	17 600	18 750	4	6	7	6	7
All fertilisers (N, P_2O_5, K_2O)	54 975	59 504	63 098	68 269	71 988	77 397	8	6	8	5	8
Exports											
Nitrogen (N)	5 557	6 582	6 530	6 810	7 157	8 143	18	−1	4	5	14
Phosphate (P_2O_5)	2 847	2 898	2 713	2 869	3 345	3 935	2	−6	6	17	18
Potash (K_2O)	7 787	8 324	9 060	9 473	10 410	11 241	7	9	5	10	8
All fertilisers (N, P_2O_5, K_2O)	16 191	17 804	18 303	19 152	20 912	23 319	10	3	5	9	12
Imports											
Nitrogen (N)	5 600	6 280	6 478	6 773	6 776	7 707	12	3	5	0	14
Phosphate (P_2O_5)	2 643	2 563	2 647	2 645	3 064	3 576	−3	3	0	16	17
Potash (K_2O)	7 726	8 011	8 855	9 268	10 096	10 865	4	11	5	9	8
All fertilisers (N, P_2O_5, K_2O)	15 969	16 854	17 980	18 686	19 936	22 148	6	7	4	7	11

(Source: ref. 8).

TABLE 4.11
Fertiliser Consumption in Relation to Arable Land, Agricultural Land and to Population, 1972/73

Continent and Country	*Consumption per hectare (kg)*								*Per capita*
	Arable land				*Agricultural land*				*Total*
	N	P_2O_5	K_2O	*Total*	*N*	P_2O_5	K_2O	*Total*	*N*, P_2O_5, K_2O
Africa	5·1	3·4	1·5	10·0	1·1	0·7	0·3	2·1	5·7
Algeria	12·5	11·3	5·9	29·7	1·9	1·7	0·9	4·5	13·4
Angola	12·4	7·1	5·2	24·7	0·4	0·2	0·2	0·8	3·8
Botswana	2·2	11·7	—	13·9	—	0·1	—	0·1	11·0
Burundi	0·5	0·1	0·1	0·7	0·4	0·1	—	0·5	0·2
Cameroon	1·2	0·2	0·6	2·0	0·6	0·1	0·3	1·0	2·4
Central African Rep.	0·3	0·1	0·1	0·5	0·3	0·1	0·1	0·5	0·6
Chad	0·2	0·1	0·1	0·4	—	—	—	—	0·6
Congo	5·7	0·2	5·6	11·5	0·2	—	0·2	0·4	7·3
Dahomey	1·5	0·8	1·2	3·5	1·2	0·6	0·9	2·7	1·9
Egypt	122·7	30·8	1·4	154·9	122·7	30·8	1·4	154·9	12·3
Equatorial Guinea	5·4	—	—	5·4	3·7	—	—	3·7	4·1
Ethiopia	0·5	0·3	0·2	1·0	0·1	0·1	—	0·2	0·5
Gabon	0·8	—	—	0·8	—	—	—	—	1·0
Gambia	1·5	1·5	—	3·0	0·5	0·5	—	1·0	1·6
Ghana	0·3	0·3	0·4	1·0	0·1	0·1	0·1	0·3	0·3
Guinea	1·1	0·1	0·7	1·9	0·4	—	0·2	0·6	0·7
Ivory Coast	1·0	0·5	2·0	3·5	0·5	0·2	1·1	1·8	6·8
Kenya	14·0	16·3	3·6	33·9	4·2	4·8	1·1	10·1	4·9
Lesotho	0·3	1·3	—	1·6	—	0·2	—	0·2	0·6
Liberia	4·4	1·9	—	6·3	2·6	1·2	—	3·8	1·9
Libyan Arab Rep.	2·8	3·4	0·4	6·6	0·7	0·9	0·1	1·7	7·8
Madagascar	2·1	1·1	1·5	4·7	0·2	0·1	0·1	0·4	1·8
Malawi	5·7	0·6	0·6	6·9	4·6	0·5	0·5	5·6	3·9
Mali	0·3	0·6	—	0·9	0·1	0·2	—	0·3	1·9
Mauritius	130·0	41·0	130·5	301·5	122·0	38·4	122·4	282·8	35·3
Morocco	8·7	6·6	4·3	19·6	4·3	3·3	2·1	9·7	8·9
Mozambique	2·7	1·5	1·0	5·2	0·2	0·1	0·1	0·4	1·7
Nigeria	0·2	0·3	0·2	0·7	0·1	0·2	0·1	0·4	0·3
Reunion	89·3	62·5	64·3	216·1	78·1	54·7	56·3	189·1	26·0
Rhodesia	32·7	20·6	16·3	69·6	9·0	5·7	4·5	19·2	23·6
Rwanda	0·5	0·4	0·4	1·3	0·2	0·2	0·2	0·6	0·3
Senegal	1·3	0·8	0·9	3·0	0·6	0·4	0·5	1·5	4·1
Sierra Leone	—	0·1	—	0·1	—	0·1	—	0·1	0·3
Somalia	2·7	0·4	0·6	3·7	0·1	—	—	0·1	1·2
South Africa	21·0	26·0	9·7	56·7	2·5	3·1	1·1	6·7	32·3
Sudan	7·5	—	—	7·5	1·7	—	—	1·7	3·2
Swaziland	14·4	15·0	13·2	42·6	1·5	1·6	1·4	4·5	14·5
Tanzania	0·5	0·4	0·2	1·1	0·2	0·1	0·1	0·4	1·3
Togo	0·1	0·1	0·8	1·0	0·1	0·1	0·7	0·9	1·1
Tunisia	3·3	3·9	0·7	7·9	1·9	2·3	0·4	4·6	6·7

TABLE 4.11—*continued*

Continent and Country	*Consumption per hectare (kg)*								*Per capita*
	Arable land				*Agricultural land*				*Total*
	N	P_2O_5	K_2O	*Total*	*N*	P_2O_5	K_2O	*Total*	*N*, P_2O_5, K_2O
Africa—*continued*									
Uganda	0·8	0·4	0·3	1·5	0·4	0·2	0·2	0·8	0·8
Upper Volta	0·1	0·1	—	0·2	—	—	—	—	0·2
Zaire	0·3	0·1	0·2	0·6	0·1	—	—	0·1	0·2
Zambia	3·8	1·2	0·9	5·9	0·5	0·2	0·1	0·8	0·9
North and Central America	32·4	19·6	16·1	68·1	14·2	8·5	7·0	29·7	56·5
Barbados	111·5	34·6	111·5	257·6	96·7	30·0	96·7	223·4	27·9
Belize	15·5	14·6	4·3	34·4	11·4	10·7	3·1	25·2	12·0
Canada	10·1	10·2	4·1	24·4	6·4	6·5	2·6	15·5	48·7
Costa Rica	26·6	25·7	12·3	64·6	11·0	10·6	5·1	26·7	32·4
Cuba	30·9	14·3	30·9	76·1	18·4	8·5	18·4	45·3	30·6
Dominican Rep.	26·7	15·4	17·6	59·7	10·8	6·2	7·1	24·1	12·6
El Salvador	99·8	24·1	10·8	134·7	49·4	11·9	5·3	66·6	23·7
Guadeloupe	63·2	63·2	52·6	179·0	48·6	48·6	40·5	137·7	30·3
Guatemala	15·9	6·1	3·3	25·3	9·4	3·6	1·9	14·9	6·9
Haiti	0·5	—	0·3	0·8	0·2	—	0·1	0·3	0·1
Honduras	21·9	2·4	9·6	33·9	4·2	0·5	1·9	6·6	9·6
Jamaica	54·8	14·5	24·9	94·2	27·0	7·2	12·3	46·5	10·9
Martinique	160·7	128·6	142·9	432·2	97·8	78·3	87·0	263·1	35·0
Mexico	18·9	5·9	1·3	26·1	5·3	1·7	0·4	7·4	13·2
Nicaragua	20·0	7·2	6·2	33·4	9·8	3·5	3·0	16·3	13·6
Panama	28·6	—	—	28·6	9·2	—	—	9·2	9·9
St. Kitts-Nevis & Anguilla	14·3	14·3	250·0	278·6	13·3	13·3	233·3	259·9	62·9
St. Lucia	61·9	57·1	142·9	261·9	54·2	50·0	125·0	229·2	45·8
St. Vincent	83·3	16·7	111·1	211·1	78·9	15·8	105·3	200·0	38·4
Trinidad and Tobago	50·4	4·3	46·8	101·5	48·3	4·1	44·8	97·2	13·6
United States	39·6	24·1	20·9	84·6	17·4	10·6	9·2	37·2	77·4
Virgin Islands (US)	64·2	24·5	5·0	93·7	25·7	9·8	2·0	37·5	9·1
South America	9·4	11·2	6·8	27·4	1·7	2·1	1·2	5·0	11·9
Argentina	1·9	1·2	0·3	3·4	0·3	0·2	—	0·5	3·5
Bolivia	2·7	0·7	0·2	3·6	0·1	—	—	0·1	1·1
Brazil	11·6	20·8	13·4	45·8	2·8	5·0	3·2	11·0	15·8
Chile	11·4	16·5	3·5	31·4	3·3	4·8	1·0	9·1	14·2
Colombia	27·7	13·9	11·7	53·3	6·3	3·2	2·7	12·2	2·6
Ecuador	3·4	2·9	2·3	8·6	2·2	1·8	1·5	5·5	5·0
Guyana	11·2	2·4	2·1	15·7	2·9	0·6	0·5	4·0	16·2
Paraguay	1·4	1·9	1·6	4·9	0·1	0·1	0·1	0·3	2·0
Peru	34·9	3·5	4·0	42·4	3·3	0·3	0·4	4·0	8·4
Surinam	92·1	7·9	5·3	105·3	74·5	6·4	4·3	85·2	9·5
Uruguay	8·5	21·6	3·2	33·3	1·0	2·6	0·4	4·0	20·9
Venezuela	6·9	4·1	3·5	14·5	1·9	1·1	1·0	4·0	6·6
Asia	17·9	7·0	3·7	28·6	8·5	3·3	1·7	13·5	6·4
Afghanistan	1·3	0·7	—	2·0	0·7	0·4	—	1·1	0·9

TABLE 4.11—*continued*

Continent and Country	*Consumption per hectare (kg)*								*Per capita*
	Arable land				*Agricultural land*				*Total*
	N	P_2O_5	K_2O	*Total*	*N*	P_2O_5	K_2O	*Total*	*N*, P_2O_5, K_2O
Asia—*continued*									
Bangladesh	16·0	4·4	1·2	21·6	15·0	4·2	1·1	20·3	2·4
Burma	2·4	0·5	0·1	3·0	2·4	0·5	0·1	3·0	2·0
China	27·2	8·2	3·0	38·4	10·6	3·2	1·1	14·9	6·1
Cyprus	38·5	26·0	5·2	69·7	31·7	21·4	4·3	57·4	47·5
India	10·7	3·5	2·0	16·2	10·0	3·3	1·9	15·2	4·8
Indonesia	19·2	3·7	1·7	24·6	12·4	2·4	1·1	15·9	3·4
Iran	6·7	4·0	—	10·7	4·0	2·4	—	6·4	5·8
Iraq	1·5	0·8	0·2	2·5	1·5	0·8	0·2	2·5	2·3
Israel	80·5	38·1	32·0	150·6	27·1	12·9	10·8	50·8	20·6
Japan	138·4	135·4	113·2	387·0	117·3	114·8	96·0	328·1	19·1
Jordan	1·7	0·5	0·2	2·4	1·6	0·5	0·2	2·3	1·3
Khmer Rep.	0·5	0·6	0·1	1·2	0·4	0·5	—	0·9	0·3
Korea, Dem. People's Rep.	118·7	55·4	16·5	190·6	115·7	54·0	16·1	185·8	24·6
Korea, Rep. of	161·2	74·0	45·1	280·3	160·0	73·4	44·7	278·1	19·2
Laos	0·1	0·1	—	0·2	0·1	0·1	—	0·2	0·1
Lebanon	104·4	47·2	23·7	175·3	101·2	45·7	23·0	169·9	18·7
Malaysia									
Sabah	8·9	5·9	19·1	33·9	8·6	5·8	18·5	32·9	11·4
Sarawak	8·1	5·1	5·6	18·8	7·8	4·9	5·4	18·1	7·5
West Malaysia	26·3	3·4	28·5	58·2	26·0	3·3	28·2	57·5	17·2
Mongolia	0·9	3·1	—	4·0	—	—	—	—	2·3
Nepal	9·1	0·8	1·2	11·1	4·5	0·4	0·6	5·5	1·9
Pakistan	20·1	2·5	0·1	22·7	15·9	2·0	0·1	18·0	6·6
Philippines	10·3	3·6	3·5	17·4	9·8	3·4	3·3	16·5	4·7
Saudi Arabia	1·5	1·0	—	2·5	—	—	—	—	0·3
Sri Lanka	28·7	4·9	17·7	51·3	23·5	4·0	14·5	42·0	7·7
Syrian Arab Rep.	5·6	2·5	0·3	8·4	2·3	1·0	0·1	3·4	7·6
Thailand	4·4	4·0	3·0	11·4	3·9	3·5	2·6	10·0	4·1
Turkey	13·6	8·9	1·0	23·5	7·0	4·6	0·5	12·1	25·2
Vietnam, Dem. Rep. of	5·5	20·8	4·2	30·5	2·8	10·5	2·1	15·4	2·8
Vietnam, Rep. of	47·6	9·5	5·1	62·2	24·9	5·0	2·7	32·6	10·5
Europe	75·3	58·1	56·9	190·3	46·2	35·7	34·9	116·8	58·8
Albania	58·6	37·8	3·6	100·0	26·2	16·9	1·6	44·7	24·7
Austria	80·8	74·9	90·4	246·1	34·9	32·4	39·0	106·3	55·3
Belgium	198·4	177·2	223·7	599·3	105·7	94·4	119·1	319·2	51·8
Bulgaria	78·4	51·0	13·8	143·2	58·7	38·2	10·3	107·2	75·3
Czechoslovakia	87·9	68·3	109·9	266·1	66·2	51·4	82·7	200·3	97·4
Denmark	123·6	53·8	76·4	253·8	111·5	48·6	68·9	229·0	135·4
Finland	67·1	65·3	52·9	185·3	65·9	64·1	51·9	181·9	108·8
France	87·0	107·8	85·6	280·4	50·3	62·3	49·5	162·1	103·5
German Dem. Rep.	134·2	102·7	135·2	372·1	103·3	79·0	104·1	286·4	105·8
Germany, Fed. Rep. of	146·9	111·5	141·8	400·2	88·2	67·0	85·1	240·3	52·8

TABLE 4.11—*continued*

Continent and Country	*Consumption per hectare (kg)*								*Per capita*
	Arable land				*Agricultural land*				*Total N, P_2O_5, K_2O*
	N	*P_2O_5*	*K_2O*	*Total*	*N*	*P_2O_5*	*K_2O*	*Total*	
Europe—*continued*									
Greece	57·8	34·4	5·5	97·7	23·7	14·1	2·3	40·1	39·4
Hungary	75·8	47·8	59·1	182·7	61·6	38·9	48·0	148·5	97·8
Ireland	113·2	175·7	162·0	450·9	27·0	41·9	38·7	107·6	172·4
Italy	56·2	47·4	21·6	125·2	39·5	33·2	15·2	87·9	28·3
Luxembourg	203·1	125·0	125·0	453·1	97·0	59·7	59·7	216·4	84·1
Malta	43·4	1·6	8·6	53·6	43·4	1·6	8·6	53·6	2·3
Netherlands	446·4	120·1	150·4	716·9	177·6	47·8	59·8	285·2	45·2
Norway	99·1	64·3	84·7	248·1	86·6	56·2	73·9	216·7	50·1
Poland	64·6	51·6	84·9	201·1	50·5	40·3	66·3	157·1	91·4
Portugal	33·8	18·9	6·6	59·3	29·7	16·7	5·8	52·2	23·5
Romania	40·1	16·5	4·3	60·9	28·2	11·6	3·0	42·8	30·8
Spain	31·5	22·1	12·2	65·8	19·0	13·3	7·4	39·7	41·0
Sweden	76·8	49·5	44·8	171·1	62·4	40·2	36·4	139·0	63·9
Switzerland	102·1	126·0	172·7	400·8	18·1	22·3	30·6	71·0	24·2
United Kingdom	131·1	65·0	60·2	256·3	50·5	25·1	23·2	98·8	33·0
Channel Islands	144·1	163·7	205·4	513·2	100·9	114·6	143·8	359·3	29·5
Isle of Man	57·5	50·1	26·5	134·1	38·9	33·9	17·9	90·7	50·3
Yugoslavia	41·8	25·0	21·3	88·1	23·5	14·0	11·9	49·4	34·5
Oceania	4·4	26·4	4·4	35·2	0·4	2·4	0·4	3·2	81·6
Australia	3·7	19·7	1·9	25·3	0·3	1·8	0·2	2·3	86·7
Fiji	40·4	10·3	3·4	54·1	28·0	7·1	2·4	37·5	13·8
New Zealand	38·4	419·7	143·9	602·0	2·4	25·9	8·9	37·2	173·8
Papua New Guinea	4·6	2·3	2·3	9·2	3·8	1·9	1·9	7·6	1·6
USSR	24·2	11·1	13·9	49·2	9·3	4·3	5·3	18·9	46·3
World total	24·4	15·3	12·7	52·4	8·0	5·0	4·2	17·2	20·6
Developed market economies	42·3	33·8	26·2	102·3	12·9	10·2	8·0	31·1	54·9
North America	34·1	21·5	17·8	73·4	15·9	10·0	8·3	34·2	74·7
Western Europe	77·0	61·8	53·6	192·4	43·5	34·9	30·3	108·7	52·3
Oceania	4·3	27·0	4·5	35·8	0·4	2·4	0·4	3·2	102·5
Other	57·4	58·9	41·0	157·3	9·3	9·5	6·6	25·4	21·3
Developing market economies	9·9	4·6	2·6	17·1	3·3	1·5	0·9	5·7	6·3
Africa	2·2	1·6	1·1	4·9	0·5	0·3	0·2	1·0	3·1
Latin America	13·3	10·2	6·5	30·0	2·8	2·1	1·4	6·3	12·6
Near East	11·8	5·5	0·5	17·8	3·7	1·7	0·2	5·6	8·3
Far East	13·1	3·9	2·6	19·6	11·5	3·4	2·3	17·2	5·1
Other	6·6	2·1	1·2	9·9	4·2	1·3	0·8	6·3	2·7
Centrally planned economies	30·8	14·9	16·1	61·8	11·1	5·4	5·8	22·3	21·3
Asia	28·0	9·1	3·2	40·3	7·8	2·5	0·9	11·2	6·3
Europe and USSR	32·1	17·7	22·2	72·0	13·3	7·4	9·3	30·0	56·7

(Source: ref. 8).

TABLE 4.12
Export and Farmgate Prices for Different Types of Fertiliser in Major Exporting Developed Countries

	Approximate West European export prices	*Farmgate prices* France	Germany, Fed. Rep.	Austria
		(US $ per tonne)		
Sulphate of ammonia				
1971/72	—	55·02	67·62	59·85
1972/73	85·00	63·00	74·76	83·16
1973/74	100·00	80·01	92·82	94·92
1974/75 (1st half)	170·00	79·59	n/a	91·14
1975 (April)	143·00	111·11	126·52	n/a
Urea				
1971/72	131·00	n/a	144·44	130·18
1972/73	162·00	n/a	159·62	161·46
1973/74	200·00	n/a	197·80	n/a
1974/75 (1st half)	368·00	164·68	182·16	178·94
1975 (Feb.)	339·00	206·00	238·00	n/a
1975 (May)	250·00	—	—	—
Triple superphosphate				
1971/72	115·00	70·38	144·44	111·32
1972/73	155·00	78·20	161·00	150·88
1973/74	300·00	92·00	222·18	180·62
1974/75 (1st half)	380·00	n/a	n/a	n/a
1975 (Feb.)	328·00	n/a	n/a	n/a
1975 (May)	240·00	n/a	n/a	n/a
Muriate of potash				
1971/72	60·00	57·00	63·00	57·00
1972/73	80·00	67·20	72·60	76·80
1973/74	90·00	83·40	90·60	77·40
1974/75 (1st half)	150·00	n/a	n/a	n/a
1975 (May)	150·00	n/a	n/a	n/a

(Source: UN WFC/8, 19 May, 1975).

attitude that has been adopted by the OPEC countries. Potash deposits are plentiful and potash is unlikely to be cartelised, but because of the location of the deposits developing countries will continue to need to import then and to pay for them in scarce foreign exchange.

As we shall see in Chapter 12 the FAO is making strenuous efforts to increase the quantities of fertiliser that are available to farmers in developing countries. The task will not be easy. As Table 4.12 shows, in the period from 1971/72 to 1975, prices for ammonium sulphate rose by 68 %, for urea by 91 %, for triple superphosphate by 109 % and for muriate of potash by 150%. In this inflationary situation it is very difficult for poor countries with few exploitable resources to increase the volume of their imports of materials they cannot manufacture for themselves.

The problem may be reduced through current research that is directed toward finding alternatives to present fertilisers—especially nitrogen—and through more efficient use. The FAO has no doubt about the importance of this work:

'In the short run chemical fertilisers constitute the most important single weapon in the the food production battle. The per hectare use of these nutrients in most developing countries is at present only one-quarter, often less than one-tenth, of what it is in most developed countries; it is especially low in Africa. Nevertheless, fertiliser consumption in developing countries has been doubling every five years and is expected to continue growing at 11% per year over the next decade. This rate of increase could be advantageously accelerated provided that supplies will be available at reasonable prices.

'However, fertiliser prices have trebled and quadrupled between 1971 and 1974 and at the moment there is a world-wide physical shortage. Developing countries depend on imports from developed countries for at least half their requirements, and the difficulties of the current supply situation prompted governments to agree, at the FAO Council's Session in July 1974, to the setting up of an International Fertilizer Supply Scheme including a Fertilizer Pool and other arrangements to assist developing countries in covering their minimum requirements. In the longer run massive expansion of fertiliser production capacity in developing countries is foreseen as necessary so that levels of fertiliser use become high enough to take full advantage of the HYVs and the envisaged extensions to irrigation.

'Even so, because fertiliser prices, relatively to other prices, are likely to be higher than in the past it may become important to examine how far fertiliser requirements per hectare are capable of being reduced through improved methods of formulation and of application . . .'.[3]

The 'physical shortage' was caused by a shortage of production capacity in the developed countries, caused in turn by inaccurate forecasting of demand. By itself the problem can be resolved in a year or two. However, if the rise in prices causes farmers in the developed countries to be more economical in their use of fertilisers, then demand will increase at a slower rate in the manufacturers' home markets and there will be less incentive for them to increase their output. In such a situation, prices would remain high through the simple supply–demand mechanism, and farmers in developing countries would find it no easier to increase consumption. Much more is needed, and we will consider this later when we look at the structure of world trade patterns.

REFERENCES

1. Delwich, C. C. (1970). The nitrogen cycle, in *The Biosphere:* Readings from *Scientific American*. W. H. Freeman, San Francisco.
2. Buringh, P., van Heemst, H. D. J. and Staring, G. J. (1976). *Computation of the Absolute Maximum Food Production of the World*. Agricultural University, Wageningen, The Netherlands.
3. FAO (1974). *Assessment of the World Food Situation*. UN WFC E/Conf. 65/3, Rome.
4. Revelle, R. (1963). Water, in *Plant Agriculture:* Readings from *Scientific American*. W. H. Freeman, San Francisco.
5. Kuenen, P. H. (1955). *Realms of Water*. Cleaver-Hulme Press, London.
6. McCulloch, J. S. G. (1975). Hydrology—the science of water, *NERC News Journal*. Natural Environment Research Council, London, November.
7. *Statistical Supplement No.* 10. The British Sulphur Corpn, London, November–December 1974.
8. FAO (1973). *Annual Fertilizer Review*. Rome.
9. Cooke, G. W. (1972). *Fertilizing for Maximum Yield*. Crosby Lockwood, London.
10. Bierhuizen, J. F. (1973). The effect of temperature on plant growth, development and yield, in *Plant Response to Climatic Factors*. UNESCO, Paris.
11. Cruikshank, J. G. (1972). *Soil Geography*. David and Charles, Newton Abbot, UK.
12. Penman, H. L. (1970). The water cycle, in *The Biosphere:* Readings from *Scientific American*. W. H. Freeman, San Francisco.

Chapter 5

HUNTERS AND FARMERS

Man may have existed in his modern form for 100 thousand years and the genus *Homo* may date back 2 million years. For no more than 10 or 12 thousand years he has obtained his food from farming domesticated species of plants and animals. For the very large part of his tenancy of this planet, man has lived by hunting wild animals and gathering wild plants, and farming is a recent innovation.

PLANT DOMESTICATION

It was believed at one time that the cultivation of more or less domesticated plants began in a limited number of areas and then spread by a process of cultural diffusion, as peoples moved away for whatever reason and encountered other peoples, to whom they imparted their knowledge of agriculture. It seems now that this theory is inadequate to explain what in fact occurred. At various places and at various times, different crop plants began to be grown deliberately by man. The peoples involved were usually isolated from one another and although the process of cultural diffusion must have occurred, it did so independently in different parts of the world, at different times and in respect of different groups of plants.

We can only speculate about why people began to grow crops in the first place. They did so in areas where suitable species grew wild in profusion. This ample genetic source was necessary to provide the raw material for early experiments. Yet if wild food was so plentiful why should people have gone to the trouble to cultivate that which they could obtain simply by gathering it? We cannot know, but it seems unlikely that the natural germination of spilled seed and seed thrown into middens would have stimulated sufficient curiosity to lead to its regular and organised sowing. Observations of such natural chance germination might have provided the clues needed to instruct pre-agricultural peoples, and they might have experimented, but the wild food supply still remained in fierce competition.

It is at least possible that the availability of such large quantities of food enabled populations to expand locally. As this happened villages would become larger until they became administratively unwieldy. Among many peoples, when this happens, some of the tribe leave the village and set up a daughter community some distance away. Since the most favoured sites for settlements would be close to the food supply, they would be occupied first, and as more and more daughter communities were established, their members would find themselves having to travel ever further to obtain their food. At some stage in this development, cultivation might well become more convenient than the long trek to and from the wild stands. At that point the observation that the most preferred plant species were growing naturally close to the new village, where they had not grown before, would be useful. The incentive to farm would be still greater if quarrels between the daughter and parent settlements made the collection of wild foods difficult.

This theory gains plausibility from our present experience with fish farming, which represents the domestication of a number of new animal species as sources of food. We will examine this in much more detail later, but the development of fish farming is very dependent on the market price for fish that is caught by traditional methods. As this becomes more expensive, and the fish themselves have to be sought further away from the areas in which they are eaten, it begins to become profitable to breed and raise the fish in captivity. It is not impossible that the day will come when all the fish we buy is supplied by farmers, rather than hunters.

The great Russian botanist, Nikolai Ivanovich Vavilov, discovered a number of sites, throughout the world, where relatives of modern crop plants are to be found in great genetic profusion and often in dense stands. He found it was possible to mark these areas on a map and he called them 'Centres of Diversity'. They are the areas, or centres, within which the largest number of species and sub-species of a particular plant are found. He deduced from this that the cultivation of these crops had begun in or close to the centres of diversity and so his centres of diversity were also, in his view, the centres of the origin of agriculture. The concept is over-simplified but it is elegant in its simplicity. Vavilov argued that the selective forces of the environment operate in roughly the same manner throughout the history of any species. Therefore the longer a species inhabits any particular area the greater the number of genetic variables it will produce. The centres of diversity, then, must be the sites from which the species originated, because it is there that the greatest genetic variation is found.[2]

Unfortunately for his theory, Vavilov also discovered what were clearly centres of diversity for cultivated plants very far removed from their nearest wild relative. His Ethiopian centre, for example, contains a whole range of crops in great genetic profusion, but none of them has a wild relative anywhere in that part of Africa. Vavilov modified his theory to take account of primary and secondary centres. Primary centres are those where domestication first took place; secondary centres are those in which great genetic variation affected species that were introduced by agricultural peoples.

No matter how the diffusion of crops comes to be explained, what is clear is that the basic genetic material for all the crop plants that are cultivated throughout the world today is contained in a limited number of areas. We will see the true significance of this when, in Chapter 7, we consider the genetic base of modern farming.

Figure 5.1 shows the location of Vavilov's centres of diversity. There are eight main centres and three lesser ones. Centre 1, in China, contains the naked oat (*Avena nuda*) in a secondary centre, soybean (*Glycine hispida*), adzuki bean (*Phaseolus angularis*), the bean (*P. vulgaris*) in a secondary

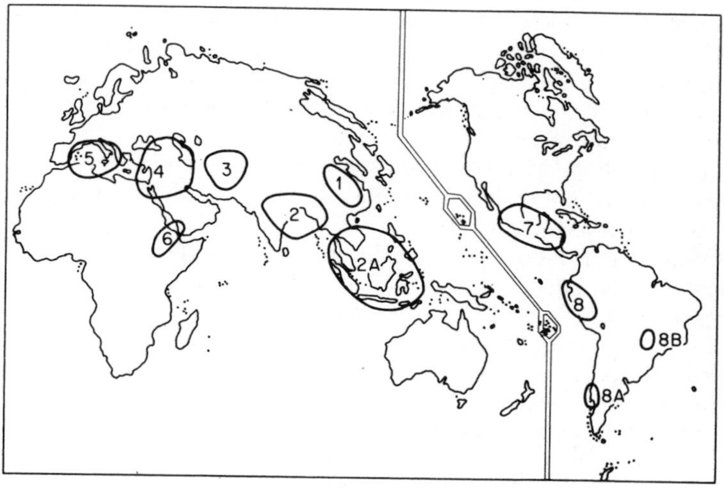

FIG. 5.1 Centres of diversity (after N. I. Vavilov).

centre, small bamboos (*Phyllostachys* spp.), leaf mustard (*Brassica juncea*) in a secondary centre, apricot (*Prunus armeniaca*), peach (*P. persica*), orange (*Citrus sinensis*), sesame (*Sesamum indicum*) in a secondary centre and China tea (*Camellia* (*Thea*) *sinensis*).

Centre 2, in India, contains rice (*Oryza sativa*), African millet (*Eleusine coracana*), chick pea (*Cicer arietinmum*), math bean (*Phaseolus aconitifolius*), rice bean (*P. calcaratus*), horse gram (*Dolichos biflorus*), asparagus bean (*Vigna sinensis*), egg plant (*Solanum melongena*), rat's tail radish (*Raphanus caudatus*), Taro yam (*Colocasia antiquorum*), cucumber (*Cucunis sativus*), tree cotton (*Gossypium arboreum*), jute (*Corchorus olitorius*), pepper (*Piper nigrum*) and indigo (*Indigofera tinctoria*).

Centre 2A, in north east India and Malaysia, contains the yam (*Dioscorea* spp.), pomelo (*Citrus maxima*), banana (*Musa* spp.) and coconut (*Cocus nucifera*).

Centre 3, in Central Asia, contains bread wheat (*Triticum aestivum*), club wheat (*T. compactum*), shot wheat (*T. sphaerococcum*), rye (*Secale cereale*) in a secondary centre, pea (*Pisum sativum*), lentil (*Lens esculenta*), chick pea (*Cicer arietinum*), sesame (*Sesamum indicum*), flax (*Linum usitatissimum*), safflower (*Carthamus tinctorius*), carrot (*Daucus carota*), radish (*Raphanus sativus*), pear (*Pyrus communis*), apple (*P. malus*) and walnut (*Juglans regia*).

Centre 4, in the Near East, contains einkorn wheat (*Triticum monococcum*), durum wheat (*T. durum*), poulard wheat (*T. turgidum*), bread wheat (*T. aestivum*), two-rowed barleys (*Hordeum vulgare*), rye (*Secale cereale*), red oat (*Avena byzantina*), chick pea (*Cicer arietinum*) in a secondary centre, lentil (*Lens esculenta*), pea (*Pisum sativum*), blue alfalfa (*Medicago sativa*), sesame (*Sesamum indicum*), flax (*Linum usitatissimum*), melon (*Cucumis melo*), almond (*Amygdalus communis*), fig (*Ficus carica*), pomegranate (*Punica granatum*), grape (*Vitis vinifera*), apricot (*Prunus armeniaca*) and pistachio (*Pistacia vera*).

Centre 5, in the Mediterranean region, contains duram wheat (*Triticum durum*), hulled oats (*Avena strigosa*), broad bean (*Vicia faba*), cabbage (*Brassica oleracea*), olive (*Olea europaea*) and lettuce (*Lactuca sativa*).

Centre 6, in Ethiopia, contains durum wheat (*Triticum durum*), poulard wheat (*T. turgidum*), emmer wheat (*T. dicoccum*), barley (*Hordeum vulgare*), chick pea (*Cicer arietinum*), lentil (*Lens esculenta*), teff (*Eragrostis abyssinica*), African millet (*Eleusine coracana*), pea (*Pisum sativum*), flax (*Linum usitatissimum*), sesame (*Sesamum indicum*), castor bean (*Ricinus communis*) and coffee (*Coffea arabica*).

Centre 7, in Central America, contains corn (*Zea mays*), the common bean (*Phaseolus vulgaris*), pepper (*Capiscum annum*), upland cotton (*Gossypium hirsutum*), sisal hemp (*Agave sisalana*) and a range of squashes and gourds, including the pumpkin (*Cucurbita* spp.).

Centre 8, in South America, contains the sweet potato (*Ipomoea batatas*), potato (*Solanum tuberosum*), lima bean (*Phaseolus lunatus*), tomato (*Lycopersicum esculentum*), sea island cotton (*Gossypium barbadense*), papaya (*Carica papaya*) and tobacco (*Nicotiniana tabacum*).

Centre 8A, in southern Chile, contains the potato (*Solanum tuberosum*).

Centre 8B, which straddles the Brazilian–Paraguayan border, contains manioc (*Manihot utilissima*), peanut (*Arachis hypogaea*), cacao (*Theobroma cacao*), in a secondary centre, rubber tree (*Hevea brasiliensis*), pineapple (*Ananas comosa*) and purple granadilla (*Passiflora edulis*).[2]

Vavilov was examining cultivated plants rather than wild ones. If we wish to discover where agriculture began we would do better to locate those parts of the world where wild relatives of cultivated plants are found. This has now been done with a number of crops, although it is notoriously difficult because of the readiness with which cultivated plants that escape revert to wild varieties. It seems, though, that possibly after a long period of experimentation and innovation, agriculture was first practised around 7000 BC in both the Old and New Worlds.

Wheat and barley were probably domesticated in the hilly country surrounding the Syrian–Mesopotamian plains in an arc that stretches from Kuzestan in Iran, through the Western Zagros, the Tauros of Turkey and eventually to the Southern Jordan hills near the Dead Sea rift.[3] Several different wild wheats and barleys were cultivated in different parts of the region and they cross-bred with one another and with wild varieties.

In the New World the first plants to be cultivated were of no great dietary importance. The cucurbits—squashes, gourds and pumpkin—were domesticated in the Tehacan Valley of Mexico by 7000 BC, but it was not until perhaps a century or two BC that maizes and beans in their cultivated forms were providing significant amounts of food. In Peru a number of food plants were domesticated by 2500 BC but sea food provided most of the day-to-day diet. Again, it was not until a few centuries BC that cultivated maize, beans, manioc, peanuts, potatoes and sweet potatoes were contributing significantly to the diet.

As the cultivated plants were taken further and further from their places of origin they were accompanied by their own peculiar patterns of weeds. This was due partly to movements of contaminated seeds but much more to the habit of a dominant species to determine the structure of the rest of the ecosystem of which it is part. Each plant species competes more or less successfully with every other species that is able to survive under similar soil and climatic conditions. Thus crops would tend to become infested with weeds of a generally similar kind wherever they were grown, although there would be local differences in weed species.

J. R. Harlan[3] has defined cultivated, weed and wild species. A cultivated species is one that is grown by man deliberately, a weed is a species that is well adapted to conditions in an environment disturbed by man, and a wild species is one that grows quite independently of man or his activities and is not much affected by them. In some cases the domestication of one race or species encouraged or even necessitated the domestication of others. Rye (*Secale cereale*), for example, probably occurred first as a weed of wheat. It proved so intractable that eventually the proto-farmers more or less abandoned the growing of wheat and cultivated the rye instead.

These very early crops were rather different from modern varieties that are the result of very many generations of breeding by man. Crop breeders simulate the processes of natural selection by imposing environmental stresses in order to collect the seed of individual plants that bear characteristics regarded as desirable. Today the wild relatives of cultivated plants sometimes occur as particularly noxious weeds among farm crops. *Aegilops squarrosa*, for example, is a wild wheat that is common in the South Caspian area and Iran and that spreads into Eastern Turkey and Western Iraq, Pakistan and Kashmir and into parts of Soviet Central Asia. In South Iran, South Afghanistan and parts of Pakistan, however, it occurs mainly as a weed among cultivated wheat. Wild einkorn wheat (*Triticum boeticum* or *T. aegilopoides*) is found in Western Asia and *Ae. speltoides*, a wild wheat grass, is common in the Eastern Mediterranean area, though it is not so widespread as einkorn. Wild emmer (*T. dicoccoides* and *T. araraticum*) is found in Israel, Jordan and Syria and to the north, in Turkey, Georgia and Armenia.

Domestication of animals

The Brothwells[1] have compiled records of animal remains from archaeological sites in four different regions of the world to show, at least for these communities, the composition of the diet. In New England, USA, 11 species of carnivore were being eaten, including the grey wolf, wild dog, foxes, bears and seals, 3 species of rodent and 4 species of deer and horse. In Borneo there were also 11 species of carnivore, including mongoose and several cats, 5 species of rodent, including squirrels and porcupines, wild pig, 3 species of deer, cattle or buffalo, elephant and 7 species of primate, including the orang-utan. In Teshik-Tash, USSR, 3 species of carnivore were being eaten, 10 species of rodent, goat and deer and horse. In Isamu Pati, in Africa, between AD 900 and 1300, 6 species of carnivore were being eaten, including leopard and lion, 3 species of rodent, buffalo, pigs and a total of 14 species of artiodactyla, zebra, rhinoceros and elephant.

Obviously not all of these species have been, or could be, domesticated. Our present range of domestic livestock should not be regarded as final, however. Throughout history there must have been many experiments designed to increase the variety and these experiments continue. In parts of Africa eland have been farmed, several deer species are being studied to this end in the USSR, in Britain the red deer may soon become a familiar farm animal in upland areas and in the USA the bison has been crossed with cattle to produce the 'beefalo', a hybrid animal intended primarily for beef production. It is very likely that in ancient Egypt the striped hyena was bred in captivity for food, and cranes, which also appeared on Egyptian menus, may also have been tamed. At various times people have regarded the hedgehog as highly palatable. Has anyone ever tried to farm hedgehogs? They may have done.

Animals that are domesticated today have all been eaten at one time or another and although their main use may have been as scavengers and hunting associates, in the case of dogs, pest controllers, in the case of cats, or beasts of burden, in the case of horses, asses and camels, all have been eaten when times were hard. It will be recalled that Roald Amundsen, Capt Robert Scott's rival in the race to the South Pole, advised Scott to use dogs rather than motor vehicles because in extreme hardship the dogs could be eaten.

The dog was almost certainly the first animal to be domesticated. A wall painting, dated at about 5800 BC, shows a hunter with a dog in Anatolia and there are suggestions that dogs may have been domesticated in Europe in Mesolithic times, with one positive dating at about 7500 BC. Dogs probably appeared in the New World much later, possibly as late as 500 BC. Wild dogs, scavenging in the vicinity of human settlements, must have grown accustomed to close contact with humans that led eventually, and probably with a good deal of random mating between tame and wild specimens, to a symbiotic relationship in which the dog assisted the hunter in return for a guaranteed food supply.

Pigs probably came next and were used exclusively for food. Probably hunting parties would bring back the orphaned litters of wild sows they had killed and these young animals would have been fattened in captivity. It is still common among some Papuan peoples to suckle young pigs with human milk, and this close contact would encourage animals to become tame and humans to permit them to survive until sexual maturity.

There are records of domesticated sheep from Iraq that date back to about 9000 BC, where lambs were killed in large numbers for meat and skins, and by 2000 BC there were a number of domesticated breeds in the Near East.

It is difficult to tell goats from sheep, when the evidence consists of no more than a few bones, but there is clear evidence of the existence of domesticated goats in the Near East by 6000–7000 BC, and by the third millenium BC there were several different breeds.

All animals in their domesticated form differ from their wild ancestors. The pig can still be compared with the wild pig, which has a distinctly different appearance and build. The original wild sheep must have been even more different to look at because the coat of the animal has changed. The wild sheep had a thin woolly undercoat over which there was a hairy outer coat. In the course of domestic breeding the outer coat has been lost and the inner coat has increased in thickness to become the modern fleece.

It is possible that all domestic cattle are descended from a single ancestor, *Bos primigenius*, the aurochs, which became extinct in the seventeenth century AD. The doubt exists because a short-horned variety has been identified and given the name *B. longifrons*, and throughout Africa and Asia humped, or 'zebu', cattles are common, descended from *B. namadicus*. It may be, then, that originally there were three species of cattle in Pleistocene times, all of which were domesticated separately. On the other hand, *B. namadicus* and *B. longifrons* may both be descended from the common ancestor, *B. primigenius*. It is certain that *B. primigenius* became very common throughout Europe in Pleistocene times, while *B. namadicus* seems to have a longer history in that remains have been found that antedate the European ones. Both *primigenius* and *namadicus* were domesticated by 2500 BC.

All modern breeds of cattle are much smaller than the aurochs and there has been much speculation about the reason for this reduction in size. It may result from no more than repeated selection by early farmers. As they found it more convenient to enclose cattle to provide a constant supply of meat and possibly of milk, they may well have chosen the smaller individuals from the wild herds. The aurochs was a very large, fierce and unpredictable animal, comparable to the wild African buffalo. Distinctly it was a creature that had to be treated with some respect. The British Chillingham herd of longhorns have been allowed to run feral since Roman times and were not even enclosed until the thirteenth century. Their behaviour now is probably very similar to that of the aurochs, and they will not permit humans to approach them. Interestingly they do not subsist exclusively by grazing, as do domestic cattle, but browse on leaves during the summer, conserving the pasture for winter consumption, when the bushes and low trees are leafless. The repeated selection of small individuals, probably stragglers, to provide the breeding population might well have resulted in new, smaller varieties of tame animals.

The Romans domesticated the rabbit and hare and also the edible dormouse (*Glis glis*).

Cattle were milked from about 3000 BC and in addition to cow's milk, the milk of sheep, goats, camels, mares, reindeer, elks, asses and yaks has been used where these animals have been tamed.

So far as is known, South American mammals were not milked. Indeed few species were domesticated at all. The llama was used mainly as a beast of burden and the vicuña was used for its wool, but the main source of meat was the guinea pig. It is still used in the Andean region as a meat animal.

Fewer birds have been domesticated and birds were not a very important part of the diet of hunting peoples, probably because those that fly are far too difficult to catch. The ostrich was in use in Egyptian times as a provider of eggs, and pelican eggs may also have been eaten. Our own domestic hens are descended from red jungle fowl (*Gallus gallus*) that lived in Northern India. They were domesticated by the time of the Indus Valley civilisation and they appeared in Egypt by the fourteenth century BC. Guinea fowl, from North Africa, had reached Greece by the fifth century BC.

The farming of fresh water fish was established in the Near East by Assyrian times, and from very early times in China, South East Asia, Russia and in North America, based on species that were available locally and considered good eating.

Crop cultivation preceded livestock farming, but once both had begun they developed together. They gave rise to quite different lifestyles. Agricultural peoples were rather sedentary, living in fairly permanent settlements. In the early stages they would not have been entirely permanent because early crop growing must have been based on swidden, or slash-and-burn systems.

The swidden farmer begins by burning off the surface vegetation after he has felled the trees and slashed down bushes. The burning cleans the surface and deposits on it a layer of ash to supply potassium fertiliser. He sows his crop on the cleared ground and goes on cultivating this ground, season after season, until either crop yields are declining or the area is colonised by weeds and returning wild plants to such an extent that further cropping is impossible. Then he moves on to a new site and begins all over again. Among different peoples there are different cultural methods for determining the year in which the tribe must move. Among some, for example, young tree saplings are regarded as sacred. On no account must they be harmed, although mature trees may be felled. So an area of forest can be cleared but recolonising trees that are allowed to grow freely will eventually make further cultivation impossible.

The system is very subtle and in terms of the amount of work required to produce the crop it is highly efficient. It is also sustainable indefinitely provided it is not required to do too much. As soon as the nutrient stored in the soil has been used, and before permanent damage can be done, cultivation ceases and the land is left to recover, usually for several years. Each tribe has a number of sites and moves every few years from one to the next, in time returning to its starting place. It is only when the human population exceeds the productive capacity of the system that farmers may be compelled to take steps to increase their crop yields or, more frequently, may be barred from one or more of their sites by the proximity of other tribes practising a similar form of agriculture. In this case they will have to return to each site before it has recovered fully. So each time it is cropped there will be a deterioration in the soil that is never repaired and great harm may be done.

Livestock farmers, on the other hand, had a much easier life but frequently a nomadic one. They became dependent on the grasslands and had to follow their herds and flocks as they grazed. At times they, too, practised slash-and-burn methods, usually to clear forest and scrub and to allow grasses to flourish. The repeated Bronze Age burning of forests has been well documented, in the case of English heathlands,[4] by pollen analyses that have made it possible to reconstruct past ecosystems that can be dated fairly accurately. Trees were felled and then burned and the emerging grasses were grazed by livestock, which also browsed the foliage on the scrub that returned with the grass. Thus the regeneration of the forest was prevented and the pattern of species changed. Those trees survived that could establish themselves quickly, and in general these were not the deep-rooting species. Then the trees vanished altogether and hazel became the dominant woody species. At about this stage, forest clearings began to be cultivated by swidden farmers. When the farmers abandoned their small fields the soil was podsolising, turning into the acid, ash-coloured, sandy soil typical of such areas today. Once begun the deterioration seems to have proceeded quite quickly, as what was once rich, mixed deciduous forest was turned into a heather and bracken desert.

Where pastoralists and agriculturalists found themselves competing for land, conflicts often resulted. The biblical story (Genesis 4) of Cain and

Abel may record such a conflict. Abel was the pastoralist, Cain the crop farmer. Both offered their produce to God, who accepted Abel's gift but not Cain's. Cain slew Abel and was punished by a curse. No man must harm him, but henceforward his crops would fail with great regularity. Cain went away to the Land of Nod, where he founded a city that he named after his son, Enoch.

The fact is that the nomadic or semi-nomadic life of the pastoralist was easy and pleasant but it could not provide the constant supply of food in one place that was necessary before a settled people could allow their population to increase. Pastoralists could not feed a city culture; farmers could. So it was Cain, the farmer, who built the city of Enoch—and eventually Jerusalem, London and New York—not Abel. It was necessary that the conflict be resolved in Cain's favour but the loss of a gentler, less arduous, less property-conscious way of life was to be regretted. So God cursed Cain but at the same time protected him.

Lewis Mumford has a theory[5] that the old paleolithic hunting culture never disappeared entirely and that once neolithic settled agriculture became established, the hunters returned to offer it military protection and became a separate caste of aristocrats and warriors. If Mumford is right, the killing of Abel takes on additional significance. Had he not been killed—had that aspect of palaeolithic culture not been excised—the hunter-turned-pastoralist might have returned to dominate and perhaps to destroy the new civilisation.

Even today there are in the world nomadic peoples who hate cities and the culture they represent, and it is interesting to note that when the conflict returned in colonial North America, our own culture recorded the exploits of the cowboys—the hunter–pastoralists–warriors–but not the duller, more stable activities of the farmers. Yet in every sense it is the farmers who are the more important and in very recent times the term 'cowboy' has come to be applied in a pejorative sense to those who enter an area, exploit its resources for their own gain and with little regard for the physical or social environment, then leave.

'HIGH' FARMING

Land could continue to support cropping reliably, year after year, only if ways could be found to restore nutrients and to maintain soil structure. In certain of the great river basins, not far from the centres where agriculture originated, nature assisted this process of soil replenishment. Where rainfall is seasonal, as it is throughout the sub-tropics and in the latitude of the Mediterranean region, rivers are liable to flood during the rainy season. In their lower reaches, the floodwater carries a rich load of silt, scoured from the lands upstream, and this silt is deposited on the surface of the flood plains and left behind when the floods recede. So a system of settled agriculture becomes sustainable where crops can be grown during the warm, sunny, dry season on soil enriched annually by silt. The annual flooding of the Nile supported the agricultural system that fed ancient Egypt and, as we saw earlier, the construction of the Aswan Dam to control the floodwater has deprived farmers of the silt and made it necessary for them to rely on chemical fertilisers.

In the Fertile Crescent of Mesopotamia and in the Indus Valley, sophisticated irrigation systems were built that regulated the flow of water, so extending the area of cropland. This was a form of high technology and it supported populations as dense as those in modern Europe until, eventually, it failed due to waterlogging and salination, probably for want of maintenance of the drainage channels.

In the wet rice growing areas of Asia, paddy fields were developed that are still in use today. Fields spend part of the year as ponds, surrounded by low walls that hold the floodwater from the river. Rice seedlings are planted in the mud as the water receded. The fertility of the soil is enhanced further by the use of every kind of organic waste, including human excrement, which is returned to the land. In terms of the amount of food produced for every unit of energy expended in growing it, wet rice farming is by far the most efficient method for producing food ever devised.

The modern Chinese have exploited their knowledge of irrigation systems to considerable effect with crops other than rice. In the Chiliying Commune, for example, situated in an arid alluvial plain in Honan Province, between 1957 and 1973, the proportion of the cultivated area that is irrigated increased from 29 to 91 %, and yields of food grains between 1948 and 1973 from 0·6 to 8·25 tonnes per ha (these are official figures from the Chinese People's Republic). Yields of cotton rose in the same period from 187·5 kg per ha to 1·16 tonnes per ha, in a commune that farms 6200 ha of land.

Increases of this order are due to more than good irrigation, of course. Improved seed, better pest and weed control, a degree of mechanisation and, most of all, the total revision of the system of land tenure, have all played a part. None the less, the figures are impressive and they show the very high yields that can be achieved by this kind of high farming without extensive use of fertilisers and other materials dependent on advanced industrial technologies. In 1973/74 the average yield for wheat in the nine EEC countries was 3·82 tonnes per ha and the average maize yield, maize being the heaviest cereal crop, was 5·52 tonnes per ha.[6]

Knowledge of hydrology is necessary for the management of very productive farming systems developed in both Old and New Worlds. Perhaps it found its most sophisticated expression in the chinampas of Mexico, still managed today but on a greatly reduced scale, in much the same way as they were in the days of the Aztec emperors, when according to Aztec records they produced tribute of 7000 tons of maize, 4000 tons of beans and other foods as well as large quantities of cotton, and fed a capital city (Tenochtitlán-Tlatelolco) with a population well in excess of 100 000 and possibly approaching half a million.

Father Acosta, the Spanish priest who wrote about the Aztec Empire in 1590, described the chinampas as 'floating gardens'. They did not float, but his mistake is understandable for it must have looked as though they did.

The valley of Mexico, in which the Aztec and the modern capital (on the same site) are located, is a high land-locked basin surrounded by mountains. In the wet summer season, five lakes used to flood and inundate a quarter of the total area of almost 8000 km^2. In the swampy south of the valley, the water table was higher than the level of the open Lake Xochimilco, and drainage channels were dug that drained the swamp and permitted the natural springs that fed the swamp to feed into the lake and from there into the deeper Lake Texcoco, further north. The mud removed in digging the canals was heaped on the surface between them to create raised islands and peninsulas.

These 'chinampas' developed as areas of raised land, surrounded by water on at least three sides, each about 90 m long by about 5–9 m wide. The sides of the chinampas were fortified with wattle fences which were often replaced in time by growing willow trees. The canals were dredged regularly to keep them open and the sediment deposited on the chinampa surface. What Father Acosta may have seen were the large rafts of water weed that are towed to the chinampas and also placed on the surface. Thus each 'garden' has its own compost heap made from a layer of water weed, topped with mud from the canal bottom or soil from old chinampas that had grown too high. During the wet season the plots retain sufficient moisture, but during the dry season they must be watered.

Seeds are germinated in special nurseries, where each seed is sown in a square of dried mud, made by spreading canal sediment over a layer of water weed, allowing it to dry in the sun, then cutting it into squares, called chapínes. When the seeds have germinated, the young plants are set out, still in their chapínes.

Since there was no external outlet from the valley, the mineral salts carried down by the summer rains and then concentrated by the evaporation of the surface water would have destroyed the whole system within a few years, were it not for the constant supply of fresh water fed from underground springs. By the fourteenth century these were no longer sufficient, owing to the expansion of the city and of the area of cultivated land that fed it, and so impressive aquaducts were built to carry fresh water from other springs, further away. In the fifteenth century, probably owing to a slight change in climate, flooding of the chinampas by saline water became an acute problem and this, too, was solved by Aztec engineers, who built a dyke 16km long to enclose the chinampas in a fresh water lagoon.[7]

This entire system of farming used no chemical fertilisers or pesticides, no fuels and no implement more elaborate than a digging stick.

Impressive drainage and irrigation systems were built in Europe, too, especially in eastern England and part of Somerset, England, where low-lying peat bogs were drained by mediaeval monks, but most of all in The Netherlands. Most of Holland lies close to or below sea level and the maintenance of the dikes has been of major national importance throughout Dutch history. Traditionally each farmer held his land only so long as he took part in maintaining his particular section of dike. When he became too old or too sick to continue with this arduous work, he left his shovel on top of the dike wall. A younger man with no land of his own could then take up the shovel and move into the farm.

Both the Chinese and the Mexicans combined their hydrological farming with fish culture, using the flooded fields or canals to breed and fatten fish. In the Middle Ages, European monks also used ponds to store and fatten fish that were eaten on Fridays, when the eating of red meat was forbidden. The name 'Fishpond' still survives in many places in England, although the pond itself disappeared many years ago. This was not true fish farming, for fish were not normally bred in fishponds, only stored there.

In Europe, livestock and arable farming were merged quite early. This meant on the one hand that meat formed a much more important part of the European Diet than it did of the Chinese or Mexican diets, while on the other hand, cattle were used as beasts of burden. This made it possible to use heavier implements, including larger ploughs.

Ploughs probably developed from the digging stick, and the Egyptians were using ploughs by 3500 BC. Babylonians had ox-drawn ploughs, combined with seed drills, by about 1300 BC, the Egyptians used them, and the Greeks based their ploughs on Egyptian models. Egyptian drawings show how digging sticks were adapted to make long-bladed hoes, the metal-tipped curved blade being attached by thongs to a handle of nearly equal length. The hoe was used in a chopping motion and with a rather more robust construction and a larger frame it was very similar to the early plough.[8]

Roman ploughs were more diverse, being adapted to varying conditions and soils, and the Anglo-Saxons used much larger ploughs, pulled by eight oxen. In parts of Southern Europe, the Near East, India, other parts of Asia and South America, the plough did not advance much beyond the early Egyptian models. These primitive ploughs simply scratched the surface and did not turn the soil over. Mouldboard ploughs, that undercut and turn the furrow over, came later, although probably they were being used by the Romans.

The Anglo-Saxon farming system was based on strips of land, each about 20 m wide and about 200 m long, growing arable crops and grass in a simple rotation that allowed the land to lie fallow while it recovered. The eight-oxen ploughs made deep furrows for sowing cereals and also helped with drainage.

By Tudor times the fertility of the land was declining. The introduction of sheep into the rotational system made better use of the pasture, returned some manure and made many fortunes. There are countless English towns and villages that were built, or that have buildings that were erected, out of the profits of the wool industry that thrived from the fifteenth century.

Farmers had still not succeeded in solving the most serious problem associated with mixed livestock and arable farming in a temperate climate, however, which was how to feed animals during the winter. Animals continue to eat during the part of the year when plants do not grow. Surplus stock had to be slaughtered in the autumn, leaving little more than a basic breeding population to be fed from limited pasture, hay and such surplus grains as there were during the long winter months.

Eventually the problem was solved in North West Europe, and the techniques on which that solution was based were introduced into eastern England in the eighteenth century. Knowledge of them spread, although rather slowly, until most of Britain had adopted what was called the New Husbandry.

The New Husbandry included in the farm rotation root crops that could be harvested and used for winter feed, and the plant used most widely was the turnip. Lord Townshend, a wealthy landowner, who introduced the new rotation on his farms and encouraged others to do the same, earned himself the nickname 'Turnip' Townshend.

The rotational system on which the New Husbandry was based was called the Norfolk four-course. It consisted of roots, barley undersown with grass, grass, then wheat in a four-year cycle. It started with the root crop, which was heavily dunged with animal manure, leaving the land well manured and free from weeds for the barley which followed. As the barley grew, the grass grew beneath it, so that when the grain was harvested to feed humans and animals a temporary pasture, called a 'ley', was already established. The following spring, animals were turned out to graze the pasture and hay crops were also taken. In the autumn, when the grass was finished, the land, enriched by the mat of fine grass roots that improved the structure of the soil, and dunged by the manure from the animals that had grazed it, was ploughed up and sown to winter wheat, the 'hungriest' crop in the rotation.

As this classical rotation became more widespread, so farming reached levels of productivity that were higher than they had ever been before. Some people even go so far as to suggest that in the eighteenth and early nineteenth centuries, British yields for cereals were higher, on average, than modern yields. It is difficult to say whether in fact this was so, for records were sparse and often inaccurate. Indeed one of the principal aims of agricultural reformers was to persuade farmers to keep records of their production and of the ways in which the fields had been treated. However, wheat yields of 2 tons to the acre (about 5 tonnes per ha) were reported sufficiently frequently for them to have been fairly common on the very best farms.

At the same time, this rotation was actually improving the fertility of the soil. All previous systems of farming had tended to deplete it, even though the depletion had taken many centuries to become evident. Impressed by the success of these new, more advanced methods, the wealthier farmers did all they could to encourage smaller and less prosperous farmers—many of whom were their own tenants—to follow their example. In the nineteenth century most of the county agricultural societies were formed, mainly to exhibit and promote 'scientific' farming, a role they have not quite lost to this day, with their livestock sections dominated by keen competition for prizes, and sometimes with associated competitions in ploughing and other rural crafts and skills. It was this development that paved the way for the 'industrialisation' of farming that took place in the second half of the present century, during which time the classical four-course rotation has been abandoned almost entirely.

That British farming did not advance more rapidly that it did during the late nineteenth and early twentieth centuries is due to the long period of depression that was caused by the repeal of the Corn Laws in 1846. This reform deprived farmers of any kind of economic protection and opened the British market to produce from all over the world. By the 1890s, and the completion of the colonisation of North America and Australasia, and the invention of methods of refrigeration that made it possible to ship fresh meat over long distances, Britain was flooded with cheap farm produce with which its own farmers could not compete. Agriculture became deeply and chronically depressed, recovering only during the two world wars, when shipping routes were partially blockaded.

The traumatic experience of World War II, which Britain entered very unprepared and with an agriculture characterised by abandoned and semi-derelict farms, bankrupt farmers and unemployed farmworkers, led the post-war government to initiate an agricultural support policy that encouraged investment and expansion in the industry. Thus the modern phase of agricultural growth can be dated from the late 1940s.

Although European agriculture was protected during the long period when British farmers were exposed to the vagaries of world markets, two wars fought over their lands did not permit farmers to modernise to the extent that they might have done. So, for somewhat different reasons, the modern development of continental farming can also be dated from the beginning of the postwar period.

In the next chapter we look more closely at the effects and implications of the recent industrialisation of food production.

REFERENCES

1. Brothwell, D. and Brothwell, P. (1969). *Food in Antiquity*. Thames and Hudson, London.
2. Zohary, D. (1970). Centers of diversity and centers of origin, in Frankel, O. H. and Bennett, E. (eds), *Genetic Resources in Plants: Their Exploration and Conservation*. IBP Handbook No. 11.
3. Harlan, J. R. (1970). Evolution of cultivated plants, in Frankel, O. H. and Bennett, E. (eds), *Genetic Resources in Plants: Their Exploration and Conservation*. IBP Handbook No. 11.
4. Dimbleby, G. W. (1965). The origin and use of heath soils, *J. Soil Ass.*, **13**(6), 473 and **13**(7), 569.
5. Mumford, L. (1961). *The City in History*. Penguin, Harmondsworth, UK.
6. MAFF (1974). *EEC Agricultural and Food Statistics*. Ministry of Agriculture Fisheries and Food, London.
7. Coe, M.D. (1964). The chinampas of Mexico, *Scientific American*, W. H. Freeman, San Francisco, July; reprinted in *Plant Agriculture*, 1970, W. H. Freeman.
8. Partridge, M. (1973). *Farm Tools Through the Ages*. Osprey, Reading, UK.

Chapter 6

FARMS AND FACTORIES

Comparisons made between modern farming and the more primitive methods of obtaining food that preceded it tend to compress a process that has been developing over 10 or 12 thousand years. Any compression of such a long period of history is bound to lead to gross distortions and none can be grosser than to imagine that the productivity of farming systems has increased in some kind of regular fashion, so that it might be possible to estimate the position of a civilisation on this steady curve simply by measuring the yields of its crops. The truth is that, historically, more agricultural systems have collapsed than have survived, and that the present phase of agriculture in the developed countries is less than half a century old and is based on scientific knowledge acquired not much more than a century ago.

The problems that face farmers today are not new and even the solutions to them have parallels in the approaches adopted by earlier peoples. Where we rely on sophisticated technologies the civilisations of the Fertile Crescent of Mesopotamia and of the Indus Valley, not to mention the chinampa farmers of Mexico, relied on similarly sophisticated techniques of water management to husband the resource that was limiting their levels of production. Where we have come to use fossil fuel energy in the form of machines and agricultural chemicals partly as a substitute for trained farmworkers, so the Romans used slaves as a substitute for members of farmers' families. As some people in our society deplore the use of machines and our dwindling labour force, so Roman writers deplored the rather similar changes they saw taking place in their own farming, and they described them in words that have a familiar ring today.

Columella, for example, in his *De Re Rustica*, attributed the decline in Roman agricultural productivity partly to the introduction of slave labour to manage the estates of the Roman nobility and partly to the starvation of the soil caused by the failure to return manures to it. Roman efforts to maximise short term gains by indulging in farming systems that were exploitive were made simpler by the substitution of slaves for the farmer and his family, which encouraged the appearance of a system dominated by absentee landlords who neither saw what was happening to their land nor cared much, since their status was based on the possession of land rather than on the use to which that land was put. In the end this 'mining' of the fertility of the soil proved ruinous, not only in Italy but in much of North

Africa and other parts of the Mediterranean area as well. Victor Hugo is alleged to have said that 'the fertility of Sicily went down the sewers of Rome'.

It may not be over-fanciful to imagine that the decline in the productivity of its agriculture played a part in the final collapse of Rome as a military and political power. It is very expensive to defend long supply lines that continue to grow as the metropolis demands commodities that have to be brought over longer and longer distances. Once these arteries are severed, sooner or later the heart must die.

There arose from the old Roman farming system a pattern of peasant farms that still persists. A rule of inheritance that requires land to be divided into smaller and smaller lots as it passes from one generation to the next, ensures that the peasants are always poor, but it also ensures that they utilise the resources available to them with great ingenuity. Thus the steep and generally dry and infertile farmlands of most of Italy have been terraced, laboriously, to minimise erosion, and wastes of all kinds have been returned to the land. Now it seems that history may be about to repeat itself, because attempts to improve the material prosperity of the peasants have encouraged the mechanisation of Italian farming. Tractors cannot work the steep terraces except by moving directly up and down them, so the terraces are systematically broken down. This process is bound to accelerate the erosion of the top soil and, if it continues, the productivity of Italian farmers will be reduced rather than increased, while the pollution of the rivers from leached nutrients and silt will increase. The fertility of Italy may be draining into the Mediterranean.

Modern concepts of agriculture date from the work of nineteenth century European chemists, who discovered that the beneficial effect of returning manures to the land arose from the chemical composition of those manures, which supplied growing plants with the range of simple salts they require. At the same time they enunciated another principle that ecologists realised later (at the time there were no ecologists, of course) had profound implications within their own discipline: if species require for their sustenance a limited range of chemical substances, then the size of their populations will be limited by the availability of the least abundant of those substances.

The British Association for the Advancement of Science invited the eminent German chemist, Baron Justus von Liebig, to summarise the work in this field, as a result of which von Liebig wrote his *Organic Chemistry in its Application to Agriculture and Physiology*. Von Liebig was an extremely opinionated, egotistical man and in his book he summarised all the relevant research, included those conclusions with which he agreed, and then claimed that all the work was his own. His own evaluation of himself came to be accepted and so, conventionally, von Liebig is credited with formulating the theories that led eventually to the development of chemical fertilisers in their modern form.

Somewhat later, in 1885, he wrote another book, *Principles of Agricultural Chemistry with Special Reference to the Late Researches Made in England*, in which he announced 50 principles regarding the nutrient requirements of plants, the relationship between nutrient availability, plant growth and soil fertility, and the need for bulky organic manures to supply the soil with the structure that permits aeration, the free percolation of water and the development of plant root systems. The concept is purely chemical; no one took account then of the role played by soil micro-organisms not simply in the decomposition of organic matter but more directly in nutrient availability: the existence of such microscopic organisms was barely suspected, far less understood. The over-simplification is revealed when von Liebig sums up his 50 principles, quite mechanistically, by saying they are all contained in one principle:

'...namely, that the nutrition, the growth, and the development of a plant depend on the assimilation of certain bodies, which act by virtue of their mass or substance. *This action is within certain limits directly proportional to the mass or quantity of these substances, and inversely proportional to the obstacles or to the resistance which impede their action*'.[1]

This suggests that it is possible to calculate accurately the increase in yield of a crop that will result from the application of a given quantity of a particular fertiliser under given conditions. While this may be true in a laboratory, the extreme variability of local conditions, both in space and time, ensures that instinct and guesswork retain their traditional roles in farming practice. Mistakes can be costly both economically and in their effects on the environment.

The production of fertilisers on an industrial scale and, rather later, the great and then rapid increase in the use of machines to replace horses and to perform a wide range of farm tasks, was made posssible by the prior existence of an expanding urban industry using cheap and plentiful sources of fuel: first wood, then coal, then oil and natural gas.

So the sequence was that a prosperous agriculture generated capital for investment in industry, and industrial growth generated still more capital for reinvestment in the industrialisation of farming.

In the late eighteenth and early nineteenth centuries, British agriculture was very prosperous. Mediaeval farming, based on long strips of land in a fairly open landscape of large fields surrounded by forest, had depleted the fertility of the land. The fallow periods were insufficient to permit the complete restoration to the soil of nutrients removed by cropping and the system was running down, when, in Tudor times, there was a major increase in sheep farming. The need for more pasture and the symbiotic relationship between livestock and the land led to a recovery, and many landowners became very wealthy indeed from the profits of the wool trade. Then that system, too, began to decline.

In the eighteenth century, progressive English landowners imported new ideas from Holland. These required that the land be enclosed in smaller fields and that enterprises be integrated, so that the ideal farm produced a wide range of arable and livestock products. All the crops, including grass in the more fertile areas, were rotated, so that each crop visited each field once every four years or so. In the last chapter we saw that the New Husbandry, promoted by the agricultural societies, brought considerable benefits.

There were heavy social costs, however. The enclosure of what had been common land deprived the rural working population of an important source of wild food, for themselves and for their livestock, and of fuel, leading to extreme hardship in many cases. It must be remembered that the English countryman is not a peasant, owning his own small patch of land from which he aims to feed himself and his family, but a landless labourer, working for wages. So living conditions became very harsh and many people left the land to find work in the expanding towns.

In many cases the appalling conditions of life in industrial urban areas in the nineteenth century—the conditions described by Mayhew and Marx—were preferable to rural conditions at the same time. This pattern of relative urban prosperity and relative rural poverty, all contained within a context of living conditions that are generally very low and within which there is a very wide disparity between rich and poor, is characteristic of a society that is industrialising. In varying degrees it was observed throughout Europe during the early part of the industrial revolution and today it is found in many developing countries.

The low living standards and the dependence of farmworkers on a cash income were exacerbated by very high food prices, blamed at the time on the Corn Laws, which permitted farmers and merchants to store food in order to force up prices, and to sell abroad if foreign prices were better than those obtaining in the domestic market.

Since the mid-eighteenth century, and despite any improvements in yields that may have occurred, Britain had been a net importer of wheat. Again the situation is analogous to that found in many developing countries today. The population was increasing in numbers and in prosperity. This created an obvious rise in the demand for staple foods, but quite soon a threshold was crossed that led to a sudden jump in demand. In this case the new, more expensive food was not meat but white bread. Since classical times white bread had been a luxury food item reserved for the wealthier classes in society. A small increase in incomes brought it within reach of many more people and demand increased, probably for reasons of prestige as much as for its greater palatability. Milling techniques at the time removed about 20% of the whole grain in order to make a white flour. Modern white flour uses only about 70% of the whole, a rate of extraction made possible by milling techniques that were not introduced until later. The by-products—mainly the husk (bran) and germ—are not wasted. They are fed to livestock or, nowadays, sold to human consumers at high prices for their health-giving properties. This dietary shift increased the demand for grain.

Even so, the quantities of wheat that were imported remained small until well into the nineteenth century, suggesting that rising demands were being met by dramatic increases in production. Statistics from that period are very incomplete but it seems fairly certain that the second threshold, into grain-fed meat consumption, occurred much later. During the early years of the nineteenth century it is possible that meat consumption fell.[2]

The blockade of Britain imposed by Napoleon, beginning in 1806, made farmers even more prosperous, and it was reinforced by the Milan Decree, which declared that any ship trading with Britain could be seized lawfully by the French. A series of cold winters and wet summers depressed yields and by 1812 the price of wheat reached 29s 6d a hundredweight, a price that was not reached again until 1952! After the war, however, the depression that lasted from 1818 to 1822 caused prices to fall sharply and led to much hardship. In 1795, magistrates at Speenhamland, in Berkshire, had devised a scale that related the price of bread and the size of families to a minimum income. If a worker was paid less than this minimum, he might apply to the parish for an income supplement. Once the postwar depression began to bite, these allowances kept agricultural wages down to the barest minimum, and by 1830 they had pauperised large areas of rural England.[2] The allowances were abolished in 1835, by which time the price of wheat had fallen to 9s 2d a hundredweight.

While wheat prices had been high, poor people had come to depend more and more on potatoes as a staple food. In Chapter 7 we shall look more closely at the narrow genetic base that led to the events of 1845 and 1846, but for the moment it is enough to record that those were the years of the Irish Potato Famine. It was not only Ireland that was affected, however. The potato crop failed throughout the British Isles. It is simply that it was in Ireland that the effects were felt most severely. Grains held in store were not released to relieve the famine because of the effect this would have had on prices, and the pressure to repeal the infamous Corn Laws became irresistible. They were repealed in 1846, having been on the statute book for 31 years.

John Burnett[2] suggests that the effect of the Corn Laws was exaggerated. They forbade the import of wheat until the home prices stood at 80s a quarter (one quarter is eight bushels, or 480 pounds) or more, but in order for them to have held prices artificially high we must assume that other European countries had surpluses of wheat they could have exported. This is far from certain and even if they had the cost of transporting them would have increased their price to at least that of British wheat, and probably more. If this analysis is correct the repeal may have removed protection from farmers before it had any real influence.

If the Corn Laws themselves had little effect, neither did their repeal.

Europe was divided by wars, and the North American continent was still being opened up, while the United States themselves were torn by the dissent that led to the Civil War of 1861–65. The third and final expansion of the American frontiers took place between 1840 and 1890 and was accompanied by the building of rail links between the middle west and the eastern seaports. In 1867 the invention of Reece's freezing machine prepared the way for the transport of meat over long distances, while in Australasia British migrant farmers were cultivating vast areas of land and preparing to export food to their homeland.

In Britain there was a series of crop failures that ended in 1879, but had increased the price of wheat to a peak of 10s 10d a hundredweight in 1878. So home-grown food was expensive and there was no economic protection against the import of cheap food. Suddenly the cheap food began to arrive, grown on huge continents where land was cheap and production costs low. By 1894 the price of British wheat had fallen to 5s 4d a hundredweight and agriculture was deeply depressed.

While it is possible to trace the progress of wheat prices from the beginning of the nineteenth century to provide a guide to the state of the market for the most important single food crop, it is very difficult to adjust the prices not simply for the inflation that has occurred from time to time, reducing the value of money itself, but also of changes in public taste and so in the relative importance of different items within the economy. There is a further check, however, in the estimates made every year of the total area of land sown to arable crops. These are traced in Fig. 6.1. From a high level around 1870 the graph shows a steady decline in cultivation until World War I. The war served only to interrupt the trend temporarily, however, and it resumed with the postwar depression. Wheat prices had risen during the war, from 7s 5d a hundredweight in 1913 to a maximum of 17s 8d in 1917. By 1939 they were down to 5s a hundredweight and British farming was at rock bottom. Then World War II increased dependence on home-grown food and the cultivated acreage increased rapidly. In the depression that followed the ending of the Napoleonic War, farmers said they needed another war to help them. The record of the twentieth century seems to support this view.

After World War II, wheat prices continued to rise but probably they did so at less than the general rate of inflation, so that in real terms it was likely that farmers would find themselves poor once again. Also the labour force that had been augmented by the Women's Land Army and by the use of pacifists, prisoners-of-war and internees, was depleted as these temporary farmworkers returned to their peacetime occupations and homes. So the area of cultivated land began to fall again and apart from small fluctuations from one year to another it continued to fall until 1955. Then it began to increase again to a level at which it has more or less stabilised. In 1974 the total area of arable land under cultivation in the UK was 17 677 thousand acres (7153·88 thousand ha). This figure cannot be shown on the graph because data from Northern Ireland were not included in earlier figures, so that the present UK figures are not directly comparable. In June 1975, the total area of arable land in England and Wales was 13 555 thousand acres (5486 thousand ha).

In most countries, farmland is being lost to urban development, to road building programmes, for airports and for the countless other apparent

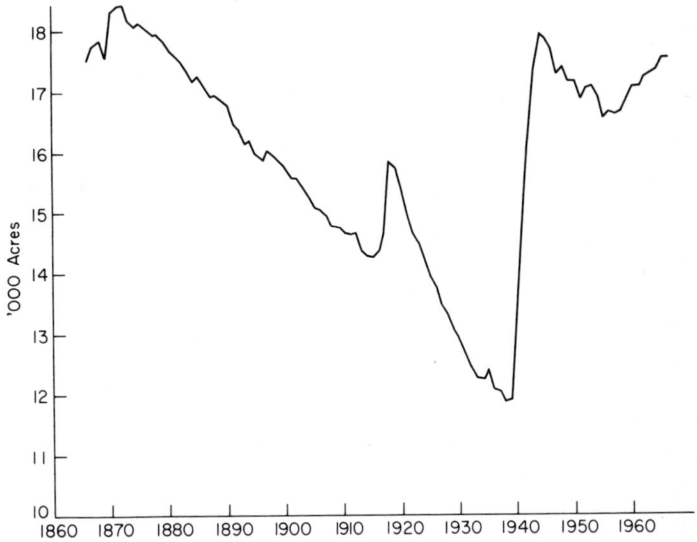

FIG. 6.1. Area of arable land in Great Britain, 1866–1966 (Source: ref. 11).

necessities for modern life. The actual rate of loss in the UK is a source of some controversy but a guess can be made from the figures in Table 6.1. Between 1963 and 1965 there were an average of 18 372 thousand acres (7435·15 thousand ha) under arable cultivation. That figure is the highest in the table, but the difference between it and the lowest figure for 1974 is only 4%. Some of this land, perhaps much of it, was lost to the increasing area occupied by farm buildings and roads. If their areas are added, the difference disappears. Indeed, apart from a small drop in 1973, the area of arable land plus farm building has actually increased each year.

It would be premature to assume from this, however, that urban expansion is eating only an insignificant amount of farmland, because during the same period the total area of rough grazing also declined. Rough grazing land was being improved to make good pasture and good pasture was being ploughed up and sown to arable crops. Thus the net loss of rough grazing should represent a gain somewhere else. That it does not do so

TABLE 6.1
Crop Areas and Livestock Numbers (at June of each year)[a]

	Average of 1963–65	1970	1971	1972	1973	1974	1974 *metric equiv.*
A. Crop areas (thousand acres)							(thousand hectares)
Total area	48 602	47 255	47 234	47 045	46 920	46 974	19 010
wheat	2 223	2 495	2 710	2 786	2 831	3 046	1 233
barley	5 047	5 542	5 654	5 653	5 603	5 471	2 214
oats	1 145	929	896	777	695	624	253
mixed corn	84	196	137	150	126	104	42
rye	20	11	16	16	13	11	5
maize	—	—	3	5	3	3	1
Total cereals[b]	8 519	9 174	9 416	9 386	9 271	9 260	3 747
potatoes	762	669	634	584	555	532	215
sugar beet	440	463	471	468	480	482	195
oilseed rape	—	10	13	17	34	61	25
hops	21	17	18	17	17	16	7
vegetables grown in the open	376	505	452	441	462	480	194
orchard fruit	210	160	154	146	141	136	55
soft fruit[c]	50	45	45	45	45	44	18
ornamentals[d]	34	37	36	38	40	38	16
Total horticulture[e]	670	751	690	674	694	704	285
Total tillage[f]	11 548	12 088	12 139	12 021	11 905	11 955	4 838
temporary grass[g]	6 824	5 700	5 718	5 825	5 798	5 722	2 316
Total arable	18 372	17 788	17 857	17 846	17 703	17 677	7 154
permanent grass	12 292	12 217	12 172	12 132	12 143	12 157	4 920
rough grazing[h]	17 938	16 537	16 501	16 342	16 320	16 220	4 564
other land[j]	—	712	704	725	753	920	372

B. Livestock numbers (thousand head)						
Total cattle and calves	11 762	12 581	12 804	13 483	14 445	15 227
dairy cows	3 192	3 244	3 234	3 325	3 436	3 402
beef cows	1 004	1 300	1 378	1 476	1678	1 889
heifers in calf	767	863	831	954	988	1 049
Total sheep and lambs	29 637	26 080	25 981	26 877	27 943	28 639
ewes	11 899	10 544	10 422	10 668	10 921	11 213
shearlings	2 516	2 263	2 263	2 438	2 733	2 673
Total pigs	7 406	8 088	8 724	8 619	8 979	8 621
sows for breeding	754	794	862	832	859	791
gilts in pig	154	159	121	128	156	107
Total poultry	116 231	143 430	139 016	140 045	144 079	139 957
table fowls (incl. broilers)	28 649	49 783	49 730	50 933	58 366	56 781
laying fowls[k]	50 772	55 237	53 705	53 831	51 766	50 130
growing pullets	26 967	24 599	22 465	21 678	18 808	18 958

[a] The coverage for 1973 and 1974 includes all known holdings in the UK with 40 standard man-days or more (a standard man-day (smd) represents 8 h productive work by an adult male worker under average conditions). All holdings with less than 40 smd in Scotland are excluded; in England and Wales and Northern Ireland, holdings with less than 40 smd are excluded only if they have less than 10 acres of crops and grass and no regular whole-time worker. The same criteria applied in Great Britain in the years 1970–72 except that the threshold for standard labour requirements in those years was 26 smd; prior to 1970, the figures related to all known agricultural holdings exceeding 1 acre in extent. The figures for Northern Ireland, before 1973, related to holdings of 1 acre or more, except for numbers of livestock which were collected from all owners irrespective of the size of the holding as well as from landless stockholders. The introduction of the changes of definition in Northern Ireland in 1973, following similar changes in Great Britain (which excluded some 14 000 statistically insignificant holdings in 1970 and about 8000 in 1973), resulted in the elimination of about 6000 or so holdings from the Northern Ireland census.

[b] For threshing.

[c] Includes small area of soft fruit grown under orchard trees in England and Wales.

[d] Hardy nursery stock, bulbs and flowers.

[e] Most of the difference between total horticultural area and the sum of individual sectors is made up by the glasshouse area.

[f] Includes acreages of other crops and bare fallow not shown in the table.

[g] Includes lucerne.

[h] Includes common rough grazings.

[j] Returns of 'other land' were collected for the first time in England and Wales in June 1969. From June 1969 to June 1973 'other land' in Great Britain was collected as woodland and areas under roads, yards, buildings, etc., the use of which was ancillary to the farming of the land; in Northern Ireland it included land within agricultural holdings which was under bog, water, roads, buildings, etc., and waste land not used for agriculture. In June 1974 the definition was changed in England and Wales to include all other land forming part of the holding and in Scotland it was extended to include ponds and derelict land. The Northern Ireland definition is unchanged.

[k] Figures for years earlier than 1964 are for fowls 6 months old and over in Great Britain and 5 months old and over in Northern Ireland.

(Source: ref. 10)

suggests that arable land was also being lost. If all the figures for the area of farmland are totalled (arable land, plus permanent grass, plus rough grazing, plus farm buildings and roads) it appears that between 1970 and 1974 there was a net loss of some 280 000 acres (113 320 ha) of farmland or a rate of loss of about 28 000 ha (70 000 acres) a year.

It may be, of course, that rough grazing land is being lost directly to urban expansion and that the better quality farmland is being conserved. Unhappily this is unlikely, despite repeated demands and assurances that good farmland will not be taken out of the food producing system if development can be directed to inferior land. By and large the rough grazing is in the uplands, in areas that town dwellers think of as remote. History works against the UK farmers, for the fact that the uplands are remote is only another way of saying that their ancestors built towns on fairly level lowlands, in the bottom of valleys, on the better land close to the farms that supplied their food. Attempts are made nowadays to find development sites that have less agricultural value, but not to the extent of building new towns in the Pennines or in the Scottish Highlands.

So improvements in farming have made it possible to compensate for losses to urban development. How have they achieved this? The two Agriculture Acts, of 1947 and 1957, provided farmers with a degree of stability they had not known for a century or more. The aim was to encourage agriculture to expand and the Acts approached the problem with a complex system of support. Minimum prices were guaranteed for the main commodities, in some cases with deficiency payments should market prices fall below the guaranteed level. Subsidies were introduced to help farmers to buy some of their materials, such as fertiliser and lime. Grants were paid toward a wide range of capital improvements. Each year the price guarantees and rates for subsidies and grants were adjusted, after consultation between the Ministry of Agriculture, Fisheries and Food and the National Farmers' Union.

The system was far from perfect and by the time it was dismantled, to enable Britain to adjust to the support system that operates within the EEC, it had become very intricate indeed. The main weakness of any system of this kind is that it must predict how much of each commodity will be produced and consumed in the coming year. It may seek to predict production either by setting quotas, as was done with potatoes and partly with milk, or simply by multiplying the acreage sown to a particular crop by the average yield. In either case, and despite the most sophisticated statistical modelling, the result is largely a guess, and guesses are often wrong. The error can be embarrassing, as it was when the acreage that was calculated early in 1975 to be sufficient to supply the country's potato requirements in 1975/76 failed to take account of the drought that occurred later in 1975, or it may be expensive, as it was during the early 1950s, when yields of arable crops rose more rapidly than had been anticipated, leading to lower market prices and consequently to very large deficiency payments that had to be made by the exchequer.

In spite of its shortcomings the system did succeed in stimulating investment in agriculture. Between 1956 and 1969 the annual formation of gross fixed capital in UK agriculture increased from £94 million to £208 million, calculated at constant prices.[3] Most of the technology was not new. The principle of fertiliser use had been known for half a century at least and many farm machines had been on the market since before the war, but until the late 1940s most farmers simply could not afford to buy them. Farming began to mechanise and to 'chemicalise'. Figure 6.2 shows how the number of tractors on British farms has increased, while the labour force has decreased. The comparison is necessarily crude, for the tractor is only one kind of farm machine, but at least it is the machine that is used on farms of all kinds. It is easier to count tractors than it is to compare combine harvesters with milking machines! The disadvantage is that over-simple conclusions may be drawn.

The tractor replaced the working horse, so that its effect on the human labour force was to release workers who previously had tended horses, while its dependence on fossil fuel energy released the land that previously had been needed to grow the energy requirements of the horses. It is difficult to argue, on any grounds, that this was not a major advance. For some tasks the tractor is far more versatile than the horse had been and it is much stronger, but for other tasks it has been replaced by more specialised machines. At present there are more tractors on British farms than there are workers employed (not counting the farmers themselves).

Table 6.2 shows how the size of the labour force has changed and it includes figures showing the size of the contribution from the Women's Land Army and from prisoners of war. It can be seen that in 1966 the labour force was less than half the size it had been in 1921, but that while the fall between 1921 and 1955 was about 27 %, an average of about 0·8 % a year, the fall from 1955 to 1966 was about 35 %, an average of 3·2 % a year. So although the size of the labour force fell throughout the entire period the rate at which it fell accelerated from about 1955. This, as we saw earlier, was the year when arable acreages began to increase again. Agriculture was becoming more capital-intensive and labour was being displaced.

There are lessons here for countries that seek to follow the western pattern of agriculture. Heavy capitalisation increases the cost of food production and so increases the cost of each work place, every worker being supported by an expensive array of machines. Thus the labour force declines and unless there is an industrial sector in the national economy that is expanding rapidly, rural unemployment is bound to become a serious problem.

In Britain this shift of labour out of agriculture was encouraged by keeping wages low and hours long. Tables 6.3 and 6.4 show average earnings

TABLE 6.2
Numbers of Agricultural Workers in Great Britain, 1921–1966 (in thousands)

Year	England and Wales				Scotland				Great Britain			
	total	regular whole-time	part-time	seasonal and casual	total	regular whole-time	part-time	seasonal and casual	total	regular whole-time	part-time	seasonal and casual
1921	869	685		184	127	104		23	996	789		207
1922	—	—		—	125	102		22	—	—		—
1923	772	625		147	120	101		19	892	726		166
1924	806	645		162	117	100		17	924	745		179
1925	803	639		164	122	102		20	925	742		184
1926	795	654		141	126	103		23	921	757		164
1927	774	650		125	119	102		18	894	751		142
1928	773	651		122	117	101		17	890	751		139
1929	770	644		126	118	101		17	888	745		143
1930	742	630		112	116	99		16	857	729		128
1931	717	616		100	112	97		15	829	714		115
1932	697	598		100	111	97		14	809	694		114
1933	716	596		120	112	96		16	828	692		136
1934	688	576		112	113	97		16	801	673		128
1935	673	568		105	113	98		16	787	665		121
1936	641	547		94	111	96		15	751	643		108
1937	632	536		96	111	95		16	742	631		112
1938	593	513		80	104	91		13	697	604		93
1939	607	511		96	104	90		14	711	601		110
1940	608	502		106	104	87		17	712	588		124
1941	650	508		141	110	94		16	759	602		157
1942	708	541		167	115	100		16	824	640		183
1943	719	543		177	124	102		22	843	644		199
1944	741 [a]	589 [a]		151	122	101		21	863	690		173

1946	774	643		131	115	96		19	889	739		150
1947	777	645		132	115	94		21	891	739		153
1948	741 [a]	592 [a]		149	109 [b]	90 [b]		19 [b]	849	682		168
1949	749	595		154	107	90		17	855	685		171
1950	737	582		155	105	88		17	843	670		172
1951	708	554		154	104	88		16	812	642		171
1952	702	534		168	102	85		18	804	618		186
1953	683	520		163	96	80		16	780	600		179
1954	658	505		152	97	78	7	12	755	583		172
1955	639	479	79	81	93	76	7	10	732	554	86	91
1956	610	455	75	80	90	73	7	10	700	528	83	90
1957	607	448	79	80	90	72	7	10	696	520	86	90
1958	591	432	73	85	88	71	7	11	679	503	80	96
1959	585	425	72	88	85	69	7	9	669	493	79	97
1960	562	406	72	84	83	67	7	8	645	473	80	92
1961	535	384	63	88	82	66	8	9	617	449	71	97
1962	513	368	60	85	76	62	7	7	589	430	67	92
1963	496	357	59	81	73	60	7	7	569	416	66	87
1964	476	333	61	82	68	56	6	6	544	389	67	88
1965	451	313	58	80	64	52	6	6	514	365	64	86
1966	430	295	54	81	58	47	6	5	488	342	60	86

[a] England and Wales: includes

	Women's Land Army*	Prisoners of War
1944	47 861	25 273
1945	43 124	57 763
1946	23 017	82 686
1947	17 682	78 734
1948	16 492	11 411
1949	11 210	—
1950	6 824	—

[b] Scotland: Prisoners of war were not returned separately prior to December 1954. Includes

	Women's Land Army*		Prisoners of War	
	regular	casual	regular	casual
1946	1 659	590	4 620	4 060
1947	1 163	602	4 442	1 548
1948	868	372	—	—
1949	615	264	—	—
1950	354	152	—	—

* A minority of the WLA were part-time, seasonal or temporary agricultural workers.
(Source: ref. 11)

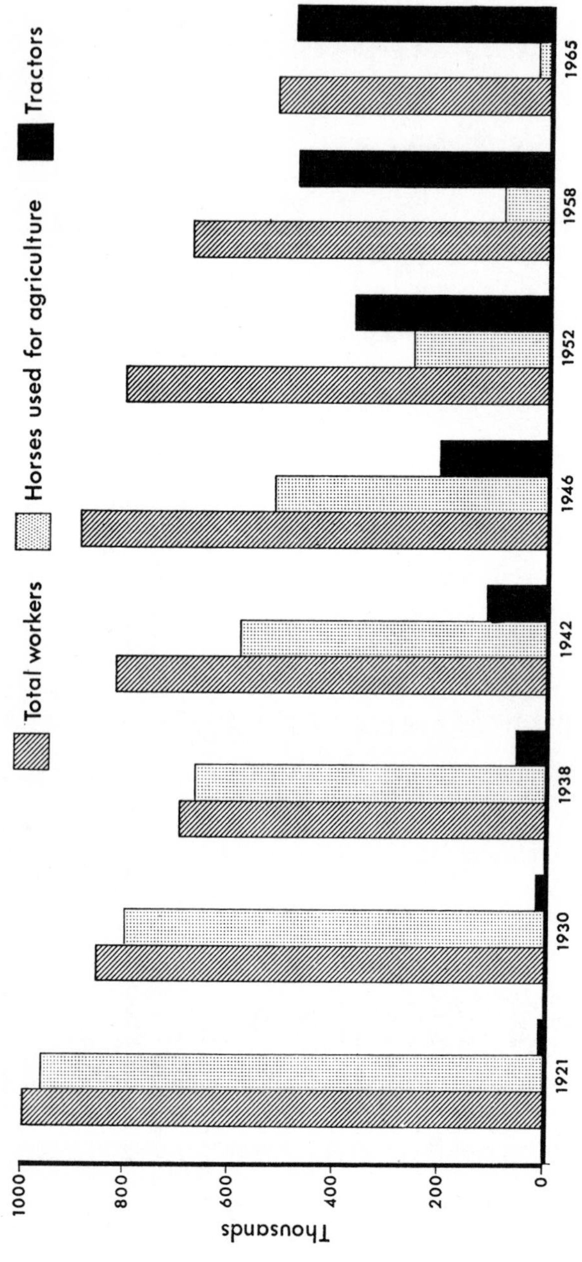

FIG. 6.2. Labour, horses and tractors in Great Britain, 1921–65 (Source: ref. 11).

TABLE 6.3
Estimated Annual Average Contract Wages and Total Earnings of Hired Regular Whole-Time Men (England and Wales)

Years ending 30 *Sept.*	*Minimum wage per week*		*Contract wage per week*		*Total earnings per week*		*Total earnings index* 1945/46 = 100	*Total hours*[a] *per week*	*Index of Retail Prices*[b] 1946 = 100
	s.	d.	s.	d.	s.	d.			
1945/46	72	2	82	9	88	9	100	53·1	100
1946/47	80	10	92	0	96	6	109	51·4	106
1947/48	90	0	100	10	106	5	120	51·4	114
1948/49	92	2½	103	4	109	9	124	51·1	117
1949/50	94	0	106	1	112	10	127	50·9	120
1950/51	99	4	111	6	119	4	134	51·0	132
1951/52	108	1½	120	7	129	6	146	51·4	143
1952/53	113	9½	127	7	136	10	154	51·2	148
1953/54	120	0	135	3	146	9	165	51·6	151
1954/55	124	10	141	10	157	7	178	52·5	157
1955/56	132	8	151	11	166	8	188	51·6	165
1956/57	141	0	160	10	179	8	202	52·1	171
1957/58	149	4	171	1	189	0	213	51·8	177
1958/59	155	7	177	9	198	10	224	52·1	177
1959/60	158	5	183	2	203	9	230	51·3	179
1960/61	166	8½	192	5	216	3	244	51·2	185
1961/62	172	7	201	9	224	5	253	51·0	193
1962/63	181	9	212	0	239	4	270	51·7	197
1963/64	189	1	223	7	253	4	285	51·2	203
1964/65	198	10½	237	3	265	9	299	50·0	231
1965/66	207	11½	251	8	285	6	322	50·1	221

[a] Basic hours plus contractual and non-contractual overtime.
[b] Calendar years up to the December following the end of the periods stated in column 1.
(Source: ref. 11)

and hours of work for farmworkers in England and Wales and in Scotland, respectively. Although wages increased, indeed they trebled between 1945 and 1965, it was not until the late 1950s that they began to increase significantly faster than the index of retail prices, and throughout the period they rose more slowly than did wages in factory-based industries. Hours remained long. There was every incentive, therefore, for workers to move into the towns, to better paid, easier jobs, and better working conditions.

TABLE 6.4
Estimated Annual Average Contract Wages and Total Earnings of Hired Regular Whole-Time Men (Scotland)

	General workers					*All hired men*[d]	
Year (June/May)	*Minimum wage per week*	*Contract wage per week*	*Total earnings*		*Total hours per week*	*Total earnings*	
			per week	*index*[c]		*per week*	*index 1945/46 = 100*
	s. d.	s. d.	s. d.			s. d.	
1945/46	70 0	—	81 4	100	—	86 0	100
1946/47	76 11	—	86 7	106	—	92 5	107
1947/48	85 11	—	95 7	118	—	102 6	119
1948/49	90 1	97 11	100 8	124	—	108 1	126
1949/50	94 0	103 4	106 8	131	—	114 2	133
1950/51	95 7	105 4	108 7	134	—	117 9	137
1951/52	104 7	115 8	119 10	147	—	130 0	151
1952/53	108 0	123 8	128 4	158	—	138 7	161
1953/54	113 8	129 7	135 0	166	—	146 10	171
1954/55	118 4	135 1	141 4	164	—	155 1	180
1955/56	125 10	147 2	152 7	188	—	165 8	193
1956/57	133 4	155 6	161 7	199	—	176 2	205
1957/58	141 4	165 1	171 6	211	—	188 11	220
1958/59	148 1	176 1[a]	181 8[a]	223	—	200 1	233
		172 10[b]	178 5[b]	(223)	48·4		
1959/60	152 3	178 5	182 7	228	47·6	203 6	237
1960/61	159 7	187 5	191 3	239	47·3	208 1	242
1961/62	166 3	191 8	194 4	243	46·5	214 10	250
1962/63	174 1	203 10	206 7	258	46·3	224 8	261
1963/64	182 6	213 3	216 7	271	46·0	239 10	279
1964/65	194 5	226 6	230 3	288	45·2	254 11	296
1965/66	206 6	237 9	240 4	300	44·7	269 0	313

[a] Excluding old-age pensioner general workers, as in the years 1945/46 to 1957/58.
[b] Including old-age pensioner general workers, and in 1959/60 and subsequent years.
[c] Up to 1958/59 the index of total earnings (general workers) is based on 1945/46 = 100. The series is then continued by basing the index including old-age pensioner general workers on 1958/59 = 223.
[d] As grieves and shepherds work 'customary hours', it is not possible to give total hours per week for all hired men.

Since 1966, wages have risen more rapidly but they are still markedly lower than industrial wages.

The rising capital cost of farming led to the merger of many small farms into larger operating units. This trend toward a reduction in the number of small farms, which still continues, has been part of official policy for some years and it is part of the EEC's Common Agricultural Policy (CAP). Table 6.5 shows the extent of this change over a five-year period from 1969 to 1974. In every arable enterprise the average acreage of farms has increased and the average size of all herds and flocks of livestock has also increased. In the case of poultry, and most of all of broilers, this increase has been dramatic, as the poultry industry has moved toward ever larger intensive indoor units. In each case, too, except that of beef herds, the number of farms has decreased. The increase in the number of beef herds reflects a change from dairying to beef production. If dairy and beef herds are counted together, the total number of cattle enterprises has fallen.

The size of farm businesses is sometimes measured in units called 'standard man days' (smd). The smd is a measure of the full-time labour required for a particular enterprise or type of farm. The concept was introduced to eliminate from statistical surveys a new type of 'small farmer' who was distorting the data. An intensive livestock farmer with pig or, more usually, poultry houses, may accommodate a very large herd or flock with little more land than is occupied by the buildings themselves.

Such systems are undoubtedly part of animal husbandry but it is arguable that they are not agricultural, if agriculture is taken to mean the growing of plant crops. The enterprise is capitalised very heavily indeed and all feedingstuffs are imported. If the acreage required to grow the feed for the livestock is added to the size of the unit, what is physically an apparently small farm becomes a very large one indeed. A battery hen may consume about 104 lb of feed grain a year (47 kg), so a flock of 5000 such birds—and 74·7 % of Britain's laying poultry are in flocks of 5000 birds or more—will consume about 236 tonnes of grain each year. The 1974/75 average yield of wheat in the UK was 4·89 tonnes per hectare, so it requires some 48 hectares to grow 236 tonnes. Immediately, a tiny farm of perhaps 1 ha or less becomes quite a substantial farm and if its economics are included with data from genuinely small farms, the picture that emerges is inaccurate. By setting definite limits to the number of workers allowed against a particular enterprise, the smd concept encourages economies in the use of labour.

This is important, or it has been considered important, because the efficiency of British farming in particular is often measured in terms of the output per worker. On this basis, agriculture compares very favourably indeed with other industries and with agriculture in other countries. Table 6.6 compares the size of farms in the nine EEC countries, and also the number of workers and the number of employees per hectare. In the EEC as a whole, 35 % of all farms are larger than 50 ha, while in UK, 69 % of farms

TABLE 6.5
Number and Size of Holdings and Enterprises[a] (at June of each year)

			1969	1974
Crops and grass acreage	Number of holdings (thousands) with	$\frac{1}{4}$ to 49$\frac{3}{4}$ acres	160·3	128·2
		50 to 149$\frac{3}{4}$ acres	98·5	89·2
		150 to 299$\frac{3}{4}$ acres	36·6	34·8
		300 acres and over	19·7	21·2
		Total	315·1	273·4
	Average acreage per holding (crops and grass)		95·7	109·1
	Per cent of total crops and grass acreage in holdings	under 50 acres	10·3	8·6
		300 acres and over	34·4	39·2
Size of business (smd)[b]	Number of holdings (thousands)	under 275[c] smd	142·9	115·4
		275[c] to 599 smd	83·2	66·5
		600 to 1 199 smd	56·6	55·0
		1 200 smd and over	34·2	41·1
		Total	317·0	278·0
	Holdings 275[c] smd and over	Average size of business (smd)	953	1 114
		Average acreage per holding (total area)[d]	222·8	238·9
		Contribution to total output (%)	92·2	94·3
	Estimated number of full-time farms (thousands)[e]	Under 600 smd	102·0	84·5
		600 smd and over	88·1	91·6
		Total	190·1	176·1
Total cereals[f]	Number of holdings (thousands) with	$\frac{1}{4}$ to 19$\frac{3}{4}$ acres	72·1	53·3
		20 to 99$\frac{3}{4}$ acres	51·6	45·7
		100 acres and over	26·2	26·6
		Total	149·9	125·6
	Average acreage		60·9	73·9
	Percent of total acreage in acreages of 100 acres and over		67·2	71·0

	10 to 49¾ acres	14·4	12·3
	50 acres and over	2·1	2·0
	Total	81·6	59·3
Sugar beet[g]	Average acreage	7·5	9·0
	Percent of total acreage in acreages of 50 acres and over	28·4	32·7
	Number of holdings (thousands) with ¼ to 9¾ acres	9·3	5·4
	10 to 49¾ acres	9·7	8·9
	50 acres and over	2·2	2·7
	Total	21·2	17·0
Dairy cows	Average acreage	21·0	28·3
	Percent of total acreage in acreages of 50 acres and over	42·9	53·0
	Number of holdings (thousands) with 1 to 19	57·1	32·3
	20 to 49	42·1	31·2
	50 and over	18·7	24·2
	Total	117·9	87·7
Beef cows	Average size of herd	28	39
	Percent of total dairy cows in herds of 50 and over	44·4	61·5
	Number of holdings (thousands) with 1 to 19	83·0	75·9
	20 to 49	13·4	20·5
	50 and over	4·5	8·9
	Total	100·9	105·3
Breeding sheep[h]	Average size of herd	12	18
	Percent of total beef cows in herds of 50 and over	30·0	40·7
	Number of holdings (thousand) with 1 to 99	62·7	46·1
	100 to 499	32·3	30·6
	500 and over	4·6	5·5
	Total	99·5	82·2
	Average size of flock	128	162
	Percent of breeding sheep in flocks of 500 and over	30·9	36·4

TABLE 6.5—*contd.*

			1969	1974
Breeding pigs	Number of holdings (thousands) with	1 to 9	47·6	25·9
		10 to 49	19·5	12·6
		50 and over	3·6	4·7
		Total	70·6	43·2
	Average size of herd		13	21
	Percent of total breeding pigs in herds of 50 and over		37·6	60·0
Laying fowls	Number of holdings (thousands) with	1 to 999	143·3	86·9
		1 000 to 4 999	6·6	3·4
		5 000 and over	2·1	2·1
		Total	151·9	92·4
	Average size of flock		350	543
	Percent of total laying fowls in flocks of 5000 and over		52·2	74·7
Broilers[i]	Numbers of holdings (thousands) with	1 to 9999	3·3	2·1
		10 000 to 49 999	0·6	0·6
		50 000 and over	0·2	0·2
		Total	4·0	2·9
	Average size of flock		9 298	19 280
	Percent of total broilers in flocks of 50 000 and over		57·3	73·4

[a] Figures adjusted to take account of changes in census methods in 1970 and 1973.
[b] Figures include holdings with no crops and grass acreage which are excluded from the first section of the table.
[c] 250 smd in Scotland; 200 smd in Northern Ireland.
[d] Figures relate to the total area of 'other land', the definition of which has changed slightly between 1969 and 1974.
[e] Includes an estimate of upwards of 14 000 full-time farms which have under 275 smd (or equivalent) based on their cropping and stocking and assuming average labour usage. Adjustments have been made for holdings which, though run as separate farming units, are in the same occupancy.
[f] Includes maize for threshing in 1974, not included in 1969.
[g] England and Wales only.
[h] Figures for Scotland and Northern Ireland relate to the December censuses in 1968 and 1973.
[i] Figures for Scotland relate to the December censuses in 1968 and 1973.
smd = standard man days, a measurement of the size of a farm enterprise based on an estimate of the labour required to run it.

TABLE 6.6
Farm Size (EEC, 1972) Measured as Percentage of Total Agricultural Area; and Employment (EEC, 1973/74)

Ha	*WG*	*F*	*I*	*N*	*B*	*L*	*Dk*	*Ir*	*UK*	*Av* '9'
1–5	7	3	22	5	8	3	2	3	1	7
5–10	12	5	16	12	16	5	7	7	3	9
10–20	28	15	15	33	31	15	20	21	6	18
20–50	39	39	14	40	32	60	44	37	21	31
50–100	10				10				24	
		{38	{32	{11		{17	{28	{32		{35
100+	4				3				45	

Workers per hectare, including farmers, their families and employees

	WG	*F*	*I*	*N*	*B*	*L*	*Dk*	*Ir*	*UK*	*Av.* '9'
	0·14	0·08	0·19	0·15	0·11	0·11	0·08	0·06	0·06	0·11
Employees/ha										
	0·02	0·017	0·069	0·034	0·008	0·006	0·017	0·007	0·034	0·03

(Source: ref. 12)

are of 50 ha or more, and 45 % are more than 100 ha. Britain has by far the largest average farm size in Western Europe. It also has the smallest proportion of small farms.

Not surprisingly, since it is what has been encouraged, there are fewer farmworkers on British land than anywhere else in the EEC area, except for Ireland. With 0·06 workers per ha, the UK has barely more than half the average degree of labour-intensity, but because its farms tend to be much larger than the average, it does have a fairly high proportion of employed workers. The Netherlands has a similar number of employees per hectare but only Italy has more.

It is only fair to farmers elsewhere in Europe to point out that this transition from a labour-intensive to a capital-intensive pattern has been easier in Britain because of its agricultural history. There is no tradition of peasantry in Britain, so the farming structure has not included large numbers of independent landowners, each holding a tiny area of land with determined ferocity. The typical British country dweller is either an independent farmer or a landless labourer, working for wages. As the cost of mechanisation fell in comparison with the cost of employing labour, the employed workers could be dislodged fairly easily and then it could be shown that the small farm was becoming uneconomic as a high degree of mechanisation benefits from economies of scale.

So it can be said that the object of British agricultural policy has been to create a mechanised, capitalised, streamlined industry in which labour is used as efficiently as possible.

Of course, productivity per worker is only one way of measuring efficiency. We may also measure output per hectare and we may measure the economic cost of production. Which of these parameters is more relevant will change from time to time. If a country is industrialising and so needs workers to move into factory-based industry, then output per worker may be the most relevant. If the need is to increase overall production of food then output per hectare becomes more important. If energy costs begin to rise rapidly the cost per hectare may become important.

To some extent the three cannot be separated. If the output per worker increases, it is not unreasonable to suppose that the output per hectare will also increase. If labour is used more efficiently, it is not unreasonable to suppose that reduced labour costs will be reflected in reduced costs per hectare of land, or other unit of production. So while the labour force was being reduced, output per hectare was also increasing.

Average yields of wheat may be taken as typical of what happened in every sector of the industry and Fig. 6.3 traces the history of wheat yields from 1885 to 1966, by which time they had more or less levelled out. The graph shows a general, slow rise that accelerates around the mid-1940s, then steadies in the early 1960s. It would seem that the reduction in the size of the labour force had no adverse effect on yields. This may be true but unfortunately there is no way for us to know.

In a sense British agriculture performed a vast experiment during the 20 years between 1945 and 1965, but it performed it in an uncoordinated way and without any control against which its effects might be measured. During that period farms became much more mechanised, the labour force was reduced, consumption of fertilisers increased, pesticides were introduced partly to improve the degree of control of insect pests, weeds and fungal diseases, partly to reduce labour requirements, and new crop varieties with improved characteristics were grown. All that we can measure is the combined effect of all these changes. There is no way we can even guess what would have happened had only some of them been made. So it is far too simplistic to assume that, because yields increased while the size of the labour force decreased, a direct causal relationship exists between the two. Had the labour force increased, or remained the same, or decreased but by a smaller amount, then yields might have risen even further than they did.

The history of this period may be obscured, too, by the fact that increases in output are measured, necessarily, against those from an agriculture that was chronically depressed and so gravely under-capitalised. If today resources are used more efficiently than they were, we must remember that in the whole of the earlier period it was not possible to use resources except very inefficiently. Again we do not know what would have happened had agricultural prosperity improved in the late nineteenth century, say, or in the period between the two world wars. There are no clear answers but in

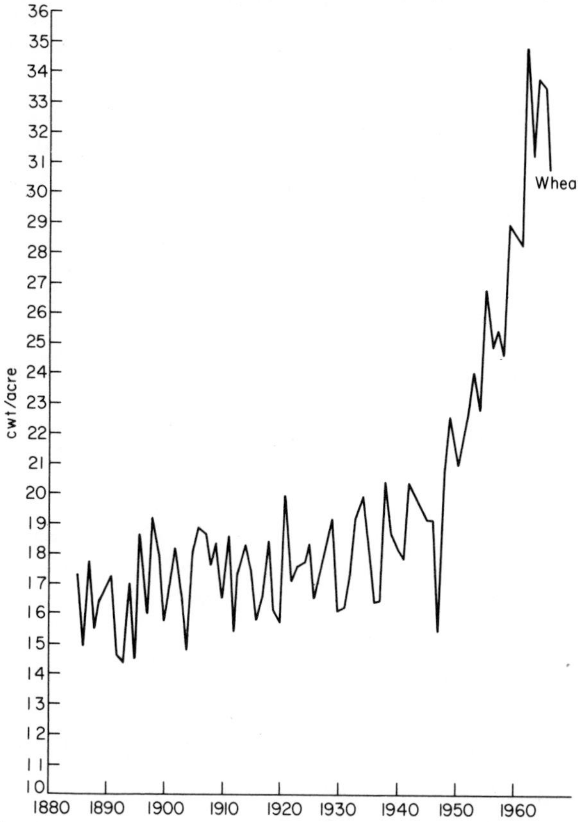

FIG. 6.3. Yield per acre of wheat in Great Britain 1885–1966 (Source: ref. 11).

Fig. 6.3 there are one or two hints, from the war years themselves. Prosperity did improve during the two wars, the decline in the labour force was arrested during World War II and the acreage sown did increase. Yet average yields did not change; they continued on the same, generally upward, trend.

Comparison with Britain's EEC partners suggests, however, that Britain has struck a good balance. Table 6.7 gives indices of production and costs for all nine Member States. It shows that UK yields are slightly below EEC averages, although yields of the most important commodities—wheat, barley, potatoes and milk—are high. It contradicts the belief that British farms are the most highly mechanised in Europe. Only Ireland has fewer tractors per hectare than Britain, while West Germany has nearly three times more. British farmers use rather more nitrogenous fertiliser than

TABLE 6.7

Indices of EEC Agriculture, 1973/74 (unless otherwise stated); West Germany = 100

	WG	*F*	*I*	*N*	*B*	*L*	*Dk*	*Ir*	*UK*	*Av.* '9'
Production (yield/ha)										
wheat	100	101	56	118	112	72	99	98	98	86
barley	100	98	57	107	116	86	96	103	100	98
oats	100	87	48	120	111	82	96	100	106	93
rye	100	77	62	97	105	89	101	—	87	97
Average all cereals	100	91	56	110	111	82	98	100	98	94
sugar beet	100	92	85	106	109	—	—	96	86	94
fodder beet	100	58	57	83	103	56	—	—	64	—
potatoes	100	81	57	129	99	105	74	93	103	93
average all roots	100	77	66	106	104	81	74	95	84	94
average all arable	100	84	61	108	108	82	86	98	91	94
milk/cow	100	64	—	114	99 (B + L)		107	50	108	—
pigmeat/ha	100	101	—	103	108 (B + L)		76	101	83	
eggs/hen	100	64	60	95	96 (B + L)		84	50	75	—
average all livestock	100	76	60	104	101 (B + L)		89	67	89	—
Inputs (machines/ha; 1972)										
tractors	100	38	38	64	55	60	57	19	34	48
harvesters/threshers	100	35	11	29	41	112	112	11	40	42
Fertiliser/ha (1971/72)										
N	100	55	42	21	126	109	125	24	110	73
P	100	84	47	69	134	80	66	53	66	74
K	100	51	15	65	119	65	71	33	43	52
Input costs/ha (1972)										
feedingstuffs	100	32	66	411	331	97	62	22	93	73
fertiliser and lime	100	56	29	109	161	60	61	26	52	58
fuel and repairs	100	38	4	91	—	24	8	9	46	40
Total input cost/ha	100	40	39	214	181	55	45	17	71	59

(Source: ref. 12)

average, although farmers in Belgium and Denmark use more. In terms of its cost, British farming is more expensive that that of France, Italy, Luxembourg, Denmark and Ireland, but rather less expensive that that of The Netherlands and Belgium. Indeed the cost of imported raw materials in The Netherlands is so high that Dutch agriculture can be regarded as mainly a processing industry, converting primary produce that is imported into more valuable secondary produce, much of which is exported.

For many years, probably since Britain first became a permanent net importer of food, there has been a running debate as to whether the country should produce more of its own food and how much it might be possible to produce. Earlier in this century several investigating committees concluded that 'self-sufficiency' would be out of the question. More recently, however, increases in output from their abnormally low level earlier have altered the picture and now most agronomists agree that if Britain decided to produce all of its own food it could do so. The argument is usually highly theoretical, for 'self-sufficiency' is itself a very abstract concept, despite its emotive connotations. In the real world, a country either imports food or it exports it.

The worst of all possible worlds is the one in which sometimes it does one, sometimes the other, for the chances are very high that in those 'good' years, when it has surpluses to export, other exporters will also have surpluses and prices will be low, while in years when it needs to import conditions will also be poor elsewhere, supplies will be short and prices high. A country that invariably exports can set one year off against another, as can a country that invariably imports. If any country seeks to produce exactly the quantity of food it consumes—to become fully 'self-sufficient'—then the techniques of forecasting, based on a simple multiplication of acreages planted by average yields, are bound to ensure that when conditions are favourable there is a surplus and when conditions are adverse there is a deficiency, since it is quite impossible to predict the many variables that affect farming. Rather than export surpluses and import food to compensate for deficiencies, the country might choose to maintain its own stockpiles, at least of the less perishable commodities. So in good years food would be taken into storage and in poor years it would be released on to the market.

Internationally, of course, this is the aim of FAO policy, and internationally it can succeed because supplies are moved from one part of the world to another: it is not only their own surpluses that countries aim to store. Nationally, however, a country whose production matches demand very closely may find that the limits to its physical storage capacity and economic flexibility are reached rather quickly, so that several successive years of surplus or deficiency will defeat the system. Further, the response to successive years of one condition or the other is liable to be an over-reaction in the opposite direction. So it is not only the technique of forecasting itself that tends to produce instability but natural human reactions to instabilities in earlier years. The accumulation of 'mountains' of produce within the European Community is a case in point, although the size and significance of these mountains has been exaggerated by the British press, which cannot wean itself from the urban-oriented philosophy of an entirely free, open market for foods.

It is probably much more sensible to follow the Swedish example and to aim to produce around 85% of the food consumed. This leaves the country a net importer but on a much reduced scale, and it ensures an adequate margin to prevent the accidental accumulation of surpluses. In times of real need a modification in patterns of consumption, moderated by short term rationing if necessary, combined with a modest but rapid expansion in agricultural output, will make good the final 15% and provide for survival in siege conditions. It is wise for any country to allow for the possibility that one day it may be besieged, although this is not at all the same thing as assuming siege conditions to exist when they do not. There are dangers of producing correct answers to the wrong questions.

If Britain seeks to increase its total output of food, Table 6.7 suggests that further intensification of mechanisation and increased use of chemicals may prove very expensive. Essentially, Britain would be aiming to follow the example of West Germany, The Netherlands and Belgium. These are the only EEC countries that produce more arable crops per hectare of land as well as more livestock products per hectare. Ireland's arable yields are generally higher than the UK's but the livestock sector is less productive in total. If Britain were to follow West Germany it might expect something like a 10% overall increase in yields at a 29% increase in costs. If it followed Belgium, output might increase by about 14·5% but costs would increase by around 110%. If it followed The Netherlands, output would increase by around 16% but costs would increase by about 143%. The figures are very crude, of course, especially those that compare the British and Dutch farming systems, but they do suggest that any attempt to increase UK food output by further application of the kind of methods that have been so successful in the past 20 years should be viewed with very great caution.

In Ireland, on the other hand, arable production is high but livestock production is low. It is very likely that livestock production could be increased at an acceptable added cost, since Irish costs are by far the lowest in the Community. In Italy the problem is different again, for here costs are low but so are all yields. If yields are to be increased in this situation, more may be needed than simply additional investment: the structure appears to be wrong.

Obviously all production systems that are based on a relationship between input and output will experience diminishing returns. Plotted on a graph, a comparison of yield increments in response to additional input might produce a curve similar to that in Fig. 6.4, which in fact is based on an American experiment in which the effect of additional applications of nitrogenous fertiliser was measured against increased yields. After a certain point each additional application of fertiliser produces a smaller increment in yield. Clearly a point will be reached at which it is inadvisable or impossible to continue to increase inputs in order to increase output.

The final, absolute limit is in this case a biological one. Beyond a certain point the crop plant will cease to respond to more fertiliser. Before that point is reached, however, there are two other points on the graph beyond

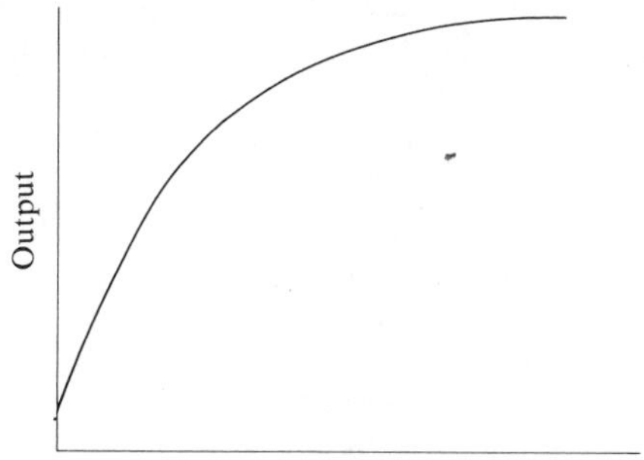

FIG. 6.4 Diminishing returns.

which the farmer probably should not go. The first is the economic limit, at which the additional income he receives from the sale of the increment in his yield is insufficient to pay for the cost of the additional fertiliser required to produce it. This point will be flexible, depending on the relative cost of fertiliser and the price he receives for his crop. In our comparison of EEC farming systems it is possible to argue that British farmers have reached that point. The other limit is an environmental one, at which the adverse effect on the environment of the use of more fertiliser cannot be justified in terms of the benefit to the community of growing more food. In some parts of Britain that point may have been reached.

Some evidence that fertiliser consumption in Britain has fallen as prices have risen suggests that an economic limit may be close. This evidence is patchy and largely subjective, and it is complicated by the fact that during 1975 there were shortages of fertiliser caused by insufficient plant capacity. However, there are other indications that tend in the same direction. The large increases in yields per hectare of arable crops occurred during the late 1940s, 1950s and early 1960s. Since then they have stabilised, although there are small, steady rises for some commodities.

Fertiliser consumption has also tended to stabilise but this levelling off occurred a year or two after arable yields steadied. This suggests that farmers reached the economic threshold at which diminishing returns from additional applications of fertiliser were felt some ten years ago. It is difficult to be certain because the pattern of fertiliser use also changed, with a levelling off of use on arable crops and an increase in use on grass. Grass yields are not recorded, except as hay, and hay yields per hectare have increased, but by an amount that is far too small to explain the whole of the additional fertiliser consumed after arable yields stabilised.

It may be that 'industrial' farming is reaching its economic limits. Its effect has been to increase food production per hectare of land and to effect great economies in the use of labour. Or, to put it the other way, to displace workers. This has helped to feed the process of urbanisation and to provide a steady supply of new workers for manufacturing industry: in many industrial countries the urbanising trend has now slowed almost to a standstill and in some it shows a slight reversal as people move out of the cities rather than into them.

Industry grew, but urbanisation also necessitated greater investment in transporting, preserving and processing food, which in turn employed more labour. Today the British food industry—as opposed to the agricultural industry—is one of the largest industries in the country, employing 8% of the national labour force. If we add together the labour forces of agriculture, the agro-supportive industries of farm machinery manufacture, marketing and servicing, fertiliser and pesticide manufacture, marketing and distribution, and the food industry, it is probable that some 13% of the labour force is engaged full time in the production, processing and distribution of food. Thus the change in the use of labour is seen to be less of an advantage than it seemed at first. The economic advantage is considerable, however, since the value added to produce contributes directly to the GNP.

Countries seeking to follow the 'industrialising' pattern should beware, however, that in releasing labour for factory industry they are not also creating a need for a food industry that will mop up the liberated labour.

It is probable that environmental thresholds are about to be reached as well. Clearly, any form of farming that necessitates human management of the landscape must have ecological effects. There is and can be no such thing as 'natural' farming. In ecological terms the farmer aims to exploit the tendency of an ecosystem to develop to a climax. During the successional stages of its development a surplus of nutrients exist within the system that potentially are available to immigrant species.

When the climax condition is reached all niches are occupied and there is a surplus of neither nutrient nor space. The farmer clears away the existing ecosystem, or part of it, and substitutes his crop plants for the species that naturally would invade the area. The crop plants utilise the available nutrients and from then on the farmer must aim to maintain the system in a kind of suspended successional state. To do so he must prevent its invasion by unwanted species that are able to compete successfully with his crops. These may be naturally wild species, but more often they are weeds, plants adapted to survive in disturbed environments. If the ecosystem is allowed to re-establish itself, eventually most of the weeds will vanish as wild plants rob them of space, nutrient, water and sunlight.

So the farmer must weed his crop and he must also compete for it with rival consumers. By providing concentrated stands of particular plant species he will tend to attract herbivorous animals that can subsist on that species. So he must control pests.

It can be seen that the farmer interferes with the natural system in several distinct ways. Some of his effects will be beneficial to other species, as when forest is cleared and its place taken by a pattern of fields surrounded by hedgerows, with a certain number of trees being allowed to remain in small stands or in the hedgerows. Such a habitat affords more niches for species than does woodland. Some of his effects will be harmful to other species but beneficial to man. Some, however, are harmful to other species and also have a harmful effect on man, so that the tolerable environmental impact of a farming system can be assessed, albeit crudely, by evaluating the relative benefits and costs of that system.

Beyond a certain point the sustainability of the system itself may be called into question. Ecological critics of modern farming are concerned principally with its effects on the structure of soils, on wild species of flora and fauna, with the side effects of the over-use of fertilisers and the use of pesticides, with pollution from intensive livestock units and with possible effects on human and animal health of the non-therapeutic use of drugs.

Although it is possible to isolate such especially sensitive areas the criticisms are really directed at modern farming as a whole, for it is the whole approach to food production that gives rise to them. The belief, that can be traced back a century to von Liebig and his contemporaries, that plant nutrition can be explained in purely chemical terms led inevitably to the view that fertilisers manufactured in such a way that they provide plants with soluble nutrients in readily available forms can replace the much more haphazard recycling of crop residues and animal and human wastes. This being so, there was no longer any reason for livestock enterprises to be run as integral parts of mixed livestock and arable farms. Animals could be divorced physically from the land that produced their food.

Once animals were gone the need for grassland was also gone, and the better grassland was ploughed up to grow barley. The barley is fed to the livestock, which is housed indoors. The removal of livestock and a large area of grassland in favour of more intensive cereal cultivations favoured the introduction of larger machines. These needed more room to manoeuvre than was available in the small meadows that used to be grazed, the hedges were no longer required to retain animals and so in Britain, in parts of East Anglia especially, the 'prairie' landscape began to make its appearance, with fields of 20, 40 or 60 ha or more. As monocultural arable systems became more common, so pest and weed problems became more acute and the incentive to reduce crop losses was increased by the economic pressure applied to farmers to make them grow more each year in order to earn a similar return on their investment. So dependence on pesticides increased.

The improvement in the efficiency of farming may have been more apparent than real. Certainly farms took on a 'modern' look and a culture that believed that the mechanisation of all operations was intrinsically good was suitably impressed. The landscape, especially in the cereal growing regions, became monotonous, resembling nothing so much as the factory floor so familiar to town dwellers. Yet many farmers held that the powerful tools provided for the modern farmer and the scale on which he was beginning to operate, actually encouraged inefficiency. It was easier than it had ever been for an indifferent farmer to make a good living, provided he did as his advisers told him.

SOIL STRUCTURE

In the 1960s, UK farmers themselves were becoming concerned about the condition of British soils. Following a survey conducted by the National Farmers' Union among its members, the government set up an official inquiry under the auspices of the Agricultural Advisory Council. The investigating committee, chaired by Nigel Strutt, issued its report, which became known as the Strutt Report, early in 1970.[4]

The report found that, in some parts of the country, soils had been damaged by the use of heavy machinery at the wrong times of year, by overstocking and by poor drainage. It suggested that the organic matter content of some soils was lower than it should be and it expressed concern about the decreasing use of lime to compensate for the acidity caused by heavy fertiliser dressings. It concluded, however, that so far the deterioration in the structure of the affected soils had not impaired their fertility.

The report was surprisingly controversial. On the one hand there were those who welcomed it as a timely warning of the future effects of farming methods that had been taken too far. Others, on the other hand, expressed surprise that there could be farmers so ignorant of basic farming principles that they could so batter their soils. Still others remarked that the investigation followed an unusually wet period and so it was surprising that the condition of soils was not even worse.

The attitude of the committee to the relationship between soil structure and fertility was curious. If the inherent fertility of a soil is assessed on the basis of a simple analysis of its nutrient content, and if nutrients are supplied principally by fertilisers, then fertility is a function of fertiliser applications and nothing more. Thus no matter what happens to the structure of the soil its fertility will not be impaired so long as the fertiliser industry continues to produce and market nutrients. If the soil is more than an inert substrate, then this concept falls.

Plant roots obtain their nutrients from dissolved salts carried in water, called the 'soil solution'. Nutrients are made available by the action of aerobic micro-organisms. Therefore regardless of their origin plants depend for their nutrients on the porosity of the soil, on its capacity to permit the circulation of air and water. This is its structure and so it is quite artificial to separate structure and fertility as though they were wholly independent concepts.

Although the fertility of a soil is related to its structure, its structure is not necessarily related to its organic matter content. Generally structure is supplied by bulky organic residues. As these decompose, spaces and channels are left in the soil, their sides lined with jelly-like substances produced by colonies of bacteria, which tend to secure these channels against collapse. There are a few soils, however, in which an adequate structure is provided by the mineral constituents. So the amount of organic matter that a particular soil should contain is widely variable and no general rule can be applied to the country as a whole.

In spite of the controversy some conclusions were irrefutable. While the damage that had been caused was far from irreversible, all the same, in the words of the report itself, 'Some soils are now suffering from dangerously low levels (of organic matter) and cannot be expected to sustain the farming systems which have been imposed on them'; and, 'We have tried to show the danger of treating the soil so roughly in one or two years for immediate gain that it will be disastrously unresponsive for several years to come. We are not concerned with price incentives or any other form of aids to investment. We merely draw attention to what is happening and point to the improvements which are desirable to obtain the best results from the soil if it is properly treated'.[4]

It seems, then, that modern farming cannot be pursued too far without imposing an intolerable strain on the soils that support it and we should remember that Britain has some of the most robust soils in the world.

Fertilisers

A proportion of all soluble salts will be washed out of soils by rainfall and it is the leaching of nutrients from the land that provides the primary food base for fresh water ecosystems.

If too much fertiliser is applied the loss through leaching may represent on the one hand a loss to the farmer and on the other hand it may lead to the pollution of water. Excess fertiliser that does not leach from the soil may harm the crop itself, sometimes reducing yield and sometimes affecting its nutritive value adversely.

A few years ago, 'eutrophication' was a fashionable word. It means, simply, 'over-enrichment'. The eutrophication of fresh water—invariably relatively still water in ponds, ditches or slow-moving rivers—stimulates the excessive production of aquatic plants, often algae that can multiply very quickly into a 'bloom'. This has an immediate effect of increasing the loss of water by transpiration and a secondary effect of causing the depletion of the water's free dissolved oxygen, through the aerobic bacterial decomposition of plant residues. The reduction in free oxygen may cause the death of certain animals, especially those fish species whose oxygen requirement is close to the normal oxygen content of the water in which they live. Thus the ecosystem begins to deteriorate. Higher animals die and eventually all vertebrates will die from asphyxiation, and beyond a certain level the water contains insufficient oxygen for the decomposition of organic matter, which tends to accumulate and decompose, anaerobically, much more slowly.

Putrefaction can occur and its effects can be unpleasant, especially in rather larger lakes where the thermal stratification of the water leads to seasonal upheavals in which trapped putrefying matter is brought abruptly to the surface. Eutrophication is an ageing process and if it is allowed to continue, the removal of water by transpiration combined with the accumulation of organic debris will cause the water to be lost. In time the area will become swamp, then marsh and finally dry land.

Nitrate nitrogen that is ingested by humans, either from nitrate-enriched water or from crops in which it has lodged in quantities that exceed those the plant can metabolise, can harm health. Bacteria in the gut of susceptible individuals, and especially of young infants, can reduce the nitrate to nitrite, which is able to pass through the gut wall and into the blood stream. There it can form a stable compound with haemoglobin, methaemoglobin. So stabilised, the haemoglobin is unable to form the unstable compound oxyhaemoglobin and so the victim is deprived of oxygen in a condition called methaemoglobinaemia. This can produce a range of symptoms and, in its most extreme form, death by asphyxiation.

It is also possible that nitrates may combine in the environment with naturally occurring secondary amines to form nitrosamines that are known to be carcinogenic. Nitrate nitrogen may also harm livestock. In the winter of 1975/76, cattle in the south west of Britain were made ill and some were killed by excess nitrate that accumulated in turnips.[5]

No one knows precisely the proportion of fertiliser nitrogen applied to British soils that leaches into the surface waters, but it is known that the total amount of nitrogen reaching surface waters in and around the UK from land drainage and sewage is equal to more than 40% of the total nitrogen applied as fertiliser.[6] It is likely that in many lowland areas, where potable water is abstracted from rivers, nitrate levels are as high as they should be allowed to rise, and in some places it may be desirable to reduce them.

It is clear that the over-use of fertiliser, and especially nitrogenous fertiliser, presents an immediate or potential threat to the environment and to health, as well as being a waste of a valuable resource.

Pesticides

The dangers to wildlife of pesticides are well known. In 1970/71 there were nine fish kills in Britain caused by pesticides. The most dangerous of the cumulative organochlorine compounds, such as dieldrin, aldrin and DDT, are banned or strictly controlled in Britain and in many other industrial countries, but still mistakes are made. Trithion, introduced as an alternative to dieldrin as a seed dressing, has no effect on the pigeons and pheasants on which it was tested, but since it has come into use it has been implicated in the deaths of 700 wintering greylag and pink-footed geese. There may be risks to some swans, including the whooper and Bewick's swans, which also feed on farmland. The world population of Bewick's swans is estimated at about 10 000 and about 20% of them winter in Britain.

Some earlier fears about pesticides have not materialised, however. It seems that the cumulative organochlorine compounds do not remain indefinitely in mammalian body fat and that a peak is reached in fat concentrations after which the compounds are excreted. Nor have the problems of pest resistance to pesticides reached the proportions that were feared, although some countries have not fared so well in this respect.

The over-use of herbicides can exacerbate pest problems by depriving insect species of sources of food, so leaving them no alternative but to attack crops. The difficulty of killing weeds among crop plants to which they may be rather similar has tended to alter weed patterns. Monoculture exacerbates this difficulty. Among cereal crops, for example, it is easiest to kill out broad-leaved weed species. These are replaced by other species which are killed in turn, but as time passes the surviving weeds are those that are more and more closely related to the cereals themselves and so most difficult to remove. Sprayed conventionally, herbicides may also depress crop yields by covering leaf surfaces with an oily film that inhibits photosynthesis.

The problems are far from simple when substances that are highly potent biologically are disseminated at random in the environment. In January 1976 there were reports from Hopewell, Virginia, of extensive damage to fish and to the health of at least 30 people who were admitted to hospital, from a little known organochlorine insecticide called kepone.[7]

The dangers of the use of pesticides are well known and the FAO announced in October 1975 that in collaboration with UNEP (the United Nations Environment Programme) a programme was to be launched for monitoring the movement and accumulation of pesticide residues in the environment on a global scale.

Intensive livestock

The indoor housing of large concentrations of livestock, often far removed from the land that grows their food, has led to two problems. The first relates to the disposal of manure and slurry that previously was returned to the land, the second to the health of the animals themselves.

Where no land is available the manure and slurry problem has been 'solved' by storage in lagoons. The cost of treating this waste to standards high enough for it to be discharged safely into rivers precludes any other approach, and even where land is available the spraying on to it of excessive quantities of semi-liquid material is offensive, effectively sterilises the land and may overload the natural purifying effect of slow filtration through the soil. The environmental load can be high. The excreta of a cow have a biochemical oxygen demand (BOD) eight times that of human excreta, so that a large unit can produce as much sewage as a small town.

Where livestock are housed in large numbers and in close proximity to one another the risk of disease is obvious. Initially to prevent disease outbreaks antibiotics were administered prophylactically through feeds. Then it was discovered, for reasons that still are not clear, that in minute doses antibiotics also stimulate growth. Thus the use of drugs as growth stimulants became widespread. Predictably, populations of bacteria exposed to very small but repeated doses of drugs acquired resistance and it was found that this resistance often covered not just one drug but a wide spectrum of similar drugs. Then it was found that resistance could be transferred 'infectively' from one strain of bacteria to another. In various parts of the world, including Britain, there have been outbreaks of enteric disease in human populations that have been traced back to intensively-reared livestock and that have proved difficult to treat with antibiotics.

The two problems of waste disposal and drug-resistant bacteria are related, in that seepage of effluent into water is one route by which resistant bacteria may reach human populations.

In January 1976 the World Health Organisation announced the findings of a consultation, held late in 1975, into the public health aspects of antibiotic-resistant bacteria. The main conclusions and recommendations were:

more precise information is needed concerning the way in which antibiotics can promote growth;

more information is needed on the possible role in the dissemination of resistant bacteria played by food and animal feeds;

there is a need to find out more about all the factors that may affect the presence of resistant bacteria in the environment, such as the presence of heavy metals, organic chemicals, disinfectants, detergents and other substances found in industrial and domestic wastes;

there should be investigation of levels of concentration of resistant bacteria in surface waters, sewage and wastes from livestock units and abattoirs, surface vegetation, soil, sewage sludge, air in livestock units and wildlife.

It is not only the use of antibiotics that gives cause for concern. Hormones are also used from time to time, amid a storm of controversy, and there is some risk that these substances may escape into the environment outside the livestock unit itself.

The latest hormone to be considered is an analogue of prostaglandin, called Estrumate, developed by ICI. This drug makes an animal ovulate at a given time and its advantage to dairy farmers is very real, for the production of both milk and calves. The optimum calving interval—the interval between the birth of one calf and the birth of the next from the same cow—is 365 days. So if each cow bears one calf every 365 days the herd as a whole will be achieving its maximum efficiency from the farmer's point of view. The average calving interval is 30 days longer than this, however, and it has been calculated that this represents a loss to the farmer of 70p for every day the cow exceeds the 365-day optimum, or £14 for each heat that is missed entirely. In a large herd of 100 cows or more, this can be costly. If an injection of Estrumate causes the cow to ovulate, she can be inseminated accurately and the breeding cycle of the herd can be controlled.

Controlled breeding of this kind is encouraged by the British Ministry of Agriculture, Fisheries and Food, which offers its artificial insemination service at a reduced charge for groups of cows presented for insemination 10 or more at a time.

If the economic advantage is obvious, so is the environmental danger if such a drug should find its way to humans or, indeed, to any non-target mammalian species.

DESTRUCTION OF HABITAT

Over most of Britain the natural climax vegetation is mixed deciduous woodland. When this is cleared to make farms, the hedgerows that border fields are very similar ecologically to woodland edge. Thus provided there is an appropriate total length of hedgerow the removal of woodland can produce an overall ecological gain for the area, since woodland edge is an ecotone richer than the woodland ecosystem proper. Hedges also provide routes for migrating species, so linking isolated small areas of woodland.

The removal of livestock from the land and the introduction of large machines encouraged the removal of hedges in Britain at an average rate of about 3500 km a year between 1946 and 1970. The effect on wildlife was serious locally. In the eastern cereal growing areas, 'prairie' landscapes appeared that afforded very poor habitat. More recently most hedgerow removal has been concentrated in western Britain, where fields were always much smaller. There the effect has been to increase the average field size from 2 to 2·5 ha which cannot be considered unduly damaging to wild species.

The destruction of habitat is an obvious disadvantage but the agricultural arguments surrounding the value of hedges are complex. On the one hand it is argued that they occupy land that could be cropped, that they shelter crops leading to uneven ripening and consequent difficulties in harvesting, and that they harbour pests. Opposing this view there are others who hold that in some areas the removal of too many hedges can cause drainage problems and even wind erosion, that the shelter afforded by hedges is beneficial as well as harmful, in that it raises the temperature at the soil surface in the lee of the hedge, and that hedges harbour balanced populations of pests and their predators, so that if a pest population should increase and then migrate into the crop, this increase will trigger a proportional increase in the size of the predator population that will assist in control.

The arguments in favour of some hedgerow removal are often valid. Many fields are too small and would benefit from being made somewhat larger—they would be farmed better. The arguments in favour of removing all hedges are simple rationalisations of the real reason, which is economic. With a diminished labour force, hedges are difficult and expensive to maintain properly and with farmers, especially arable farmers, being pressed hard to produce as much food as they can, the additional cropping area that hedgerow removal liberates can be important. Many farmers are now aware of the hazards to wildlife and there is a growing tendency for farm management programmes to incorporate conservation programmes.

CONCLUSIONS

The picture that emerges is of industrialised farming systems that have been carried about as far as they can be carried in a particular direction. There is little doubt that the productivity of these systems could be increased but to do so might require structural changes that would take agriculture into new directions.

In developing countries such problems may appear remote but we should remember that farmers in the tropics and sub-tropics usually work with soils that are poorer and less robust than those in Britain and with climates that are harsher. The problems encountered by farmers everywhere are likely to be more acute, especially pest and weed problems, soil erosion can set in earlier, and be more difficult to remedy, and responses to these problems that base themselves too closely on the industrial model may accelerate the appearance of ecological side effects.

Certain aspects of European farming are quite inappropriate. It makes little sense to economise in the use of labour when unemployment is a serious problem. It makes even less sense to encourage heavy capital investment in advanced technologies when capital for investment in manufacturing industry is difficult to obtain. So, no matter how attractive they may appear superficially, large-scale mechanisation or intensive indoor livestock units have little to offer. Indeed it is arguable that such systems cannot be sustained for much longer in the developed countries as rising input costs reduce their profitability.

REFERENCES

1. von Libeig, J. (1885). *Principles of Agricultural Chemistry with Special Reference to the Late Researches made in England*, p. 34.
2. Burnett, J. (1966). *Plenty and Want*. Nelson, London.
3. Donaldson, J. G. F. and Barber, D. (1969). *Farming in Britain Today*. Pelican, Harmondsworth, UK.
4. AAC (1970). *Modern Farming and the Soil*. Agricultural Advisory Council, HMSO, London.
5. *Western Morning News*, 3 November 1975. Plymouth.
6. Owen, M. (1973). Resources under pressure: water, in *Intensive Agriculture and the Environment*. CICRA Symposium, An Foras Talúntais, Dublin.
7. *The Times*, 29 January, 1976. London.
8. Pollard, E., Hooper, M. D. and Moore, N. W. (1974). *Hedges*. Collins, London. Estimates were made by the Nature Conservancy Council using aerial photographs.
9. ADAS (MAFF) (1976). *Wildlife Conservation in Semi-Natural Habitats of Farms*. HMSO, London.
10. MAFF (1975). *Annual Review of Agriculture*. HMSO, London.
11. MAFF (1968). *A Century of Agricultural Statistics*. HMSO, London.
12. MAFF (1974). *EEC Agricultural and Food Statistics*. HMSO, London.

Chapter 7

JOULES AND GENES

The 'energy crisis' that resulted from the increase in OPEC prices for oil had repercussions in the agricultural systems of the industrial nations. Prices for fuels and most chemicals rose sharply. In some places there were shortages of fuel or nitrogen fertiliser caused directly or indirectly by the interruption of oil supplies. Aware of the essentially finite nature of fossil fuel resources, a small number of workers in Britain and the USA had been preparing 'energy budgets' for some time—budgets that evaluate the performance of an industry by the efficiency with which it uses energy rather than monetary resources. They considered a wide range of industries, including agriculture. Thus they showed the extent to which modern farming methods are dependent on the availability and price of fossil fuels. The 'energy crisis' brought an awareness of this dependence to a rather wider audience.

The principle of energy budgeting is very simple. Since the units in which energy is measured are universal, in the sense that they may be applied to energy in any of its forms, the whole of the work done in the production of an article can be calculated and added together to give an energy cost for the product. The technique can be used to compare the efficiency with which energy is used in different factories producing similar goods, so it becomes possible to say, for example, that production of motor cars is more efficient in this factory than in that.

Energy budgeting has certain advantages as an economic tool over financial accounting. Most obviously, financial accounting must compensate for inflationary or deflationary effects over periods of time if comparisons are to be made. If they are to be made between one country and another it may be necessary to allow for differences in patterns of consumption that affect values. This is especially true when comparisons are made between market economies and centrally planned economies, where to a high degree prices are controlled and related to an imposed system of relative values. Energy is constant and no value need be attached to it. If it costs x joules to produce a refrigerator in Czechoslovakia, this fact can be used to compare the efficiency of refrigerator production in that country with refrigerator production in Japan, where each refrigerator costs y joules to produce.

It is suggested by some ecologists that the technique is more valuable still, in that it measures a flow that is more immediate and relevant than the flow of money. Energy is expended to convert a raw material into a manufactured article. The expenditure of this energy is rewarded by a flow of money which moves in the opposite direction, from the sale of the manufacture to the expender of energy. In systems jargon it forms a feedback loop that acts positively while demand exceeds supply and the price remains high, but becomes negative when supply exceeds demand and the price falls.

However, if the behaviour of the total economy is measured in terms of the rate at which money flows within it, the flow that is measured actually moves in a reverse direction—from the sale to the producer—and it moves after the event: no money can flow until the manufacture has been sold. So the conventional economist must measure a flow that moves late and backwards.

Energy flow, on the other hand, moves forward and immediately. The energy is expended while the manufacture is being produced. Thus an economist who bases his calculations on the flow of energy will be in a better position to act quickly and accurately should he wish to regulate the economy in any way.

Finally energy can be costed, its price being related to the current price for primary fuels, so that an energy budget can be converted into a monetary budget quite simply, while retaining its forward flow and its immediacy. Its disadvantage, of course, is that while it may say a great deal about production and distribution, it says nothing about the market.

The technique was applied to agriculture first in the USA, and the results led the American ecologist Howard Odum to make a remark that earned itself a place in the history of the environmental movement. He said that modern industrial man 'no longer eats potatoes made from solar energy; now he eats potatoes partly made of oil'.[1]

Unlike any manufacturing industry, agriculture derives most of its energy from direct solar radiation. In accounting terms, if a power station burning coal or oil is consuming the earth's capital, as stored solar energy, then agriculture operates on income, as incident solar energy.

Energetics is well established as a branch of ecology. Incident solar energy can be measured directly and accurately, and its subsequent flow through an ecosystem can be monitored. Energy accounting works in the same way, but applied to agriculture a distinction must be made between the natural, or residual, energetics of the agricultural ecosystem and the energy subsidy contributed by the farmer. Unless this distinction is made the calculations are largely irrelevant to agricultural economics.

Farming begins with a natural ecosystem. Left to itself the system will continue to flourish as energy flows through it. In order to grow his crops the farmer clears away much of the natural vegetation. To do this he expends energy, in this case his own energy, derived from the food he ate. It can be measured and an appropriate allowance made for the 'residual' energy demand of the bodily functions that are necessary to keep him alive and that will be consumed whether he works or not. A figure remains that represents the additional energy he expends in doing work. Of course, his expenditure of energy does not end there. The natural vegetation must be prevented from re-establishing itself. He must weed and hoe and, at last, he must harvest his crop.

The food crop can be evaluated in energy terms as food energy, measured in joules, just as is energy in any other form. Unlike manufacturing industry the energy efficiency of agriculture can be measured directly as an input: output ratio. The total energy expended can be compared with the energy produced. In this way farms can be compared in any number of ways and the energy cost of producing particular nutrients, most commonly protein, can be evaluated under different conditions.

Most of the work on British agricultural energetics has been done by Gerald Leach and Malcolm Slesser, whose work is gaining wide acceptance. In West Germany the energy costs of food production are now included in the official yearbook of agricultural and food statistics.

The method requires, then, that every input to food production be identified and the energy cost of producing it determined, and then the input costs added and compared with the energy value of the food produced. Since some kind of baseline is required against which comparisons can be made, it is usual to follow the historical development of agriculture. This can be seen to have passed through a number of distinct phases.

The earliest transition from hunting and gathering was to a swidden, or slash-and-burn, kind of primitive farming. The next stage requires a settled kind of farming based on much harder and more skilful work by the farmers. Animals may be used as a source of power that make it possible to cultivate the soil more thoroughly than the physical strength of a man would permit. Finally, machines are introduced and agricultural chemicals. The use of these tools increases until, as in modern industrial farming, the system comes to depend on them economically.

Obviously, for as long as food production requires energy to be expended only by humans, or by animals fed from the produce of the farm, there is no fossil fuel subsidy; the energy cost is paid out of solar income, although it does cost space in the shape of the land required to feed working animals. When a fossil fuel subsidy is introduced it can be used—and invariably is used—to replace human and animal labour. Land is released to feed more humans and human workers are released for manufacturing industry.

What was overlooked until detailed energy budgets were compiled was the very high cost of these inputs themselves. Every farmer appreciates that his tractors consume fuel. He may be less aware of the quantity of fuel consumed in their production, going all the way back to the mining of the metallic ores from which they are made and to the extraction of the fuels themselves.

TABLE 7.1
Energy Inputs for a Typical Hour of Tractor Use, UK 1968

50 *horsepower* (37·3 *kW*)[a]	£/h	MJ/£	MJ/h
6 000 h life; 900 h/yr			
depreciation	0·138	200	27·6
repairs	0·074	200	14·8
tax, etc.	0·011	—	—
fuel[b] (3·18 l/h)	0·046 7	2 949	137·7
oil, grease[b]	0·015 6	550	8·6
Total	0·285	662	188·7
non-fuel input as % of fuel: 37·0			
65 *horsepower* (48·5 *kW*)			
7 000 h life; 900 h/yr			
depreciation	0·172	200	34·4
repairs	0·091	200	18·2
tax, etc.	0·011	—	—
fuel (3·68 l/h)	0·056 7	2 949	167·2
oil, grease	0·017 8	550	9·8
	0·349	658	229·6
non-fuel input as % of fuel: 37·3			
90 *horsepower* (67·2 *kW*)			
7 500 h life; 900 h/yr			
depreciation	0·373	200	74·6
repairs	0·200	200	40·0
tax, etc.	0·017	—	—
fuel (6·73 l/h)	0·098 9	2 949	291·7
oil	0·020	550	11·0
	0·709	589	417·3
non-fuel input as % of fuel: 43·0			

[a] Averages of data given for 45 and 55 h.p. (33·6 and 41·0 kW) machines.
[b] Fuel and oil are given combined as £0·062 3 per hour. The National Institute of Agricultural Engineering estimates that the 'year round' fuel consumption for this size of tractor is typically 3·18 l/h, giving £0·046 7 per hour at the average 1968 fuel cost of £0·014 7 per litre. The same proportional costs for fuels and oils have been assumed for the larger machines.
(Source: ref. 2).

It is possible to estimate the energy cost represented by each pound or dollar invested as capital or operating cost, and Table 7.1 shows how such a calculation is performed and its results. A quite small tractor consumes 417·3 MJ/h (MJ = megajoule, i.e. joules × 10^6). What is interesting is that while the ratio of the horsepower of the smaller to the larger tractor is 1·8,

TABLE 7.2
Energy Inputs for Field Equipment per hectare (Depreciation plus Repairs)

	Energy input MJ/ha		*Energy input MJ/ha*
Plough		Cereal drill	
2-furrow reversible	176	3·5 m	66
3-furrow	86	2·5 m, combine	158
5-furrow	121	Self-propelled tanker–combine	
assumed	120	harvester	
Rotovator	316	2·5 m	770
Cultivator	108	3·0 m	908
Harrow	18	4·2 m	814
Roller, 3-gang	41	*assumed*	820
Fertiliser		Pick-up baler, hay or straw	330
distributor	66	Grass mower (per cut)	104
spinner	25	Hay tedder (per cut)	45
assumed	45	Hay windrower (per cut)	22
Sprayer, low volume	34	Bale handling equipment	270

(Source: ref. 2).

the ratio of the energy they consume is 2·2. It appears that the efficiency of energy use decreases as tractor size increases, despite the fact that the larger tractor has a longer life. The tractor does not work alone: it is used to operate other equipment and implements. Table 7.2 evaluates the energy cost of depreciation and repairs for a series of common agricultural machines, in terms of the energy input cost for each hour of operation.

It costs energy to produce fertilisers, especially nitrogenous fertilisers. The nitrogen they contain, which is actually the plant nutrient element required, is derived from the atmosphere, where nitrogen is plentiful and free. Fixing it in a compound in such a way as to enable it to be supplied to crop plants in an available form is far from cheap, however. To form ammonia or ammonium compounds by the Haber process, a hydrocarbon feedstock must be supplied. Today this is most commonly natural gas, although naphtha, an oil by-product, is also acceptable. Ammonia is formed under great pressure and at high temperatures in the presence of a catalyst. Thus fossil fuels supply not only the energy to fuel the process but the feedstock as well.

Phosphorus and potassium fertilisers also require energy to be expended in their mining, beneficiation and subsequent processing, but much less. Table 7.3 gives the energy cost of the most common fertilisers.

Most pesticides, on the other hand, consume very much more than even

TABLE 7.3
Energy Inputs for Fertilisers, UK 1968–73

Fertiliser type (ingredients as %; $P = P_2O_5$; $K = K_2O$)		*Bagged; factory gate[a] MJ/kg product ICI*	*Leach*	*Bagged; delivered to farm Product MJ/kg*	*Element MJ/kg*
Ammonium nitrate	34·5 N	25·4	25·9	26·2	76·0 N
Urea	46·6 N	36·8	38·6	38·9	83·5 N
Liquid ammonia	82·4 N	50·5	51·2	51·5	62·5 N
Ammonium sulphate[b]	21·0 N	—	16·9	17·2	81·9 N
Diammonium phosphate[b]	18 N 46 P	—	19·5	19·8	76·5 N 13·0 P
Compounds 15–15–21	15 N 15 P 21 K	16·2	16·2	16·5	83·8 N 14·4 P 8·3 K
22–11–11	22 N 11 P 11 K	19·7	19·7	20·0	80·6 N 13·7 P 7·9 K
9–25–25	9 N 25 P 25 K	13·7	13·7	14·0	87·0 N 15·2 P 7·9 K
17–17–17	17 N 17 P 17 K	17·5	17·5	17·8	82·6 N 14·0 P 8·2 K
Potassium salts	100 K				9·0 K
Weighted average nitrogen	100 N				80·0 N
phosphate	100 P				14·0 P
potash	100 K				9·0 K
Lime (ground limestone)					2·0

[a] No packaging charge applied to ammonia.
[b] Calculated from ref. 19 with 4% surcharge for capital and fixed costs, packaging added.
(Source: ref. 2).

nitrogenous fertiliser. They are truly the product of a sophisticated energy-intensive industry that can operate only on a large scale; it is very doubtful whether they could be produced economically in smaller units or in ones isolated from other chemical engineering processes.

As we saw in the last chapter, our heavy investment in the industrialisation of agriculture has been accomplished by large absolute increases in the quantities of food produced. The really big gains, however, have been in the productivity of labour employed on farms, and it is usually in terms of labour productivity that the efficiency of industries is measured.

On this scale modern farming looks very efficient indeed. Hunter-gatherers, such as the !Kung bushmen, can typically produce about 4·3 MJ for every hour spent working.[2] A simple subsistence farmer produces between 25 and 40 MJ per hour. A modern American farmer, using all the chemicals and machines available to him, produces around 3000 MJ per hour, a figure that varies somewhat from crop to crop.

So on the face of it there is a very significant gain. A closer examination shows at least that there is another side to the picture. If grain grown on capital-intensive farms that employ little labour and so achieve a high output per man-hour is fed to livestock, total productivity per man-hour may fall to as little as 50 MJ, which is not much better than the productivity of peasant farmers growing cereals in the tropics. Indeed the final figure is actually much lower, because the peasant farmer grows food for local consumption, while the European or American farmer grows food for processing and for consumption a long way from the farm. When these 'downstream' costs of transport and processing are included, output may be 35 MJ per man-hour or less.

There has been a substantial saving in the size of the labour force engaged in producing and supplying food, but this saving must not be exaggerated. The change in agricultural methods has permitted a much higher degree of urbanisation and this, in turn, has necessitated a much more elaborate system for food preservation and distribution. So while the farm labour force has decreased, the labour force engaged in distributing the food has increased. Agriculture itself requires the supportive labour of those engaged in manufacturing, servicing and selling machines and chemicals. According to Leach's estimate[2] the total number of persons engaged in the production and distribution of food in the UK and in industries that support them is almost 3 million, or about 12·7% of the national labour force.

In terms of efficiency ratios, energy expended compared with food produced, modern farming makes rather a poor showing, and the more highly industrialised it becomes the poorer the showing it makes. Subsistence farmers in the tropics, for example, may produce 60 or 70 times more energy than they expend, while British barley growers may produce about 2·5 times more. Broiler poultry production is much less efficient even than this, consuming 10 times more energy than it produces, and fishing using powered vessels is the most inefficient of all, consuming anything from 20 to 100 times more energy than it yields. Figure 7.1 shows the energy input per acre of land for various UK farm enterprises and Tables 7.4 and 7.5 show how the total energy input to UK agriculture is computed.

The true relevance of figures such as these must not be misunderstood. The aim is not to show that primitive farmers are vastly more efficient than farmers within an industrial society. Even if it were true, such an item of information would contribute little to any discussion of the future development of agriculture and so it would hardly warrant the work

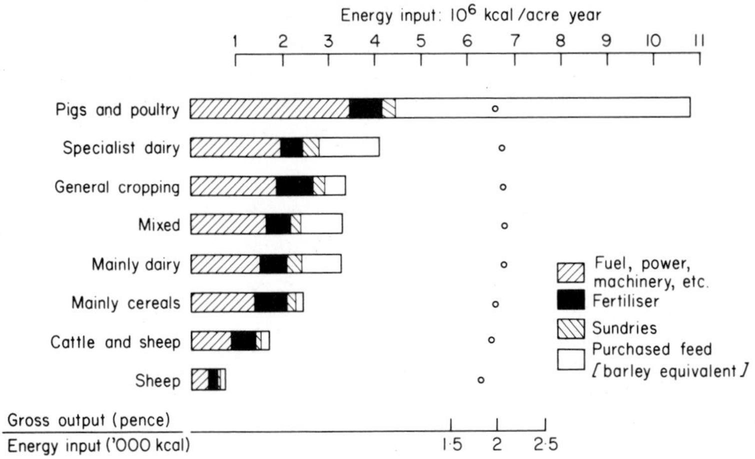

FIG. 7.1. Energy input per acre of land for various UK farm enterprises. (Source: ref. 3).

required to substantiate it. It is much more to be seen as a tool, whereby we may discover the effects of past changes in technology and calculate the benefit we may hope to derive from any proposed innovation in the future. It can help us to distinguish between that which is genuinely advantageous and that which is merely profitable in the short term for the operator. It may show us where the real constraints on our activities may appear. In the words of Gerald Leach:[3]

'The true constraints on man's ability to manipulate the environment for his own ends are ultimately set not by printed notes but by physical or "real" resources such as land, minerals, soil nutrients, water, the pollution absorbing capacity of a region, time (that is, labour), skills, and energy. Human ingenuity may mask this fact for a period, but almost invariably it does so merely by relieving pressures on one resource at the expense of increasing pressures on others—as, for example, when we use extra energy and machinery to reduce pollution, or grow more food on the same land area.'

When we consider the energy cost of actual food items, some of the true resource costs of industrial lifestyles become apparent. The Center for Science in the Public Interest has produced a list of such items produced and consumed within the US food system. A 12 oz bottle of Coca Cola, for example, costs about 7·4 MJ; peanut butter costs 22·9 MJ per lb; 1 lb of grain-fed beef costs 44·9 MJ, while 1 lb of grass-fed beef costs 31·3 MJ.[4]

A computation of the total energy used in the US food system made in 1974 by J. S. and C. E. Steinhart is described in Table 7.6. Measuring in

TABLE 7.4
Major Indirect Energy Inputs to Agriculture, UK 1968

Purchases from:	*Purchases*[a] *M£*	*Assumed* *MJ/£*[b]	*Energy* *MGJ*
Agric. machinery	54	215	11·61
Tractors	36	217	7·81
Pumps	1	142	0·14
Other non-electrical machines	3	129*	0·39
Electrical machines	1	176	0·18
Timber + furniture, etc.	1	91	0·09
Distribution on capital purchases	15	71	1·07
Total capital purchases	111		21·29
Agric. machinery	17·3	215	3·72
Tractors	5·0	217	1·09
Rubber	8·2	337	2·76
Motor vehicles	2·4	234	0·56
Other machinery, metal goods	13·9	mix	2·35
Total machinery non-capital	46·8		10·48
Pharmaceuticals	7·8	342	2·67
Paint	2·3	512	1·18
Soap + detergents	0·7	388	0·27
Other chemicals	15·2	287*	4·36
Total chemicals	26·0		8·48
Bricks, etc.	4·7	624	2·93
Cement	2·1	1 500	3·15
Timber	21·7	91*	1·97
Other building materials	18·6	517	9·62
Construction	40·5	126	5·10
Total buildings	87·6		22·77
Miscellaneous (quarrying, textiles, clothing, packaging, printing, communications)	26·1	mix	4·28
Water	6·0	296	1·78
Rail transport	3·7	185*	0·68
Road transport	28·6	120*	3·43
Other transport	5·3	76*	0·41
Miscellaneous services	54·0	58*	3·13
Distribution	96·5	71	6·85
Total transport, services, etc.	194·1		16·28
Overall total	491·6	(171)	83·58

[a] Purchases from *Input–Output Tables for UK*, 1968 (ref. 20).
[b] All MJ/£ data from Chapman (ref. 21), except * items which are from Wright (refs. 22, 23).
(Source: ref. 2).

TABLE 7.5
Energy Inputs to Agriculture, UK 1968

	Quantity	*Energy, MGJ*
Coal	0·172 Mt	5·62
Coke	0·10 Mt	3·31
Electricity	(3·444 TWh)	(49·59)
60 % for non-domestic	2·066 TWh	29·75
Petroleum: power units		
diesel or gas-oil	0·645 Mt	33·79
fuel oil	0·034 Mt	1·70
vaporising oil	0·060 Mt	3·18
lubrication	0·011 Mt	0·91
50 % motor spirit	0·111 Mt	6·01
Petroleum: heating, drying, etc.	0·484 Mt	24·15
(Total petroleum)	(1·345 Mt)	(69·74)
Total direct energy		108·42
Fertilisers		
N	0·783 Mt	62·64
P	0·482 Mt	6·75
K	0·459 Mt	4·13
lime	4·20 Mt	8·40
Total fertilisers	5·924 Mt	81·92
Machinery		
capital	111 M£	21·29
non-capital	46·8 M£	10·48
Total machinery	157·8 M£	31·77
Chemicals	26 M£	8·48
Buildings	87·6 M£	22·77
Miscellaneous	26·1 M£	4·28
Transport, services etc.	194·1 M£	16·28
Total other inputs	333·8 M£	51·81
Feedstuffs		
food industries	15·13 Mt	51·3
grow imports	(7·01 Mt)	35·2
ship imports	(7.01 Mt)	18·0
Total feedstuffs	15·13 Mt	104·5
Overall total (rounded)		378 MGJ

Total output: 2 380·2 £M. Input/output: 159 MJ/£.

(Source: ref. 2).

TABLE 7.6
Energy Use in the US Food System. All Values are multiplied by 10^{12} kcal

Component	1940	1947	1950	1954	1958	1960	1964	1968	1970
				On farm					
Fuel (direct use)	70·0	136·0	158·0	172·8	179·0	188·0	213·0	226·0	232·0
Electricity	0·7	32·0	32·9	40·0	44·0	46·1	50·0	57·3	63·8
Fertiliser	12·4	19·5	24·0	30·6	32·2	41·0	60·0	87·0	94·0
Agricultural steel	1·6	2·0	2·7	2·5	2·0	1·7	2·5	2·4	2·0
Farm machinery	9·0	34·7	30·0	29·5	50·2	52·0	60·0	75·0	80·0
Tractors	12·8	25·0	30·8	23·6	16·4	11·8	20·0	20·5	19·3
Irrigation	18·0	22·8	25·0	29·6	32·5	33·3	34·1	34·8	35·0
Subtotal	124·5	272·0	303·4	328·6	356·3	373·9	440·5	503·0	526·1
				Processing industry					
Food processing industry	147·0	177·5	192·0	211·5	212·6	224·0	249·0	295·0	308·0
Food processing machinery	0·7	5·7	5·0	4·9	4·9	5·0	6·0	6·0	6·0
Paper packaging	8·5	14·8	17·0	20·0	26·0	28·0	31·0	35·7	38·0
Glass containers	14·0	25·7	26·0	27·0	30·2	31·0	34·0	41·9	47·0
Steel cans and aluminium	38·0	55·8	62·0	73·7	85·4	86·0	91·0	112·2	122·0
Transport (fuel)	49·6	86·1	102·0	122·3	140·2	153·3	184·0	226·6	246·9
Trucks and trailers (manufacture)	28·0	42·0	49·5	47·0	43·0	44·2	61·0	70·2	74·0
Subtotal	285·8	407·6	453·5	506·4	542·3	571·5	656·0	787·6	841·9
				Commercial and home					
Commercial refrigeration and cooking	121·0	141·0	150·0	161·0	176·0	186·2	209·0	241·0	263·0
Refrigeration machinery (home and commercial)	10·0	24·0	25·0	27·5	29·4	32·0	40·0	56·0	61·0
Home refrigeration and cooking	144·2	184·0	202·3	228·0	257·0	276·6	345·0	433·9	480·0
Subtotal	275·2	349·0	377·3	416·5	462·4	494·8	594·0	730·9	804·0
Grand total	685·5	1 028·6	1 134·2	1 251·5	1 361·0	1 440·2	1 690·5	2 021·5	2 172·0

kilocalories, rather than megajoules, the figures show the extent to which the total energy demand has increased in a 30-year period from 685·5 $\times 10^{12}$ kcal in 1940 to 2172 $\times 10^{12}$ kcal in 1970, an increase of 316 %. In the 20-year period between 1952 and 1972, the energy demand from UK agriculture (not the entire food system) has risen by 70 %, while the monetary value of the food produced has risen by 64 %. Table 7.7 reduces inputs and outputs to indices based on a single year, which makes comparisons simpler.

TABLE 7.7
Index Numbers of Energy Input, £ Product and Man-Years, UK 1952–72 (1952 = 100)

	1952	1960	1965	1968	1970	1972
Index energy input	100	119	135	157	164	170
Index £ product	100	120	138	143	152	164
Index labour man-years equivalent	100	81	67	59	56	54
Index $\frac{\text{energy}}{\text{£ product}}$	100	99	98	110	108	104
Index $\frac{\text{energy}}{\text{man-years}}$	100	147	201	267	293	315
Index $\frac{\text{£ product}}{\text{man-years}}$	100	148	206	242	271	304

(Source: ref. 2).

In the USA, maize growing now requires an average of about 6·5 GJ (1 gigajoule = 10^9 J) per acre, soybean production requires about 1·2 GJ per acre and wheat production costs about 2·6 GJ per acre.[5] Similar studies have shown that US beef production requires inputs ranging from 1·9 GJ to 13·4 GJ per 100 lb, the lower figure relating to animals that are largely grass fed, the higher figure to those that spend almost all their lives in feedlots, consuming grain.[6]

This great increase in energy use has done more than release labour. It has permitted, and in recent years positively encouraged, a high degree of specialisation. Figure 7.2 shows the distribution of types of farming in England and Wales. There have always been areas in which it was difficult, sometimes impossible, to grow cereals, but apart from this climatic limitation and the more obvious topographic ones experienced in the uplands of Wales, until quite recently most of these regions produced a fairly full range of commodities. They needed to do so, not simply because of the inadequacy of a primitive marketing and distribution system, but because animals were needed as a source of manure.

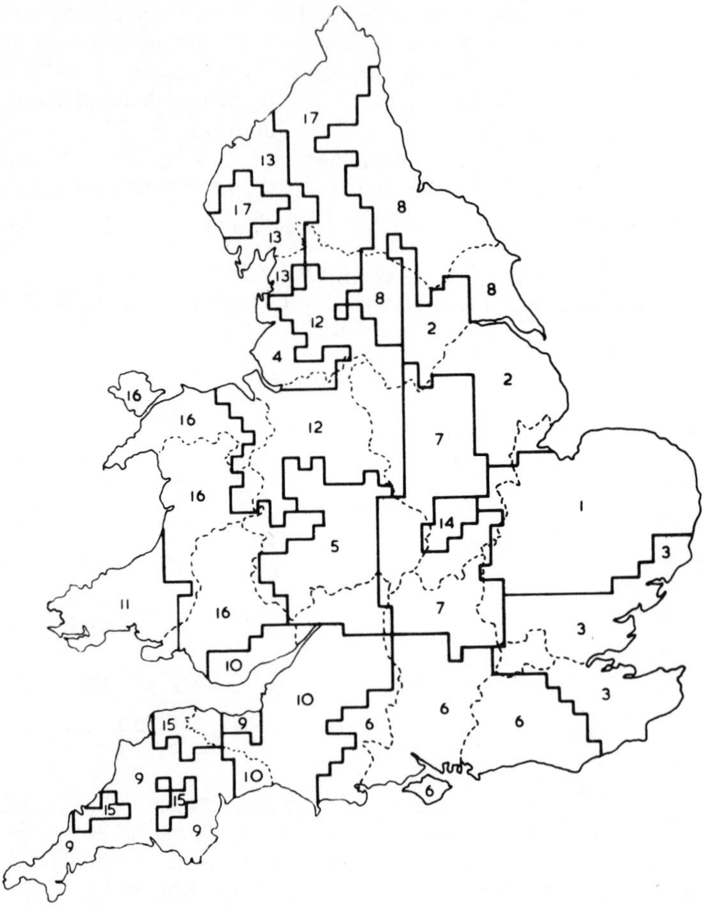

Region type		*Region*	*Region type*		*Region*
Mainly arable	1	E. England	Mainly dairying	10	W. England
	2	E. Midlands		11	W. Wales
	3	Home Counties		12	N.W. Midland
	4	S.W. Lancs		13	N.W. England
Mixed arable and dairying	5	W. Midlands	Livestock and upland farming	14	E. Midlands
	6	S. England		15	S.W. England
	7	E. Midlands		16	Wales (excl. W
	8	N.E. England		17	Pennines and Lake Distri
	9	S.W. England			

FIG. 7.2. Farm type regions of England and Wales. (Source: ref. 18).

The almost symbiotic relationship between livestock and arable land was of very great importance. The introduction of chemical fertilisers on a large scale, produced industrially, allowed that relationship to recede in importance. Farmers were able to specialise, each one growing those crops that could be grown most easily and most profitably.

Figure 7.2 illustrates this rather well. It shows how arable farming has come to dominate in eastern and south eastern England, with an additional small pocket in south west Lancashire, that mixed arable and dairy farming covers most of the central regions, and that dairying and livestock farming has been concentrated in the western areas, with additional pockets in the uplands elsewhere. We should not assume that this farming pattern is absolute or traditional. Although climate and topography have imposed constraints, so that there have always been regions where certain enterprises were too unreliable to be pursued, the most adaptable regions, where all enterprises are feasible, supported most enterprises most of the time. The principle of rotational mixed husbandry based on cereals, roots and grass to feed cattle and sheep, was introduced into Britain from East Anglia, and as we saw earlier the rotation was called the 'Norfolk Four-Course'.

Table 7.8 shows the pattern of fertiliser use in England and Wales in 1974, broken down by crops and including most of the important field crops and permanent and temporary grass. Tables 7.9 and 7.10 show how this pattern has changed over a six-year period. They show that the use of nitrogenous fertiliser on arable crops has declined a little since a peak in 1972, but that fertiliser use on grassland is still increasing.

To what extent is such an energy-intensive system appropriate in developing countries? Indeed to what extent is it sustainable within the countries that are already industrialised?

The concept of the Green Revolution, based as it is on the improvement of yields by the substitution of new cereals varieties that are more responsive to high-technology inputs, demands cultural changes in recipient societies. This is a matter that will be considered in more detail in Chapter 11 but it is one that was overlooked when the FAO plans were devised. Unless the recipient of the products of a particular technology is able to reproduce them within his own society, he must become more and more dependent on the donor. Thus if the new cereal varieties require the use of pesticides to limit losses from the insect pests, weeds and diseases to which they are especially susceptible, then ideally the recipient should be able to buy pesticide chemicals manufactured within his own country. This would ensure that the increased flow of cash and energy (remember that the two are partly interchangeable) would be contained entirely within the local system and the increased cost of more sophisticated farming methods would be recouped from increased farm incomes and these, in turn, would be paid out of higher wages received in an expanding industrial sector of the economy.

TABLE 7.8
Fertiliser Use in England and Wales, 1974

	Fields	*Acres (thousands)*	*Overall units p.a.* N	P_2O_5	K_2O	*% area receiving* N	P	K	FYM	*Actual units p.a.* N	P_2O_5	K_2O
Spring wheat	187	145	55	31	30	95	88	85	—	58	35	35
Winter wheat	2 198	2 628	71	36	30	92	79	73	—	78	45	41
Spring barley	3 034	4 106	58	31	31	97	94	91	—	60	33	34
Winter barley	420	408	72	40	36	98	93	89	—	74	44	41
Spring oats	303	235	46	30	27	93	91	89	—	50	33	31
Winter oats	184	156	55	40	37	96	93	93	—	57	44	40
Mixed corn	106	91	40	39	27	86	84	78	—	46	47	35
Rye	36	27	60	23	18	79	50	47	—	76	46	38
Maize	60	39	91	53	53	92	87	87	—	99	61	60
Early potatoes	75	48	127	136	154	99	99	100	—	127	136	154
Maincrop potatoes	368	308	140	147	196	100	100	100	—	141	148	196
Sugar beet	472	466	118	73	145	100	94	100	—	118	78	146
Swedes and turnips (stock)	222	130	51	68	54	84	87	82	—	61	78	66
Mangolds	48	11	92	69	90	90	86	88	—	102	80	102
Kale and cow cabbage	289	164	84	41	40	95	82	79	—	88	50	51

Rape for stockfeed	84	82	89	63	41	96	94	90	—	93	67	46
Beans for stockfeed	154	115	8	18	16	16	35	32	—	46	52	49
Other stockfeed	91	64	54	43	43	79	78	78	—	68	55	55
Peas for human consumption	185	221	6	20	25	27	52	54	—	23	39	46
Broad beans	15	24	9	20	21	52	52	52	—	17	39	40
Runner and French beans	27	24	110	69	76	92	100	100	—	120	69	76
Brussels sprouts	53	42	181	99	157	99	99	99	—	184	100	158
Cabbages	48	47	122	77	120	100	90	89	—	122	86	135
Cauliflower	25	25	142	103	152	98	93	93	—	145	111	164
Carrots	33	23	67	55	100	76	76	76	—	88	72	130
Onions	25	14	100	101	155	93	98	98	—	107	103	158
Small fruit	30	14	55	29	61	67	60	85	—	83	49	72
Top fruit	88	112	83	18	39	82	49	64	—	102	36	62
Hops	26	23	126	60	141	97	84	95	—	130	71	148
Oil seed rape	29	33	149	51	49	100	100	95	—	149	51	51
All tillage	9170	10059	68	41	45	92	87	84	—	74	47	54
One year leys	77	71	73	28	19	80	49	48	—	91	57	41
Two- to seven-year leys	3754	4518	105	28	23	86	63	60	—	122	45	38
Permanent grass	4093	7386	53	18	12	61	42	39	—	86	42	31
All crops and grass	17094	22034	71	31	29	80	67	64	—	88	46	46

(Source: ref. 18).

TABLE 7.9
Fertiliser Use on Tillage, Leys and Permanent Grass, 1969–74

	1969	1970	1971	1972	1973	1974
			(units per acre)			
N						
tillage	66	70	72	73	71	68
leys	74	85	78	94	99	105
permanent grass	38	41	41	46	47	53
All crops and grass	58	62	62	67	67	71
P_2O_5						
tillage	42	45	43	45	43	41
leys	36	34	30	31	34	28
permanent grass	22	19	22	20	19	18
All crops and grass	34	33	33	34	33	31
K_2O						
tillage	48	49	47	50	48	45
leys	25	25	20	22	25	23
permanent grass	14	14	12	12	12	12
All crops and grass	32	32	29	31	30	29

(Source: ref. 18).

TABLE 7.10
Use of N in Compounds and 'Straights' on Tillage, Leys and Permanent Grass 1969–74

	1969	1970	1971	1972	1973	1974
			(units per acre)			
Tillage						
compounds	47	47	47	47	44	42
straights	19	23	25	26	27	26
Leys						
compounds	31	34	29	31	35	34
straights	43	51	49	63	64	71
P.G.						
compounds	19	18	19	19	18	19
straights	19	23	22	27	29	34
All C. & G.						
compounds	34	34	33	34	33	33
straights	24	28	29	33	34	38

(Source: ref. 18).

Economics is the one sphere of human activity where it really is possible for a community to raise itself by pulling on its bootstraps! However, if the input products are to be manufactured within the society, then that society must already have reached a level of industrial and technological development and competence to provide the resources of capital, plant, personnel and research and development it requires. If this situation obtains, then the transference of the technology is unlikely to be necessary, for it will exist already.

The relationship between donor and recipient will be similar to that between European and North American societies: technologies and scientific information are exchanged as between equals, in both directions, and there is a donor and a recipient for each item but no net donor or net recipient. If the recipient society is not in this position, then it can accept only a part of the cultural complex: the desired technology itself.

Since the technology does not exist in isolation it must remain dependent on the parent culture for the support the technology requires. So the farmer who wishes to use pesticides must buy them from the technological society that introduced him to them. He may be enabled to produce more food but little is done to stimulate the rest of the local economy in ways that would increase the effective demand for his produce. Meanwhile his additional production costs must be paid to a manufacturer overseas. The result could be a net drain on the foreign exchange reserves of the recipient country with little overall economic improvement to show for it. Perhaps the view is jaundiced but it can be argued that the attempt to transfer technologies crudely from the industrial to the non-industrial world guarantees the growing and possibly perpetual dependence of the latter upon the former. If this is the harshest interpretation, the most generous must allow that the alteration of farming technology offers no certain guarantee of economic independence and prosperity.

Agricultural technologies devised in industrial societies may be inappropriate in non-industrial societies for other reasons. As we have seen, the energy accounting applied to British and American farming practice shows that the industry has received a very large injection of energy in the form of fossil fuel power. To some extent this must have increased efficiency but inevitably it has also displaced human workers. At one time not only was a large area of land required to feed working animals, but a large labour force was also required to manage them, on the farm. That labour force has left agriculture, most of it having been transferred to urban-based agricultural supportive industries. Farms have merged to form larger units, a process that continues. It is part of the same process, since the increase in energy-intensiveness has been accompanied by an increase in capital-intensiveness.

It is said that each worker in British agriculture now has the support of a larger capital investment than a worker in almost any other industry.

Machines and chemicals are expensive. It is necessary, therefore, to achieve economies of scale by employing the technology over a large enterprise. Just as fields must be made larger physically to accommodate large machines, so farms themselves must become larger. It is not economic to maintain a complete 'kit' of modern equipment on each of a large number of small farms. The machines cannot achieve their optimum workload even if the small farmers, whose incomes reflect the size of their businesses, could afford investment on this scale. So fields become larger, farms become larger and the human labour force falls still further.

We choose to interpret this as improved efficiency, in the sense of increased output per worker, but there are also losses. Small fields on steep land that could be cultivated with horse-drawn equipment cannot be cultivated with tractors and so they are withdrawn from cultivation entirely. The area inside the gate of each field that is damaged by the movement of machines to such an extent that its fertility is virtually destroyed has grown with the size and weight of those machines. Added, all these small 'islands' on most farms would comprise a considerable acreage of potentially fertile land that at present is unused or under-used.

In developing countries, economies in the size of the rural work force simply cause more unemployment, either in the countryside or in the cities where country dwellers move in search of work that often does not exist. So wealth tends to concentrate in the hands of a dwindling number of people and demand for food fails to grow, while hunger increases.

Now that we have established that in Britain the fossil fuel used to subsidise food production approaches close to and sometimes exceeds the energy value of the food produced—to paraphrase Odum, we are eating many food items that are made entirely from oil and with some, such as intensive poultry production, we are throwing away a substantial part of that oil—what happens to agriculture if fossil fuels become more expensive or scarce? It is very difficult to assess the effect on agriculture or food prices in Britain of recent increases in fuel prices. This is because agriculture is slow to react to changes: it takes at least a full year to see the effect of any change in arable cropping and even longer to see the effect of changes in dairying and beef production. It is difficult, too, to separate out the effects caused by rising fuel costs and those caused by rises in grain prices that occurred at the same time. According to Leach:

'Any attempt to analyse the short-term response of farming and the rest of the food system to higher fuel prices is therefore well-nigh impossible. Broadly speaking, though, it is clear that in the UK at least higher fuel prices have had little effect on farming as a whole—except to push up farmgate food prices. The rise due to energy alone has certainly been as much as 20% in real terms and probably considerably more if one counts indirect effects.'[2]

Leach estimates that a doubling of energy prices will lead to a 10% increase in farmgate prices. If these are passed on to the consumer they will be considerably more than 10% by the time they reach retail outlets, because of the higher downstream processing and distribution costs.

In the USA an attempt has been made to determine the effect on agriculture of increased energy costs. The Center for the Biology of Natural Systems at Washington University, St. Louis, Missouri, has compiled energy budgets for a wide range of farm enterprises, but budgets that differ somewhat from the total energy budgets used elsewhere to evaluate the overall energy dependence of food production. The aim here was to consider only that part of the food system over which the farmer has immediate control. Thus the energy cost of fixed equipment and buildings, purchased before the rise in energy prices, is omitted, as are all downstream costs.[7]

A total of 29 crop systems was considered, covering most of the important arable crops in different localities to allow for variations in climate and soils. In general the results show that energy input costs rose on average between 55 and 75% between 1970 and 1974, most of the increases falling between about 63 and 67%. It is more difficult to estimate how much of this increase was passed on to the consumer. The prices paid to farmers for many commodities increased before the effect of increased oil prices had worked through to affect input costs. Thus the fraction of the price received by farmers that can be set against input energy costs has sometimes risen, sometimes remains constant, but in many cases—19 out of the 29 investigated—it has actually fallen, showing that prices have risen faster than energy input costs.

The conclusion must be that, when seen in a total economic situation, energy costs represent only one factor in determining food prices. In a free market economy, supply and demand exert a much more dominant effect. American wheat prices rose much more rapidly than the energy costs for wheat production because demand for wheat was strong. High costs for feedingstuffs led to a reduction in beef production and so prices for alfalfa (called lucerne in Britain) and hay fell, although the cost of producing them had risen. The price of ammonia fertiliser rose more rapidly than the energy cost of its production—rapid though that was for this energy-intensive commodity—because demand for ammonia increased. Overall, then, increased oil prices had a rather minor effect on food prices. The CBNS team conclude that:

1. For every crop, the energy component of production costs has risen sharply, typically by between 50% and 75% from 1970 and 1974.
2. Other variable production costs have also risen sharply—generally by about the same fraction as energy costs. However, for a few crops energy costs have risen at a rate significantly different from that of other costs,

sometimes more rapidly, sometimes more slowly. The main factor is the specific form of energy needed to produce the crop.

3. For most crops, the increase in the price received by the farmer has been proportionately larger than the energy price increases.

However, the fact that rises in fuel costs have had a fairly minor effect on food prices does not mean they will not do so in the future. The report warns:

'... the present relationship between input costs and crop prices will not necessarily continue indefinitely. Successive good world harvests could soon cause crop prices to level off or even to fall somewhat. This would not subsequently cause a drop in energy prices, nor even a halt to energy price increases.'

A subsequent study[8] attempts to assess the vulnerability of particular crops to changes in energy costs. Again the conclusion is that while, at present, energy costs are a minor factor in total costs and prices, the situation could change and the price and availability of energy could become critical.

No one can know where such a critical point will be encountered, since it will be experienced by farmers quite subjectively. Individual farmers do not base their plans on assessments of the world food situation, or even of the national situation, except in so far as they try to guess at the relative demand for different commodities. They look at their own income and their own costs. Consequently it is they who determine at what point changes are made in farming technology and the nature of such changes, and they do so in order to maximise their incomes, rather than for idealistic motives.

If energy costs increase, and these increases are reflected in increased chemical prices, at what point will farmers begin to use less chemicals? What will happen if they do? In Chapter 9 we consider the possibilities of making substantial reductions in the use of agricultural chemicals, as one of the options open to farmers in the future. More immediately the CBNS comparison of organic and conventional farms in the US corn belt[9] in 1974 shows that the lower energy input costs for the organic farms more than offset their rather lower yields, although the differences in yields were not very large. So under 1974 conditions organic farmers, who differed from their more conventional colleagues only in that they used no artificial fertiliser except rock phosphate, no insecticides and very little herbicide, had a slight edge.

For the conventional farmers 1974 was a bad year. The weather was poor. 1975 was a much better year, and the CBNS study continued, showing that yields on the conventional farms improved and the conventional farmers regained the economic advantage. Should energy costs rise further, organic farmers may find they have a more permanent competitive edge, and should food prices fall, since prices are determined by the market and not by input costs alone, their lower input costs could cushion the effect.

In the most extreme situation, in which energy prices were rising while the price of food was falling, organic farmers might become so self-evidently more prosperous than their neighbours that a swing toward organic farming methods could occur. In a sense this is happening already. After all, as the CBNS report points out, 'organic' and 'conventional' farming systems are points on a continuum, not systems that are fundamentally different. There is a wide area within which compromises are possible and individual farmers may select the most suitable point on the continuum according to their own requirements. In Europe, interest in organic farming and the advantages it may confer—environmental advantages as well as economic ones—has stimulated much interest in recent years and there can be little doubt that some farmers are modifying their methods in the direction of organic principles and that many more would like to do so.

This being so, we may wonder whether or to what degree it is appropriate to consider transferring from industrial to non-industrial societies technologies that, in the absence of the cultural context within which they evolved, are liable to cause as many economic and social problems as the agricultural ones they solve, at the very time when the economics of farming in industrial societies may be suggesting a move away from those very technologies.

If modern agricultural technology is vulnerable to changes in the price and availability of the fossil fuel energy on which it has become so dependent, it is also vulnerable genetically and this is far more serious.

The initial alteration of an ecosystem, whereby the natural living community is removed to make way for a more limited number of those species of plant and animal favoured as sources of food, represents an ecological, or genetic, simplification. The range of genes contained within the area is reduced by the exclusion of certain species. As a limited range of crop plants continues to be grown year after year, random in-breeding, out-breeding and cross-breeding with nearby wild relatives of crop plants leads to the development of crop varieties that may all look roughly similar, but that in fact are different genetically. This has advantages and disadvantages for the farmer, and it is the disadvantages that are likely to become apparent first.

Such genetic diversity makes it very difficult to control the crop. Among the characteristics acquired genetically are those which govern rates of seed germination, the time interval between flowering, fruiting and the setting of seed, the ease with which seed is shed from the plant and dispersed, the reaction of the plant to more or less water and more and less nutrient. If these characteristics can be standardised, productivity can be improved. A crop will respond uniformly to particular treatments and it will ripen together, so making harvesting easier and reducing losses in the field caused by seed that has ripened too early being shed. It will reduce problems caused by the germination of such seeds among following crops.

Modern plant breeding aims essentially to achieve just this kind of uniformity, although uniformity is not always the immediate overt goal. The development of the Green Revolution hybrid cereal varieties, as a simply technological response to a complex range of problems, provides a classic example. The problem was how to increase crop yields in tropical and sub-tropical regions where cereals developed for temperate climate conditions would not thrive.

More specifically the problem was that when additional fertiliser and water were applied to many traditional cereal varieties in developing countries, the plants responded by growing much taller as well as by producing larger ears. The weight of the heavier ears was too great for the stem and in moderate wind or rain the stem would fail mechanically and the plant would fall over, or 'lodge'. A lodged crop is difficult to harvest at the best of times, although a modern combine harvester can cut close to the ground provided—a big proviso—there are no large stones on the surface, hidden by the crop, that will damage the cutting blades. Inevitably, though, losses are heavy. Moreover, should the fallen grain become damp it may germinate, which will destroy it altogether as a useful grain. Shed grain may complete its own natural cycle by re-sowing itself. Cereal grains actually bury themselves by the alternate flexing and straightening of the fibrous beard in response to changes in atmospheric humidity. So they may become weeds that interfere with the following crop.

The search began to find new varieties that were short-stemmed and thus more robust mechanically, that responded to increased fertiliser by depositing more nutrient in the 'sink'—the seed—that grew more seed for less leaf and stem, and that matured and ripened in a shorter time. As we saw in Chapter 3 the search was successful. The new varieties were developed and if they were not adopted on the scale the breeders might have hoped, this was not the fault of the research institutes that produced them.

Other searches, which continue all the time, are for crop plants, especially cereals, that are resistant to fungal disease and to a lesser extent to infestation by insect pests. In both cases susceptibility to attack is transmitted genetically; fungi and some insects are attracted to particular qualities in the target, qualities that are inherited.

Most plant breeding is a laborious business involving the growing of thousands of plants, from which those bearing the desired characteristics are isolated to be grown again. It may take many generations to achieve a new variety that has commercial potential. In Chapter 3 we saw just how difficult was the process that led to the new hybrid high-yielding cereals.

There is an alternative, however. While conventional plant breeding is based on the random mixing of the ingredients in a particular, closed, gene pool, it is possible to alter genes deliberately, to induce mutations. In nature, mutation occurs in all species at random. The vast majority of random mutations confer new characteristics that have no survival value and the mutant strain dies out. From time to time, however, one will prove successful. Natural mutations do occur in normal plant breeding, of course, but in recent years research institutes all over the world have been experimenting with induced mutations. By inducing mutations deliberately, the rate of mutation can be made to increase dramatically above the normal level. While the majority of mutations will continue to be valueless, the small proportion that are useful will be represented by a much larger actual number of plants.

Much of the work on mutation induction is co-ordinated by the International Atomic Energy Authority of the UN, which holds meetings and symposia at which workers may discuss their findings. Almost every crop plant is the subject of experimental work in this field, and positive results are beginning to emerge in the form of varieties that carry desirable, and new, characteristics. Tolerance against one or more diseases has been induced in wheat and millet and information has been collected on the genetic factors that confer disease resistance or susceptibility. In many vegetatively propagated crops, some of which, like banana, cacao, cassava, citrus, coconut, coffee, rubber and sugar-cane, are of great economic importance in the tropics, it is difficult to conduct conventional breeding experiments. In some, generative reproduction may be uncommon, while in others the breeding cycle is so long as to make conventional breeding programmes impossibly lengthy.[19]

Mutations are induced chemically by applying known mutagenic substances to seeds or by exposing seeds to ionising radiation, which explains the interest of the IAEA. There can be no doubt that great benefits are to be derived from such work but there are other, subtler, dangers once the results of the breeding stations come to be applied in the wider world outside.

Imagine what would happen if breeders were to develop a new variety of wheat that yielded four times more grain than existing varieties. At first the seed would be very expensive and for this reason, and because farmers are conservative in their habits and not all of them read their newspapers and trade magazines, little of the new wheat would be grown. The farmers who did grow it would earn much larger incomes and this fact would not be lost on their more cautious neighbours. So more farmers would begin to grow it. As soon as average yields began to rise, prices for wheat grain would begin to fall owing to the increase in the supply. Farmers would then need to grow larger yields in order to earn satisfactory incomes. So eventually almost all farmers would be compelled to grow the new variety and those who lacked the finance to invest in any new technologies or inputs required, or who were too set in their ways, would be squeezed out of wheat production entirely.

A point would be reached when a very large part of the national stand of wheat would be of a single variety. Every plant would be, genetically, the identical twin of every other plant. This new situation would replace the present one, where farmers may choose from a list of varieties—each genetically different from the others—so that the national wheat stand contains considerable genetic diversity. If this genetically uniform stand were suddenly to prove susceptible to a particular disease or pest, the entire national crop would be at risk, since the characteristic that rendered one plant susceptible would be present in all plants.

Could this happen? Yes, it could. Crop breeding is tending in this direction as it tries to develop cereal varieties that will do for temperate climate agriculture what the Green Revolution varieties promised to do for tropical and sub-tropical farmers. So the wheat variety may be produced. It will be impossible to predict its resistance to disease for more than a year or two in advance, with even the most exhaustive screening, because of random mutations among the pathogenic fungi.

Crop varieties that are bred for resistance to particular diseases usually lose their resistance after five or six years because the fungus mutates into a new form that the variety is unable to resist and so the disease becomes virulent. While a wide range of varieties is grown the effect is not serious nationally, although it can be very inconvenient for individual farmers. In 1972, in Britain, two popular varieties of wheat—Joss Cambier and Cama—were attacked by the disease they had been bred to resist and the yield from these two wheats fell between 25 and 30 %.

The danger of genetic uniformity is illustrated more clearly, however, by the most spectacular plagues of modern history. In 1870, for example, Sri Lanka was the world's leading producer of coffee. By 1885 it was exporting no coffee at all. The entire industry collapsed—and carried a bank with it—because of a fungal disease (*Hemileia vastatrix*) which killed all the plants. The planters changed to tea as quickly as they could and the British became a race of tea drinkers. In 1917, Americans had two wheatless days a week because of the devastation caused in the previous year by red rust. Red rust is the disease mentioned in the Bible as that which, together with the moth, 'corrupts'. The Romans named a god, Robigus, after it.[11]

These outbreaks are largely forgotten today. The Irish potato famine is remembered. The potato was introduced to Europe, probably from Colombia, in the sixteenth century, but it was not until the eighteenth century that varieties were developed that could be grown widely in the European climate. A very restricted range of varieties was produced in Ireland, where the potato rapidly became the staple food. The principal disease of potatoes is blight, caused by a fungus, *Phytophthora infestans*, and the potato plants that were brought across the Atlantic were not infected with it, so they were able to grow in the absence of this natural control. All potatoes of a particular variety are genetically uniform because potatoes are reproduced vegetatively.

Technically all potatoes of any particular variety are the same plant. In the 1830s, *P. infestans* crossed the Atlantic. Particular weather conditions were required for it to begin to multiply rapidly and it was not until 1845 and 1846 that these occurred. The result is history. The human population of Ireland was halved.

The most recent severe outbreak of disease was the the southern cornleaf blight that reduced American maize production by 15% in 1970. The severity of this outbreak was the direct result of plant breeding programmes.

In 1917 Donald F. Jones, then a graduate student, discovered a way of producing hybrid maize commercially, to produce yields 25% higher than those being produced at the time. Unfortunately his technique was very expensive. The maize plant is self-fertile. The tassels at the top are the male flower. To produce a hybrid the two varieties had to be planted in alternate rows, but in order to ensure that plants in one row were fertilised only by plants in the next row the tassels had to be removed from the plants that were to be fertilised. Detasselling was done manually by schoolboys.

In 1931 a variety was developed in which the male flower was sterile. This obviated the need to detassel the plants manually but the progeny from the cross also proved sterile. Further research revealed that sterility was transmitted genetically, not through the cell nucleus but through the cell cytoplasm of the female. The new and useless hybrid suffered from cytoplasmic male sterility. Eventually a gene was discovered that would restore fertility to the progeny and this was incorporated. The restorer gene occurred in a mutation that was found in Texas and the strain bearing it was called the T (for Texas) strain. It became the basis for all subsequent maize breeding until, by 1970, nearly every commercial maize variety in the country carried T cytoplasm. In other words almost the entire national maize crop was based on cytoplasm that was identical, although the cell nuclei differed.

In 1962 two maize breeders working in the Philippines, Mercado and Lantican, published a note in the *Maize Genetics Cooperative Newsletter* in which they pointed out that a fungal disease caused by *Helminthosporium maydis* was particularly virulent among plants carrying T cytoplasm. In 1965 they published a second paper on the subject. Neither they nor anyone else foresaw the risk of a major epidemic, perhaps because *H. maydis* itself was so well known. It had been present in North America since the arrival of the first settlers and it had never caused serious problems. Each year it would kill a few plants and occasionally it would mutate to a more virulent form, but the virulent forms never managed to establish themselves. The observations from the Philippines were assumed to relate to tropical conditions that favoured the fungus in some way.

Then *H. maydis* mutated again. The epidemic began in the early spring of 1970 in Florida. Weather conditions were favourable for it and it spread rapidly north. By the time scientists realised that it was the T cytoplasm that rendered plants vulnerable to it, it was too late. Virtually the entire national crop was at risk. In 1971, T cytoplasmic varieties still dominated commercial maize production because they had displaced all other varieties. Fortunately the weather in that year did not favour the disease and so the epidemic was contained.

The effect of the southern cornleaf blight epidemic was serious enough to stimulate a full investigation by the National Academy of Sciences into the degree of genetic vulnerability of major US plant crops.[12]

The report found that a high degree of genetic uniformity exists in a number of important crops. Most wheat breeders have concentrated on a single cytoplasmic sterile type, placing as much emphasis on this (called the *Triticum timopheevi* type) as maize workers placed on T cytoplasm, and the risk may be especially great among the new dwarf varieties. Of sorghum the report said:

'... the genetic diversity in parents is not sufficient to give adequate protection against a catastrophic epidemic and a real threat exists'.

It found that rice is highly vulnerable. Ninety percent of the southern US rice acreage is sown to five varieties and virtually all the Californian acreage is sown to three varieties.

Potatoes are being cultivated on a very narrow genetic base and although no threat is known to exist, if a new disease should arrive the degree of vulnerability to it could be high. In 1970, 68·8 % of US sweet potatoes were of a single variety and more than 90 % of the country's sugar beet carried similar cytoplasm. Genetic uniformity was also pronounced in soybeans, peanuts, peas, many brassicas and upland cotton.

The danger is obvious and it is one that the Green Revolution programmes increase by replacing a wide variety of traditional crops by uniform stands. It is made even more serious by the fact that the populations of the world depend for the bulk of their food supply on a very small range of crop plants. More than half the world population depends on rice for most of its dietary energy, and more than 60 % depends on rice, wheat, maize, sorghum or barley. Most of the remaining energy is supplied by potatoes, sugar cane, cassava, bananas, beans and soybeans. Altogether there are no more than about 20 plant species that supply almost all our food. The first risk, then, is that increasing genetic uniformity will threaten one or more of these plants over a wide geographical area.

There is a second genetic risk, only partly related to the first. As agriculture expands into new land and as existing agriculture becomes more intensive, a large number of wild plants are destroyed. It is estimated that at present there are some 10 000 species of wild plants that are threatened with extinction. The risk to these plants is recognised by UN agencies and gene banks are being established in a number of places.

The concern for endangered wild species is not merely sentimental: there is a hard, practical core to it, for the extinction of species depletes the global gene pool. Once a plant or animal ceases to exist there is no way in which it can be recreated. All our domesticated plants and animals have been developed from wild ancestors. At some time in the future it is certain that a need will arise for new plants or animals that have commercial potential as sources of food. They may be required either for cross-breeding with closely related domesticated varieties in order to transfer such desirable characteristics as, for example, might facilitate the adaptation of a species to a particular environment, or for full development as a new crop species.

For some years eland have been raised in parts of Africa and they appear to have certain advantages over imported cattle, especially in their adaptation to environments cattle find hostile. In North America the bison, which almost became extinct, is now crossed with imported cattle to produce the 'beefalo', a hybrid animal that carries many of the advantages of both varieties. Soviet workers have experimented with the domestication of indigenous species of deer and in Scotland the red deer may soon be farmed commercially in areas that cannot produce beef.

The value of plants is less well known but the US National Research Council has listed 36 tropical plants that have 'significant potential' as new sources of food or raw material.[13] An investigating panel examined 400 plant species and found that 9% of them were potentially useful. In some cases they may prove very useful indeed. There is the winged bean, that has an unusually high protein content, the joroba bean, which produces an oil similar to sperm oil, a tree that can provide forage for sheep and that grows on extremely salty soils, and a Texan shrub that produces more rubber than the rubber tree.

The problem of the conservation of species also has a moral aspect. Although we may not wish or need to exploit the potential of a species that at present is wild, we have no way of predicting the conditions that may obtain in the future. By depleting the gene pool we restrict the freedom to manoeuvre of those who will follow after us. We have no right so to compromise future generations.

Conservation is not a simple matter. Seed banks can store seeds over long periods but to do so is not natural. From time to time the seeds must be germinated and grown, for no seed lasts forever. As time passes, the workers who must grow these plants will become less and less familiar with species that are long extinct in the wild and so the risk of accidents increases. Furthermore by conserving seeds in this way the species are removed from the natural environmental pressures to which they would adapt. Should the time come for them to be sown again, in the wild or commercially, conditions might have changed so drastically that they were no longer able to survive.

A similar problem exists with obsolete varieties of cultivated plants. These are under pressure from two directions. On the one hand, as we have seen, the trend of scientific research and agricultural development is to encourage ever larger stands of ever fewer varieties. On the other hand, national and international policies to protect growers can also limit the number of varieties grown.

EEC regulations require all commercial seeds to be registered.[14] After a period for registration the official list was published and thereafter it became illegal to sell seeds of any variety not included in the list. It is not an offence to grow such a variety, only to sell the seed from it. The regulations were introduced after a period during which commercial seedsmen had, in any case, been shortening their lists of traditional crop varieties to make way for new, improved varieties.

One of the voluntary organisations most concerned with this threat in Britain is the Henry Doubleday Research Association, which comments:

'The Regulations have the following effects:

'1. They make it impossible for a specialist seedsman to collect scarce varieties from amateur gardeners, peasants, or overseas sources, list them and sell to connoisseurs, plant breeders or universities at a price which allows for the small demand. He can apply for permission to have the variety brought back on the list to be tested at Cambridge for two years. He will then have the responsibility of keeping it stable and true to name. The cost of this is prohibitive to any small seedsman in any of the Nine. This means that the survival of old varieties depends on keen gardeners with old fashioned tastes who are a dying race in all countries.

'2. Each variety is in the National List under its correct name, with its traditional synonyms which are permanent, and its non-traditional synonyms, which will be deleted on 30 June, 1980. The correct name must be used before the selection name, which will be accepted until and unless the first is removed from the list. As an example: Bedfordshire Champion is the correct name of the onion which has Brown Globe as its traditional synonym. Its non-traditional synonyms are Bedfordshire Champion, Hurst Reselected, Golden Globe and Nuttings Golden Ball. Seedsmen have grown onions under these names for many years, and there is no way of being certain that they do not have special qualities we may need in the future. It is not possible to measure the taste of an onion, or its "strength". There is no publication setting out the mineral, vitamin, or amino-acid analysis of the varieties of onions or any other vegetable. It may well be desirable to breed vegetables for any of these qualities yet all will cease to be available in 1980.

'As an example of the wide variation possible between varieties that morphological and taxonomical opinion considers identical, Bedfordshire Champion is highly susceptible to downy mildew (*Peronospora destructor*) yet Up-To-Date, which is regarded merely as a selection of it, is highly resistant in both leaves and foliage (sic).[15]

'3. Seedsmen will gain by conforming to EEC regulations, which will make it easier to export to European seedsmen, and easier for these to export to us. Many catalogues contain an increasing number of European kinds. This will mean increasing pressure to reduce the number of older varieties to make room for new kinds which can be printed large and black and pushed as major improvements. The effect of this will be that fewer and fewer seedsmen will list any of the older kinds, which will be discarded as the National List and the EEC Common Catalogue are reviewed, and varieties which have ceased to be "top of the pops" are deleted.'[16]

The Henry Doubleday Research Association serves amateur gardeners, many of whom are recruited to take part in trials and rather informal experiments and investigations of various kinds, including the testing of techniques and products as well as observing ecological situations in their own gardens. It proposes that its members support the establishment of a central seed bank for traditional varieties of vegetables to prevent their extinction and loss.

It is at least possible, then, that the industrialisation of agriculture may bring threats from two directions. By increasing the energy input to the system it increases productivity, but it does so by creating a growing dependence among farmers on fossil fuels, whose availability and price cannot be predicted accurately. Within industrial countries farmers may respond to rising energy costs by shifting toward more organic methods. This suggests that it might be appropriate to investigate much more deeply than anyone has done so far the possibilities for adapting not organic farming techniques—for the transference of any technology from industrial temperate to non-industrial tropical cultures is fraught with difficulties—but the approach to husbandry of organic farmers who have had many years of experience of practising their methods in an economic climate that has not favoured them. This same increase in dependence on energy subsidies for food production also displaces labour and favours the wealthier farmers and landowners, so its social and economic effects may be very different from those desired.

At the same time, the new technologies may erode the genetic base of agriculture and so the genetic stability of the systems of farming they replace.

Perhaps we should consider in more detail the desirability of widening the genetic base of our food supply, by widening the range of crop plants on which we depend and by increasing the variety of crops of individual species. The danger of serious disruption from widespread epidemics is very real. Some of these issues will be dealt with in Chapter 9, where we consider some of the options open to us in the future and some of the work being done at present to explore them.

REFERENCES

1. Odum, H. T. (1971). *Environment, Power and Society*. Wiley, London.
2. Leach, G. (1975). *Energy and Food Production*. International Institute for Environment and Development, London.
3. Leach, G. The energy costs of food production. Mimeo.
4. Fritsch, A. and Dujack, L. (1975). *Energy and Food*. CSPI, Washington.
5. Lockeretz, W., Klepper, R., Gertler, M., Fast, S. and O'Leary, D. (1975). *Energy in Corn Belt Crop Production*. Center for the Biology of Natural Systems, Washington University, St. Louis, Mo.
6. Lockeretz, W. (1975). *Agricultural Resources Consumed in Beef Production*. CBNS, Washington University, St. Louis, Mo.
7. Commoner, B., Gertler, M., Klepper, R. and Lockeretz, W. (1974). *The Effect of Recent Energy Price Increases on Field Crop Production Costs*. CBNS, Washington University, St. Louis, Mo.
8. Commoner *et al.* (1975). *The Vulnerability of Crop Production to Energy Problems*. CBNS, Washington University, St. Louis, Mo.
9. Lockeretz, W., Klepper, R., Commoner, B., Gertler, M., Fast, S., O'Leary, D. and Blobaum, R. (1975). *A Comparison of Organic and Conventional Farms in the Corn Belt*. CBNS, Washington University, St. Louis, Mo. This study continued and a further report was issued in 1976, comparing data for 1974 and 1975.
10. FAO/IAEA (1973). *Induced Mutations in Vegetatively Propagated Plants*. Vienna, 1973.
11. Allaby, M. (1973). Miracle rice and miracle locusts, *The Ecologist*, **3**(5), 180.
12. NAS (1972). *Genetic Vulnerability of Major Crops*. National Academy of Sciences, Washington.
13. *New Scientist*, 25 March, 1976, p. 659.
14. The Seeds (National Lists of Varieties) Regulations in the Plant Varieties and Seeds Acts, 1964, as amended by the European Communities Act, 1972.
15. MAFF. *Diseases of Vegetables*, Bulletin No. 23. Ministry of Agriculture, Fisheries and Food, London.
16. *Vegetable Seed Library, Preliminary Proposals*. Henry Doubleday Res. Assocn, Braintree, UK, 1975.
17. Steinhart, J. S. and Steinhart, C. E. (1974). Energy use in the US food system, *Science*, **184**.
18. MAFF (1974). *Survey of Fertiliser Practice*. HMSO, London.
19. Slack, A. V. (1967). *Chemistry and Technology of Fertilisers*, Wiley Interscience, New York.
20. CSO (1973). *Input-output tables for the United Kingdom* 1968. Central Statistical Office. HMSO. London.
21. Chapman, P. (1975). *Energy analysis of the UK Census of Production* 1968. Report ERG 006, from Energy Analysis Group, Open University, Milton Keynes, Bucks., England.
22. Wright, D. J. (1973). The natural resource requirements of commodities. Paper to conference on energy analysis, Imperial College, London, July 1973.
23. Wright, D. J. (1974). Goods and services: an input–output analysis. *Energy Policy* **2,** 307–15.

Chapter 8

THE IMPORTANCE OF CLIMATE AND WEATHER

The weather is the subject of endless jokes about the British interpretation of the art of conversation. It is one of those subjects about which everyone has an opinion and, more confusingly, a memory. Memory does confuse us because we tend to remember phenomena that are exceptional. We remember the 'memorable' but the ordinary, the average, passes without notice, even in Britain. So as we grow older the summers and winters we recall from our youth are the long hot ones and the hard, cold snowy ones. In other words we remember the exceptions to the rule and when we gaze from our windows or sit, damp and miserable, contemplating the ruin of a washed-out summer holiday, it is the exceptional weather from the past with which we compare it. Inevitably the weather appears to be getting worse.

This is the conventional view and obviously there must be some truth in it. Yet what if our memories were not playing us false? What if the weather in the late 1970s really is worse than the weather we knew as children? After all, climates are not constant. If we extend our time scale from that of human lifetimes to something closer to geological time, we can count several full ice ages, one quite recently. We can count periods when Britain had a climate much more like that of the Mediterranean today. We can even find evidence, admittedly from much further back in time, of even warmer periods. If this is so, then it may not be impossible that the climate is changing within our own lifetimes, and that we are witnessing the change. Indeed if we accept that climates are not fixed eternally, it becomes inevitable that the weather patterns are changing constantly. So our memories may not be playing tricks with us. The weather of 20 years ago very possibly was rather different from the weather we see today. What we have not determined is whether today's weather is 'worse' or 'better' than that of the recent past.

Superficially it would appear that the British weather is becoming warmer and drier. This is the subjective view, based on what we actually observe, even if we allow for the possibility that the weather we have experienced recently is exceptional (memorable!) and that soon it will return to its more usual pattern, leaving the golden summers of 1975 and 1976 to linger in the memories of our children, who will use them in their old age as 'evidence' that the weather is deteriorating.

The true evidence does not support this view. Indeed it runs directly counter to it, so that a rather wider picture of what has been happening elsewhere in the world is required in order to make the current theories more credible.

In March 1976, Wisconsin experienced the worst 'ice storm' ever. For a week, freezing rain fell heavily over much of the state. As it impacted it froze. Thick layers of ice grew on the ground, on buildings, on trees and on power lines. The trees that line the streets of Milwaukee and Madison were bent over by the weight of the ice and finally broke. The trees are planted to provide shade from the summer heat. Eventually the rain stopped, only to be followed by icy winds blowing south from Canada. It was the wind that broke the trees and brought down the power lines. The ice short-circuited insulation points on pylons, so that spectacular fireballs ran along the remaining lines and whole areas were deprived of power.

People began to try to heat their homes by open fires lit in their decorative and non-functional fireplaces, and fire brigades had a busy time damping down the results. Milking machines, powered electrically, would not work, so the large dairy herds in America's most important dairying state could not be milked. The milk from those that were milked had to be poured away because the milk could not be separated. Fashionable suburban homes were without water, for each had its own well, whose water is delivered by an electric pump.

Of course the ice storm ended, the wind died, the thaw came and the damage was repaired. It was a nine days' wonder (fairly literally) and the tale will be told and retold until, much improved, it is filed away as part of the folk lore of that part of the world. Yet something had happened to the weather. Was it just a freak or did it indicate some deeper change?

American farmers have been struggling with adverse weather for several years. Drought when rain was needed, floods when in most years the weather was dry, weather that was hotter or—more usually—colder than usual, all have reduced agricultural output. On at least one occasion unusually early frosts delayed the Canadian grain harvest. It is argued now that for the past 30 years the American grain growing areas have enjoyed unusually good weather, that it is the period from the 1940s to the 1970s that was exceptional and that we may anticipate a return to more usual, and much worse, conditions.

In other parts of the world, competition for scarce water had led to tense international situations. India, for example, has dammed the River Ganges some 200 miles north of Calcutta in order to divert the main flow of the river south into the Hooghly, so as to flush out the port of Calcutta of accumulated silt. The conflict arises because naturally the Ganges flows in a more easterly direction, through Bangladesh. Bangladesh is thus deprived of water which is critically important during the annual dry season.

Upriver storage reservoirs collect Ganges water during the wet season for irrigation in the Indian states of Bihar and Uttar Pradesh during their dry season, but Bangladesh farmers derive no benefit from this at all. The Indians now propose to build a canal through Bangladesh to link the Ganges with the Brahmaputra, to the east. This would improve the scheme, since the Brahmaputra rises earlier than does the Ganges, so the water could be diverted westward to compensate for the dry season before the dry season began. The Bangladesh farmers would then have access to water for irrigation as well as the Indian farmers. However, the very existence of the canal would cause a certain amount of agricultural disruption in Bangladesh and, much more sinister these days, it would place absolute control of Bangaldesh's two main rivers in Indian hands.

In the Near East, trans-frontier relations have been strained by competition for river water, especially from the Jordan.

The weather is what we experience from day to day—the immediate manifestation of climate, which is determined by the behaviour of very large air masses. If meteorology deals with immediate phenomena and detailed observations and predictions, climatology deals in more majestic concepts and time scales. Conflicts over water resources, farmers' worries over poor growing conditions, may seem unrelated to possible changes in the world's climate, but the picture is much too complex for anyone to be certain.

In Chapter 1 we saw how the failure of monsoons, the very long drought in the Sahel Zone of Africa and drought in the USSR had caused local famines and had contributed to the disruption of world food balances in 1972 and 1973. Yet the southward spread of the Sahara into the Sahel, or border region, may be caused as much by human activity as by climatic change. Certainly this is the view of Mr Mostafa K. Tolba, Executive Director of UNEP, the UN Environment Programme. 'I believe man is more to blame', he told the press in Geneva in September 1976.[1] 'It is he who is aggravating what nature is doing', and he warned that each year more land is lost to desertification and to urban expansion than is brought into agricultural production. In 1977, UNEP is to sponsor a major conference on desertification.

People react to environmental changes, and the reaction to a natural change that causes a desert to spread may eventually cause it to spread further.

The Sahel is a vast, remote area, populated sparsely by people pursuing a mainly nomadic, pastoral way of life. The vegetation is too poor to permit of any kind of settled livestock husbandry, far less of cropping, so herds of animals are driven from pasture to pasture. As the desert encroaches on traditional pasture lands, so the farmers find themselves crowded more closely on the land that remains and this pasture, never good and now weakened by drought, is over-grazed.

As the vegetative cover is destroyed its root system dies and the soil loses some of its structure. It is covered by blown sand, it erodes or compacts, and so the desert spreads a little further. The farmers move again and the pattern repeats itself, as the herds are driven further and further in an attempt to escape from the desert they are creating. The problem is made even worse by the exploitation of the herdsmen by merchants in the cities who have found lucrative markets for indifferent meat and so encourage farmers to increase the size of their herds, and by veterinary advisers who try to improve the economic status of the farmers by reducing mortality among the herds, so enabling the population of animals to grow.

The story is tragic and the choices that face advisers are agonising. The reduction in the incidence of disease in cattle can have a significant effect. The most serious cattle disease in tropical climates is trypanosomiasis, transmitted by parasites carried by the tsetse fly. Since the tsetse fly also causes sleeping sickness in humans there is good reason to wish for the insect to be controlled. Intense efforts to achieve such control began in the 1960s, initially based on moving people—and herds—out of infested areas. Then pesticides were used intensively and infested forest areas were cleared to destroy the fly's habitat.

According to Dr W. E. Ormerod, of the London School of Hygiene and Tropical Medicine, 'increasing wealth of the coastal nations has led to a massive increase in demand for high quality meat in the big towns such as Accra, Abidjan and Lagos, and disease control has enabled quick profits to be made out of vast herds even when losses are high on the long treks.'[2] At one time, trypanosomiasis was estimated to cause the death of about 3 million cattle a year in Africa. Its reduction means the size of herds increases. Nor does it end there, for the clearance of forests to destroy tsetse fly habitat simultaneously opens new areas for grazing—and over-grazing. As the herds move out of the Sahel they are moving into the Sudan.

The FAO continues to press for funds to bring the tsetse fly under control, and it sees the consequent expansion of herds as unequivocally good:

> 'A massive but long and difficult campaign to eradicate the tsetse fly could boost herds in tropical Africa from 20 million to 120 million head—opening up one of the world's greatest potential untapped sources of protein food and almost doubling Africa's total number of cattle on the hoof.'[3]

To be fair the FAO does acknowledge the risk of over-grazing, but its attitude may seem somewhat casual:

> '. . . there is the danger of over-grazing, if the growth of herds and land use is not properly planned and controlled. However, experts from industry express confidence that a concerted effort and a political will to control tsetses and trypanosomiasis would benefit both wildlife reserves and grazing resources because of the increased attention that would focus on them.'[3]

This rather delightful example of official casuistry proceeds in a neat circle. It takes for granted that independent, semi-nomadic peoples, whose contact with Europeans is small, can be organised so that their behaviour is 'planned and controlled'. It anticipates great benefits to wildlife from the destruction of the habitat it shares with the tsetse fly. Finally it solves all of its problems by asserting that these will disappear if outside advisers watch them closely enough, a conclusion that may not be warranted by past experience of industrial assurances that its activities will produce effects that are only beneficial.

Clearly the political and ethical problems are difficult. To what extent can one oppose measures taken to control the insect that spreads a disease which takes a heavy toll in human life and suffering? Yet a doubt remains, a suspicion that the real motive is profit, short term profit to be found in the wealthy markets of the oil-rich capitals by traders, and that all else is no more than lip-service to the environmental lobby and, incidentally, to the needs of the pastoralists themselves.

All deserts are spreading. The US Agency for International Development (US AID) has estimated that in the past half-century some 650 000 km^2 on the southern edge of the Sahara have become barren. In the 1950s acacias were common around Khartoum. By 1972 the nearest trees were 145 km further south. The Chilean Atacama Desert is advancing about 2 km a year. The Mexican Chihuahua Desert, formed during the past few centuries, continues to advance. The Indian Thar Desert, in Rajasthan, expands at the rate of about 13 000 ha a year; already the desert is larger than the whole of France. Dr Erik Eckholm, of US AID, is outspoken on the subject:

> 'The population of arid North Africa has multiplied six-fold since the beginning of the century and the destruction of vegetation in Morocco, Algeria, Tunisia and Libya has accelerated, particularly since about 1930 when the population of these countries began to rise steeply. Over-grazing, the extension of unsustainable grain farming and firewood gathering have all contributed to the deterioration of the agricultural environment. The result is the degradation to desert-like conditions of about 100 000 ha of land each year.'[4]

This would suggest that human agency is responsible for the spread of deserts and thus for any climatic changes consequent upon that spread. Is this entirely true? It is an example of the complexity of the situation in which so many independent variables act upon one another.

Actual measurements of what is happening to climate are difficult. In the northern hemisphere there are sufficient weather stations to feed a constant stream of reliable data, but in the southern hemisphere, which consists mainly of ocean, stations are very few and far between. Thus the picture is much more complete for the northern than for the southern hemisphere. Even in the north, however, the changes are so small as to be dwarfed by normal season variations, so that figures remain tentative and controversial for some time before they can be confirmed. It is known, for example, that in the north the average temperature has fallen over a 30-year period. If this is so, you would expect the northern polar icecap to have increased in size. It is said to have done so by most climatologists.

Discussing climate change in an article in *The Guardian* on 3 November, 1975, for example, James Taylor stated that net solar radiation had decreased and that 'this has been shown by the advance of the polar icecap'. On 1 December, 1975, however, Pearce Wright, Science Editor of *The Times*, quoted a paper published in the monthly magazine of the Meteorological Office by Dr R. M. Sanderson:

> 'An investigation of the so-called ice-limits, made possible with special satellites circling the Earth in a polar orbit, shows that there has been a steady decline each year in the total area of sea over which ice forms.'

Within a few weeks of one another, two specialists disagree publicly over a fundamental issue.

Clearly there are dangers in any attempt to interpret climate change on the basis of inadequate data, and these dangers become greater if the attempt is extended to relate climate change to human activity. In the past, historians have tried to explain historical events in terms of climate change. The result has usually been a distortion of both histories—that of the climate and that of human institutions.

Climates do change through historical time but there is no reason to suppose that they do so according to any regular, repeating cycle. At any particular time, three cycles at least are operating together. There is a long term oscillation between glaciations or other major climate patterns that occupy periods of time measured on a geological scale. So at present and during the whole of recorded human history, we live in an inter-, or post-glacial period. It is inter-glacial if one assumes that it will be followed by a further glaciation, in which case, technically, the Holocene Epoch has not yet begun and we are still living in the Pleistocene. There are many scientists who hold this view. It is a post-glacial period if no further ice ages are to come, and in that case we do live in the Holocene.

Within this—from our point of view—very long oscillation there are smaller ones that operate over centuries. Within those changes there are still smaller ones that operate over decades or even shorter periods. So the fact that a particular year is relatively warm or cool, wet or dry, may amount to no more than a local swing around a median that is determined by a short term secular change (decadal warming or cooling) which in turn may be a short term variation from another median, and so on. This makes very long range forecasting exceedingly difficult, if not impossible.

It is known that the earth has experienced several periods of glaciation, when the climate has been generally cold. Obviously the average temperatures experienced during recorded history have been much higher than those experienced then, although one must be wary even with a statement so apparently obvious, since there were periods of remission during the glaciations that would have brought warmer weather for periods amounting to several human generations.

One of the best reviews of the history of climate was written by Professor Ladurie,[5] whose work is of such careful, dedicated and one might almost say loving scholarship that it deserves a much wider currency than it may have received. Prof. Ladurie has studied historical records and compared these with dendrochronological findings, the changes in the position of glaciers in Europe and elsewhere, and with records of wine and other agricultural harvests, to produce an account of the changes that have taken place in climate over the past 1000 years and, in some instances, for much longer.

Between 1400 and 1300 BC the Alpine glaciers extended themselves, according to the scientists who studied them,[6] further than at any time since the Ice Age. Between 900 and 300 BC the glaciers extended themselves again, in two thrusts separated by a century or a century-and-a-half of withdrawal.

During Roman times the climate was much warmer, but between AD 400 and 750 the glacial extensions reached another maximum. They withdrew again, advancing once more from about AD 1150 or 1200 to about AD 1300 or 1350. The climate grew warmer, only to be followed by the 'Little Ice Age', during which the glaciers extended again, and which lasted from about AD 1550 to 1850.

So the weather is sometimes warmer, sometimes colder. Yet its phases form no regular cycle, except to the extent that a maximum must be followed by a decline, a minimum by a rise—what goes up must come down! Glacial extensions reach maxima that may last 100 years (1400 to 1300 BC) or 300 years (AD 1550 to 1850).

Since about 1850 the climate has grown warmer again. Thus the pictures we have of extremely cold winters in Dickensian times are related to fact: the winters were much colder in those days.

The warming was a trend only, and there were variations from median. In figures quoted by H. H. Lamb,[7] for example, average temperatures fell sharply during the first decade of this century and slightly during the 1930s. Following the maximum reached in about 1942, however, the general trend has been toward a cooling, which began to slow down in the mid-1950s, reversed and became a warming from about 1959 to about 1961, then resumed.

It was possibly the temporary reversal around 1960 that caused some of the confusion among those interested in interpreting climatic trends in the late 1960s, when the data were being made available. While one school of thought held that the trend was downward, another school held that that trend had 'bottomed out' and was reversing. We can see now that the reversal was only temporary. The cooling has affected sea temperatures as well as those on land, again with the short term reversal. Sea temperatures in the North Atlantic averaged for nine Ocean Weather Ships, reached a maximum in 1950 and by 1968–72 were more than 0·5 °C lower.

The most extreme effects are seen in the arctic, however. Again according to Lamb, during the 1960s the number of months during which temperatures were below the average values for 1931–60 increased year by year, from 5 months in 1960 to a maximum of 10–11 months in 1968. Over the whole decade, 64 per cent of all months were cooler than average. Unless the other months were exceptionally warm to compensate, this suggests a general fall.

The fall was maintained in the period from 1970 to 1973, with 8–9 months below average in 1970, 7–9 in 1971, 7–8 in 1972 and 7 in 1973: 62·5 % of all months. During this period the cold centre around which northern hemisphere weather circulates moved from Siberia to northern Canada, for reasons that are not known, and the growth of snowbeds and glaciers in parts of Canada is causing concern. During the 1960s and early 1970s only 8·4 % (1960s) and 4·2 % (1970s) of all months were warmer than average.

It is winter temperatures that lead climate changes. There is evidence that at earlier times when the glaciers were extending, a series of cold wet winters were followed by the beginning of the growth of the glaciers. The theory of sudden full glaciation, the subject of a major BBC television documentary that caused some unnecessary alarm, is based on this fact. If winters become colder and longer, and summers consequently cooler, then a point may be reached where winter snows do not disappear entirely during summer. This would increase the albedo—reflectivity—over the area, so reflecting back into space incoming solar radiation and contributing to further cooling. The theory is attractive but it is no more than a theory.

In the UK the mild winters since 1970 have raised 1971–73 average winter temperatures to a level with those of the 30-year period up to 1960, though springs and summers are cooler. During the period 1960–69, overall mean temperatures were 0·3 °C below the average for the previous 30 years.

Rainfall distribution has also changed. The Climatic Research Unit at the University of East Anglia has used figures for rainfall distribution as the basis for statements about more general weather patterns.

As we have seen, all along the southern edge of the northern hemisphere deserts, rainfall has decreased. Something rather similar seems to have happened in the southern hemisphere. In the tropics, rainfall has increased. Further north (and presumably south), in the Mediterranean latitudes, rainfall has increased. Beyond this belt, both north and south of the Equator, areas of increased and decreased rainfall alternate. In the northern hemisphere they form rather vertical patterns, in the southern hemisphere the divisions are oriented more NE–SW. In latitudes higher than this, snowfall has increased.

These changes have been sufficient to produce severe droughts, as in the Sahel, and acute local difficulties, but in general it seems that the reductions in rainfall are greater in the lower latitudes, close to the Equator, than in the higher latitudes.

When data for temperature and rainfall are compared with figures for average pressures it appears that average pressures have fallen a little at the Equator and at both poles, and that both northern and southern middle latitudes have come to be dominated by bands of relatively higher pressure. This new pattern of pressure distribution is all that is needed to provide much of the explanation for changes in rainfall. In the Sahel Zone, for example, prevailing winds now come from the north east, across large land masses in Asia and Europe. This accounts for the apparent paradox that the Sahel Zone is now in an area of mainly low pressure that one would usually associate with wet weather. What does all this mean? Lamb offers the following conclusions:

(*i*) Forward computation of the solar radiation available in different latitudes and seasons over the Earth with the slow cyclic changes of the orbital arrangements seems to imply development towards an ice age situation (possibly less extreme than the last glaciation) about 10 000 years hence.

(*ii*) The operation of superposed fluctuations on time scales from about 200 to 2000 years, possibly attributable to solar output fluctuations and changes of the combined tidal force of sun and moon, must be expressed to produce long periods of climatic recovery (increasing warmth) or of apparent long-continued stability of climate, followed by sharp (step-like) cooling, superposed on any slow general decline of temperature level in the millennia ahead. These shorter term changes must of course be much more apparent to the people living at the time than the 10 000-year trend, but at some point within the next few millenia one of these combinations may be sufficient to change the climate near 50 °N in Europe rapidly to one favouring pine rather than oak forest and the possibilities of cultivating grain and fruit crops accordingly. The corresponding changes to be expected in Africa and elsewhere in low latitudes might be partly elucidated by studying evidence of the tendency during analogous climatic fluctuations in the past.

(*iii*) There seem to be similarities between the course of the climatic fluctuations that have taken place during the present century and those that occurred just 200 and 400 years earlier. The parallel with the sixteenth century may be the closer of the two, but both are in some respects impressive.

Two hundred years ago there was a further cooling within the already cold period.

The problems of dealing with data collected over a comparatively short period in order to make statements about much longer periods is demonstrated by the fact that, speaking on 17 March, 1976, Dr B. J. Mason, Director-General of the Meteorological Office, appeared to use the phenomenon of the recent mild winters to conclude that the cooling trend had been arrested. 'There is no real basis for the alarmist predictions of an imminent ice age,' he said,[8] 'which have been largely based on extrapolation of the 30-year trend of falling temperatures in the northern hemisphere between 1940 and 1965. Apart from the strong dubiety of making a forecast from such a short-period trend, there is now evidence that the trend has been arrested.' He went on to suggest that comparisons with the 1931–60 period, on which Lamb's calculations are based, may be misleading, since that period 'was probably one of the most abnormal 30-year periods in the last thousand years'.

This argument is rather unsatisfactory. If comparisons with the 1931–60 period are invalid we are thrown back either on the observation that, in general, temperatures have risen since about the middle of the nineteenth century, with the 30-year period of cooling being dismissed as aberrant, or on the experience of the mild winters of the early 1970s. In either case, evidence seems to be dismissed on the grounds that it does not support a theory, and this is bad science.

In the temperate latitudes the general weakening of weather systems has led to an increase in anticyclonic patterns in the mid-Atlantic. The 'blocking' anticyclones that used to hold back or divert cyclonic weather in its movement eastward towards Europe now last for much longer periods. They are rather stronger than they were, so permitting depressions to fill more rapidly. In north west Europe we would expect this change to result in a marked reduction in westerly weather. The mild wet air that used to reach us in westerly winds from the Atlantic, that moved anticlockwise around cyclones located to the west or north west of the British Isles, has given way to much drier air from the east or north east, as air moved in a clockwise direction around anticyclones.

Records have been kept of the number of days each year when general westerly winds blew over the British Isles. These show[7] that in the mid-1860s there were about 95 such days each year. The number fell slowly until about 1885, when it began to increase again, continuing to increase with a brief lapse around 1915 until it reached a peak of almost 110 days during the late 1920s. Then it fell again, recovered during the 1940s, resumed its downward trend and, by 1970, had reached a figure of about 75 days a year, lower than at any time for more than a century. So indeed the incidence of westerly weather is decreasing.

It is difficult to derive from this any clear picture of the changes to be expected in day-to-day weather, except that it will conform less closely to the patterns of the past. In other words, summers and winters may be warmer, cooler, wetter or drier than those we think of as normal. It is likely that in Britain weather will assume more continental characteristics with long dry periods interrupted by violent rains, but from time to time giving way to more traditional westerly weather. In the long term the trend is toward cooler weather in all seasons.

During the late 1960s and early 1970s there was considerable speculation about the effects human, and especially industrial, activity might be having on climate. As we saw earlier, intensive agriculture, especially over-grazing by livestock, can and does accelerate the spread of deserts, with a consequent feedback to the local climate: a reduction in plant cover increases albedo and at the same time reduces the amount of water reaching the atmosphere from transpiration and the amount of dew that is held by plants. Albedo increases, surface evaporation increases, transpiration decreases and the climate becomes drier.

It was suggested that two factors were acting in opposition to one another. Increased combustion of fossil fuels was releasing into the atmosphere quantities of carbon dioxide that were sufficient to disturb global radiation, and so heat, balances. This was called the 'greenhouse effect', although the name is not really accurate. Carbon dioxide molecules absorb long wave radiation but not short wave radiation. The earth receives solar radiation in a wide spectrum but much of it is concentrated in the short wavebands as visible light. This radiation reaches the surface. As the surface or objects on it or in the atmosphere are warmed, they begin to emit long wave radiation. Much of this escapes into space, so balancing that part of the incoming radiation that is not utilised elsewhere in the system. Long wave radiation that encounters carbon dioxide molecules is 'trapped' by them. They are warmed and then they emit long wave radiation in all directions, some of it out into space but some toward the surface. So an increase in atmospheric carbon dioxide will lead to a general atmospheric warming.

A similar effect may be produced by water vapour in the atmosphere, and a further by-product of the combustion of fossil fuels is water vapour. Although this is called a 'greenhouse effect', in an actual greenhouse the heating is due mainly to the enclosed space that does not permit cooler air to enter and the trapping of outgoing long wave radiation by the glass. Carbon dioxide and water vapour play a minor role. At all events the 'greenhouse effect' should lead to a general warming.

The combustion of fuels also warms the atmosphere. Whenever fuel is burned—or indeed whenever energy is expended in any purpose—a proportion is lost as low grade heat into the environment so that, in accordance with the second law of thermodynamics, eventually all energy gradients are reduced to zero. The extent of the warming that occurs is a direct function of the amount of energy that is used and so industrial activities also raise the temperature of the atmosphere.

The picture is complicated by the fact that while water vapour will amplify the 'greenhouse effect', the formation of cloud will increase the planetary albedo, reflecting back incoming radiation and cooling the atmosphere. So water vapour effects the atmosphere in both ways.

The effect of carbon dioxide molecules in air is different at different heights. In the lower atmosphere, long wave rays warm the molecules and long wave radiation is emitted by them in all directions. The lower in the atmosphere the molecule is, the greater is the chance that the radiation emitted from it will encounter another carbon dioxide molecule, when the process will be repeated and the proportion of radiation lost to space will become smaller and smaller.

In the stratosphere, however, the atmosphere is much rarer, especially above the molecule, and the chances of a random encounter with another molecule are more remote, so the proportion lost to space is much greater. In the stratosphere, then, there is little or no warming effect. At the same time the chances of a carbon dioxide molecule encountering incoming long wave radiation are also greater, and so a proportion of incoming radiation will also be lost by re-radiation into space. Thus the net effect is to cool the upper atmosphere, warm the lower and increase the lapse rate.[10]

It has been estimated[11] that a doubling of atmospheric carbon dioxide, from 300 to 600 parts per million, might lead to an increase in temperature of about 2 °C in the lower troposphere and a cooling in the stratosphere ranging from about 2 °C at 25 km to about 12 °C at 40 km, the radiative cooling increasing from about 1° to about 1·1 °C per day at 25 km and from about 4° to about 5 °C per day at 40 km. The cooling in the upper atmosphere would decrease the frost point, which determines the quantity of water vapour needed for the formation of cirrus-type clouds, so cloudiness might increase. Such clouds are extremely tenuous, however, and it was considered that they would have no significant effect on radiation balances.

The carbon dioxide effect, leading to a general warming in the lower atmosphere, was believed to be countered by an increase in atmospheric particles which tended to cool the atmosphere. Particles are released into the air naturally, especially by volcanoes, and as a result of human activity. Aerosols—minute particles with a fairly long residence time in the atmosphere—absorb heat and scatter radiation. The backscattering of incoming radiation has a cooling effect similar to that of increasing the planetary albedo. The absorption of heat has a generally warming effect in the troposphere, but in the stratosphere, because the heat is absorbed so far from the earth's surface, the effect at the surface is felt as a cooling.

Until fairly recently it was believed that in the troposphere the backscattering effect of aerosols was much greater than any compensatory absorption effect, so their presence could be associated with a general cooling. Today the picture is less clear, because some workers[10] believe that certain man-made aerosols that contain carbon, iron oxides and some other materials may absorb more heat than they scatter. Aerosols also act as condensation and freezing nuclei, so their presence may lead to increased cloudiness.

It was postulated, then, that man may influence global climate in two ways and that in general these two mechanisms opposed one another. Since an atmospheric cooling has been observed, it was argued that the effect of aerosols must be the dominant one.

This was not the effect that would be predicted on the basis of a simple calculation of the quantities of carbon dioxide and aerosols released into the atmosphere. In fact carbon dioxide was not accumulating at the rate it was being emitted at the surface. The reason for this is the existence of 'sinks' into which carbon dioxide is absorbed. Green plants, for example, utilise carbon dioxide in photosynthesis, and an increase in atmospheric carbon dioxide might stimulate an increase in plant growth which would release oxygen and so increase the atmospheric content of that gas, and this would dilute the remaining carbon dioxide, probably to the level that had obtained originally.

Carbon dioxide is also slightly soluble in water and so the oceans represent a further—in fact the major—sink. No one knows the total absorptive capacity of the oceans, so that if surface emissions of carbon dioxide continue indefinitely, a point may be reached beyond which the sinks will absorb no more and atmospheric levels begin to rise rapidly. Even if this should happen—and it is not likely because of limitations on the total reserves of fossil fuels that are available to be burnt—there is considerable leeway within the system before climatic changes become serious and, of course, they act counter to the aerosols which this model of the world's atmosphere holds to be dominant. So initially the effect would be benign.

Bryson holds that the changes observed in surface temperatures and rainfall since the 1940s can be attributed to human activity, since the extent of this activity is sufficient to account for the changes within the models he uses. He deals with both carbon dioxide and aerosols.

Since, as we have seen, the effect of carbon dioxide is to increase air temperatures at low altitudes but to decrease temperatures in the upper air, so increasing the lapse rate, on his model of the behaviour of air governed by the Hadley and Rossby regimes we should expect the ITD to be confined more closely to the Equator, which is what has occurred. If as he suggests the average increase in surface temperatures attributable to carbon dioxide since 1940 (forgetting the counterbalancing effect of aerosols) is in the order of 0·1 °C for known emissions, lapsing to nil at a height of 3 km, then he calculated that the sub-tropical anticyclone belt should have been displaced towards the Equator by about 15 km.[9] This would produce an annual decline of rainfall in northern Nigeria and, he suggests, throughout the Sahel of about 75 mm.

Aerosols have not been emitted at the same rate in all parts of the world.

Indeed they are associated particularly with industrial activity. Thus they are concentrated more heavily in the higher latitudes of the northern hemisphere. So one would expect a reduction in radiation reaching the surface that is greater in the higher latitudes than in the lower. Even if emissions were distributed evenly, the angle of incidence of incoming radiation is such that it has a longer passage through the atmosphere in higher latitudes than in lower ones, so the effect would be the same. For one reason or another, incoming radiation is required to pass through more turbid air in the north than in the south. The steepening of the pole–Equator temperature gradient suggested by this hypothesis has been observed.

The extent to which human activity can be held responsible depends on the size of the human contribution to total aerosol emissions. Bryson states that according to his own calculations about 17% of all temperature variance caused by increased turbidity over the past century is attributable to agricultural, industrial and other human activities. In recent decades, however, this contribution amounts to much more like 30%. The remainder comes mainly from volcanic activity. So according to Bryson, while human behaviour cannot be indicted positively as a cause of the present climatic change, this behaviour has occurred on a scale large enough to account for the change.

So is what is happening natural or is it induced by man? No one knows but there is a plausible theory based on natural change. In the 1920s a Yugoslav scientist, Milutin Milankovich, suggested that long term climatic oscillations, those that produce ice ages, are caused by changes in the earth's orbit around the sun. The idea was interesting but it could not be tested because insufficient data existed about past climates. In recent years, as we have seen, intensive research into past climates has produced much of the information needed and the Milankovich theory is attracting support.

A team at Columbia University, New York, led by Dr James D. Hays, has tested the theory and is convinced by it. In a statement issued at Columbia in late November 1976, they said:

'We are certain now that changes in the earth's orbital geometry caused the ice ages. The evidence is so strong that other explanations must now be discarded or modified.'[1]

At present the earth is heading for another ice age and the cooling during the last 30 years is expected to continue:

'This cooling trend should continue for on the order of 20 000 years. In that length of time I think there is not much doubt that we will build up substantial ice on the Northern Hemisphere continents.'

Man may also be altering the composition of the upper atmosphere by the injection of chemical compounds that react with ozone. In recent years the effects on the ozone layer from exhaust emissions from aircraft and from the chlorofluorocarbons used as 'freons' to propel substances from aerosol cans, have been considered in this context. Most of the concern has been over the possible effect on health of an increase in radiation in the ultra-violet band that reaches the surface. It is possible, however, that interference with atmospheric ozone might have climatic effects.

Ozone is formed in the upper atmosphere by the bombardment of oxygen by ionizing radiation. Oxygen molecules split ($O_2 \rightarrow O + O$) and a proportion of them reform as ozone (O_3), which is ionised again by further bombardment in a continuous process that derives its energy from the radiation, so absorbing it. It is estimated that about 3% of incoming radiation is absorbed in the ozone layer and about 20% in the remainder of the lower atmosphere. It is this 3% absorption that accounts for the relatively high temperatures encountered between about 25 and about 50 km above the surface.

Effectively this process blankets out the radiation it absorbs and it absorbs rays preferentially in the ultra-violet waveband, so that the ozone layer forms a partial shield against ultra-violet radiation that otherwise would reach the surface: unless, of course, an increase in the amount of radiation that passed through the upper layers simply led to the dissociation and recombination of oxygen and ozone at lower altitudes, where the air contains more molecules per unit volume, so that the weakening of the ozone layer led to a general increase in the ozone content of the air at lower levels. It would not produce another ozone layer as such, because this depends on air that is much more stable mechanically than is the lower air. This possible compensatory effect may have been overlooked.

Ozone is highly unstable chemically, so that the introduction into the upper atmosphere of chemical substances with which it can react may lead to the formation of relatively stable compounds, thus depleting the reservoir of ozone and ionised oxygen. This, so runs the theory, could weaken the ultra-violet shield.

It could also have other effects. If a smaller proportion of incoming radiation were absorbed, then the temperature of the upper atmosphere might fall. At the same time the increase in the radiation passing through the ozone layer would permit an increase in absorption in the lower atmosphere and an increase in the amount of energy received at the earth's surface. This warming of the lower atmosphere and cooling of the upper atmosphere would sharpen the lapse rate, with climatic implications.

Man's influence on local climates and weather patterns is well documented, but at present his influence on global climate remains controversial and highly theoretical, even in the short term. Since the 1972 UN Human Environment Conference in Stockholm, steps have been taken to improve the monitoring of the atmosphere for pollutants and to provide better information on weather patterns. Orbiting satellites observe the atmosphere constantly. The day may come when it will be possible to say with more certainty whether or not man has, or can have, a significant effect on a system that is powered, after all, by an energy source far greater than anything he can muster. Probably such influence as he has will be caused by leverage exerted at weak points in the system rather than by massive interventions that override natural tendencies.

Meanwhile the more plausible explanation is the purely natural one. Climates change naturally, they have done so throughout the history of the planet without the aid of man, and the present change is neither so large nor so rapid as to require any additional explanation.

Studies of some of the very ancient changes in climate have been made at the Geography Institute of the Georgian Academy of Sciences in the USSR. Studying deposits in a cave that date back for 100 000 years, certain clear changes have been detected in the last 35 000 years. There have been six brief, but sharp, cold periods and seven much longer phases of moderate and warm weather. The scientists conducting the investigation believe these changes cannot be accounted for by geological processes on earth, such as mountain folding, vulcanism, the contraction of land or invasions by the sea. They suggest some extraterrestrial cause, such as the Milankovich orbital geometry theory.

It does seem as though climate is changing, for whatever reason. Any such change is bound to affect plant growth and so food production may increase or decrease.

In the sub-tropics conditions are likely to remain very difficult. According to both Bryson and Lamb the average rainfall in marginal areas is likely to remain lower than it was earlier this century, so regions where rainfall was already low may become desert for climatic reasons, regardless of human activity. It would not be realistic, therefore, to plan for increased production along the southern edge of the northern hemisphere deserts or to direct investment there.

Further north, in the temperate regions, growing seasons are shorter. An examination of records at six agricultural stations within the US corn belt shows that since 1945 the growing season has grown shorter by between 22 and 39 days.[12] At present the average length of the growing season, calculated from the end of the spring frosts to the beginning of the autumn frosts, is about 165 days. Since the new hybrid maizes require between 100 and 130 days from sowing to harvest, little further deterioration can be tolerated.

The immediate problem, however, is not the average length of the season so much as the variations around the mean that can produce sufficient good seasons to warrant continued investment but occasional bad seasons that cause substantial losses. We can say that while it may be possible to estimate maize yields once sowing has been completed and one end of the growing season has been passed, it will not be possible to use any past figures as a basis for estimates of yields in future years. The conditions are inherently unstable and crop failure is more probable than it used to be. Nor can we expect vigorous attempts to be made to expand production if these would require further capital investment, for the risk will be too great.

Further north, in Canada, difficulties have been experienced already with cereal crops, as the shortening of the growing season has made for late spring sowing and harvests damaged by early autumn frosts. Climatically the entire grain growing region of Canada is marginal and a continued cooling need not proceed much further before cereal cropping becomes very difficult indeed and perhaps impossible. The Canadian situation is made worse by the shift of the arctic anticyclone from Siberia to Canada. At present, according to Lamb, it is centred between north east Canada and Greenland. This means the prevailing winds over the prairie provinces are now north-westerlies, blowing down from the Arctic Circle. In western Canada, possibly including parts of Alberta, winds may be more westerly but the moist air they bring in from the Pacific will be shed over the Rockies. Alberta was already a rather dry area.

The increase in pressures immediately to the south of the arctic will also bring prevailing northerly winds over much of the grain growing region of the USSR. Again these winds will be cold, but in this case wet, so agricultural conditions in the Soviet Union will be complicated. Colder weather will make most cropping more difficult, but wetter weather will be beneficial. Apart from the 1972 drought the trend has been towards wetter weather. Further east a fall in pressures over central Asia may bring somewhat milder conditions but in central parts of Siberia prevailing winds will be more easterly, bringing dry air across the European land mass.

In the maritime parts of Europe, growing seasons have also become shorter. In Britain, for example, the growing season is about 10 days shorter than it was in the 1940s.

In South East Asia, away from the monsoon areas which must be regarded as agriculturally unreliable, conditions should remain largely unchanged, although an increase in easterly winds across the South Pacific could lead to increases in rainfall. Recent trends have been toward drier weather, however.

In the southern hemisphere the general cooling will shorten growing seasons and there, too, deserts are spreading. In Australia the desert has become somewhat drier than it was but the areas surrounding it have become wetter. Probably this represents a net improvement in farming conditions. New Zealand has slightly more rainfall than it had, as does the coastal belt around southern Africa. Apart from part of southern Brazil and northern Argentina, which are wetter than they were, most of South America south of the tropics is drier than it was formerly.

Except in marginal areas that are very sensitive to quite small changes, the effects of climate change so far have been slight. Indeed it is not so much the increase or decrease in rainfall, or the decrease in average temperatures, that creates problems, so much as the instability that makes predictions more difficult. A weakening of weather systems means that the old clearly defined seasonal changes are less reliable.

The overall effect of climate change as it has been experienced, and the increasing effect should recent trends continue, is to make agriculture more difficult in most regions, including the main cereal growing areas. This does not necessarily mean production will fall but it does mean the climate must be taken into account if plans are made to increase output. Part of the effort directed to increasing production may be needed to sustain present levels. It means, too, that research into new techniques and new crop varieties must aim for more efficient utilisation of solar energy so as to shorten the time taken for plants to mature, and so far as it involves the development of new machines, these machines must be able to work on land that is less robust than land is today, without damaging it. Machines may need to become smaller and lighter, for they may need to get on to land that is wetter and possibly colder than most present-day farmers would consider it desirable to work.

REFERENCES

1. UN Environment Programme (UNEP) (1976). *Uniterra*, p. 2. Nairobi, September.
2. Quoted in *The Guardian*, 15 March, 1976.
3. FAO press release, 5 April, 1976. Rome.
4. Quoted in *The Guardian*, 9 January, 1976.
5. Ladurie, E. L. (1972). *Times of Feast, Times of Famine*. Allen and Unwin, London.
6. Aario, L. (1945). Ein nachwärmezeitlicher Gletschervorstoss in Oberfernau, *Acta Geographica*. Finland; and Mayr, F. (1964). Untersuchungen über Ausmass und Folgen der Klima und Gletscherschwankungen seit dem Beginn der postglazialen Wärmezeit. Ausgewählte Beispiele aus den Stubaier Alpen in Tirol, *Zeitschrift für Geomorphologie*, cited by Ladurie, op. cit.
7. Lamb, H. H. *The Current Trend of World Climate: A report on the early* 1970*s and a perspective*. Climatic Research Unit, School of Environmental Studies, University of East Anglia, Norwich, UK.
8. Quoted in *The Times*, 18 March, 1976.
9. Bryson, R. A. (1973). Drought in Sahelia: who or what is to blame?, *The Ecologist*, **3**(10), 366.
10. Matthews, W. H., Kellogg, W. W. and Robinson, G. D. (1971). *Man's Impact on the Climate*. MIT Press, Cambridge, Mass.
11. *The Times*, 1 December, 1976.
12. *Nature*, **260,** 420.

Chapter 9

OPTIONS FOR THE FUTURE

To many people the 'world food problem' is seen as a simple failure of supply to meet a growing demand. This is partly true, of course, but it can be grossly misleading if it is followed by a simplistic assumption that no more is needed than an increase in total food output based on the transfer of western technologies to the regions where hunger is endemic. Perhaps the euphoria engendered by early accounts of the 'Green Revolution' encouraged this attitude. If so, such accounts did a grave disservice by diverting attention from the deeply complex nature of the very real problem that exists and that cannot be solved by any kind of 'technological fix'. In Chapter 1 we saw that a clear distinction must be made between 'need' and 'demand', and in Chapter 3 we saw that the Green Revolution is subject to a number of resource constraints that have reduced its contribution to levels well below those that were anticipated.

Yet there is a technological dimension to the problem and the growing doubts about the desirability or even possibility of large-scale transfers of technology from one culture to another have emphasised the need to re-assess technologies of all kinds.

Essentially the aim of technology must be to make the most efficient use of resources. These resources include solar energy, fertiliser—the fossil fuel energy subsidy to agriculture—water, land, labour and finally food itself. It is sometimes argued, for example, that the additional fertiliser used each year by farmers in the industrialised countries to produce very small increments in yields, might be applied more profitably in developing countries, where the potential increments are much greater. In Britain, for example, fertiliser use on cereals increases very slowly, but yields per hectare remain more or less constant. In other words the economic threshold of diminishing returns has been reached and further increases in fertiliser applications will be justifiable only if there is a substantial increase in grain prices to pay for them. Each additional tonne of grain will be very expensive in terms of fertiliser. In most of the world each additional tonne of fertiliser produces about 6 tonnes of grain and in some countries, including India and Pakistan, it produces 10 tonnes.[1] So if additional fertiliser is available it may be sensible to find ways of directing it to these countries, where it can be turned into the largest quantity of food.

Agricultural scientists have considered this possibility in detail at the Dutch Agricultural University at Wageningen. In January 1976, Mr van

Monsjou, who works for a subsidiary of Dutch State Mines, repeated the argument at a meeting of the British Fertilizer Society, suggesting that the potential for food production in the tropics and sub-tropics is actually much higher than in the temperate regions and that in the years to come the really major food producers will be found in what are now developing countries. He had in mind Tanzania, Kenya, Uganda, Mozambique, Malagasy and parts of Zaire, as countries with particularly high potential.

'Solar energy is free', he said. 'It may be worth while to intensify agricultural production in the tropics and sub-tropics, where crop yields are potentially very high, and to concentrate fertiliser application there, instead of areas with lower potential like Western Europe.'[2]

His approach, then, is to optimise the use of energy and land area, by increasing output in those areas that receive the most intense solar energy, through improving the nutrient status of their soils. Of course this is the Green Revolution argument again, and it runs into all the constraints of the real world and the economic and monetary systems that the world has created. It does indicate, however, what might be possible were the world to achieve a more equitable economic regime—a subject to which we will return in later chapters.

The main 'backbone' of the technological development of agriculture in the tropics and sub-tropics is, as we have seen, the new hybrid cereals that respond to additional inputs of fertiliser and water by increasing the amount of food stored in the seed, rather than by increasing the overall size of the plant. An alternative approach, and one that requires no additional input of scarce resources, might aim to increase the efficiency of photosynthesis itself.

This is less bizarre than it may seem. Some years ago it was discovered that plants may be divided into two broad groups: those with and without mechanisms for photorespiration. There are other differences as well, in leaf structure and in the biochemical pathway by which carbon dioxide is fixed, but the main difference is in the mechanism of photosynthesis. At high temperatures and in intense light, plants that do not photorespire photosynthesise faster than those that do. So they achieve a more efficient utilisation of the solar energy available to them and they grow more quickly. Plants with low photorespiration include a number of tropical grasses, some of which are crop plants—sorghum, maize and sugar cane in particular. This has been known for some time. What is newer is the realisation that photosynthetic mechanisms may be altered within existing species.

One would imagine that the difference in photosynthetic mechanisms is so fundamental that all species within any genus must possess the same system. It was found, however, that anomalies exist. Several were discovered, including one variety of tobacco with a rate of photorespiration much lower than that of other tobaccos and with a consequently higher rate of photosynthesis.[3] If such differences exist naturally in plants that are related so closely, then it should be possible to introduce the quality, at least into some crop species. In one set of experiments French beans were made to behave like tropical grasses by reducing the oxygen concentration in the air from 21 % to between 2·5 and 5 %. After periods of from 6 to 17 days, dry weight was doubled.[4]

The percentage of total radiation that is converted into glucose by photosynthesis in three major temperate climate crops was measured at the Rothamsted Experimental Station, in Britain. Cereal grains, yielding 7 tonnes per ha, converted 2 % of solar energy into glucose; sugar beet, yielding 50 tonnes per ha, converted 2·4 %. The theoretical maximum rate of conversion is 18 %[5] and so there is considerable potential for improvement.

This improvement might be achieved by altering the leaf structure of crop plants. Since photosynthesis occurs in green leaves, the proportion of available energy that is utilised by a plant must be related directly to the size of its leaf area exposed to the light. This does not necessarily require plants to grow larger leaves. In many cases it requires modification in the arrangement of leaves to allow the penetration of light to the leaves that are lower down and shaded by the canopy above them. In the case of the grasses, including cereals, it may be a matter of modifying the angle at which the leaves grow, in order to expose a larger proportion of the leaf. The death of leaves might be made to occur later, allowing photosynthesis to continue for a longer period.

This offers an alternative, and an additional approach, to the more conventional one of rearranging the distribution of dry matter within the crop plant so that a larger proportion is translocated to the sink—the seed, root or tuber in which nutrient is stored. So far the approach has not been used, largely because past experience has shown that increased leaf growth leads to increased yields only indirectly. The discovery of variability in rates of photosynthesis suggests that it will be used in the future.

Provided such physiological changes can be introduced into varieties of crop plants by conventional breeding programmes this alternative does not involve especially high technologies. The energy requirement is low and much of the work involved is routine and can be performed by workers trained in developing countries themselves. It is the conceptualisation of the initial programmes that involves scientific knowledge of an advanced kind, not the carrying out of those programmes.

With the general realisation that the high technologies characteristic of western agriculture are inappropriate in many other regions, there has been intensive effort made to develop technologies that can be transferred. The Intermediate Technology Development Group Ltd, founded by Dr E. F. Schumacher, has collected a large amount of information on machines and tools that are available, and it has commissioned the designing of some to fill particular gaps. The name of the group, 'Intermediate Technology', has rather lost favour in some areas, since it is held by its opponents to imply some kind of inferior technology, suitable for the poor but not for the rich, and to others it implies a stage in a developmental process that leads to full western industrialisation. Probably the distrust is unwarranted, and certainly Dr Schumacher and his colleagues have wide experience of problems in rural areas of developing countries, yet names can become difficult to live with! The concept is more difficult to flaw if one accepts the validity of its objectives—to provide real, practical help to poor farmers. It designed, for example, a tool bar with five different farm implements that could be interchanged easily and that could be towed by a tractor or by horses or oxen. The entire kit was cheap (it cost about £60 at 1970 prices), compact and simple enough for it to be repairable by any village blacksmith. To satisfy ITDG criteria, aid kits of this kind must be small enough to fit into the back of a Land-Rover and simple enough to be maintained by local craftsmen.

This is important. In the years immediately following World War II agricultural aid often took the form of large machines simply diverted from their natural markets in the industrial countries. It was a time when major powers were competing for political influence in countries that had not committed themselves to either of the main camps and so aid projects were intended to be flamboyant, to leave the recipient impressed by the generosity of his patron and in no doubt of his patron's identity or of the great advantages to be gained by the wholehearted adoption of his economic system. Inevitably the schemes backfired. There were too few trained mechanics, spare parts were too difficult to obtain and in time the machines that broke down were abandoned in landscapes that became littered with piles of unsightly junk.

It might be possible to argue that these misdirected propaganda campaigns were largely responsible for the decision of most of the uncommitted nations to remain uncommitted, a decision that led eventually to the emergence of the 'Group of 77' non-aligned countries, that by the early 1970s were devising common approaches for dealing with the rich nations. At the same time, mention of large agricultural machines aroused feelings of hostility in many poor, agrarian countries. There was a danger of throwing out the baby with the bath-water.

This hostility became focused on the tractor, the one machine that was taken to represent the kind of economic imperialism the non-aligned countries were determined to break. Probably this was due to the fact that more tractors were sent to developing countries than were machines of any other kind. Yet the reason for that is simple. Farmers in industrial countries had found the tractor one of the most useful machines ever invented. It replaced draught animals and by doing so it liberated vast areas of land that previously had been required to feed those animals. It is true that it did so by substituting potentially scarce fossil fuel energy for energy derived inexhaustibly from crop plants, but in this case the bargain was a sound one. The tractor can work faster than animals, which means the farmer can exploit short periods of good weather more easily than he could before. It is much more convenient to use and it consumes no energy when it is not working. It can perform a much wider range of tasks than the draught animal, mainly because it is much more powerful.

This is not to say that the tractor is invariably preferable to draught animals—which fit better into many cultural traditions and which breed their own replacements— but merely to attempt some minor rehabilitation. There are places where the tractor could be introduced beneficially, provided it is the right kind of tractor.

In some parts of the world, especially in parts of Africa, the oxen used as draught animals are also the principal form of wealth. Consequently each farmer attempts to increase the size of his herd. As anyone who has read *The Tragedy of the Commons* will appreciate, the inevitable result is serious overgrazing of the available pastures. This reduces the economic return from the herd, so tending to encourage farmers to increase the size of their herds still more to compensate, which aggravates the over-grazing in a spiralling fashion. Since the animals themselves are in poor condition from undernourishment they are less able to work. This means that the cultivation of arable land becomes more and more difficult, and slower. In areas where ploughing, cultivation and sowing must take place during a short period, this is serious, and leads to an overall reduction in output of food for humans as well as for animals.

The problem can be solved in two ways. Either the animal population is reduced—through starvation or by persuading the farmers to part with the only kind of wealth they recognise—or a substitute must be found for oxen, to ensure at least that arable cropping is not dragged down by the failure of the livestock sector.

Swaziland is such a country and a machine has been designed for it that in Europe or America might be called a 'work-horse', but that in fact is called a 'Tinkabi', which is the Swazi word for oxen. It was designed by workers in the agricultural engineering departments of local agricultural colleges to meet specific criteria: it must work more quickly and efficiently than a team of oxen; it must carry a 500 kg load; it must be easy to assemble and dismantle, for ease of maintenance; its controls must be simple and minimum servicing must be needed; it must be cheap enough for the majority of farmers.[6]

What resulted is a tractor with a very wide wheel track, which means it can be built high enough from the ground to work among growing crops. It is powered by a 16 bhp diesel engine with a hydrostatic drive to two drive motors, a hand lever that controls steering, speed and braking. Maintenance is simple. The price is within the reach of Swazi farmers, aided by existing loan schemes, but the main problem will be one of marketing a machine that can be sold only as a package, complete with an adequate facility for after-sales service and repair. The future for the Tinkabi seems hopeful but other attempts to design an 'appropriate' tractor have failed in Africa, due to marketing difficulties. So far it has been only in Thailand that such a machine has been built and sold successfully, made by local firms from old jeep parts.

Better machines and implements, designed specifically for peasant famers, can improve the efficiency with which land and labour are used. In Hertfordshire, England, a tool has been designed and made and now is being sold all over the world, that makes the use of pesticides dramatically more efficient. Micron sprayers sell for not much more than half the price of knapsack sprayers and for less than one-tenth the price of boom sprayers that need a tractor as well. They can be assembled easily, all the parts can be replaced and they consume between 1 and 10 % of the amount of pesticide used by more conventional sprayers.

The technology is simple and elegant, as good technology should be. Most conventional sprayers work rather like garden hoses or lawn sprinklers. The concentrated pesticide is diluted with water, oil or some other substance, and carried in a tank. It is pumped from the tank either to a single nozzle, in the case of the knapsack sprayer, or to a boom carrying a number of nozzles. The diluted pesticide emerges as a random mixture of droplets of all sizes that fall more or less vertically, to drench the crop from above, or from below if the knapsack sprayer is aimed upward to spray, for example, orchard trees. Any insect hit by a droplet containing a lethal dose of a contact insecticide will be killed, but since the drops travel almost entirely in one direction the reverse side of leaves may be untouched, leaves may be sheltered by other leaves between them and the source of the spray, and most of the insecticide drips to the ground. On the ground its residual effects may assist pest control, or cause subsequent environmental problems or, in some well documented cases, actually exacerbate the pest problem by exerting a sustained depressive effect on the populations of predators that spend part of their lives on the ground, climbing plants in search of food.

In order to achieve an acceptable level of control, relatively massive doses of insecticide must be used. Rather similar arguments apply to fungicides and, to a lesser extent, to herbicides. Since many pesticides are mildly phytotoxic, the covering of leaves will inhibit photosynthesis and this may be reflected in reduced yields, and since many pesticides are carried on an oily base the covering of leaves with oil will inhibit respiration and this, too, may reduce yields. Thus pesticides have been subjected to bitter but often justified attacks in the industrial countries that use them most. In developing countries such problems have not emerged because farmers cannot afford to use them in comparable quantities.

A final argument against the conventional use of insecticides is that it tends to encourage the emergence of pest populations that are resistant to them. This is to be expected, on evolutionary grounds, since the pesticide represents an environmental, or selection, pressure. Insects that have natural de-toxifying mechanisms, or that have thicker chitinous exoskeletons making penetration more difficult, will survive to breed more frequently. In time a resistant population will emerge.

The same argument applies to fungicides. In the case of herbicides the need to protect the crop against a chemical substance formulated to kill plants means that very often weeds are controlled selectively, starting with those least similar to the crop plants—the spraying of broad-leaved weeds in a cereal crop for example. In time, and in a monocultural situation, the removal of one weed species encourages the expansion of a rival that previously had been weaker, so that the pattern of weeds changes, the weeds becoming ever more similar to the crop and so ever more difficult to control.

The Micron sprayer solves many of these problems and it does so by emitting the pesticide as a mist-like very fine spray within which each droplet is of a similar size. The diluted pesticide is fed on to a disc that spins at several thousand revolutions per minute. The edge of the disc is toothed, rather like a cog wheel. The liquid spreads across the surface of the spinning disc and is driven by centrifugal force toward the edge, where it travels along the teeth to their tips. Still being thrown outward it leaves the teeth in fine filaments which break into droplets almost immediately. By altering the speed of the disc and the size of the teeth, the size of these droplets can be regulated with considerable precision, so that the most appropriate droplet size for each kind of application can be achieved.

This mist gives a very even coverage of any exposed surface, so that the statistical probability of its encountering a target is enhanced: either the target is hit immediately or a moving insect or larva cannot travel more than a very few centimetres before it crosses a deposited droplet carrying a lethal dose of insecticide. In the case of fungicide spraying, the spread of the fungicide will be prevented in the same way.

Because the mist is so light it does not fall vertically, but drifts. Carried by a very light breeze—5 km per hour is ideal—it will move into a crop laterally, so covering upper and lower sides of leaves as well as stems, and practically none of it will reach the ground. This makes it far more subtle. Furthermore, since its coverage of each leaf is more even, in fact the total leaf area covered *per leaf* is less and so any inhibiting effect on the development of the plant is reduced. Herbicides can be applied close to ground level very precisely, so that the mist moves beneath the crop, encounters the weeds but has a minimal effect on the crop foliage above it.

Quite apart from the very great reduction in adverse side effects, this sprayer system confers two great advantages. The first is that the quantities of pesticide required are reduced dramatically, the second that it is labour-intensive in its use.

The technique is known as 'ultra low volume' (ULV) spraying. ULV spraying of a fungicide to control blight in potatoes was compared with conventional spraying. Three conventional sprays were used: 1·35 kg of Mancozeb in 224 l of water per ha left 12·2% of leaves affected and produced a crop yield of 39 tonnes per ha; 840 g of Fentin plus 280 g of Maneb in 224 l of water per ha left 13·3% of leaves affected and produced a yield of 34 tonnes per ha; 1·4 kg of Osophthalonitrile in 224 l of water per ha left 6·1% of leaves affected and yielded 43 tonnes per ha.

The ULV fungicide was 98 g of copper oxychloride in 4 l of water per ha—less than one-tenth the quantity of fungicide in less than one-fiftieth the quantity of carrier liquid. After this spraying, 2·9% of leaves were still affected by blight and the yield was 42 tonnes per ha. Each trial was repeated three times.[7] In a trial of Dimethoate, a systemic insecticide used for aphis control, 350 g of active ingredient in 224 l of water per ha produced an aphid score (the number of insects found as the mean of 3 repetitions of 20 samplings) of 8·3 after 14 days; 39 g in 4 l of water per ha, sprayed at ultra-low volume, gave an aphid score after 14 days of 0·6.[7]

The economic implications of a sprayer that gives much better control using very much less of an expensive pesticide are obvious. The sprayer itself is simple and robust. The spinning disc atomiser is made of plastic and is housed at the end of a tubular arm, also made of plastic. It is powered by a 12 V electric motor which runs on torch batteries inside the arm. The feed pipe is also contained in the arm. The reservoir fits at the other end of the arm. In some models the reservoir consists of the bottle supplied by the pesticide manufacturer, so to fit it the operator need only remove the screw cap and screw in the arm. It is easy to dismantle, all parts are replaceable and good parts from old sprayers can be 'cannibalised' as replacements, giving the sprayers a long working life. They are light and easy to handle and since they must be used in a light breeze, which carries the mist away from the operator—repeated trials have shown that the pesticide does not carry more than 50 m downwind—the operator has little risk of contamination so, except with the most toxic preparations, protective clothing is not required. The only real risk to operators occurs when attaching the bottles and this occurs with sprayers of all types.

Since it is designed primarily for use by hand, although there are larger models designed to be attached to a vehicle, it is labour-intensive. This means that in areas of high rural unemployment, workers are not being displaced, and because the operator is so close to the crop it is possible to achieve much greater accuracy and sensitivity. The operator is able to make sure that every plant is treated and as he works he is able to examine the crop closely for early signs of other problems that may require treatment. ULV sprayers have been used to spray fertiliser–pesticide mixtures, by using liquid seaweed manures as the carrier liquid and so saving what otherwise would be a separate application of a foliar feed.

This then is an example of a contribution made by advanced technology toward the more economical use of chemicals and so toward the more efficient use of working capital, labour and land. Micron Sprayers Ltd are a commercial success and have proved very popular in many parts of Africa and Asia.

Yet might it not be possible to avoid the use of pesticides entirely? This is the aim of the organic farming movement, at which we shall look in a moment. To some extent pests, weeds and crop diseases can be controlled by cultural methods, such as the rotation of crops to prevent a build-up of parasites and cultivations timed to kill annual weeds as soon as they germinate and before the crop is sown. Beyond that, biological methods may be used. There have been notable successes in the use of natural predators to control pests, but there have been many failures as well. Much of the work has been done in environments where pesticides were difficult to use.

The Glasshouse Crops Research Institute, in England, relies largely on maintaining pest–predator balances and has devised management techniques that keep pest damage within limits that are economically acceptable. Glasshouses are special environments rather different from the fields outside. Crop plants are grown much more densely to make optimum use of the costly space. In a commercial glasshouse all the plants in a particular house will be at the same stage of development at the same time. The glasshouse is more or less sealed from outside influence. The crop itself is very valuable. If a pest outbreak occurs the insects find a virtually limitless source of food. Should their population size increase to a point at which in the open it would divide, sending new colonies in different directions, it is trapped and has no access to the 'next field'. If sprayed the chances are high that this isolated population will acquire resistance to pesticides quickly. So in a sense an alternative to pesticides had to be found, and with a number of important pests it was.

Progress in biological control is slow, however, and always fraught with danger, for many of today's pests began as species introduced into an alien environment accidentally—as was the rabbit into Australia, or deliberately—as was the rabbit into Britain. A new development was announced in December 1976 that may lead to improvements in disease control. The disease is crown gall, produced by the bacteria *Agrobacterium tumefaciens*. It produces rough heavy growths at the base of the trunk and on the roots of trees—it is especially a problem in the production of tree fruits—which block the routes by which water and nutrients reach the upper part of the plant, so producing stunted growth.

An Australian scientist, Dr Allen Kerr, tried inoculating healthy trees with a non-virulent form of *A. tumefaciens* and he found this conferred the kind of resistance to attack that is conferred by inoculation in mammals. His work was checked by Dr William J. Moller, of the University of California Davis, and Professor Milton N. Schroth, of UC Berkeley. Using

1040 one-year old seedlings of almond, plum, peach and apricot, they inoculated one-quarter, treated one-half chemically and left one-quarter untreated except for dipping in water. They then planted all of them in soil infested with *A. tumefaciens*. Of the untreated trees, 157 survived, 84 of them had six galls or more and only 10 had no galls. Of those dipped in the harmless bacteria, 201 survived, 148 had no galls at all and only one had six or more. It seems possible that the technique can be developed a little to give a simple but almost entirely effective control of crown gall.[8]

In general the approach to control of fungus disease is still based on breeding resistant varieties, but since resistance lasts only for five or six years on average, new emphasis is being placed on the advantages of planting a range of varieties rather than uniform stands of the most popular ones. In Britain the National Institute of Agricultural Botany at Cambridge has produced a detailed plan to guide farmers in choosing varieties of wheat and barley.[9]

To what extent is this work relevant to the needs of developing countries? Edward Bals, the Austrian founder of Micron Sprayers Ltd, worked in Asia for many years and since then has travelled widely in Africa. He has seen for himself the nature of the problems with which poor farmers must deal in tropical and sub-tropical climates. It was for them that he designed his sprayer.

This close contact is vital. As we shall see in later chapters far too many programmes for the tropics and sub-tropics have been formulated in industrial countries with temperate climates and economic and social conditions very different from those in which the programmes are intended to work. So far as possible, research should be conducted close to the areas it is hoped to benefit, and developments that seem exciting should be approached with great caution, for they may contain hidden dangers.

We saw earlier, for example, that late in 1975 British scientists introduced a new drug, called Estrumate, which is an analogue of the hormone prostaglandin and which will regulate ovulation in dairy cows and so bring the average calving interval closer to its biological limit.

It sounds, and is, very profitable, but only so long as adequate information is available to the farmer and to everyone else involved, and so long as intensive management systems are available to exploit the improvement in production. Without these the possible gain will be much reduced, perhaps lost entirely, and farmers will be left dealing with an extremely potent chemical substance that could cause grave harm to cattle if used wrongly, and that certainly would have serious effects on other mammals, including man, should it escape into the wider environment. This then amounts to technology of a very high order, a technology that can be used only under the most stringent controls within the most sophisticated systems, and even then with the greatest caution. Indeed it is possible to argue that it should not be used at all. It can be of little use commercially in non-industrial countries. It is a technology that cannot be transferred.

So far as possible, research should be concentrated close to the farmers it aims to benefit. On 25 November, 1975, this view was endorsed by the First Commission to the governing council of the FAO, meeting in Rome, in a resolution which:

'... expressed the conviction that national research services in developing countries must be created, or further strengthened and improved, to provide new means of improving food and agricultural production and post-harvest technology. Countries were also urged to improve extension and other supporting services to ensure the effective application of research results.

'All member nations already having advanced research systems were requested to reinforce their efforts, through bilateral and international arrangements, to assist developing countries to build up their national research capabilities. They were also requested to devote an increasing share of their own research efforts to the specific problems of tropical and semi-arid agriculture.

'The resolution requested further that the Director-General of FAO contemplate the establishment, wherever necessary, of regional research and agricultural documentation centres in homogenous geographic regions. The principal task of such centres would be to support and complement agricultural research efforts undertaken within a national framework by the countries of the same ecological area.

'The creation of such centres was to be considered in conjunction with the Consultative Group on International Agricultural Research (CGIAR) which is co-sponsored by FAO, the World Bank and the UN Development Programme (UNDP). FAO provides the secretariat for the Technical Advisory Committee that advises the CGIAR on research priorities, specific research proposals for which Group assistance may be sought, and on the status of existing international research programmes.'[10]

At the same meeting the same commission passed another resolution calling for the highest research priority to be given to work on the natural fixation of nitrogen as an alternative to nitrogenous fertiliser. We saw earlier that an ethical argument can be advanced for making very much more fertiliser available to farmers in developing countries, but if the need for nitrogen fertiliser can be reduced or even eliminated, the gain is real and immense. More than half the total fertiliser used by farmers is nitrogenous.

Even in the most advanced countries most of the nitrogen reaching crop plants is supplied naturally, by the soil ecosystem itself. The fertiliser added by the farmer is by way of a bonus to stimulate more rapid and greater plant growth. For centuries farmers have known that this additional nitrogen can be supplied by animal manures and by the growing of leguminous plants, which at one time were believed to fix their own atmospheric nitrogen. Later it was discovered that legumes have a symbiotic relationship with certain groups of micro-organisms, which live in nodules attached to the plant root system, and that it is these organisms that fix nitrogen which the plant uses. The growing of leguminous crops enhances the nitrogen content of the soil because after harvesting the roots are left in the soil—or should be—complete with their associated nitrogen-fixing nodules that continue to function for some time, to the advantage of the crop that follows.

The industrial fixation of atmospheric nitrogen is, as we saw earlier, a very energy-intensive process. It needs to be, because the inert molecular gas (N_2) reacts only when its very strong triple nitrogen–nitrogen bond is broken. By the usual Haber process this requires a temperature of about 500 °C, a pressure of about 400 atm and a catalyst. Then, in the presence of a hydrocarbon—such as a coal product, methane or oil—atomic nitrogen will combine with hydrogen to form ammonia (NH_3). Ammonia is the basic nitrogen fertiliser. Although liquid ammonia is used as a fertiliser it is not used in this way on a large scale, because losses by evaporation are high unless it is injected below the surface. Most nitrogen fertilisers contain their nitrogen in the form of ammonium compounds (NH_4), or nitrates (NO_3) or in an organic form. Yet it is as ammonia that nitrogen is used by plants, and nitrates, although they are made available quickly in soils, are lost readily owing to the high solubility in water which is what makes them commercially attractive.

In the soil itself atmospheric nitrogen is fixed to form ammonia in immense quantities, at ambient temperatures and normal atmospheric pressure. This is one of the main nitrogen sources for plants. The other principal source is the natural recycling of nutrients, as proteins, containing nitrogen, are decomposed in the soil by bacteria to yield some ammonia and some nitrate. Nitrogen is also contributed by lightning, which supplies the energy for the fixation of atmospheric nitrogen, and by volcanic ash. There is little anyone could do—or would wish to do!—to increase volcanic activity, and the action of lightning is similar to the normal industrial process. Organic farmers in particular, and good farmers in general, supply their soil with as much organic waste matter as they can in order to provide proteins for bacterial decomposition—a process that can be accelerated by composting. The most interesting process, and the one about which least is know, is that of bacterial fixation.

In fact, though, two approaches to the subject are possible, and both are being pursued. The chemist would argue that what occurs involves chemical changes and so might be replicable chemically. It is known that an enzyme, nitrogenase, fixes atmospheric nitrogen (dinitrogen). A number of groups are working intensively, especially in the USA, the USSR and the UK, to unravel the complexities of nitrogenase and its action. It is known that the enzyme consists of two proteins. One has a molecular weight of about

200 000 and consists of two molybdenum atoms, between 22 and 36 iron atoms and a similar number of sulphur atoms. The other protein has a molecular weight of 60 000 and consists of four iron atoms and four sulphur atoms. Neither protein fixes nitrogen by itself, but when they are mixed and provided with ATP (adenosine triphosphate) as an energy source, and with a reducing source, they convert dinitrogen to ammonia and hydrogen. Attempts are being made to model nitrogenase but the purpose of this work is mainly to provide the chemist with information about the behaviour of dinitrogen.[11]

Other chemical pathways are known. Dinitrogen does combine fairly readily with certain metals at room temperatures. However, these metals, which include lithium, calcium and, at higher temperatures, magnesium and titanium, are themselves highly reactive and some of them are explosively reactive with water. So they cannot be involved directly in the damp, oxygenated conditions of the soil. Other systems have been devised, especially by M. E. Volpin in the USSR, A. E. Shilov in the USSR, J. E. Bercaw in the USA and E. E. van Tamelen in the USA, in which dinitrogen is fixed chemically in anhydrous conditions to form a nitride which, when hydrolysed, releases ammonia. They are single processes, however, in that hydrolysis prevents any further nitrogen fixation.

Certain compounds, when mixed to form a 'soup', will fix dinitrogen in very small quantities but with the disadvantage that the soups themselves are so complex that it is difficult to tell precisely what is happening or why. Late in 1975, however, G. N. Schrauzer, who works with a group in California, announced that he had discovered an aqueous system that is more effective than earlier ones, converting dinitrogen to ammonia considerably faster. The work seems promising but so far it has not advanced very far.

For a number of years and intensively during the past decade, attempts have been made to trap dinitrogen on metal complexes. This has now been achieved at the Unit of Nitrogen Fixation at the University of Sussex, UK, where nitrogen fixation by all pathways—chemical and biological—are being studied. The process they have developed requires very complex reactions but it can be performed by very weak acids and it can occur in alcohols and probably—though this has not yet been achieved experimentally owing to the water-insolubility of the initial compounds—in water.

It is therefore quite possible that the day is not far distant when it will be possible to fix dinitrogen chemically by processes that require neither hydrocarbon feedstocks nor the expenditure of large amounts of energy.

This represents only one approach. The other is biological, and apart from the unit at Sussex University it is being studied intensively at the Rothamsted Experimental Station of the UK Ministry of Agriculture, Fisheries and Food. There are two main possibilities. The first is to isolate, identify and then culture the nitrogen-fixing bacteria themselves. Free-living bacteria have been identified and once they can be cultured conveniently it may prove possible to inject them into soils to enhance the nitrogen status of those soils in a fairly permanent way.

In September 1976 a team of scientists at the University of Florida announced what appeared to be a major step forward. They had isolated the nitrogen-fixing bacterium, *Spirillum lipoferum*, which is associated with certain tropical grasses, and they inoculated with it a set of field plots sown to pearl millet (*Pennisetum americanum*) and a forage crop, guinea grass (*Panicum maximum*). They found that the inoculated crops required less nitrogenous fertiliser than those that had not been treated in order to achieve similar yields, and they calculated that on the pearl millet crops up to 42 kg of nitrogen per ha, and on the guinea grass plots up to 39 kg of nitrogen per ha, could be contributed by the bacteria. The association between *Spirillum* and other bacteria and tropical grasses is less well understood than that between legumes and *Rhizobium* spp., but if the results achieved so far can be repeated in larger trials the nitrogen fertiliser requirement for cropping in the tropics and sub-tropics could be reduced considerably.[12]

Even so there are dangers. It is at least possible that if the population of one species is increased dramatically within an ecosystem that previously was stable, the consequent change in the overall system may result either in the restoration of the original balance by the elimination of the invaders, or in the elimination of competing species, some of which may be useful to the farmer.

It may not be only nitrogen that can be supplied to crops by bacteria. Other nutrients in a natural system are recycled biologically, and work at the Department of Biological Sciences at the University of Dundee, led by Michael Daft, has identified the sequestration of phosphate by 'versicular-arbuscular' fungi. These fungi were found to infect certain plants—but not all—that were colonising the inhospitable environment of coal tips. Associated with nitrogen-fixing bacteria in nodules, they were sustaining plants by making nutrients available to them under very difficult conditions. The fungal spores were washed from the roots of infected plants and added to the roots of maize being grown in sand. Sixty percent of the maize plants became infected, the dry weight of the roots trebled and the dry weight of the shoots doubled. Maize and lucerne (alfalfa, a legume) were then planted together on coal tips, but both were killed by the acidic conditions. When planted on anthracite waste, with lime added to counteract the acidity, both plants thrived. It is possible that some kind of nodule–fungus combination can be produced commercially. Immediately it is envisaged that it would be used to speed the colonisation of spoil heaps, but the reclamation of waste land also has far reaching agricultural implications.[13]

The ability to fix nitrogen is transmitted genetically and so it may be possible to isolate the relevant genes. Again, this is being studied. If and when it succeeds it may prove possible to introduce the gene into crop plants, to produce varieties of, say, wheat, that require no fertiliser because they can fix their own nitrogen. An alternative might be to develop the natural symbiosis that exists between legumes and nitrogen-fixing bacteria to produce 'leguminous' cereals.

Such modification of crop plants seems promising but it carries very real hazards. In Chapter 7 we saw how undesirable it is to replace whole ranges of traditional crop varieties with new varieties whose genetic base is much narrower. The agricultural system itself becomes vulnerable to mutating microfungi or insects. It is possible to imagine a very dangerous situation developing should several of these research programmes be successful. A crop plant whose rate of photosynthesis is increased dramatically, or one that can fix its own supply of nitrogen—indeed that contributed to the nitrogen requirement of the crop that followed—would be so attractive commercially that it might well sweep the market and in a few years come to dominate production of that particular crop over wide areas. After that it would be only a question of time before the entire national, or even regional, crop would be threatened by outbreaks of disease or pest infestations.

Might it not be possible, though, to conceive of a highly productive agricultural system that was not heavily dependent on costly inputs that must be bought out of foreign exchange and that maintains a high degree of genetic diversity? Indeed such a system is possible. In Britain, America and Australasia it is called 'organic' farming and in continental Europe, 'biological' farming. Neither name is in the least accurate, for of course all agriculture is both organic in its chemistry and biological in its techniques and pathways.

In Britain the 'organic farming movement' was denounced for years as the 'muck and mystery' school because it advocated the composting of wastes and, so far as possible, the maintenance of the integrity of whole biological cycles and because, in doing so, it spoke of matters that were not well understood. Today the situation has changed and organic farming methods are attracting much more attention.

At its best, organic farming is farming that requires a high degree of skill and a very detailed knowledge of the soil and local environment. By abandoning the chemical 'tools' that make it possible to manipulate conditions in rather crude ways, it begins by demanding very high standards of husbandry.

Unfortunately the 'movement' has been kept alive for a generation or more by devoted enthusiasts, very few of whom were practising farmers, and while attempts have been made at research these have been generally weak or indecisive, probably because they were initiated in a defensive spirit. The experimenters felt a need to justify a belief—a belief that organic methods were in the long term more beneficial to the condition of soils and capable of producing food of a higher nutritional quality. Both tenets may be justifiable but so far they have not been justified. Indeed proof is very difficult and the investigations needed to produce it expensive. What has emerged was not foreseen and is much more interesting. It is that organic methods are evidently capable of producing sustainable yields at relatively low cost. In years that are bad for more conventional farmers, organic farmers find their yields may be higher, in good or average years yields are rather lower, but the margin between organic and conventional farming profitability is now so narrow that even quite slight increases in conventional production costs that occur through rising input prices can give organic farmers an edge.

This was demonstrated during 1975 by a series of studies performed by the Center for the Biology of Natural Systems at Washington University, St. Louis, Missouri, for the National Science Foundation Program of Research Applied to National Needs. The aim of the studies was to determine the resources, and especially energy resources, consumed in US agriculture and then to evaluate the effect on agriculture of price increases for oil and its related products. In the course of this they examined farms that did and did not use chemical fertilisers and pesticides. It was found that during 1974, which was a poor year for conventional farmers, the economic difference between the two kinds of farming practice were very narrow, so demolishing the conventional argument that if fertilisers and pesticides were abandoned, farmers would be bankrupted.

'... our results permit us to conclude that there can be no more than a small difference, if any, between the economic returns per acre realised by two groups of farms: an organic group that does not use inorganic fertilisers or pesticides, and an otherwise comparable group of conventional farms that do use these inputs. On the conventional farms, expenditures for fertilisers, other soil amendments, and pesticides constituted about one-half of variable operating costs, amounting to an average of $23 per acre ($57 per hectare) of cropland. This compares to an average of $7 per acre ($17 per hectare) on the organic farms. Our data show that this considerable additional expenditure for fertiliser and pesticides by the conventional farms, as compared with the organic ones, results in no net gain in income. The slightly higher value of the crops produced (estimated at 8 %, not a statistically significant difference) is offset by higher production costs. Because the organic farms achieve the same economic returns and production as the conventional farms without the use of pesticides or inorganic fertiliser, they use only about one-third as much energy as the conventional farms for about the same level of output.'[14]

The implications of results such as these relate not so much to the economic comparison itself—the conventional farmers regained their competitive edge the following year when the weather was better—as to the effect on both kinds of farming of further increases in fertiliser and pesticide prices, increases that in part could be caused by rising energy costs and then could be exacerbated by them. Clearly in this situation the organic farms would begin to show a definite increase in profitability. At the same time the organic farmers are protected more securely against a fall in crop prices, since a smaller fraction of the total value of their production is accounted for by operating costs. In the study the organic farms were found to spend 19 % of production value in operating costs, against 27 % on conventional farms. So as prices fall the organic farm is seen to be more profitable than the conventional farm and to remain economically viable for longer. It may be that the pattern of conventional farming has begun to change already, for in 1974, when energy costs were rising, 47 % of the conventional farmers in the study were using less fertiliser than they would have liked, either because they could not obtain the fertiliser they wanted or because it was too expensive.

This study was followed by another, which examined much more closely the differences between conventional and organic farmers. Sixteen farms were chosen in each category and they were selected carefully so that they would be as similar as possible in every respect except their use of chemicals. They were farming similar areas, with similar soils, with a roughly similar mix of livestock and arable enterprises.

Yields were found to be very similar on both kinds of farm and the average value of crops did not differ to an extent that is statistically significant. In the words of the report:

> 'with 90 % confidence, we can say only that in value of production per acre, the organic group is from \$32 below to \$5 above the conventional group (assuming no systematic biases in our data).'[15]

In fact the results show a difference of \$14 per acre (\$35 per ha) in favour of the conventional farms. The difference in production costs, \$16 per acre (\$40 per ha) in favour of the organic farms, cancels out the gain. It was found, then, that the organic farms in the study were more profitable than the conventional ones, by \$2 per acre (\$5 per ha). This is not statistically significant. With a 90 % profitability the difference between organic and conventional farms would range from −\$14 to +\$18 per acre (−\$35 to +\$44 per ha). In the following year, of course, the conventional group moved ahead, though not by much. It was in energy-intensiveness that large differences appeared. The conventional farms consumed nearly three times more energy than the organic ones. This makes the organic farms much less vulnerable to rises in energy costs and to falls in crop prices, so confirming the conclusions reached in the other study.

The difference in vulnerability to rises in energy prices has stimulated new research into organic farming. The American Delphian Foundation announced early in 1976 that it would build what it called a 'Low Entropy Agricultural Facility' on a 526 ha site near Sheridan, Oregon, where all kinds of technologies will be investigated and demonstrated, including solar and wind energy, aquaculture, methane production, the recycling of by-products, biological filtration and polyculture. Algae will be grown in ponds to break down sewage products and the algae are to be fed to fish. Both algae and fish will be harvested to make fertiliser and livestock feed, while the purified water will be used for irrigation. The composting of wastes generates heat that will be used to heat greenhouses, and methane will also be produced from organic matter. 'The idea is to combine technologies that depend on continuously available energy resources such as the sun to produce food and insure the future of the environment we live in.'[16]

In Canada, McGill University has established what may be the world's first university centre for the study of organic farming, under the auspices of the Faculty of Agriculture. Directed by Dr Stuart B. Hill, Major Professor of Zoology in the Department of Entomology, already the centre has collected a formidable bibliography of literature pertaining to organic farming and has outlined programmes for teaching, research and extension. The research objectives are 'long-term, problem oriented, holistic, and multidisciplinary and will cover such areas as: soil organic matter, productivity, and food quality; low-energy systems of food production; marginal land use; recycling; preventive and integrated pest control; nutrition and health'.[17] Eventually the centre hopes to construct a building where the recycling of wastes and solar and wind energy technologies will be practised.

In Europe, too, interest in organic farming is growing. The International Federation of Organic Agriculture Movements (IFOAM), based in France, collects information from member societies all over the world and publishes digests in its quarterly newsletter. Founded in 1972 by five associations, IFOAM now has 50 members in 17 countries. These are mainly in developed countries but many of them showed a marked interest in the problems of tropical and sub-tropical farming. Since the first concern of an organic farmer is to the health of his soil it is very possible that the movement may be able to contribute much, especially in areas subject to severe erosion.

There are centres, though, where information is collected or produced that is of more immediate and practical help to farmers. The tradition of research into organic farming in Britain can be traced back to the inter-war period and the founding of the famous 'Haughley Experiment', a comparative investigation of farm practices on sections of an 80 ha farm in Suffolk. The findings of the Haughley Experiment were inconclusive but the work, and the farms have been taken over by the Pye Research Centre, founded in 1971—in the best tradition of experimental farms—by an interested and wealthy individual, Mr J. A. Pye.

As it becomes more established the hard agricultural information needed by IFOAM will be provided by the new International Institute of Biological

Husbandry, also located in Suffolk, England, and directed by a former member of the staff of the Soil Association, David Stickland. The institute is looking clearly and very directly at the needs of farmers in developing countries. Within weeks of its creation its advisers were drawn from Argentina, Canada, France, India, Italy, Switzerland and the USA, and it had information on organic farming systems that were functioning in Taiwan, Western Samoa, India and Costa Rica.

In spite of the ridicule it has attracted, organic farming is based upon premises that are perfectly sound. If agriculture is regarded as a cyclical process, from the soil to the crop plant, from the crop plant to man and to livestock, from livestock to man, and from crop residues, livestock and human wastes back to the soil again, then any attempt to accelerate the cycle may be applied at any point in the cycle. Conventional agriculture has chosen to accelerate crop production, the upward movement of the cycle as it were, by adding synthesised nutrients to stimulate growth. The organic farmer seeks to accelerate the descending side of the cycle by concentrating on the rapid decomposition of wastes and their return to the soil. Either approach is valid, although the conventional one may seem the more obvious.

There is a danger, however, that too much attention paid to one part of the cycle may lead to too little emphasis being paid to the other. Thus the organic farmer argues that in his search for higher yields, grown more rapidly, the conventional farmer is too wasteful of the residues that should be returned to the soil to maintain its structure and biological integrity and this, in the long term, will lead to a progressive reduction in fertility. The conventional farmer argues that by emphasising the maintenance of the biological cycle, the organic farmer is content to accept lower yields.

Since it is the conventional farmer who has dominated agricultural economics for the past generation (it is why he is regarded as 'conventional'!) it is not surprising that the profitability of a farm enterprise is calculated on the basis of his levels of yield. It is the rise in energy costs that have changed the situation by showing that greater attention paid to the descending part of the cycle is economically, as well as biologically, justifiable, and that if he can produce similar yields, but with lower production costs, the organic farmer may have more to offer farmers in developing countries than his energy- and capital-intensive colleague. In the end it is this despised minor section of western agriculture that may supply the key to agricultural development in the future, in industrial and non-industrial countries alike.

As an opportunist species, man is very adept at turning adversity to advantage, in agriculture as much as anywhere else. As we saw earlier, it is probable that rye was domesticated because it became an uncontrollable weed of wheat crops. Rather more recently another weed has been considered for its uses. The water hyacinth (*Eichhornia crasspipes*) was taken to the USA from Venezuela in 1884 by Japanese exhibitors at the Cotton Exposition in New Orleans. It established itself, spread, and now it is a major weed of many of the world's rivers between 32° N and 32° S. In warm, nutrient-enriched water the hyacinth can double its numbers every 8–10 days and form huge floating mats. The Mexicans learned to use water weeds, which may have been water hyacinth, in their chinampa system, and now American workers have devised a very advanced complex to use it.

The National Space Technology Laboratory of the National Aeronautics and Space Administration (NASA) is growing water hyacinth. The remarkable efficiency with which the plant takes up nutrients, and its rapid growth, make it very suitable for treating human sewage. So the plants are grown on sewage and pure water is returned to the fresh water cycle. The hyacinth is then used to produce biogas (methane) as a feed for livestock and as a bagged fertiliser. The gas is used to provide some of the energy for the operation, the drying of the crop is powered by solar panels, and the livestock (cattle and poultry) wastes are treated by the plants. The technique is suitable, obviously, only in the tropics and sub-tropics, but while this excludes widespread application in temperate climates—except possibly in warm water from power stations—it may be of great value in developing countries.[18]

Another approach to crop growing in the tropics has been devised by a German biology teacher, Rudolf Sessler, who worked for some years in Peru. It is rather similar to the chinampa system but it aims to solve the most acute problems of tropical agriculture: the rapid oxidation of organic matter owing to the high soil temperature and humidity, the leaching of nutrients in the heavy rain, the rapid drying out of the top soil in the very hot sun and the inherent fragility of tropical soils that makes them prone to laterisation (if they are lateritic) and to the loss of structure.

Herr Sessler digs a series of ditches, rather less than a metre wide, and lines them with impermeable sheeting. The mud that is excavated is heaped on raised beds between the channels and water flows along the channels. The proximity of the water cools the soil, reducing the rate of oxidation. Leaching is prevented by the impermeable lining that protects the beds and such nutrients as are lost from the beds move only as far as the water, where they can be made to support aquaculture. The general improvement of the environment, and the return to the beds of sediment dredged from the channels, makes it possible to maintain the structure of the soils. The system has been tried only on a small scale but Herr Sessler's own trials seem to confirm the viability of it (R. Sessler, private communication, 1976) and the FAO has shown interest.

Increasing production is only one approach to increasing the quantity of food available. Another is to reduce food wastage.

Following the Sahelian drought there was a plague of rats. By the spring of 1976 the rat population outnumbered the human population in Senegal by more than 300 to 1. Quite apart from the obvious threat to human health, rice production in the Senegal Delta was reported to be reduced by 60 %.[19] Rats were climbing corn stalks to reach the ripening ears, farmers were having to dig up rat holes to recover part of the groundnut crop that had been taken by the rats and stored below ground, young vegetables were being eaten as soon as they appeared above ground and in the first nine days of January 1976, 10 000 young trees on a 25 ha reforestation perimeter—designed to prevent the spread of the desert—were destroyed. A similar plague of rats occurred in Kenya in 1962. In some areas it destroyed the cereal crop entirely. In 1967 the WHO estimated that the total world loss of stored cereals and rice for which rats are responsible was 33 million tonnes a year.

In many developing regions, crop losses after harvest amount to 40 % or even more. The problem is not solved easily, for too little is known about the behaviour of tropical rodents and control measures that work in temperate climates often fail, especially where they require the animal to ingest repeated doses of a poison.

In Europe and America, Warfarin is the most widely used rodent poison. It is attractive because it can be applied in ways that protect other mammalian species from exposure and because a rodent killed by Warfarin is not poisonous to other species. Warfarin (200 Coumarin) is an anti-coagulant. The affected animal dies from loss of blood that can result from quite minor wounds, internal or external. Unhappily rodents themselves have partially adapted to it and a strain of 'supermice' and 'superrats' have appeared that are quite resistant. The females of one British strain of supermice can grow and even breed on a diet of nothing but Warfarin. These animals survive because their blood is more inclined to coagulate than that of susceptible animals so, ironically, they can sometimes be killed by witholding Warfarin, which can lead to thromboses.

American research suggests an alternative approach to rodent control.[20] Working at the Ecology Research Center, Miami University, Oxford, Ohio, ecologists fed house mice with a female sex hormone, diethylstilbestrol (DES), which makes males sterile. Two groups of mice were released into two fields and provided with straw for nesting. When the populations were established each group was fed peanut butter, the experimental group being given peanut butter treated with DES. After 11 weeks the population in the control field was the same as at the start of the experiment, but the experimental population had virtually died out. The results were confirmed by replication in the laboratory.

DES has been used to sterilise male farm livestock and to improve weight gain, and it has attracted much criticism for the risks its use poses of contaminating produce or of its being released accidentally into the wider environment. Its possible use as a means of rodent control is to be viewed with some caution, but it may prove safe and practical in certain circumstances, especially where there is a danger of a population explosion among the pests but little risk that bait fed to them will be eaten by non-target species.

The plague that all farmers in the dry sub-tropics fear is from locusts. A few years ago it was believed that the locust problem had been overcome by the use of insecticides. Now the pest is emerging again. In July 1976 the FAO warned that a new and major outbreak was possible in north-west Africa, and that it might prove more severe than any outbreak in the past because of the much greater dependence of farmers on large stands of crops being grown commercially, rather than on small patches that used to be typical of a peasant culture. By the autumn heavy rains in the locust breeding grounds brought reports of swarms from Saudi Arabia, Sudan, Algeria, Libya, India, Pakistan and Mali. These were brought under control but isolated locusts continued to be found in several countries, and the FAO warned of possible population increases and possible locust migrations. The suspect areas were under constant surveillance, including satellite observation. The satellites provide information on cloud cover which can be used to estimate rainfall, and on the vegetation coverage in regions where vegetation appears only when rainfall has exceeded a certain level. From this information it is possible to identify areas of risk that can be examined by ground surveys. Once locusts are located, killing them presents no great problem.[21]

In many cases, wastage after harvest can be reduced by more efficient facilities for storing, drying and distributing grain. Food wastage is not a phenomenom confined to developing countries. The industrial nations also waste very large quantities. In the UK most estimates suggest that 20–25% of all food harvested or imported is wasted—in the sense that it never reaches the human consumer for whom it was intended, or reaches a consumer but exceeds his or her nutritional requirement, for over-consumption is also a form of waste.[22]

Over-eating is now quite characteristic of the rich countries and it causes severe health problems. A whole range of 'diseases of civilisation' have been associated causally with the over-consumption of specific food items, especially refined carbohydrates[23] and animal fats.[24] The cost for medical treatment and in lost production amounts to many millions of pounds each year. A reduction in this wastage would confer clear social benefits and the economic benefits would include reduced costs for medical treatment, reduced food import costs and increased industrial production. Such a reduction requires changes in consumption patterns.

So far there is little information on the practical measures that might be taken to bring about a voluntary change in diet or whether they would be effective. Norway has proceeded further in this direction than any other country by taking steps to persuade people to eat a higher proportion of food that is produced at home. In Britain the Food Policy Unit of Earth

Resources Research Ltd, funded by the Anglo-German Foundation for the Study of Industrial Society, undertook a study of the future of food supplies and the implications for food and agricultural policy, devoting much of its attention to this neglected area. An essential first step is to improve communication between agriculturists and nutritionists, for it is only too easy to design policies that are nutritionally admirable but agriculturally impossible and vice versa.

In many countries, especially in developing countries, food storage facilities could be improved at low cost and a quite disproportionately high benefit. Some years ago experiments were made in the USA on the irradiating of food in sealed containers as a method of preservation. Such a technique must be evaluated very carefully indeed before irradiated food can be marketed, but after exhaustive testing, in September 1976, a meeting of scientists sponsored jointly by the FAO, IAEA (International Atomic Energy Agency and WHO (World Health Organization) and held at the WHO headquarters in Geneva, recognised five food items—potatoes, wheat, chicken, papaya and strawberries—as 'conditionally safe' for human consumption following irradiation. Three foods—rice, fish and onions—were given 'provisional' approval and one—mushrooms—was referred for later evaluation. That the approach was cautious is shown by the fact that research was conducted in 23 countries and evidence of research carried out all over the world in the course of the past 25 years was taken into account.[25]

Some forms of food processing also lead to considerable wastage. Where the production of butter and cheese takes place on the farm or in small village plants, the skimmed milk and whey by-products can be fed to pigs. When production becomes concentrated in large factories the quantities of by-product make this impossible, owing to the cost of moving a bulky low-value material or of drying it to make it more compact. Other processes produce wastes that do not offer even this possibility of a direct outlet. Conventionally such wastes are discharged into surface waters, but the tightening of regulations governing the quality of discharges has required the food industry to consider ways of reclaiming nutrients from their effluent and, having reclaimed them, of using them to manufacture subsidiary products. Sophisticated techniques have been developed for converting wastes from the food industry into proteins or, less commonly, carbohydrates suitable for livestock feed, and one day, possibly, for direct human consumption.

These techniques[26] often base themselves on the growing of microfungi or bacteria on nutrient substrates derived from the waste, then harvesting the micro-organisms. These are techniques developed for single-cell protein production elsewhere. The oil industry has found ways to culture organisms on hydrocarbon substrates. Organisms have been cultured successfully on cellulose materials such as wastes from the timber industry. Abattoir waste, livestock effluent and human sewage, indeed any organic material, have been used or probably could be.

Much of the work that has been done is designed to use wastes or by-products of other industries, and while the technologies required are not necessarily high by western standards, they do require capital investment on a scale that is seldom to be found in developing countries where, in any case, the wastes may not exist as feedstock materials. In the case of the food processing industry especially, the solution to wastage is not still more advanced technology but to contrive a marketing system wherein most food is eaten fresh, and to carry out unavoidable processing in units small enough to provide wastes in quantities that can be managed more easily. There are two exceptions: crop residues that could be processed into food for humans, and sewage.

In most forms of crop production, only a part of the plant is eaten—often only a very small part. It is possible to extract nutrients from the remainder of the plant and so increase the nutrient yield of the crop very dramatically. However, there is a danger here, too. Conventional agriculture requires that crop residues be returned to the soil. Should the whole plant be sent off the farm for processing there could be a serious reduction in soil organic matter and, especially in tropical or semi-arid conditions, this could be disastrous, since problems of soil erosion would be exacerbated. If on the other hand the fibrous residue from protein extraction—the significance of the technique is that it makes available proteins that otherwise are unavailable to non-ruminants, which have no mechanisms for digesting celluloses—is returned to the land on which the crop was grown, this additional cost may prove uneconomic, raising the price of the end product too high. The problem can be solved by on-farm primary processing but this requires new skills of the farmer.

The recycling of sewage is an obvious economy that all countries should practise, but few do. Applied in its raw state, as 'night soil', human sewage can encourage the proliferation of intestinal parasites and so be injurious to health, but composted sewage is safe: the thermophilic organisms involved cause a high-temperature fermentation and the high temperature kills the parasites. Pathogenic bacteria cause few problems in either case, for they cannot survive for more than an hour or two at ambient temperatures.

Some workers have suggested, however, that sewage could provide a feedstock for the production of a high-protein feed for livestock, especially for non-ruminants. Samuel H. Smith and Harry Rothman, at Manchester University in England, have developed to the pilot stage a process for achieving this (S. H. Smith, private communication, 1976).

Tables 9.1 and 9.2 show the potential of this process and Table 9.3 compares a commercial chicken feed with a chicken feed prepared from sewage, the commercial feed being one that was in use some years ago. Smith, in the same communication, comments:

'With the exception of Methionine which is a little low, the constituent values in the feed compound using sewage base feed compared favourably with a conventional feed of the period indicated. However, recent studies and evaluations of components which could be used instead of grasses, etc., and based on more up to date animal feed formulations indicate more exciting results. This is particularly so when the pig and Bovine are included.'

The process requires no micro-organism to be cultured on a sewage-derived substrate. It can be carried out at the sewage works and it takes about 4 hours, from primary sedimentation to completed and bagged feed. The most promising application may be as a feed concentrate rather than as a compounding component:

'This process produces a detoxicated and sterile granule. It offers immediate use as a concentrate to farm produced feed components.

'If we consider the efficiency of farm production of animal feeds and basing this on grains, then, including the straws, this efficiency could be taken at 7 tonnes per hectare. These crops are expensive in energy, fertilisers, pest and fungi controls, labour and also demand the best soils and climates.

'Now, if leaf and root crops were grown as the bulk and supplements to animal feeds and using this sewage feed concentrate to top up the nutritional levels to those necessary, then acreage production levels could be increased to around 49 tonnes per hectare according to crop. Further, these crops may not need the best soils, climates and very probably could be

TABLE 9.1
Analysis of Protein in Human Sewage

Protein	%
Arginine	0·969
Histidine	0·386
Isoleucine	0·750
Tryptophan	0·189
Leucine	1·394
Lysine	0·744
Methionine	0·325
Valine	1·078
Cystine	0·306
Tyrosine	0·537
Threonine	0·537
Glycine	0·812
Phenylalanine	0·671

grown nearer to the tree line on lands which are presently virtually non or least productive. Furthermore, pesticides, insecticides and some fertilisers could be reduced from agricultural practice as we could exercise some control on these problems on a botanical (biological) level, which is more effective than using one species of fauna to destroy another.'

The Manchester team has shown that the process could be profitable in a sewage works serving a population of 250 000 or more, at mid-1975 prices for feedingstuffs.

TABLE 9.2
Nutrient Analysis of Human Sewage

Nutrient	%
Total carbohydrates	56·030
Fat extract	5·110
Fibre	7·277
Crude protein	16·389
Ash	3·076
Met. energy 2 795·294 kcal/kg	

The direct processing into food of inedible crops grown specifically for that purpose has been studied for many years. Technologically there is no great difficulty in producing a protein concentrate from grasses and herbs, whose high cellulose content makes them indigestible except to ruminant animals. Using low technology, on-farm equipment, leaf protein could be sold either to feed livestock elsewhere—which might, for example, reduce physical damage to pastures from overgrazing—or as an extender in food for humans.

Many routes for augmenting human and animal diets are under consideration. The WHO held one of many such symposia, on Animal Wastes, at Bratislava, from 28 September to 5 October, 1975.

In the industrial countries, alternatives to meat are being considered as 'extenders' to be used in meat products. Apart from single-cell or leaf proteins, these are derived mainly from cereals or from beans, especially soya. These techniques, requiring the texturing of bean or cereal proteins by spinning or extrusion, have been described by the UK Food Standards Committee.[27] The argument against them is that, from time immemorial, people have found it possible to eat beans as beans, so it seems unnecessary to expend energy to disguise them as something else, although the sophisticated palates of the west may require some education and the peoples of the west may require some refresher courses in cookery.

We have considered some of the ways in which food may be used more

TABLE 9.3
Nutrient Comparison between Commercial Chick Feed and Chick Feed using Sewage Base

Nutrient	*Growers' feed (percent)*	*Sewage-based feed (percent)*
Arginine	1·190 75	0·969 00
Glysine	0·591 00	0·812 25
Histidine	0·469 23	0·386 00
Isoleucine	0·838 00	0·750 00
Leucine	1·554 75	1·393 50
Methionine	0·355 25	0·324 50
Cystine	0·257 25	0·306 00
Phenylalanine	0·792 75	0·671 25
Tyrosine	0·622 00	0·570 50
Threonine	0·864 25	0·536 50
Tryptophan	0·234 75	0·189 00
Valine	1·172 00	1·078 25
Total carbohydrate	53·711 00	56·030 00
Fat extract	4·225 00	5·110 00
Crude fibre	5·885 00	7·277 00
Crude protein	19·009 50	16·388 50
Ash	4·351 00	3·076 00
Met. energy (kcal/kg)	2 770·584 00	2 795·284 00

effectively and in which production might be increased by the more efficient use of resources. We have not answered the big question that haunts those whose view of the future is defiantly euphoric: will the desert bloom?

The short answer is no, it will not. As we saw in Chapter 8 the climate is more likely to become worse than better, and so conditions in arid and semi-arid areas will not improve. If water is the major limitation, in areas where there is absolute scarcity and little wastage not much can be done. A great deal of research has been performed into the desalination of sea water and there are a few plants in operation. Desalination, based on the distilling of water to remove the salts, requires very large expenditures of energy and such plants as there are are often associated with large power stations. Even if desalinated water were cheap, which it is not, the irrigation of inland desert areas would require its transport over very long distances. Central Chad, for example, is 1600 km from the nearest coast and the route passes through the rainforest. At its eastern extremity the Indian Thar Desert is about 1000 km from the sea. It is difficult to see how water could be conveyed over such long distances safely, reliably and sufficiently cheaply for it to be of real benefit to poor farmers.

What is possible is the halting of the process of desertification by careful management in the desert edge areas. In many places trees have been found to bind the soil and to act as a windbreak to prevent sand from being blown on to the cultivated land nearby. As the soil is built up carefully behind the shelter belt, a further belt can be planted, so that gradually the insidious process is reversed. The technique can work only where the supply of groundwater is adequate to support the trees. Groundwater may be available even if rainfall is low, and some species of trees will grow well under very dry conditions.

Good progress has been made in some parts of the Sahara, and now it is being suggested that the trees themselves might produce a crop that could be sold or fed to livestock. The carob tree is being studied to this end. The tree cover may one day enable farmers to grow grass, so providing grazing for animals, whose manure may help in the soil-building process that could lead to successful agriculture, but only in more favoured areas. These are large but in all the world's deserts most of the area is too dry for any kind of agriculture in the foreseeable future. Most of the successes have been achieved in the Sahara, which is by no means the world's driest desert.

A great deal of improvement is possible, based on technologies that exist today or that will exist in the very near future. In many regions, however, the problem of hunger is caused not by the inadequacy of farmers but by the poverty of the people who are unable to exert an effective economic demand. It is a political problem not an agricultural one, and here too there are some answers to be found in the experience of countries such as China and Tanzania that have devised for themselves directions for development that are appropriate for their circumstances and that offer the most exciting opportunities for others. We shall return to this in Chapter 11.

REFERENCES

1. Allaby, M., Blythe, C., Hines, C. and Wardle, C. (1975). *Losing Ground*. Earth Resources Research, London.
2. Quoted in *The Guardian*, 5 January, 1976.
3. Zelitch, I. and Day, P. R. (1968). Variation in photorespiration. The effect of genetic differences on net photosynthesis in tobacco, *Plant Physiology Lancaster*, **43,** 1838–44. University of Lancaster, UK.
4. Bjorkman, O. L. (1967). Effect of Oxygen Concentration on Dry Matter Production in Higher Plants, *Yearbook of the Carnegie Instn*, *Washington*, **66,** 228–32.
5. Thorne, G. N. (1971). Physiological factors limiting the yield of arable crops, in Wareing, P. F. and Cooper, J. P. (eds), *Potential Crop Production*. Heinemann, London.
6. Muller, M. (1976). Tinkabi—mechanical ox for Africa, *New Scientist*, **69**(988), 404, London.

7. Heath, E. D. (1969). The ULV ground application of oil based formulations, *Proc. 5th Brit. Insecticide Fungicide Conf.*
8. *New Scientist*, 2 December, 1976, **72**(1029), 530.
9. *The Times*, 13 September, 1976. Report by Leonard Amey.
10. FAO press release 75/114, 25 November, 1975. Rome.
11. Leigh, J. (1976). A chemical fix for nitrogen?, *New Scientist*, **69**(988), 385.
12. Report in *The Times*, 13 September, 1976.
13. *New Scientist*, 2 December, 1976, **72**(1029), 531.
14. Lockeretz, W., Klepper, R., Commoner, B., Gertler, M., Fast, S., O'Leary, D. and Blobaum, R. (1975). *A Comparison of the Production, Economic Returns and Energy Intensiveness of Corn Belt Farms That Do and Do Not Use Inorganic Fertilizers and Pesticides.* CBNS, Washington University, St. Louis, Mo.
15. Lockeretz *et al.* (1975). *A Comparison of Organic and Conventional Farms in the Corn Belt.* CBNS, Washington University, St. Louis, Mo.
16. NERC (1976). *NERC News Journal*, **2**(1), 10. Natural Environment Research Council.
17. *The Macdonald Journal*, December, 1975–January, 1976. McGill University, Canada.
18. Wolverton, B. and McDonald, R. C. (1976). Don't waste waterweeds, *New Scientist*, **71**(1013), 318.
19. UN Development Programme (1976). *Development Forum*, p. 8. UNDP, Geneva, May.
20. Johnson, R. F. and Barrett, G. W. (1976). Effects of diethylstilbestrol on feral house mouse (*Mus musculus* L) population dynamics under field conditions, *J. Applied Ecology*, **12**(3), 741.
21. FAO (1976). Press releases 76/39, July 7, 76/60 October 21, 76/65 November 8. Rome.
22. Roy, R. (1976). *Wastage in the UK Food System.* Earth Resources Research, London.
23. Cleave, T. L. (1974). *The Saccharine Disease.* J. Wright, Bristol, UK.
24. Blythe, C. (1976). Problems of diet and affluence, *Food Policy*, p. 91. London, February.
25. WHO (1976). Press release WHO/35, September 7. Geneva.
26. Birch, G. G., Parker, K. J. and Worgan, J. T. (eds) 1976. *Food from Waste.* Applied Science, Barking, Essex, UK.
27. MAFF (1974). *Food Standards Committee Report on Novel Protein Foods.* Ministry of Agriculture, Fisheries and Food, HMSO, London.

Chapter 10

THE OCEANS AS A FOOD SOURCE

It is tempting to imagine that the seas are a cornucopia, capable of supplying an inexhaustible harvest of high-grade protein. After all they cover four-fifths of the surface of the planet, an area exceeding by many times the cultivable area of dry land, even when the most imaginative schemes for farming rainforest or desert areas are included.

The illusion is interesting. It may be one of the last cultural reminders of industrial man's more primitive forebears. When we think of the sea we think as hunters, hunters moreover, who see no limit to the territory we can exploit for game: although the creation of exclusive economic zones and their jealous defence represents a modern version of tribal territoriality.

Almost without exception the fishermen of the world are hunters and we should not allow ourselves to be deceived by the sophistication of modern fisheries technology into believing otherwise. Fishing is hunting, qualitatively no different from the kind of hunting practised by present-day primitive peoples. The point requires emphasis, for in considering the future for the fishing industries of the world we cannot use the criteria we apply to agriculture. A farmer ensures that the crop he harvests this year is replicable in future years. The fisherman does this, too, when he relates his catch to his estimate of the annual yield the exploited species can sustain, but he takes no further steps to husband the resource on which he depends.

When we talk of increasing agricultural yields we imagine this may be achieved in a sustainable manner, by the growing of one crop after another. When we think of increasing the yield from fishing we may be proposing the erosion of the resource base.

Since the early 1950s there have been various estimates of the total maximum sustainable yield of fish. Some of these figures have been very high but a middle estimate might be in the region of 100 million tonnes a year. This yield has never been achieved in practice and with the decline in total yields in the early 1970s, many people came to believe that stocks were declining as a result of over-fishing.

As we saw in Chapter 1, most of the decline in world catches can be explained by the failure of the South American anchovy industry, for reasons that are not clear but probably include over-exploitation as one prime cause. For the rest of the world we should not jump to the conclusion that a decline in yield reflects a decline in stocks. It might be that fishermen were less skilful, or went to sea less frequently, or stayed at sea for shorter periods. Such behaviour may seem much more improbable that it is in fact. Rising operating costs, especially the price of fuels, may act as an effective constraint if consumers are not prepared to pay more for fish.

There is every reason to believe that in most countries fish as a food is not especially favoured by the majority of the population, and thus demand is likely to be very sensitive to price rises. An expanding industrial sector within a national economy may offer better-paid work, more congenial hours and better conditions than fishing can hope to do , and thus industry may attract labour that is difficult to replace. A highly selective consumer demand may lead to the over-exploitation of particular species, with a corresponding decline in the size of the populations of those species, leading to a reduction in catches of the only fish that people will buy; but other species may remain as plentiful as ever they were, so that it is inaccurate to speak of a decline in stocks as though, in aggregate, the sea contained less fish than it contained formerly.

The issues are complex and it is not surprising that it is so difficult to find areas of agreement. The problem is made worse by the poor state of our knowledge. Most farmers know how many animals they have of each species and how much of their land is devoted to each plant crop. A fisherman has only a vague notion of the size of the population he hunts, and with many species no one knows with any certainty what a sustainable yield might be. Conservation quotas, imposed for many commercial species, are based not on any scientific estimate of the sustainable yield but only on the size of actual catches averaged over a number of years.

Such events as the thrice-repeated 'cod war' between Britain and Iceland may suggest that commercial fishing is becoming more viciously competitive and this, in turn, may suggest that certain fish species are threatened. Almost certainly this is so, and the reasons for it are worth examining.

Part of the fishing industry has adopted a high level of technological support and this has made it very capital-intensive. Meanwhile most of the world's fishermen, including those in many of the rich industrial countries, work on a small scale in small boats, in a kind of marine version of a cottage industry. It may be that history will consign them to oblivion or at best to some corner of a museum where they will earn a living of a kind entertaining tourists, but there are good reasons for supposing that this would be undesirable.

Much modern fishing technology is developed from military technology and it is designed to facilitate the location of fish shoals and to aid navigation. It is expensive, and to pay for it catches have had to increase. In order to increase the size of the catch the size of vessel had to increase. So a spiral is created in which the size of catch must increase in order to pay for the technology employed to increase the size of the catch.

All is well so long as stocks can sustain such an increase and, as we saw earlier, they increased dramatically during the late 1940s, 1950s and 1960s. This increase in catches justified further investment and so the spiral tightened. The situation becomes desperate should catches begin to fall or even should they fail to increase at the planned rate, for individual firms and possibly entire fleets may find themselves over-capitalised.

On theoretical grounds alone, this form of industrialisation may be inappropriate for fishing. At the very least it will necessitate strict and effective limitations imposed by international agreement and policed, if for no other reason than to protect the fishermen from their own excesses. To revert to the analogy with primitive hunters, it is as though the tribe learned nothing of farming but suddenly found itself capable of employing aircraft, bombs and automatic weapons. The size of the kill would increase but a substantial increase would be needed to pay for the new weapons. Since something rather like this has happened repeatedly when actual primitive peoples have encountered representatives from industrial civilisations, we know very well the inevitable outcome. The game becomes extinct or it alters its habitat or behaviour in order to place itself beyond the reach of the hunters, and the tribe disappears either by starvation or by becoming lost in a larger, more industrial culture, to which its members cannot adapt successfully. So the application of advanced technologies to any form of hunting must be viewed with the greatest caution.

Another, closer analogy may be drawn with whaling, which is also a form of hunting. At one time whaling was practised on a small scale, using relatively small vessels. As the capacity to locate and kill whales increased, so did the annual catch, and it was a catch that was concentrated on the most attractive species—the right (which earned its name for the very reason that it was the right one to catch), humpback, blue and grey whales. It continued until these species vanished commercially, in the sense that their numbers became so few that the cost of hunting them could not be justified by the return from their products. It was at this stage that the hunting of them was forbidden in order to allow stocks to recover. Commercial interests invariably overrode scientific advice, although the scientific advice itself was never precise because of insufficient information about whale numbers or behaviour. The loss of one species always increases pressure on other species, so that one by one the whales came to bear the brunt of the assault.

At the 1972 UN Human Environment Conference in Stockholm a resolution calling for a 10 year moratorium on all whaling was agreed overwhelmingly. Since more than 90% of the world's whale catch is accounted for by the USSR and Japan it is not difficult to secure overwhelming agreement to save the whale species, but it is almost impossible to implement it. The International Whaling Commission, which meets annually in London to agree quotas for the coming year, has 16 members, including Britain whose own whaling fleet went out of business in the early

1960s, and even their pressure on the two major whaling nations is likely to result only in their leaving the commission and so depriving the whales of the little protection they have. The reason is not human wickedness but merely economic necessity—the pressure of the capitalisation spiral. A 10 year moratorium would be tantamount to a permanent end to all whaling and it is unlikely that any government could persuade its own people of the need to close down a profitable industry under pressure from other nations.

At the 1976 meeting of the commission a new quota system was devised, rather more subtle than earlier systems, that did offer some improvement in the rate of over-hunting. Yet the fear remains that the commercial hunting of whales will be checked finally only by the collapse of the resource on which the industry depends.

Thus it has been with fish, once allowance is made for the rather larger number of species involved and the larger populations. Each technological advance both facilitates and necessitates a larger catch.

It is not only fish stocks that suffer. What we may call the 'capital imperative' of modern industrial methods of fishing also operates against the interest of the smaller scale inshore fishing fleets.

Actually these supply the bulk of the fish caught in many countries. In Britain, one of the most industrialised fishing nations, the inshore fleet supplies from 42 % (the estimate of the Ministry of Agriculture, Fisheries and Food) to 70 % (the estimate of British United Trawlers Ltd, one of the leading companies owning and operating large deep-sea trawlers) to 75 % estimated by the inshoremen themselves.[1]

At this point we need one or two definitions. 'Inshore' fishing is defined in Britain as fishing from vessels of 80 ft (24·4 m) in length or less. Such vessels do not usually travel very far from their home ports, but there are many exceptions and it is quite common for the larger of them to be away from home for days on end. The large trawlers that work the distant grounds stay away for weeks on end. Nor is it quite accurate to imagine that the inshore vessels are without modern aids. There are many very small open boats engaged in commercial fishing but most of those more than about 50 ft (15 m) in length carry modern navigation systems, echo meters and the radios that are required by law in Britain at least.

'Industrial' fishing has two meanings, both of which are in current use. In Britain the word is taken to mean fishing for the processing industry; in effect, fishing for fishmeal production. In other countries the word means fishing by industrial methods which, in practice, are very difficult to specify accurately. Both inshore and distant water fleets engage to some extent in industrial fishing, according to either definition.

Vertebrate fish are caught by line or net. Hand-lining, or long-lining, is used commonly by inshore boats but very rarely by larger vessels. A very long, stout line is lowered into the water. This line has numerous smaller lines attached to it, each of them bearing a hook. Thus if a small line is lost the long main line remains intact. A hand line catches hundreds, perhaps a thousand fish at a time, depending on the gear used to winch it in. Winched by hand, about 30 kg of fish is as much as a strong man can haul from the sea at a time. The hand-lining technique is much favoured for catching large mackerel for human consumption.

There are three main kinds of net, the drift, the trawl and seine nets. The drift net hangs like a curtain in the water, weighted at the bottom and supported by a head-line of floats above. The catch is brought aboard by securing one end of the net to the boat and bringing in the other end.

If the net is shot in a circle, to surround the fish, this is seining, and it can be performed from the shore by a rowing boat. Leaving one line ashore, the boat shoots the net in a circle, returning to shore with the other end. The net is then hauled ashore by fishermen on the beach.

Trawling is the hauling through the water of a net shaped like a sock. The fish that enter through the open end are driven down to the narrow end, where they are trapped. The trawl net is weighted at the bottom and floated at the top, and the sides are kept open by 'otter boards', which are fastened at the sides and so arranged that when towed they tend to move away from one another. The trawl net is winched aboard the boat using a gallows on the side or stern (determining whether the vessel is a side or stern trawler), both sides being hauled together until the otter boards reach the gallows. These are secured and then the whole net is taken aboard. The size of trawl that can be towed is determined by the engine power of the vessel but a much larger net can be used if two vessels work together. This is 'pair trawling'. A heavy beam along the bottom of the net is used for beam-trawling, but in recent years a new, industrial type of beam-trawling has been introduced in which a much heavier beam is attached to the bottom of a much bigger trawl. This ensures that almost everything on the bottom—and a good part of the bottom itself—is netted, which causes considerable damage to the benthic fauna.

A seine net that is closed at the bottom to form a 'purse' is used for purse-seining. Modern beam-trawling and purse-seining are clearly 'industrial' methods of fishing, but all the others are used by vessels of all sizes and to all intents and purposes they are very similar to methods that have been used for many centuries. All that has changed are the materials used: nylon is used for nets rather than cotton, though not without complaint from a few fishermen who find nylon nets more difficult to repair. The real differences are of scale, as marine engines have become more powerful and vessels larger. What is really new is the electronic equipment used to aid navigation and to locate shoals, which also makes fishing much safer.

In the North East Atlantic area, which includes the North Sea and Channel, quotas are now imposed to restrict catches of most species. The most popular fish of all, at one time, the herring, was fished almost to commercial extinction. In the autumn of 1976, commercial fishing for herring was forbidden in all UK waters. In the early and mid-1970s the mackerel, one of the few species remaining unprotected, came under similar pressure.

In their efforts to conserve cod stocks on which their national economy depends, the government of Iceland unilaterally forbade foreign vessels from fishing within a 200 mile band until agreement had been reached on fish quotas that the foreign fishermen considered unacceptable. All fishing was banned in certain areas where the cod spawn. This unilateral action, the third in a series whereby, over the years, Iceland has extended the sea area over which it claimed exclusive economic control, was disputed fiercely by Britain. Icelandic waters provide a traditional and fruitful fishing ground for the British distant water fleet. Eventually the dispute was resolved, although by the end of 1976 no long-term agreement between the EEC, or Britain unilaterally, had been reached with Iceland and British ships were withdrawn from Icelandic waters entirely, the 200 mile limit having been followed by similar limits to the waters of a number of—and eventually to all—maritime nations, including the members of the EEC. The harassment of trawlers as well as the eventual settlement itself, which was inevitable, forced the big ships to work closer to home. There the herring quota was fished out quickly and the ships had to move to other stocks. The effect was upon the industry as a whole, rather than upon individual boats. The ships that began fishing for mackerel were not necessarily the same ships as those that formerly had worked in Icelandic waters.

It was not only the political confrontation with Iceland or the shortage of fish that caused the problems faced by the big trawler companies. Operating costs were rising. Since the large rise in oil prices, fuel costs had made long sea voyages very expensive (the oil tankers themselves could no longer afford to sail at full speed for long distances). Wages had risen. Insurance premiums were high and so were interest charges on borrowed capital. The British government helped where it could. Grants and loans were available for the purchase of large ships and subsidies were paid for each day spent at sea on a sliding scale that began with boats of 40 ft (12·2 m) and ended with boats of 135 ft (41·2 m). Vessels smaller than this, which included most of the inshore fleet, received no assistance and vessels larger than 135 ft received no additional assistance. Other costs had risen, too. When away for long periods, crews must be taken home—by air if necessary—for leave every fortnight or so, and fares had risen as well.

High fixed costs meant the ships could not afford to lie idle in port. So they sailed, but once they had sailed, the high operating cost—up to £1500 a day by early 1976—meant they had to catch fish, and in large quantities.

Mid-water trawlers from several European countries began working the profitable mackerel shoals off south-west Britain and later they were joined by some purse-seiners.

The inshore mackerel fleets, meanwhile, had been doing well for some years, although, as it turned out, 1976 was the year in which the really huge shoals of fish did not return and inshore (in the sense of close to the shore) catches were poor. Their small boats were cheap to buy, equip and operate, so they were much better protected against rising costs, much as organic farmers were in comparison with their heavily capitalised and energy-intensive colleagues. The fishermen's association and then the producer organisations, recognised by the EEC, had worked hard and successfully to develop markets for the mackerel for human consumption. This was no mean achievement, for the mackerel is not a popular fish in Britain. Much of the catch was exported, especially to France. The inshoremen do not work for wages. Each fisherman takes a share of the catch and the boats each receive a share to cover maintenance costs. No special social status accrues to the owner of the boat. Some people prefer to own a boat and are prepared to accept the responsibilities that this entails. Crews vary from one man to 10, and boats are seldom away for more than a day or two unless, for a few weeks, they are working from a neighbouring port.

The arrival of the purse-seiners threatened markets. One purse-seiner can catch as much in a single night as several dozen small boats, fishing with hand lines. The markets glutted, prices fell and the purse-seiners began to fish for meal—'industrial fishing' by the British definition—because it was economically preferable for them to fish for meal than not to fish at all. It was at this point that the inshoremen began to fear for the fish stocks.

The main problem, however, arose in 1975 from the 'slipping' of catches. The purse-seiner skipper sails with an order to catch a specific quantity of a particular species of fish, and the size of fish acceptable for human consumption is also specified. His equipment locates shoals and gives him sufficient information for him to estimate its size and density. From this he can determine its weight. Since he is able to catch a whole shoal at a time, he hunts until he finds a shoal that fills his requirements, meanwhile informing other skippers of the shoals he finds but does not catch, a service that is appreciated by the inshoremen. Having decided to catch a shoal he shoots his net. It is not until the fish are brought to the side of his ship that he can see them and so identify their species and size. If they are suitable they are pumped from the net directly into the hold in a clean, fast, efficient operation. Unfortunately its very speed ensures that it is quite impossible to sort fish should the shoal be composed of more than one species or of individuals of different sizes. So should the fish he sees be unsuitable the bottom of the net may be opened and the net hauled in from around them. This is slipping a haul. Theoretically the fish swim away unharmed. In practice most of them die from the jostling.

In 1976, although the scandal of haul-slipping ensured that if hauls were slipped it was done more discreetly than in the past, more powerful ships appeared, some of which could overtake a shoal moving away from them with their gear lowered. Always the problems are of degree. All fishermen catch some fish that are useless—'rubbish'—and throw them back. There is a difference, however, between the hand-liner who throws back a few kilogrammes of fish and the purse-seiner who throws back perhaps 100 tonnes at a haul. One ship is known to have slipped 500 tonnes in a single night in 1975.

The problems of Britain's fishing industry are relevant to the rest of the world, for they typify what can happen when a modern technology confronts and competes with a traditional craft. Successive Law of the Sea Conferences have crystallised the concept of a 200 mile Exclusive Economic Zone for all maritime states, and yet a major stumbling block remains as land-locked states try to claim some rights at sea. It is the argument that, in the autumn of 1976, was proving divisive within the EEC, whose Treaty of Rome is founded on the principle of resources to which all Member States should have equal access. Does this mean that non-maritime states have a right to develop maritime interests in competition with maritime states whose economic activities at sea are structured into their way of life? The major fish resources in EEC waters are located around the shores of the British Isles, and fishing provides much needed employment. It is understandable that the UK and Ireland are unwilling to allow their waters to be opened to the distant water fleets of other countries.

The problem is a philosophical one and if it can be resolved the economic and political problems are not especially difficult. Essentially all modern states that aspire to a fishing industry must decide at an early stage on the structure of that industry. Shall it be characterised by a small fleet of very powerful, fast boats, able to move around coastlines following the fish, but working out of a limited number of home ports, or shall it consist of a much larger number of much smaller boats working locally?

There are arguments for and against both courses. Modern technology makes the first course feasible, if expensive. Some of the cost may be recouped by the better economies of scale that can be achieved by a limited number of large short installations. On the other hand the system has an in-built tendency to destroy its own resource base and this tendency is very difficult to regulate. The inshore fleet has the advantage of being much less efficient, in that the catch capacity of each boat is much smaller. Because they work closer to home, fishermen become intimately familiar with local grounds and fish and they are able to conserve stocks more easily and with smaller cost to themselves. There is a big difference between rejecting a few fish that are too small and throwing back many tonnes, as we saw earlier. For what it is worth, the inshore fleet also provides more employment, dispersed around the coast in areas where other jobs are often difficult to obtain. Britain is deciding now on the future structure of the industry, but many other countries will have to reach decisions on this issue in the years to come.

Of course, compromise is possible. Once the philosophical issue is agreed and a government knows the structure of fleet it wishes to see, measures can be devised to ensure that it takes the required form. The slipping of hauls can be controlled by requiring vessels to land all the fish they catch. Since most of a slipped haul is doomed anyway, and since the size of holds is limited, the effects on stocks would be minimised and the regulation would stimulate efforts to devise subtler methods. It is possible to sample a shoal before shooting a full-sized net, for example, perhaps by catching a few fish on a hand-line. Rather than establishing catch quotas or attempting to control fishing methods, it should be possible to draw a series of bands around coasts and limit the size of ship that is allowed to work inside each of them. This would reserve the inshore band for the existing inshore fleet but leave the more distant grounds for the boats best equipped to spend longer periods at sea. Nor would this violate the EEC principle of shared resources, since no special provision would be required to bar vessels from the waters of another state: the threatened inshore boats do not travel very far and there is little risk of 20 m Italian or German boats fishing off Norfolk. Even if they did they could do little damage.

From the surface the sea looks much the same all over the world. It is not surprising, then, that many people imagine that because fish is plentiful in certain areas it must be plentiful everywhere. This is very far from true. Large areas of deep ocean are biological deserts and the rich fishing grounds occur on the continental shelves.

On the continental shelves, nutrients draining from the land and reaching the sea from rivers support the plant life that forms the basis of food chains. In the deep oceans, although nutrients may be present in the bottom mud, there is insufficient light to support photosynthesis and so there is no base on which complex ecosystems can be constructed. Those animals that do live in such waters depend on nutrient that descends from above, and this is inevitably scarce. It is not to say there are no fish at all in deep oceans—any more than there are no living spècies in deserts. Indeed there are, but they tend to be dispersed widely and often they live at such depths as to be quite inaccessible to conventional fishing techniques.

Where fish are plentiful at sea there is often some unusual phenomenon to explain it. The rich anchovy stocks off the South American coast were supported by numerous upwellings in the cold Peru Current that brought nutrients from the bottom close to the surface so they could be utilised by green plants. If we were to try to catch fish in the deep oceans, as some people have suggested we should, we would need to devise new, even more powerful fishing techniques. This would be very expensive and there is very little chance that the fish would sell for a price high enough to justify the operation on economic grounds. We are drawn back to the point that has been made many times before: food can be produced commercially only if an economic demand exists for it.

We are very conservative in our choice of foods and this conservatism applies to fish as much as it does to food from any other source. A main British argument in the quarrel with Iceland was that the British are devoted to the eating of cod, and when a journalist asked a spokesman for the industry whether the large trawlers might not turn to mackerel instead, he replied that the British do not like eating mackerel and so there was insufficient demand. Other species are available but usually they can be sold only after processing has made them unidentifiable. The blue whiting has been suggested as a species with great commercial possibilities. Closely related to the true whiting, *Gadus merlangus*, the blue whiting, *G. poutassou*, occurs most commonly in Mediterranean waters, but it has been located much further north. Although the British Ministry of Agriculture, Fisheries and Food suggests it may exist in very large quantities, so far few have been caught and no great enthusiasm seems to exist in Britain for it. It may be the fish of the future and then again it may not. If it is, should we plan now to protect the stocks of it?

Research is intensifying into the fish resources of more remote regions. Early in 1976 a Soviet–American project was announced, in which a specialised US satellite would collaborate with surface vessels to survey the Atlantic off the west coast of Africa. The experiment lasted for six weeks, during which time the satellite flew over the area three times, and by early May the Soviet vessels were sailing for home.

'The main purpose of the experiment is to study the remote areas of the world, not coastal zones. It is believed that with the use of the comprehensive research to assess the stocks of fish in the whole ocean it will be possible to bring world catches of fish to 90–100 million tonnes a year.

'Soviet specialists believe that the maps of currents, the charts of temperatures of the water surface and the positioning of feed grounds drawn up with the use of space photography will make it possible to work out scientifically substantiated recommendations to regulate the catches of fish on a global scale and to ensure constant replenishment of stocks of fish and preserve rare species of marine life.'[2]

It is interesting to note that 100 million tonnes is the figure that was quoted many years ago as the annual sustainable world catch. Was that figure grabbed out of the air?

Given the structure of the modern fishing industry and the kind of fleet that will be required to work the more remote South Atlantic grounds, it seems unlikely that developing African countries will benefit from any discoveries that are made there. It is very probable that the grounds will be worked, if they are worked at all, mainly by the Soviet and American fleets and that the catch will be used, probably entirely, for fishmeal fertiliser or to provide a high-protein feedingstuff for farm livestock.

The imminent imposition of a 200 mile zone inside which maritime states will have absolute jurisdiction over resources is leading to new forms of collaboration whereby industrial fishing fleets gain access to valuable fishing grounds. On 1 March, 1976 the FAO announced that discussions were being held between commercial fishing companies and the governments of a number of developing countries. The aim was to form 'successful partnerships between Third World countries and commercial companies in developing mutually beneficial fishing operations'.[3] 'The company representatives expressed keen interest in new joint ventures with governments of developing countries to harvest untapped fish resources but said they were short of the appropriate expertise, basic knowledge and field organisation possessed by FAO for carrying out preliminary feasibility studies. However, some delegates criticised the "lack of profit orientation" in many preliminary feasibility studies by public or international bodies. Robert Payne of the South China Seas Fisheries Programme of FAO replied it was FAO's policy to develop areas, not companies. One aim was the creation of quasi-commercial fishery operations with subsidies when commercial fishery was not profitable.'

If the limitations of modern industrial fishing techniques are self-evident, is there no hope that man may learn to domesticate at least some species and so begin to farm, rather than hunt them?

Fish farming is not new. Indeed it may be as old as any other form of husbandry. Traditionally it has been practised most extensively in fresh water but fish are also cultivated in brackish water and today there is an increasing amount of research directed to the farming of marine fish.

Asian wet rice farmers and mediaeval European monks are two examples of members of very different cultures who arrived independently at an essentially similar technique of fresh water fish farming. The Chinese farmers cultivated fish in their flooded fields to provide an additional crop of protein. The monks either managed their fish ponds to provide a high-protein food for meatless Fridays, or insisted on meatless Fridays in order to provide an outlet for their fish, depending on one's view of history. In both cases the industry was based on herbivorous fresh water species and the nutrient base of the food chain was human sewage, which promoted plant growth. The most popular species of fish was the carp.

There are both advantages and severe limitations in the cultivation of fresh water fish. The advantages are that the farming system can be integrated into a conventional farming system and that the fish are likely to be herbivorous. The principles of fish husbandry are not vastly different from those underlying the intensive husbandry of any other animal species and so the farmer experienced with one may succeed with the other. Most edible species of marine fish and most edible fresh water fish are carnivorous, but there are some edible fresh water herbivores such as members of the carp family although carp also tolerate brackish water. The yield of edible product is bound to be higher from a herbivorous species than from a carnivorous one, and the shorter food chain (typically fertiliser, algae, fish) makes for simpler management. The principal disadvantage is that the ponds occupy space that might otherwise be producing conventional agricultural products.

The disadvantage of lack of space can be overcome by moving to a brackish water environment, as in an estuary or, in Scotland or Scandinavia, a sea loch or fjord. There is a range of species of edible fish that can tolerate brackish water, although yields may be generally rather lower

TABLE 10.1
Total Areas of Fish Farms in Brackish Water

Location	*Size (ha)*
Hawaii	1 300
India	9 000
Arcachon (France)	300
Italy	100 000
Philippines	120 000
Java	80 970
Celebes	20 240
Sumatra	3 850
Taiwan	16 000
USSR	41 000
	392 660

(Source: ref. 4).

than in fresh water. There is a long history of estuarine farming. Man-made tidal barrier traps are common in, for example, Mauritius and in Hawaii, where they are more elaborate. The Hawaiian traps can enclose up to 100 ha each, are generally made from basalt and equipped with sluice gates. In Luzon (Philippines) traps can enclose a quarter of a hectare. In the Black Sea, Russian fish farmers close off bays with sand bars and raise mullet. At Biguglia, Corsica, there is a 1500 ha lagoon. The Japanese cultivate the yellowtail (*Seriola quinqueradiata*), puffer fish (*Fugu*) and prawns, especially in the Inland Sea. There are traces of old tidal traps in Britain.[4] Table 10.1 shows the location and total area of brackish water fish farms in present use. Throughout the world a total area of about 400 000 ha is being farmed in this way. The area is small but it is estimated[5] that the total world yield from fresh water and brackish water fish farming is around 3 million tonnes a year. This is 3% of the suggested maximum sustainable yield for fisheries.

Yields from brackish waters may be only one-half of those from fresh water or even less. At Chesapeake Bay (USA) and in the Sea of Azov (USSR) yields of 80 lb per acre per year (about 15 kg per ha) have been reported. In the southern North Sea (considered as brackish water in this respect because it is almost completely enclosed by land and its salinity is lower than that of the Atlantic) 52 kg per ha was being produced in 1948, and in the northern North Sea yields in the same year were 26 kg per ha.

Pond construction can be expensive and usually the main limitation on brackish water farming is the shortage of capital for investment in the initial construction that is needed. Tidal movement is used to change the water and to bring in nutrients, so that although fish are sometimes given extra food, this is less than in intenisve fresh water farming and so the economics of the operation must balance lower yields against lower operating costs. The ponds must be designed so as to control the salinity of the water. The normal estuarine environment is very harsh because of the great changes in salinity which occur with each tidal movement. Carp can tolerate up to 9 % or sometimes even 12 % salinity, which is very salt indeed. The salinity of sea water varies from place to place but averages around 35 parts per mille (3·5 %). The species best suited to brackish conditions are milkfish (*Chanos chanos*), grey mullet (*Liza* spp.), *Tilapia mossambica*, penaeid prawns and eels. Salmonids (salmon and trout) which spend part of their life cycles in fresh water and part in the sea, as do eels, are also being considered for rearing in an entirely brackish water environment. Tilapia can grow to 450 g in 8 months, but usually they are cropped at rather more than 250 g.

The food chain of which the fish are part does not include plankton and so the growth of plankton is not encouraged. The fish are bottom-feeders, depending on organisms that grow on the bed. Thus the accumulation of detritus is valuable, since this stimulates the growth of benthic diatoms. The greater the salinity the larger the number of animals there is likely to be on the bed of the trap, because a higher salinity means the trap receives a larger quantity of sea water, bringing in nutrients and organisms. The food chain is benthos, algae sometimes fed with additional fertiliser, fish. If the fish are given extra food this usually takes the form of grain or legume meals. Fertilisers used should be slow-acting in order to promote algal growth on the bottom, rather than plankton growth.[6]

There is a clear relationship between the organic matter content of the water and bottom mud and the yield of algae and of fish. Table 10.2 illustrates this. An increase of about 240 % in the organic matter content approximately doubles the yield of algae and fish. In this table about 8 % of the algae is being converted into fish, by weight.

It is likely that estuarine farming could be expanded. Whether it will be depends first of all on the availability of capital for would-be farmers and then on the future of estuaries themselves. All over the world they are the recipients of water-borne pollutants of all kinds. While ordinary sewage might improve farming conditions, fish are very susceptible to a wide range of toxic substances released into water by industry and agriculture. Most pesticides and even urea fertiliser kill fish.

Estuaries and coastal wetlands are also popular with developers, who often see in them potential holiday resorts with marinas, water-skiing, bathing and large hotels built on land that has been drained. This is not the place to argue whether or not such developments are desirable. Everywhere

TABLE 10.2
Algal and Fish Yield in Relation to Organic Matter Content of Water (Brackish Water)

Organic matter (%)	*Algae* (*kg/ha/yr*)	*Fish* (*kg/ha/yr*)
0·39	—	—
1·23	15 000	1 200
2·41	18 750	1 500
3·27	25 000	2 000
4·17	28 250	2 500

(Source: ref. 4).

there are conflicts over the use of land and coastal waters and these conflicts are not likely to diminish in intensity as the growth of population in some regions and the general trend toward urbanisation increase the demand for recreation and amenity. Perhaps, then, it would not be wise for anyone to plan an estuarine fish farm at present. The risk is too great that the enterprise would have to close before it could repay the capital invested in it.

The cultivation of fish in fjords or sea lochs is different. In general these areas are not threatened, and this is true marine fish farming. Again it has been the subject of research going back over a number of years.[7] During World War II a fresh water pond of 0·8 ha and a salt water pond of 1·2 ha were created in a Scottish sea loch at Ardtoe, Argyll. The Ardtoe farm was stocked with plaice produced at Port Erin, Isle of Man, where there is an experimental plaice hatchery. In France, which has the largest oceanographic institute in Europe (and the third largest in the world), the Centre Océanologique de Bretagne, there have been experiments with sea bream and considerable success with sea bass, turbot and sole, as well as several species of shellfish. There has been much research, too, in the USA, Canada and Japan.

The choice of species is critical, mainly for economic reasons. In Japan the yellowtail (*Seriola quinqueradiata*) is most popular. Work in North America has concentrated on the Pacific and Atlantic salmon (*Onchorynchus* spp. and *Salmo sala*), common pompano (*Trachinotus carolinus*) and the 'black cod' or sablefish (*Anoploma fimbria*)[5] and Tilapia.

Mackerel have been raised experimentally by the US Bureau of Commercial Fisheries in California.[8] In Britain most work has been concentrated on the flatfish: plaice (*Pleuronectes platessa*), Dover sole (*Solea solea*), turbot (*Scophthalmus maximus*) and lemon sole (*Microstomus kitt*). All of these fish can be spawned under artificial conditions, and plaice and Dove Sole larvae have been grown to a marketable size.

The species are chosen because it seems likely that demand and prices for them will remain high. In Britain, for example, the 10 most valuable species,

TABLE 10.3
Estimated Annual Production Rates and Gross Returns for 10 Species of Marine Fish

Species	*No. of fish per m^2*	*Total production (kg/m^2)*	*Age when marketable (yr)*	*Production ($kg/yr/m^2$)*	*Gross returns (new pence/ yr/m^2)*
Turbot	27·9	17·1	2·8	6·1	244·0
Halibut	36·8	10·0	2·0	5·0	189·0
Hake		15·0	2·8	5·4	176·9
Dover sole	64·5	8·0	2·7	3·0	171·7
Red mullet		15·0	3·9	3·8	77·0
Brill	28·0	10·4	2·9	3·6	93·6
Grey mullet		15·0	2·2	6·8	136·4
Plaice	49·5	6·9	4·0	1·7	24·1
Lemon sole	43·2	7·8	3·7	2·1	56·7
Red sea bream		15·0	4·1	3·7	51·2

(Source: ref. 5)

based on the mean annual value in 1969–70, are, in this order: Dover sole, turbot, halibut, hake, lemon sole, brill, red mullet, grey mullet, plaice and red sea bream. There seems little point in exploring the potential of species that will prove less profitable for the farmer. Table 10.3 shows the estimated annual production rates and gross returns for the 10 most popular species, ranging from £512 to £2440 per ha per year. As Table 10.4 shows, however, up to half this sum may be represented by the cost of food. Even so, it is obvious that marine fish farming has commercial possibilities.

In Europe these are not the most valuable species, however, even at the high prices quoted, and everywhere, including Britain, salmon and trout are much more profitable both for food and for sport. Consequently the development of fish farming has proceeded much further with them than with any other fish. In France annual production of fresh water species, about half of them trout, amounts to about 30 000 tonnes and it is considered that this figure could be increased by a further 50 %.[9] In Britain about 800

TABLE 10.4
The Cost of Food with Increasing Age for 10 Species of Fish

Age (yr)	*Average conversion ratio*	*Species*									
		Dover sole	*Turbot*	*Halibut*	*Hake*	*Lemon sole*	*Brill*	*Grey mullet*	*Red mullet*	*Plaice*	*Red sea bream*
(a) Value of fish, in new pence per fish											
2		3·71	14·72	10·83	3·23	1·30	4·99	3·66	2·46	0·52	0·80
3		8·70	27·72	32·26	7·79	3·08	10·11	8·08	3·62	1·12	1·74
4		13·69	42·92	68·86	14·42	5·56	16·25	14·00	4·48	1·97	2·90
5		17·86	58·88	121·71	22·97	8·56	22·75	21·02	5·04	3·07	4·19
6		21·00	74·68	190·87	33·13	11·85	29·22	28·72	5·38	4·34	5·46
(*b*) Cumulative cost of food, in new pence per fish											
2	4·2:1	0·27	1·54	1·21	0·41	0·20	0·80	0·78	0·52	0·16	0·24
3	5·0:1	0·70	3·17	4·03	1·10	0·54	1·79	1·88	0·80	0·37	0·58
4	6·1:1	1·22	5·49	9·90	2·32	1·10	3·23	3·68	1·06	0·74	1·08
5	8·0:1	1·80	8·68	21·04	4·40	1·98	5·23	6·50	1·29	1·36	1·82
6	10·5:1	2·36	12·83	40·14	7·63	3·26	7·84	10·54	1·47	2·32	2·77
(*c*) Food cost as percentage of value of fish											
2		7·3	10·5	11·2	12·7	15·4	16·0	21·3	21·1	30·8	30·0
3		8·0	11·4	12·5	14·1	17·5	17·7	23·3	22·1	33·0	33·3
4		8·9	12·8	14·4	16·1	19·8	19·9	26·3	23·7	37·6	37·2
5		10·1	14·7	17·3	19·2	23·1	23·0	30·9	25·6	44·3	43·4
6		11·2	17·2	21·0	23·0	27·5	26·8	36·7	27·3	53·5	50·7

(Source: ref. 5)

tonnes of salmon are produced each year and in Norway production is about 2000 tonnes a year.[10] At a meeting of the Royal Society of Edinburgh, held in March 1976, scientists argued that the deeply indented coastline of Scotland offers a total of more than 1000 ha of suitable sites for salmon farming, and that if all of them were exploited, yields might reach a total of about 50 000 tonnes or more each year.

The salmon and trout spend part of their lifecycles in fresh water and part at sea. It has proved possible to farm them by taking over their migratory habit and carrying them from the fresh water where they hatch to the salt water where they mature.

Marine Harvest Ltd, a subsidiary of Unilever Ltd, has invested in salmon farming and runs its own laboratories in Aberdeen, where a practical system has been devised. Between October and December, adult fish are stripped of their eggs and milt. Fertilised eggs are hatched in trays through which filtered river water flows. Larvae hatch between March and May and once they begin to feed they grow rapidly into parr. The following spring the parr begin to turn silver in colour, indicating that they are now smolts, ready to migrate to the sea. They are carried in tanks to the marine farm, where they are placed in floating cages. Those smolts that mature after only one year in salt water are harvested as grilse, but the remainder are harvested after several years in the cages, as fully mature salmon. The cycle is completed by selecting individuals for breeding.

The system is more complicated than it may sound. The condition of both fresh water and sea water must be considered carefully. The chemical composition of British salmon rivers varies widely, for example. The Unilever farm located its hatchery on an existing salmon river, thus providing water that is known to be suitable for hatching eggs, rather than trying to replicate such water. In the sea water, salinity, oxygen content and temperature must all be kept within certain limits. Salinity changes with changes in the inflow of fresh water and the state of the tide. Oxygen content is determined by the water flow and in some lochs the rate of tidal flow at times is insufficient to supply the oxygen the fish require and they are dependent on fresh water flowing above the sea water. The temperature can be changed by the wind, which under certain conditions can cause fresh water to accumulate and form ponds of warm water. Warm water contains less dissolved oxygen than cooler water.

The natural development of the fish also causes problems because when they reach sexual maturity the rate of growth diminishes as the fish produce roe, which is valueless. There has been much experimentation to produce fish that are sterile, and in the course of this research advances have been made in cross-breeding to produce fish that grow more rapidly.

The genetic manipulation of fish is not new. Fish have been bred selectively ever since they have been bred at all. Carp have been selected over many generations for their ability to adapt to the local conditions under which they are farmed. Rainbow trout have been selected in the same way, and in both cases the result has been fish that grow much more rapidly than do wild fish in similar locations. Selection has occasionally been carried to extremes with no obvious ill effects. The ornamental goldfish that decorate many an urban garden pond exhibit the most fanciful forms, bearing very little resemblance to their wild ancestors.

In flatfish, selection for larger mature size has encountered problems of hierarchies which are common in some flatfish species and that may be unavoidable. The position of a fish in the hierarchy exerts considerable influence on its mature size, and there is wide variance. Attempts to group immature fish by size, so that all the fish of a particular length were caged together, failed because hierarchies were re-established and some individuals grew more rapidly than others until the variance was as great as among random populations, but with the added disadvantage that the size range began with smaller fish in the selected group than in the random group.[11] It is possible that better results might be obtained by selecting for egg size before hatching, rather than for the size of actual fish.

Fish hybridise very readily compared with other animals. In France salmon and trout have been crossed. Female plaice breed with male flounders in the Baltic, female turbot breed with male brill in the North Sea, and the beluga (*Huso huso*), which can weigh more than a tonne when mature, has been crossed successfully with the sterlet (*Acipenser ruthenus*) which rarely weighs more than 500 g. By back-crossing a female beluga with a male beluga × sterlet hybrid, Soviet breeders have produced a sturgeon that is said to grow faster than the beluga itself. American breeders have achieved a similar effect with rainbow trout. This technique exploits the phenomenon of hybrid vigour, in which the hybrid can grow more rapidly than either of its parents, although the effect can be confused by the artificial conditions in a hatchery because of the very great extent to which the rate of growth of a fish is dependent on environmental conditions.

British experiments have produced similar, though less spectacular, rapid growth in plaice × flounder hybrids, but the whole of the effect has been explained by the favourable conditions existing in the hatchery. Whether or not it is hybrid vigour that produces the increase may seem of only academic interest to the farmer who benefits from it. Purdom[11] suggests that a cross between plaice and halibut (*Hippoglossus hippoglossus*) might be worth examining, since it might produce a fish (haice, plaibut?) that combined the suitability of plaice for artificial culture with the more rapid growth rate and higher quality of the halibut.

Hybridisation may also be used to confer resistance to disease. In the USSR, resistance to red spot disease has been achieved by crossing common carp (*Cyprinus carpio*) which is susceptible to the disease, with crucian carp (*Carassius auratus*) which is resistant.

More direct chromosome manipulation is also possible. This has been used extensively in the breeding of poultry and plants. The most important uses of chromosome engineering are to preserve desirable characters in a population that is genetically uniform and then to cross members of this population with those of another population to produce progeny that show hybrid vigour, but that are also uniform genetically. To do this, inbred populations must be developed, requiring up to 20 generations of brother–sister mating. This is a tedious business and many lines die out before a satisfactory level of inbreeding has been achieved. Some 60 years ago, however, embryologists discovered that it is possible to stimulate eggs into embryological development using spermatozoa that are genetically inactive. It is a form of parthenogenesis and it makes it possible to produce an inbred population in one generation. Workers at the British MAFF Fisheries Laboratory at Lowestoft, Suffolk, have used the technique, called gynogenesis, with trout, plaice and flounder, and it seems likely that it will work with any species whose eggs can be fertilised and reared artificially.

There is still some confusion about what may or may not be possible when it comes to feeding. Most of the fish we eat are carnivorous, which means they may be converting one form of protein that is edible for humans into another form of protein. Table 10.5 shows the natural foods of the 10 most popular British fish species. With some species, such as sole, the presence of some live animals is necessary in order to stimulate feeding at all and in a totally controlled environment this leads to economic problems. The biological problems are solved in laboratories by culturing algae and using them to feed rotifers, which are fed to the fish, but it is difficult to see how this could be made commercially feasible.

Quite apart from the economics of feeding one kind of fish to other kinds of fish, the presence of dead fish in the water can be harmful. It may cause a build-up of sulphides, which may lead to the deoxygenation of the water.[7] It has been suggested that in cold waters in the higher latitudes the common mussel provides a convenient source of feedingstuffs, yielding up to 1200 tonnes per ha or more. Thus, said one correspondent to *The Times*, 'To replace the entire Icelandic quota of 165 000 tons by, say, rainbow trout, would require 2·5 million tons of mussels as feedstuff. This could be obtained from 5000 acres (about 2000 ha) or 5 % of the area of Morecambe Bay. The time scale for the operation is just three years.'[12] This assumes that mussels convert plankton into edible protein feed at an efficiency close to unity, and that the fish convert protein feed into protein product with an efficiency of about 15 %, or a ratio of input to output of about 1·5: 1. Others have accepted this ratio and have cited the carp as the herbivorous fish most likely to prove economically efficient.

Table 10.6 shows the amount of food actually fed to grass carp and common carp in the Kwangtung Delta, China, compared to the yields of fish. The food consisted of grass, silkworm waste and equal parts of fresh silkworm pupae and rice bran. On these figures about 2·95 % (33: 1) of the

TABLE 10.5
The Natural Foods of the 10 Main Commercial Fish Species

Species	*Juveniles*	*Adults*
Turbot	Polychaetes Crustaceans Molluscs	Fish
Halibut	Crustaceans Fish	Fish Crustaceans Cephalopods
Brill	Crustaceans	Fish Crustaceans
Red mullet	Crustaceans	Crustaceans Molluscs Polychaetes
Hake	Fish	Fish
Dover sole	Crustaceans Polychaetes	Polychaetes Molluscs
Grey mullet	—	Molluscs Crustaceans Algae
Lemon sole	Crustaceans Polychaetes	Crustaceans Polychaetes Molluscs
Red sea bream	Small crustaceans	Crustaceans Echinoderms Fish
Plaice	Crustaceans Polychaetes Molluscs	Molluscs Polychaetes

(Source: ref. 5).

total feed was converted into fish, crude weight for crude weight. The protein/protein conversion rate is obviously much higher and it is important to note that most of the material used as feed is not edible for humans.

Experiments at the Fisheries Laboratory, Lowestoft, using plaice and Dover sole, and in Japan using other species, have shown that the conversion ratios vary from 4:1 at 1 year old, to 10·5:1 at six years. These are the figures used to calculate the feeding costs in Table 10.4, the cost being based on the use of fish offal and the cheapest trash fish. The table assumes a similar conversion ratio for all species at the same ages, an assumption that may be wrong but that at present is untestable owing to insufficient data on species other than plaice and Dover sole.[5] In Denmark,

TABLE 10.6
Feeding Schedule for Common Carp and Grass Carp in the Kwangtung Delta, China

Month	*Approx. temp. (°C)*	*Estimated wt. of fish in pond*		*Quantity of food per month (kg)*			
		Increment/ month kg	*Total kg*	*Grass*	*Silkworm waste*	*Fresh silkworm pupae*	*Rice bran*
February	15	—	70·00	—	—	—	—
March	16	127·80	197·80	1 534	1 022	639	639
April	20	149·10	346·90	1 739	1 193	745	745
May	24	191·70	538·60	2 301	1 534	959	959
June	28	255·60	794·20	3 067	2 054	1 278	1 278
July	30	319·50	1 113·70	3 834	2 556	1 598	1 598
Harvested, end-July			800·00				
New stock added			513·70				
August	31	426·00	937·70	5 112	3 408	2 130	2 130
September	28	319·50	1 259·20	3 834	2 556	1 597	1 597
October	27	149·10	1 408·30	1 789	1 193	745	745
November	23	106·50	1 514·80	1 278	852	533	533
December	16	85·20	1 600·00	1 022	682	426	426

(Source: ref. 15)

fish farmers have used coalfish and young herring to feed trout and have achieved conversion ratios of 6:1. When pelleted feeds are substituted for trash fish, conversion ratios improve to about 1·25:1 or 1·5:1.

It is quite wrong to compare pelleted feeds with raw or processed mussels, and the estimate of 2·5 million tons of mussels to produce 165 000 tons of fish is far too low. A more accurate figure might be in the region of 9·9 million tons. If it is really possible to produce yields of 500 tons of mussels to the acre (1255 tonnes per ha) then the area required would be some four times greater than has been suggested: more like 20% of the area of Morecambe Bay! This level of mussel production would suggest very intensive mussel farming. Intensive farming of mussels from lines hung below rafts usually requires about 25% of the total water area to be covered with rafts. Thus to farm 8000 ha of water, it would be necessary to 'occupy' about 32 000 ha—80% of the area of Morecambe Bay! Even then the mussel yields have certainly been over-estimated for the cool waters off Britain, where in fact no one farms mussels because they are so plentiful in the wild!

These figures are important only because they show the degree to which estimates showing a large element of wishful thinking and based on inadequate or misinterpreted data, may be very wide of the mark indeed.

The economic yield may be improved by allowing the fish to find a proportion of their own food. Indeed in traditional fish farming systems the extent to which the fish are given extra food at all varies widely. Bottom-feeding flatfish tend to remain in one area provided food is available, and experimentally trout have been taught to answer signals that indicate that food is being provided. This makes it possible to allow the fish to find most of the food they need but to supplement it with protein in pelleted form to increase the rate at which weight is gained. As one might expect, yields vary equally widely. Table 10.7 gives some comparisons of different farming systems, ranging from a low 1:1·1 to 1·3 for plaice moved from one area to another in Denmark, to the quite extraordinary yield of about 170 kg per litre of water per second for rainbow trout reared in the USA in running water, a yield of 2 million kg per ha per year.

At Long Island Sound, oyster production has been increased by utilising waste heat from power stations. Waste heat has also been used in shrimp farms in Florida and prawn farms in Britain,[7] and though the work is largely experimental, results seem promising. With the growing demand for scampi in northern Europe, there is a rich prize for the farmer who first succeeds in producing penaeid prawns in cold northern waters sufficiently quickly to bring them to market ahead of the main supply, which is imported from Japan and arrives in late summer or autumn.

At the French Oceanological Centre in Britanny they are working to this end. Penaeid (Imperial) prawns are raised in France, mainly on the Mediterranean coast, by planting juveniles flown from Japan in the spring. The prawns are being bred at the centre with the aim of selecting or otherwise developing a variety that will survive through the winter in waters whose temperature is about 11 or 12 °C. At this temperature they would be almost immobile and eat very little, but when the water began to warm they could be fed additional protein (probably from mussels) and be fattened. Workers at the centre found that when they marketed farmed prawns in July they were paid 65 francs per kg, but by November the price had fallen to 42 francs.

There may be comparable gains to be made, though more easily, from the breeding or capture of the young of, for example, lobsters and scallops—for which the French demand is apparently insatiable—their protection until they are large enough to have a high survival rate in the wild, then transplanting them to protected areas where they can grow to commercial size. Again the French are experimenting along these lines.

In California another by-product of industrial society has found new uses, as old street-cars have been dumped in the sea to form artificial reefs to attract fish. Reefs may help to protect, for example, young hatchery-raised lobsters from natural predators, but beyond this the value of the reefs is doubtful.

Yet problems remain. Any animal species raised intensively, with

TABLE 10.7
Selected Examples of Aquacultural Yields by Ascending Intensity of Culture Methods

Culture method	*Species*	*Yield (kg/ha/yr) or economic gain*
Transplantation	Plaice (Denmark 1919–1957)	Cost: benefit of transplantation 1:1·1–1·3 in best years (other social benefits)
	Pacific salmon (USA)	Cost: benefit, based on return of hatchery fish in commercial catch 1: 2·3–5·1
Release of young into natural environment	Pacific salmon (Japan)	Cost: benefit 1: 14–20 on above basis
	Shrimp, abalone, puffer fish (Japan)	Not assessed; reputed to increase income of fishermen
	Brown trout (Denmark 1961–1963)	Max. net profit/100 planted fish: 163%
Retention in enclosures of young or juveniles from wild populations, no fertilisations, no feeding	Mullet	150–300
	Eel, misc. fish (Italy), Shrimp (Singapore)	1 250
Stocking and rearing in fertilised enclosures, no feeding	Milkfish (Taiwan)	1 000
	Carp and related spp. (Israel, SE Asia)	125–700
	Tilapia (Africa)	400–1 200
	Carp, (Java, sewage streams)[a] ($\frac{1}{4}$ to $\frac{1}{2}$ of water area used)	62 500–125 000
Stocking and rearing with fertilisation and feeding	Channel catfish (USA)	3 000
	Carp, mullet (Israel)	2 100
	Tilapia (Cambodia)	8 000–12 000
	Carp and related spp. (in polyculture) (China, Hong Kong, Malaysia)	3 000–5 000
	Clarias (Thailand)	97 000
Intensive cultivation in running water; feeding	Rainbow trout (USA)	2 000 000 (170 kg/l/sec)
	Carp (Japan)	1 000 000–4 000 000 (about 100 kg/l/sec)
	Shrimp (Japan)	6 000
Intensive cultivation of sessile organisms, molluscs and algae	Oysters (Japan, Inland Sea)[a]	20 000
	Oysters (USA)	5 000 (best yields)
	Mussels (Spain)[a]	300 000
	Porphyra (Japan)[a]	7 500
	Undara (Japan)[a]	47 500

[a] 25% of area covered by rafts. (Source: ref. 15)

individuals crowded closely in an environment that is controlled to a large extent by man, is prone to disease. Once an infection enters a colony it can be transmitted very rapidly. While it is feasible to give injections to a herd of cattle, or even to a flock of poultry, it is hardly feasible to inject a shoal of plaice, although efforts are being made to do the equivalent of this. Generally, though, disease control remains a matter of hygiene.

The diseases to which fish are susceptible in farms are the same as those encountered in aquaria.[13] In natural populations they are seldom serious but in the artificial conditions of a farm they can be devastating, killing a whole colony at a time. It is not easy to encourage investment in fish farming when farmers may expect to lose their entire stock of animals, that in some cases take four years to reach sexual maturity and longer to reach a marketable size, every five or six years, but this is the situation at present.

The worst diseases are caused by species of *Vibrio* and *Pseudomonas*, which cause dermatitis, tail rot and ulceration; the fungus *Ichthyophonus;* the dinoflagellate *Oodinium*, which causes 'velvet disease'; the ciliate *Cryptocaryon* which causes 'white spot disease'; and certain monogenetic trematodes, particularly *Benedenia* and *Axine*, which parasitise the gills.

Prophylaxis consists of ensuring that water and food are clean, that the pH of the water remains within defined limits and that newcomers to the farm are quarantined before they contact the rest of the colony.

The economic difficulties are caused first by the absence of any strong demand for fish, so that farmers have no cushion against rises in costs but may have to sustain periods of low prices when conventional fish catches are good.[14] The lack of any tradition of large-scale intensive fish farming in most countries means there are no institutional arrangements to encourage and protect farmers.

This can make a profound difference. In France for example, where fish farming is traditional, the would-be farmer must obtain permission to use water from only one authority, is entitled to the latest scientific and technical information and advice for the asking, and if his advisers believe his project has a good chance of success, he will receive financial assistance. In Britain, life for the fish farmer is much more difficult. In July 1975 the Fish Farmers' Union of England and Wales merged with the National Farmers' Union and probably a parallel merger of the corresponding Scottish unions will follow before long. This established that fish farming is accepted as farming by conventional farmers. The Fish Farmers' Union seek the same taxation status as farmers.

A marine fish farmer working in a sea loch has no legal title to the water. He must lease a mooring for his fish cages and make an access agreement with the owner of the land across which he must pass. If his fish should be stolen he has no redress on the grounds of theft (marine fish are wild animals and the property of no one) or poaching or piracy. Indeed if he is producing salmon or trout he may well find he is poaching himself when he harvests them, for legally they may be the property of the owner of the riparian rights. If he occupies premises ashore, they are treated in the same way as industrial buildings not as farm buildings. The difficulties under which the fish farmer works were summed up in a letter to *The Times* by the Clerk and Superintendent and the Senior Scientific Officer of the Lancashire and Western Sea Fisheries Joint Committee on 16 February, 1976:

'The siting of fish farming structures in the sea requires consent from the Crown Estate Commissioners, the Department of Trade and Industry, the Ministry of Agriculture, Fisheries and Food, harbour authorities, and usually local authority planning departments. Buildings used in aquaculture, unlike farm buildings, require planning permission and are not de-rated. There are grants payable to farmers, and grants for the construction of fishing boats, but no grants for fish farming (apart from very limited grants and loans to re-store shellfisheries). The public right to fish and to navigate in the sea is jealously guarded; this makes it extremely difficult to obtain a Several Order or a Crown lease; furthermore Several Orders afford no protection to fish held above the seabed in rafts or in fish cages.'

Will the world of tomorrow derive a major part of its protein from fish? It is unlikely. As we have seen, industrial methods of fishing are highly efficient but have an inherent tendency to destroy the resource on which they depend. The figure of 100 million tonnes, often given as an estimate of the maximum sustainable fish catch from the world's oceans, has yet to be reached, there is room for considerable doubt as to whether it can be reached and, if it were reached, whether it could be truly sustainable. If it were reached and were proved to be sustainable, it would be composed of significant proportions of fish species that have little or no value for human consumption. Since there are few countries in which fish is a genuinely popular food, what likelihood is there that entirely new species would find a market? Some people in Britain may still remember the unpopularity of whale meat and snoek when these were introduced into the country shortly after World War II when food, especially meat, was in very short supply and strictly rationed.

It is rather probable, then, that conventional fishing is contributing as much to world food supplies today as it will ever contribute, and unless it is restructured to some extent to protect stocks (and incidentally the livelihoods of fishermen themselves) catches may decline in years to come.

Fish farming may expand. Certainly there is room for it to do so, provided governments provide the necessary encouragement, which consists largely of easy credit to provide capital and then security of tenure of his piece of water for the farmer, and the recognition that farmed fish should be considered as much the property of the farmer as terrestrial animals are. Even if fish farming does expand, its potential contribution must be limited. With the exception of carp or, in warmer climates, Tilapia, most of the edible fish being considered are carnivores and so are rather costly to feed. Sites are restricted. All fish, even herbivorous species, are likely to require fertiliser. So, in many senses, fish farming competes with conventional farming for fertiliser and for many substances conventionally fed to livestock, and in its favour it can offer no significant improvement in conversion rates. Its potential, then, is that of producing limited quantities of high-quality protein from areas that otherwise produce no food at all.

As soon as fish production begins to demand advanced technologies, as it does in distant water fishing and as it may do in some forms of fish farming, it becomes a preserve almost exclusively of the rich. Even though Peru was the world's leading fishing nation for several years, virtually all of its catch was exported as fishmeal. The industry benefited the rich more than it did the poor.

It is possible, then, that fish may come to occupy a rather more prominent place in the diet and that a small absolute increase in fish consumption may seem greater than it actually is, if it is accompanied by a reduction in the consumption of meat, which may be the case in some developed countries, or by much smaller increases in meat consumption, which may be the case in some developing countries. The ways by which fish are obtained may become rather more sophisticated and the day may come when most of the fish eaten by humans is produced on farms by methods very similar to those involved in other forms of livestock husbandry.

REFERENCES

1. Allaby, M. (1976). The mackerel war, *The Ecologist*, **6**(4), 132.
2. Novesti press release. Bulletin 36846, 5 May, 1976. London.
3. FAO press release 76/9. Rome.
4. Hickling, C. F. (1970). Estuarine fish farming, *Adv. Marine Biol.*, **8**, 119–213.
5. Jones, A. (1972). *Marine Fish Farming*, Laboratory Leaflet (New Series) No. 24, Ministry of Agriculture, Fisheries and Food, Fisheries Laboratory, Lowestoft, UK.
6. Hickling, C. F. (1968). *The Farming of Fish*. Pergamon, Oxford.
7. Milne, P. H. (1972). *Fish and Shellfish Farming in Coastal Waters*. Fishing News (Books), London.
8. Iversen, E. S. (1968). *Farming the Edge of the Sea*. Fishing News (Books), London.
9. Agence Presse Environnement. (1976). *Le Mois de l'Environnement*, No. 1, June 1976, Paris.
10. Loftas, T. (1976). Day of the farmed Scotch salmon, *New Scientist*, **70**(994), 20.
11. Purdom, C. E. (1972). *Genetics and Fish Farming*. Laboratory Leaflet (New Series) No. 25, Ministry of Agriculture, Fisheries and Food, Fisheries Laboratory, Lowestoft, UK.

12. Semmence, H. R. (1976). Letter in *The Times*, 11 February, 1976.
13. Sinderman, Carl J. (1968). Disease and parasite problems in marine aquaculture, in McNeil, W. J. *Marine Aquaculture: Selected papers from the conference on marine aquaculture*. Oregon State University Press, 1970.
14. Scott, Anthony (1968). Economic obstacles to marine development, in McNeil, op. cit.
15. Bardach, J. E., Ryther, J. H. and McLarney, W. O. (1972). *Aquaculture. The Farming and Husbandry of Freshwater and Marine Organisms*. Wiley-Interscience, New York.

Chapter 11

EMPLOYMENT, INCOME DISTRIBUTION AND NUTRITION

In the years immediately following World War II, aid projects devised in the industrial countries tended to receive support to the extent that they impressed their recipients. The cold war between competing economic and political systems was fought out in developing countries as much as it was in the propaganda each side hurled at the other directly. Gifts were often large, sometimes spectacularly so, and labelled clearly 'Gift of . . .'.

At other times, aid was intended to benefit the donor rather than the recipient. In the context of the world food situation we may think of the disposal of large grain and other surpluses that otherwise might have caused acute embarrassment in the producing countries. By exporting such surpluses to countries that were suffering food shortages, the markets of the industrial nations were not affected. Food aid to post-war Europe ended as soon as the farms of Europe were producing once more. Free or cheap food imports that undercut home production would have been rejected as dumping.

The West also dumped its surpluses in hungry Asia, but because hunger was still a problem in the recipient regions the dumping charge was more difficult to make. At times, of course, such aid did relieve hunger and was beneficial. At others it simply depressed local production and all too often it was accompanied by measures, imposed as a condition of its acceptance, designed to ensure that commodities produced locally could never compete in world markets with those produced in the West.

We still live in the aftermath of those years and in the next chapter we shall look more closely at world patterns of trade that seem to guarantee that the rich grow richer while the poor grow poorer.

That particular approach to aid ended, although nothing was done to modify trading patterns, and development programmes came to be designed sincerely for the benefit of the poor. The Green Revolution programmes fall into this category, and a very high level of altruism characterises those who are seconded to administer them.

Even so, programmes were designed largely by technologists and promoted on the basis of assumptions about technologies and the societies that use them that were far too simple. So it was found, over and over again, that rapid economic development tended to redistribute wealth upward. In other words, nationally as well as internationally, the rich grew richer while the poor remained poor.

Some years ago, studies of the ways in which technologies were transferred from one culture to another concluded that four conditions must be satisfied before such transfers can succeed:

(1) The technology must be transferred in its entirety, complete with all the plant and other equipment it requires, and local personnel must be trained to work it as quickly as possible.

(2) The recipient must then assume complete control over it, and have access to such capital as is needed to develop and adapt it.

(3) The recipient must already possess a sufficient pool of scientists, technologists, and government and industrial research and development facilities, to enable the technology to develop in the ways most appropriate to local needs.

(4) The recipient must be in a position to make and implement decisions that are likely to influence the future development of the technology itself, the industries it serves and the markets in which its products are sold. In some cases the government may need to act as a major buyer.

This may present a picture that makes the situation of many developing countries, or depressed regions that lack control over their own economies, quite hopeless. Yet it is useful if it prevents further simplistic assumptions about the ease with which advanced technologies can be exported. It may, for example, encourage the development of alternative technologies for which these criteria can be satisfied.

Dr Robin Roy, of Britain's Open University, has also studied the nature of technological change.[1] He argues that the relationship between technology and society is interpreted most frequently according to one of four determinist models. These assume that one factor—technology, economics, politics or ideology—determines everything else. Thus societies develop technologies and these determine the direction of social change, so that it becomes possible to arrange societies hierarchically according to their technologies. If we do this, it is but a small and logical step to assume that societies with similar technologies are also similar in every other respect. So we can show that modern industrial societies, all using similar technologies, are growing more similar socially.

We can also indict social institutions for failing to take advantage of technological 'advances' that are available to them. We can say that they are failing to adapt or that they are lagging behind what might be possible. As Roy admits, the argument is very plausible. It is used in agriculture to show that no more than a few rather simple, if radical, changes are needed in social institutions in developing countries for them to be able to take advantage of the technological opportunities provided by more 'advanced' societies that would provide them with ample food supplies. Yet, as Roy also points out, the model does not explain how it is that some highly evolved societies, such as those of Greece, China or India, failed to employ all the technological knowledge they possessed, nor why even today and even in the industrial countries a high proportion of new technologies are never adopted.

The reason may be that the economic system prevailing in the society, or its level of economic development, may not require those technologies to be adopted. This then is the economic–determinist model, which holds that technological changes are controlled by economic and commercial forces. If a task needs to be accomplished, very often there is a wide range of technologies available. In agriculture, for example, the control of a particular insect pest may be achieved by employing one or two men and a crop-spraying aircraft, or an array of workers to remove each insect by hand. The technology that is chosen will be determined by the relative availability and cost of labour, pesticides and aircraft. These economic forces will encourage societies always to pursue the most effective course for them, and if those forces require that tasks be accomplished more quickly, more completely or more cheaply, then economic and technological advances will be stimulated. Very often this is what appears to happen but sometimes it does not.

When neither of these models fits it may be because particular sections within the society are seeking their own advantage to the exclusion of all else. Thus we arrive at the political–determinist model in which economic, technological and social changes are regulated by the conflict of competing interests. Thus in the nineteenth century Britain allowed its agriculture to run down while it concentrated on developing its manufacturing capacity, because at that time industrialists were wealthier and more powerful than farmers and could attract capital for investment. In the twentieth century the rising power of the trades unions has improved living standards for workers but may also have contributed to the search for labour-saving technologies that could reduce production costs.

So society is seen to be controlled by certain sections within it. Since these sections will, or may, hold in common certain views about the nature of society and the role of the individual within it, and will tend to use their influence to direct society in ways that conform to those views, the process of development and change acquires ideological overtones. We may assume that societies which subscribe to different ideologies may develop in quite different ways.

None of the determinist models is entirely satisfactory. All of them try to reduce a very complex process to a very few simple causal relationships. The truth, Roy suggests, is that the process really is complex, that all these factors exert an influence, but that they and other factors interact at every level. The economic and political systems within a society may reflect an ideology, may produce a particular kind of technology, but will also be shaped by the technologies it has chosen to employ.

We see, then, that attempts to 'develop' traditional agricultures simply by exposing them to teams of foreign advisers were naive. Expressed in its most extreme form, if we wish other cultures to adopt our technologies then we should begin by making them into extensions of our own culture. This is likely to be seen as an attempt at imperialism. Certainly it is the way it is viewed in China, which has developed an alternative strategy for development over which it can exert full control. At the FAO Conference in November 1975, the Chinese Vice-Minister of Agriculture and Forestry, Mr Yan Li-Kung, outlined some of the achievements in his country and the Chinese view of aid from the USA and the USSR:[2]

'In 1974 China's total grain output reached 274·9 million tons, or 240% above that of 1949 and the output of ginned cotton was 2·45 million tons, or 570% above that of 1949.

'Good harvests have been reaped for 13 years running and another good harvest has been gathered this year after conquering fairly serious natural disasters.

'However, the level of our agricultural production is still not high, and that of our per capita food consumption is not high either,' he said. 'China hopes to achieve farm mechanisation by 1980 and complete modernisation of agriculture by the end of the century.

'The fierce contention between the superpowers is bound to lead to war some day,' he said. 'China blames the world food crisis on the machinations of the two superpowers, both of whom want only to "perpetuate the exploitation of the Third World".'

One of the superpowers boasts of its food surpluses and uses them to preserve its economic superiority. Mr Yan spoke emphatically:

'To put it bluntly, its "leading responsibility" is aimed at keeping the Third World countries subservient under its wilful sway, exploitation and plunder as before'. The other superpower fares no better at Chinese hands. It buys up vast quantities of food and disrupts and dislocates markets. 'This superpower has spared no effort to peddle the Third World such trash as "international division of labour" and "economic integration" and boasts how its "economic co-operation" with the Third World has added an "international economic relationship of a new type".... In all this, it has outdone the old-line colonialism and imperialism. This superpower that is most zealous in mouthing "detente" and "disarmament" is precisely the most dangerous source of war in the world today.'

In its speeches to UN conferences, China's clear aim is to secure the leadership of the Third World. Consequently it says that it is possible for a comparatively poor country to stand up to the major powers without fear of retaliation. Chinese speeches are famous for their splendid hyperbole but this should not mask the fact that unless they expressed a view that is held widely in the Third World they would not be made in those terms. There is resentment at trading patterns that favour the rich but there is also resentment at aid programmes that appear to serve the political status quo, to perpetuate the subservient relationship between recipient and donor and, within the recipient countries themselves, to favour those with wealth and power.

To be fair the problem is recognised in the West, albeit belatedly. In April 1976 the UK Select Committee on Overseas Development published a report in which it acknowledged that poverty is the root cause of hunger and that in future aid must be concentrated in rural areas, where poverty is most acute. It estimated that about 10% of British aid goes to rural development projects and it urged that this proportion be increased. Doubling the proportion would be very difficult, it believed, and it made no firm proposals for ways in which the allocation of funds might be changed. It guarded itself, too, against charges of neo-colonialism.[3]

In March 1976 the World Bank published its atlas for 1975, showing that 61% of the world's population in 1973 lived in countries where the per caput annual income was below \$500, and 30% lived in countries where it was below \$200. Between 1971 and 1973 the number of countries with an annual per capita income of more than \$5000 rose from one (the USA) to six: USA, Switzerland, Sweden, Canada, West Germany and Denmark. A number of smaller countries are also very rich indeed—Kuwait (annual per capita income \$12 500), the United Arab Emirates (\$11 630), Qatar (\$6040) and Iceland (\$5030). The comparable figure for India is \$120 and for China \$270. The annual per capita income in the USA is \$6200 and in the USSR \$2030.[4]

If this is the result of some 30 years of overseas aid then it is clear that the poorest sections of the world community are not being helped. So what is happening?

Aid comes from industrial societies and is given to societies that are mainly agrarian. Even agriculture in an industrial society tends to structure itself on industry—the British farmer is often described as a 'businessman' and so, in many ways, he is—so that it is easy to underestimate the power of a landowner in a country whose main industry is still farming. It is equally easy to ignore or to misunderstand the very complex system of rights, privileges and responsibilities by which a traditional agrarian community operates, and the possible consequences when that system is subjected to too great a stress.

The person who owns the land has great power over those who do not. He possesses capital and, because his land can be used as a security, he has relatively easy access to credit. If his tenants or workers need capital he is one of the sources from which they are likely to obtain it. It is not surprising, then, to find that new agricultural technologies are adopted first by the wealthier farmers. The technologies require investment in irrigation, fertilisers, pesticides, seed and possibly equipment. Only the wealthy can afford this investment. So the benefits from increased yields accrue first to the wealthy.

This supposes, of course, that landlords are invariably harsh and determined to advance their own interests at the expense of the rest of the community—a distinctly industrial concept. In most cases they are not, but the fact that an income disparity that previously either had not existed because the economy did not work on a monetary basis or that did not matter because it had existed for long enough for it to be accepted and because compensations existed in the form of duties and responsibilities of the rich to the poor, can suddenly become very evident because it is much greater, stresses the system. The poor are made aware of their poverty and so they may resent the wealth of the landowner. Poleman and Freebairn, in a study of the economic and social effects of the Green Revolution, summarise a situation that is quite general:

'The most obvious of the factors determining who will receive the benefits is who owns the land. In low-income agrarian societies, a great majority of the organising institutions centre around the ownership of land. . . . For the short run, land owners would be expected to receive much of the surplus profit from the innovation.'[5]

Having said that rapid technological innovation is likely to place severe stress on any traditional society, however, the effects of that stress may vary widely from place to place. Employment, for example, may either increase or decrease from the same cause, depending on circumstances in a particular locality. If crop yields increase substantially, then more work is required at harvest time. This may cause labour shortages, leading to demands for higher wages. There have been cases where landowners have tried to resist this demand and the frustration of the workers has erupted in outbreaks of violence.

Alternatively the higher value of the crops may provide the landowner with profits that he chooses to invest in harvesting machinery and so unemployment increases. A single combine harvester, stopping periodically to unload its grain tank into a trailer drawn by a tractor, which carries the grain to the store, employs two workers or perhaps three. Harvesting with a reaper and binder might employ up to 10 workers. Harvesting by hand employs a whole village and is a social activity, usually followed by celebrations in which the whole community participates. In Europe schoolchildren still receive a long summer holiday because traditionally their labour was needed during the summer to bring in the harvest. There are few of them today who remember this!

A study in the Moquequa Valley in southern Peru, quoted in ref. 5, of the feasibility of changing a farming system based on the extensive production of cereals by smallholders into one based on intensive, small-scale horticulture, showed that capital requirements would increase by two to three times, employment would increase by 20–30% and incomes would almost quadruple.

In Mexico the aim for 50 years or so has been to reform land tenure systems in programmes that have brought well over 2 million families into the position of holders of land—either owning or leasing it—rather than labourers. At the same time, technical developments have been encouraged and farmers have been helped by better credit facilities and price supports. The effects have been uneven, depending partly on the intensiveness with which the land was farmed before the programmes began. Employment has increased from 50 to 100% over a 30-year period, output has increased annually by 3·5 to 5·8%, capital investment is from three to 12 times what it was in 1930 and the cost of inputs has generally left a satisfactory profit, although this has grown rather slowly in some regions.

Even so only the periphery of the national farming system has been affected. In more recent years the widely publicised Puebla Project, in the state of Puebla, has aimed to bring appropriate modern technologies within the reach of small-scale farmers. The project began in 1967 with 30 participants and, by 1970, 5000 farmers had joined it and found themselves earning incomes more than double those of their neighbours who still used traditional methods.

There may be a limit to the extent to which such programmes can be made to benefit the entire rural population. Improvements in incomes must be based on higher crop yields and yet even in very poor countries, where hunger is common, the elasticity of demand for food is low, as we saw in Chapter 1. If a country is a net importer of food then some expansion in home production can eliminate the import requirement and benefit a certain number of producers. Increases in production beyond this may overload the market and cause more harm than good, unless the economy is centrally planned and surplus food bought in by a central organisation that also arranges for its export. The obvious alternative, to add more value to the food produced by processing it into more costly items—as, for example, by feeding surplus grain to livestock—can succeed only where the general economic level is such that an effective demand exists for high-priced food.

In India traditional societies were organised very rigidly, in complex hierarchies where individuals at each level had relationships with those at other levels that were clearly defined and backed by divine authority. Prolonged exposure to European ways of life began the erosion of this social structure so that it is difficult to determine the extent to which more recent agricultural changes have initiated or merely continued or altered the direction of social change.

It was the colonial power that encouraged the shift from self-sufficient rural communities to communities engaged in trade and integrated into a monetary economy. Private ownership of land and property was encouraged, which made credit easier to obtain, and the demand for credit was met increasingly by moneylenders. The development of urban industries displaced many workers in hand-craft industries, farmland began to be diverted into non-agricultural uses and when the colonial power took steps to halt this trend, many moneylenders bought farms and became landowners. The number of landless increased. Of course, the effect was felt unevenly. Many remote areas were hardly affected, and in those areas that were, the erosion of the traditional social structure did not necessarily mean that the new landowners failed to meet their customary obligations.

Whether the new agricultural technologies have initiated or merely accelerated what was happening anyway, the fact is that they have the power to erode completely the traditional structures and, with them, the safeguards that are built into them to protect the poor.

The effect has been felt in two stages. In the first stage, growers are encouraged to maximise their profits. The HYV cereals offer substantially larger yields but require more expensive methods of husbandry. Thus farmers have the opportunity of growing more but also need to do so in order to cover the cost of the new husbandry. Soon all the relationships within the community are defined in monetary terms. In place of traditional privileges and obligations, services rendered and services received, wage rates, rents and crop shares are laid down in greater detail. This tends to convert workers into a rural proletariat. The fact that the new technologies work as well for small farmers as for large suggests that the benefits of them should be shared equally by the whole community. This may be resisted by the wealthier landowners, who have just begun to experience the advantages of profit maximisation, and so the small farmers, the tenants and the share croppers become engaged in political activity. The situation was summed up in 1970 by Harold Munthe-Kaas:

> 'The emergence and development of this kind of violent movement, operating outside the country's existing institutions, with the explicit purpose of breaking down the entire political and economic system, are clearly a result of the system's inability to let all social groups benefit from the general advancement of the society. While India over the past few years has achieved impressive progress on its "green revolution", the result in the countryside has been economic polarisation with the few rich getting richer and the masses getting poorer. Many are being pushed off their land and losing their property.'[6]

It was this process that led to the observation that 'the green revolution is turning red'. In East Thanjavor the local Communist front organisation changed its name in 1968 to the Agricultural Workers' Union and in various parts of rural India the Marxist Communist Party began to make substantial gains in elections. Where landowners and workers formed groups, each with their own organisations, that found themselves confronting one another, the relationship could become highly inflamed.

When members of the Agricultural Workers' Union demanded higher wages for bringing in a larger harvest— and so for performing more work—in 1968, the resulting conflict led to the burning alive of 42 workers, on 25 December, and the arrest of the President of the Nagapattinam District (taluk) Paddy Producers' Association.

The situation of tenants was not easy either. Larger crops and consequently larger profits increased the value of land, and this was reflected in increases in rents and a reduction in the security of tenure. In some places rents came to represent 70 % of the crop. Landowners tried to reduce tenants to the status of share-croppers, then to evict them entirely so they could farm the land themselves, using labourers.

Although the Indian Government had been pursuing policies of land reform, this new economic pressure made them more than ever difficult to enforce. Trends that were already observable were simply reinforced. In the Indian Punjab, the Punjab Security of Tenures Act of 1953 sought to give tenants rights of occupancy and to set maximum rents that could be charged. However, it did permit the eviction of tenants if the landowner wished to cultivate the land himself. Between 1953 and 1955 the number of tenants decreased by more than 86 %, from 583 000 to 80 000 or so.[7]

Even so, some traditional patterns of social behaviour continued, and although they had been deprived of their legal rights and security, tenants were allowed to continue to cultivate the land in many cases. Farms in the

TABLE 11.1
Area Owned Including Uncultivated Area by Size of Holdings in Pakistani Punjab

Size	*Acres (thousands)*	*Percent of total*	*No. of owners (thousands)*	*(% of total)*
Less than 10 acres	7 092	31·8	1 809	78·7
10–99	10 428	46·7	476	20·7
100–499	2 502	11·2	12	0·5
500+	2 295	10·3	1	0·1
Total	22 317	100·0	2 298	100·0

(Source: ref. 24).

Punjab, on both sides of the border with Pakistan, are small. Table 11.1 shows that in the Pakistani Punjab more than 99 % of farms, and more than 78 % of the land area, work in lots of less than 100 acres (40 ha). Most farms are less than 10 acres (4 ha) in area. Table 11.2 shows the distribution of cultivators and cultivated land in the Indian Punjab. In 1966 the Indian Punjab was divided into two states, Punjab and Haryana.

At the time the new Green Revolution technologies were introduced, only a minority of farmers, those with holdings of 8 ha or more, were in a position to raise the capital needed to exploit them fully. The most urgent need was for improved irrigation. Existing systems had been designed only to provide the minimum protection against drought. New wells had to be sunk and only the larger farmers could afford to sink them. Only farmers with larger holdings could afford to buy the seed, fertiliser and pesticide they needed. In the end it was only farmers with holdings of 20 ha or more who experienced a substantial improvement in their way of life, while those

TABLE 11.2
Distribution of Cultivators and Cultivated Areas in the Punjab by Size of Operational Holdings, 1961–62

	Less than 2 ha	2–4 *ha*	4–8 *ha*	8 *ha or more*
Percent of rural households in the group to the total sampled	37·5	24·8	23·8	13·4
Percent of the cultivated area for the group to the total	7·4	18·3	33·0	40·7

(Source: ref. 5).

with very small holdings may have suffered a decline because of their need to lease additional land to form an economically viable holding at a time when rents were rising rapidly.

In the Indian Punjab it is likely that the new technologies did not increase unemployment, although they did increase the number of workers by altering the status of those who previously had worked land in their own right. The organisation of workers led to wage increases but these were partly offset by retaliatory measures taken by landowners who denied workers the right to free fuel and other resources that had been customary.

In the Pakistani Punjab disparities in wealth had been much greater for many years. As Table 11.1 shows, although most farms were very small, 78 % of the rural population owned less than 32 % of all the land. During the late 1960s agricultural expansion was encouraged by substantial subsidies for the use of fertiliser and pesticides and by high support prices for wheat. By introducing the new HYV wheats, farmers were able to quadruple their incomes.

In 1969/70, Pakistan (then West Pakistan) became a net exporter of wheat. However, the benefits were not shared equally. The Agricultural Development Bank would provide loans for sinking wells only to farmers with 5–10 ha of land, depending on the quality of the land, and this excluded the majority of growers. There was considerable migration from rural to urban areas. Poleman and Freebairn suggest this may have been due to the desire of larger farmers to continue to farm their land but to enjoy the advantages of an urban lifestyle, and to the sale of very small farms that were proving uneconomic.[5]

The frustration of urban workers, and of farmworkers and smallholders, created political unrest that led first to the establishment of martial law, in March 1969, and finally to the overthrow of the old regime by a new party, the People's Party of Pakistan, led by Mr Z. A. Bhutto, who appealed directly to the peasants, promising to free them from exploitation.

A survey by the Indian Agricultural Research Institute in 1968[8] estimated that adoption of the new HYVs involved a doubling of the amount of family labour employed and a small increase in the employment of non-family labour. However, it has also been estimated[9] that if all the land in the Indian Punjab were sown to the new wheats, the demand for labour would increase by only 6 % and this additional labour force would be needed mainly in the harvest season. This may be a pessimistic estimate. In the case of rice it has been found that labour costs in India are roughly double (from 1:1 to 2·9:1) those for traditional varieties but this cost has not been converted into actual labour demand in the sense of the number of man-days needed per hectare of land.[10] A report on the Intensive Agricultural District Programme showed the Ludhiana District in the Punjab, which is one of the most advanced wheat growing areas in India, had increased the number of jobs faster than the rate of population growth, and that real wages increased by 16 %.[11]

When adjustments are made for local variations in social patterns, what is true for India and Pakistan is probably true for much of south and south east Asia. The People's Republic of China has approached its problems differently, of course, and the success with which it has solved most of them affords models that have influenced strongly the increasing number of centrally-planned economy countries in the region. In the future it will doubtless influence more. We shall look at the Chinese pattern in a moment.

Table 11.3 shows that in Asia as a whole, 46 % of all farmers have less than 1 ha of land, and that 88 % have less than 5 ha. However, this 88 % of farmers own only 47 % of the land. Land reform is an urgent need and probably there will be no solution to rural unemployment that does not involve further migrations from the countryside. V. K. R. V. Rao, who conducted a study of the progress of the Green Revolution for the UN Research Institute for Social Development (UNRISD), outlined the problems of the 'sub-marginal' farmers, working 0·4 ha or less:

'In the long run there appears to be no alternative to their leaving agriculture and going in for non-agricultural employment. However, their numbers are large and there is no way one can see at the moment to provide them all with non-agricultural employment. Nor can one leave them to their fate as that would either bring an unwanted and massive exodus to the

TABLE 11.3
Size of Farm Holdings in Asia, 1960

Size of holding	*No. of holders (thousands)*	*Area held (thousands)*
Less than 1 ha	45 123	21 592
1–2 ha	20 776	30 795
2–5	19 845	62 529
5–10	7 401	51 556
10–20	3 022	40 676
20–50	834	22 897
50–100	102	7 108
100–200	17	2 817
200–500	8	2 791
500–1 000	3	1 989
1 000 and over	2	6 206
Total	97 133	250 960

(Source: ref. 12).

urban areas or result in intolerable tensions in the countryside. Attempts will therefore have to be made to increase the productivity of their subsistence agriculture by organising them into production teams with opportunities for work outside the farm but in the rural areas in their vicinity by integrated rural development and supporting programmes of rural public works. Such sub-marginal farmers will have to be treated as a special case and special facilities provided for them to earn, from a combination of both agricultural and non-agricultural work, enough income to lift them above the level of poverty. Simultaneously opportunities should be provided to the younger among them to acquire new skills that would enable them to leave their land and take to industrial and tertiary occupations.'[12]

The Philippines has been studied more intensively than most developing countries. It is the home of the International Rice Research Institute, where the new HYV rices were developed and first introduced and the progress of its agricultural development has been monitored carefully.

The country was a Spanish colony from the sixteenth to the end of the nineteenth century and was subjected to many reversals of policy as the colonial power sought to protect its interests there and, simultaneously, in its American colonies. By the time the Philippines achieved their independence, much of the farmland was owned by powerful individuals and organisations, including the Church, who were exploitive and incompetent.[13] There was a fierce agrarian rebellion, followed by a more stable development of the economy, interrupted by the Japanese occupation during World War II.

Following the war the Philippines pursued a fairly conventional strategy of export-led economic expansion, but it fell increasingly under the economic domination of the USA, which led to fears that American companies were acquiring Philippine capital. The high rate of population growth prevented any real improvement in living standards. The rate of growth was never sufficient to provide full employment to a work force that was increasing so rapidly. There had been many schemes to stimulate production of rice, the staple food, and in 1936 the National Rice and Corn Corporation (NARIC) was created to regulate the industry. Dissolved during the occupation by the Japanese, NARIC was re-established after the war and was able to take advantage of the HYVs as soon as they became available.

Land tenure is complicated. Basically, land may be worked by the owner, who hires labour for a wage, undertakes all the management functions himself, bears all the economic risks and receives all the profits; or it may be worked on a share-cropping basis, in which the landlord and his tenant share costs, risks and profits, though not necessarily equally, and management decisions are also shared; or the land may be leased, in which case the landlord bears no risk and merely receives rent, while the tenant bears all the risks, makes all the management decisions and receives all the profits. Thus the person who assumes the risks is not necessarily the one who owns the land, and contracts may vary considerably from region to region and from one tenant–landlord partnership to another. To complicate matters further, land is rented in a competitive market. Very often there is no clear class distinction, since any individual may own a smallholding of his own, may be a share-cropper on another holding and may also work for wages part time. If the landlord does not farm the land himself he may be an absentee, represented by an agent or rent collector. Even if he does manage some of his own land he may do so through a manager.

Table 11.4 shows the distribution of land in the Philippines by size of farms. As in most of Asia, farms are generally small. Almost 95% of all farmers work holdings of 10 ha or less and this 95% control about 67% of the total farmland. Tables 11.5 and 11.6 show how farms are managed and how tenancies are distributed among those who pay cash, a share of the crop or a combination of the two. In 1960 almost 85% of farmers, working almost 80% of the land, were either owner-occupiers or tenants (Table 11.6), while 92·6% of all tenants, working 71·4% of all farmed land, paid their rent in the form of a share of the crop. Share-cropping is the general rule.

By the time the HYVs were adopted, rice yields in the Philippines were well below the Asian average and had been for many years. The average

TABLE 11.4
Percentage Distribution of Farm Holdings According to Size or Area of Farm Operated

Area of farm (ha)	*Total farmers* (%)	*Farm area* (%)
Less than 1	11·5	1·6
1–2	29·6	10·2
2–3	21·7	12·8
3–4	11·6	10·3
4–5	7·1	8·1
5–10	13·4	23·7
10–20	4·6	15·3
20–50	0·7	5·6
50–100	0·1	2·1
100–200	0·05	2·0
200+	0·04	4·4

(Source: ref. 26).

yield between 1934 and 1956 was 1178 kg per ha compared to the average Asian yield of 1706 kg per ha. Moreover, between 1948 and 1956 the average yield in Asia rose by about 17%, while that in the Philippines rose by only 1%.[14]

Many problems were experienced as attempts were made to introduce the new varieties and the new technologies that accompanied them. The laissez-faire administration was ill-equipped for such a task. However, the area of land under irrigation increased substantially, from 19% of the total farmed area in 1948–50 to 42% in 1968–70, and yields increased also. The new technologies were popularised by 'farmer-co-operators' selected, trained and provided with equipment and materials to act as catalysts in their areas. Even now little fertiliser is used. In 1968/69 only a quarter of all rice land received fertilisers, and the government had decided some time earlier not to introduce a fertiliser subsidy, which tends to benefit certain sections of the farming community more than others. The export of fertiliser was prohibited during the oil crisis of the early 1970s. Fertiliser prices were held stable, however, and credit facilities were provided cheaply to landlords, who passed them on to tenants as loans. It may be that this combination of stable fertiliser prices and credit facilities provided the major stimulus to increased production.[13]

As we have seen, most farms are small and most farms are occupied by crop-sharing tenants. The average size of holding has been decreasing and tenanted farms have been growing smaller more rapidly than owner-occupied farms. Among the owner-occupied farms there are some large haciendas, often working side by side with small-scale owner-occupiers.

TABLE 11.5
Distribution of Farms in the Philippines by Acreage and Type of Tenancy

Type of tenancy	*No. of farms (thousands)*	*Percent of total farms*	*Area (thousand ha)*	*Percent of total area*
Share rent-paying tenants	745·4	92·6	1 677·8	71·4
Fixed (produce) rent-paying tenants	34·1	4·3	88·9	3·8
Cash rent-paying tenants	13·5	1·6	547·0	23·3
Cash and share rent-paying tenants	10·8	1·4	34·1	1·4
Cash and fixed (produce) rent-paying tenants	0·7	0·1	3·7	0·1
All types	804·5	100·0	2 351·5	100·0

(Source: ref. 13).

However, the pattern varies somewhat from province to province. Overall the distribution of land is grossly unfair. Dr I. Palmer, of UNRISD, has commented on the need for land reform:

'Thirty percent of farm area is operated by 5·5 % of farmers. At the other end 62·8 % of farmers operate 24·6 % of farmland. Tenancies would be more heavily concentrated at the lower end of the farm scale than owner-operators. So skew is land distribution that it has given rise to the suggestion that until holdings as small as only a few hectares are brought under land

TABLE 11.6
Percentage Distribution of Farm Operators (A) and Farm Area (B) in the Philippines, by Tenure Class

All farms	1903		1918		1939		1948		1958		1960	
	A	*B*	*A*	*B*	*A*	*B*	*A*	*B*	*A*	*B*	*A*	*B*
Full owners	80·7	75·6	77·7	73·6	49·2	55·1	52·6	61·5	49·8	55·5	44·7	53·2
Part owners	—	—	—	—	15·6	12·1	10·0	8·6	10·2	9·8	14·3	14·7
Tenants	19·3	24·4	22·3	26·4	35·1	25·1	37·3	27·1	39·8	26·5	39·9	25·7
Farm managers	—	—	—	—	0·1	7·6	0·1	2·7	0·2	8·2	0·1	4·7
Others	—	—	—	—	—	—	—	—	—	—	1·0	1·7

(Source: ref. 25).

reform all tenants cannot be awarded land. The reply to that can only be that if that is harsh on landowners the present land distribution must be almost unbearable for tenants. It is worth remembering that land reform legislation does not entertain the idea of giving landless labourers land.'[13]

Share tenants have little security, since they hold their land on a year-by-year basis, and their frustration led to outbreaks of peasant resistance to the authorities and to landlords on a number of occasions. Land reform legislation aims to work in stages. There is some uncertainty about whether its aim is primarily to improve the lot of poorer farmers or whether it hopes to increase productivity and accepts that, in order to achieve this, the status of tenants has to be upgraded so as to encourage them to seek a greater degree of self-reliance and to bring them into an economic bracket that would make them eligible for credit. Whatever its aim the first stage of the reform is to declare land reform areas. Within these areas share tenants automatically become lease tenants. In the second stage the land was purchased by the government and mortgaged to the tenants. In the final stage the tenants would become the owners of their farms. Rents were fixed at a maximum of 25% of the average of the harvests in the three years preceding the fixing of the rent.

Unhappily landlords were still permited to evict tenants, and so it was not difficult to prevent tenants from experiencing the benefits to which they should have been entitled. There was confusion and great lack of coordination among the five government agencies responsible for implementing the reform and, in the end, progress was pitifully slow. In the first eight years, out of a total of 607 000 share tenants, only 182 000 had been reached by the programme and of these only 8332 had become leaseholders. In 1971 the government declared that all areas producing foodgrains were now land reform areas, but by February 1972 only about 9% of the share tenants had leases.

Predictably the peasants became more active politically, encouraging their neighbours to become more aware of their rights under the programme. This activity was repressed by local landlords, often aided by the Church and government officials, who together controlled the information media and the militia. Indeed the landlords themselves had predicted the failure of the reform. They argued that lack of capital would force lessees back into the role of share-croppers. The peasants, however, were realising that the reform itself was insufficiently radical to achieve its own objectives.

In 1972 martial law was declared, the entire country was made a land reform area and all tenants farming rice or maize were given either 5 ha of unirrigated land or 3 ha of irrigated land, which they were to buy over 15 years. The farms were valued at 2·5% of the average of the three harvests preceding the change and interest would be charged at 6% per annum. The land would be obtained by the surrender by, first, farmers holding more than 100 ha, then those holding between 50 and 100 ha and finally, by late in 1973, those holding 20 or more ha.

Small landowners protested and the maximum permitted size of holdings was increased to 24 ha. Landlords responded rapidly and decisively. They evicted tenants and forced them to become labourers. They filed criminal charges against them. They intimidated them physically and bulldozed their homes. The government had forbidden the eviction of tenants but it could hardly forbid landlords from pressing charges against tenants who threatened their lives.

The landlords were to be paid compensation, although many of them did not really understand how this was meant to work, and those that did saw that while some safeguards had been built in, it was not really proof against inflation.

The government became more determined than ever, but by early in 1974 it seemed that the average size of holdings being transferred to their tenants was 1·8 ha, rather than the 3 or 5 ha promised, and it was not clear even then whether the transfer was from share-cropping to leasing, or from leasing to mortgaging. In September 1974 it appeared that only 116 titles had actually been transferred to owner-occupiers and it is probable that about half of these have already reverted to the landlords, in a variety of informal agreements whose aim is to provide credit to the smaller farmer. Between autumn 1972 and autumn 1974 only 140 applications for leases had been received by the agency responsible for registering them, and only 88 land valuations had been transmitted to the agency responsible for paying compensation to landlords.

The martial law is not really effective against landlords and although penalties are laid down for the offences of obstructing or disobeying regulations, no landlord has been imprisoned.

Even had it succeeded the land reform would not have benefited the majority of tenants. It exempted landlords with less than 24 ha, and even a limit of 12 ha would have left 70% of all tenants unaffected. Nor did it attempt to help landless labourers, so that once a tenant had been evicted and converted to a labourer he was in an economic sense beyond help. Indeed the land reform might have made them worse off, for the pressure of population on available land is acute. As Dr I. Palmer says:

> 'Tenants and landless labourers have had the practice of asking landowners to install their mobile houses in a corner of a field. The subdivision of farms is making such non-productive use of space increasingly less desirable and already landless labourers are having difficulty finding room for their homes in lessee country.'[13]

This situation is exacerbated by the requirement that new lessees improve their farming systems in order to increase output. They must farm every last square metre of their land. Only if they do so will they be regarded as credit-worthy.

However, amid a generally dismal picture, one fear has not been realised. It was believed that the new technologies would be adopted first and most enthusiastically by the larger farmers and then percolate down through owner-operators, but leave tenants largely unaffected. The land reform programme added to these fears because it was felt that a lease rental, or mortgage repayment that was based on a valuation computed from crop yields grown traditionally, might suggest to tenants that by increasing their output they might provoke a revaluation of their land and a consequent increase in rent. It did not happen. Throughout the country the new technologies were adopted equally by farmers of all kinds working holdings of all sizes, so that the benefits did not accrue primarily to a sector that was already wealthy, so increasing social tensions even further.

An UNRISD team studied three provinces in detail: Camarines Sur, Iloilo and South Cotabato. They found that in Camarines Sur and Iloilo about 80 % of farmers were growing certified seeds, but that in South Cotabato, where farmers are crowded more closely together, seeds were being passed from farm to farm. In the country as a whole, in 1971/72, 56·3 % of the total paddy rice area and 73·4 % of the irrigated area, was sown to HYVs. HYVs are more vulnerable than traditional varieties to a range of natural vicissitudes, and on the whole the differences in yield are not so great as had been predicted, and some farmers have been changing back to the old varieties.

The introduction of the new varieties changes labour requirements. This results, in part, from changed cropping patterns. Where crops are all sown at the same time and large harvests gathered, labour requirements may become very seasonal, leading to under-employment at some times of the year. The kind and degree of mechanisation also affects the demand for labour. The introduction of four-wheeled tractors in Luzon, for example, was found to reduce the demand for labour by 30–40 %. The introduction of two-wheeled tractors on the other hand has almost no effect on numbers employed. In addition to the labour required to transplant rice and to harvest it, more careful husbandry may be needed. Crops must be kept weed free and, despite the official advice to use herbicides for weeding, in fact many farmers have relied on hand weeding, for which they require additional workers. Even spraying, however, provides some employment. Farmers have resisted the mechanisation of threshing, so that although areas whose productivity has been high for a generation or more may have adopted mechanical threshing many years ago, in areas where productivity was low and is only now beginning to rise, farmers continue to use traditional methods. In either case, large increases in output create more work at threshing time.

It is only in cultivation itself, the preparation of land for sowing, that the demand for labour has fallen generally. This could change, of course, should a rise in the prosperity of farmers encourage them to invest in a higher degree of labour-saving mechanisation. In 1968 a survey of 780 farms in Laguna showed that all but three owned a plough and 81 % owned a harrower, the two implements used in cultivation; half the farms owned a device for mechanical weeding; about one-fifth owned a pesticide sprayer; 3 % owned an irrigation pump; almost 8 % owned a two-wheeled hand tractor; and only two farms in the sample owned a four-wheeled tractor.[15] In the three regions in the UNRISD study, only in Camarines Sur was there a clear move toward increased use of tractors and mechanical weeding. In all cases where HYVs were being grown, however, cultivations were carried out more carefully and the single clear advantage that a tractor offers is speed of cultivation, which makes it much easier for the farmer to cultivate at exactly the right time—an important factor in weed and pest control.

In Central Luzon and Laguna the number of man-days of work devoted to each hectare of farm land increased from 64 in 1966 to 67 in 1970, while the number of man-days required for each ton of produce decreased from 34 to 25 in the same period.

The labour force is drawn from the families of farmers or from the pool of landless labourers. In general, members of the farmer's family will be employed in preference to outsiders, but when family labour becomes insufficient to cope with the amount of work, then other labour must be drawn in. It is not clear, though, whether work is given to members of farming families in preference to other work they may have been doing off the farm. Under some circumstances there is an incentive to hire outside labour rather than to employ members of the family, since landlords often require debts to be paid out of farm income but do not take account of income derived from elsewhere. Thus relatives who contribute to the household budget by working away from home may be best advised to remain where they are, since the cost of hired labour can be deducted from the income out of which the landlord must be paid a percentage. So the pattern of employment varies from place to place.

Other factors also influence labour decisions. The quality of the work, especially the condition of crops at harvest time, might influence the number of applications for employment, since workers would be less willing to work for a wage that was to be paid from a crop of little value. As one observer commented:

'In general, many farmers abandoned normal crop care when they saw the degree of damage on non-resistant varieties, and sought employment more vigorously or immersed themselves in the November and January election campaigns. However, it is important that normally stable harvest share and work arrangements were upset. Harvesters refused to work on badly damaged crops for the normal one-fifth or one-sixth, wet season *hunos*, or dry season *atorga*, and demanded one-quarter, one-third or even one-half of the yield or daily palay pay depending on the extent of the damage. In response many farmers who would not normally do so harvested with their own and household labour, and excluded *namumulot* gleaners, as the harvest itself was virtually a gleaning operation.'[16]

Overall, employment in the Philippines increased as a result of introducing the new technologies, but it did so from a rather low base level and it tended to favour family labour rather than the landless labourers.

The problem of rural unemployment and under-employment and its relationship to poverty and over-rapid urbanisation is well known to the FAO, and it has been part of the World Food Programme's activities to stimulate job creation, through schemes not necessarily linked directly to agriculture. On 5 May, 1976 the FAO announced that some 8 million jobs had been created in developing countries since the inception of the programme 13 years earlier. In Bangladesh, 2 million people were employed on a food-for-work basis repairing irrigation systems.

'Nearly 3·5 million jobs were connected with various programmes of human settlement. Of these some 600 000 rural settlers and an equal number of refugees had been provided work. Half a million jobs had been generated in construction activities and some 1·8 million people had been involved in voluntary self-help activities related to better living conditions in human settlements.

'The Programme's aid has helped to construct and repair nearly half a million housing units, mainly in Africa and the Near East. Thousands of kilometres of rural feeder roads and urban streets, railway lines and power lines, bridges, schools and hospitals have been built.

'The number of beneficiaries of all kinds of WFP assistance from 1963 to mid-1975 were estimate at 38·6 million. Of these nearly 35 % formed part of projects directly related to agricultural production and forestry and an equal proportion for community development programmes. Others included school children and such vulnerable portions of the population as nursing mothers.'[17]

The key to agricultural development, however, is the provision of credit. All farming works by a credit system, in that the farmer must buy seed, fertiliser and other raw materials before he has a crop from the proceeds of which he can pay for them. If he needs new equipment or wishes to invest in more or better buildings, to improve his livestock or, indeed, to make any advance, he must find a way to borrow the capital and repay it from the increase in his income he expects from it. The extent of the problem can be seen from the example of the Philippines, in Table 11.7. Farmers borrow money from private citizens, from landlords, from official agencies, from

TABLE 11.7
Cash Borrowed and Annual Interest Rate by Source and Province, Present and Pre-HYV, Philippines

Source	*Farms* (%)	*Present amount* (*pesos*)	*Interest* (%)	*Farms* (%)	*Pre-HYV amount* (*pesos*)	*Interest* (%)
Camarines Sur						
private person	30·2	377	19·0	53·3	303	29·4
landlord	19·8	265	29·3	16·7	102	2·0
FaCoMa	17·4	651	2·0	11·7	346	2·4
relatives	7·0	250	—	5·0	500	180·0
rural bank	25·6	667	10·0	13·3	856	8·4
average	100·0	479	—	100·0	389	
Iloilo						
private person	34·4	217	93·3	26·5	250	59·3
landlord	47·5	235	40·0	65·3	190	81·7
FaCoMa	4·1	459	79·2	—	—	—
relatives	2·5	225	14·4	2·1	500	—
rural bank	11·5	555	12·5	6·1	500	12·0
average	100·0	298	—	100·0	240	—
South Cotabato						
private person	48·3	235	31·2	71·4	147	14·1
landlord	41·6	171	131·7	21·4	101	84·0
relatives	3·4	180	172·2	7·2	160	40·0
rural bank	6·7	400	11·4	—	—	—
average	100·0	212	—	100·0	134	—

(Source: ref. 27).

relatives or from rural banks and they pay interest rates up to 172% per year. In the words of V. K. R. V. Rao:

'. . . credit has always been a problem for the farmer: and many of them have had to borrow from moneylenders or landlords or what are euphemistically called "friends and neighbours" and pay such high rates of interest that the produce left behind hardly gave them any incentive for putting their best into cultivation, let alone improving their agricultural practice or investing in land improvement. In many cases, the agency through which, and the the terms on which, they obtained credit resulted in the loss of land ownership and converted them into either agricultural labourers or share-croppers or what were called in Indonesia debt-work peasants.'[12]

In his travels through Asia, Rao found that not only was credit the major bottleneck but it also played a major role in distorting the agrarian

TABLE 11.8

Money and Real Net Income (pesos per season) by District and Tenurial Group, Philippines

	Owner	*Lease tenant*	*Share tenant*	*Landlord*
Camarines Sur				
net income 1967	1 513	620	493	427
net income 1971	2 725	766	1 449	1 182
net income 1971 at 1967 prices	1 879	528	999	788
percent real increase	24	114	103	91
Iloilo				
net income 1967	1 328	1 480	891	914
net income 1971	2 167	1 819	1 124	1 362
net income 1971 at 1967 prices	1 494	1 254	775	939
percent real increase	12	−15	−13	3
South Cotabato				
net income 1967	737	1 075	497	341
net income 1971	2 151	4 021	1 554	1 130
net income 1971 at 1967 prices	1 483	2 773	1 071	779
percent real increase	101	159	118	128

(Source: ref. 13).

structure in favour of landlords, moneylenders, traders and large-scale farmers.

In October 1975 the FAO held a conference in Rome to consider this problem. The World Bank had suggested that banks adopt much more flexible policies toward poor farmers, visiting them rather than waiting for the farmers to call at an office in a town, allowing production potential rather than the ownership of property as collateral against loans, advancing credit in the form of goods such as seed and fertiliser, rather than cash, and a generally closer relationship with farmers that would provide them with an assurance of continuity, while allowing the bank to reassure itself regarding their ability to repay. At the end of the conference central banks were urged to provide farm credit, in cooperation with governments and the UN Development Programme. By June 1976 the FAO was able to announce an international programme in which all member countries would be invited to participate and for which the FAO would provide a secretariat. Barclays Bank International, in London, announced that it was willing to fund the first phase of a programme to establish the needs for training materials.

The problem is huge and it will not be solved easily. Table 11.8 shows that despite the introduction of the HYVs in the Philippines, the country where their spread has been largest, the incomes of farmers have not increased as much as might have been hoped.

It seems, then, that an adequate rate of agricultural development must depend on full-scale agrarian reform. Poor farmers must be provided with access to credit on terms they can afford. To do this, and to provide a proper incentive, they must own or at least be guaranteed the secure tenure of their land. Landless labourers must be given access to land. In agrarian societies it is extremely doubtful whether this can be achieved without very radical reforms that require governments to legislate against the short term interest of their most powerful supporters, and to become landowners themselves at least for a time. Even in the Philippines, which has a rather extreme laissez-faire market economy, the government decided it had to appropriate land in order to redistribute it. Its reforms have failed so far because the government lacked the political power to implement them. An approach is required that is still more radical.

It may be no coincidence that the countries that have achieved the greatest success both in redistributing access to farmland and increasing food output are those with a centrally-planned economy—the socialist countries, both in Asia and also Cuba, the solitary Latin American socialist state. In Africa the situation is rather different, and several countries like Tanzania have realised that their development must remain under the control of those who should benefit from it, that economies and social systems must be designed that are related to traditional cultures, growing out of them as it were, rather than alien systems imposed on them from outside.

The most spectacular example of all is provided by China, which has transformed the economy of the largest nation on earth within a single generation. Before the revolution rural China was in a condition very akin to that of most Asian developing countries today. Wealthy large-scale farmers accounted for 10 % of the rural population but controlled 70–80 % of the land. The small farmers and landless labourers, representing 90 % of the population, worked 20–30 % of the land. Share-croppers were paying half of their produce, or sometimes even as much as 70–80 % of it, to the landlords in rent and interest charges.

After the initial land reform that followed the revolution, farming became based on small owner-occupied peasant holdings. Families were encouraged to cooperate in mutual aid projects and producers' cooperatives were established. Members of the cooperatives pooled their land so that many small farms came to be managed as a single unit, and the members were paid wages on a share basis related to the amount of land they contributed. The land then became the property of the cooperative. Compensation was paid for draught animals and equipment that also became common property, and wages became tied more closely to the amount of labour each member contributed. This linked incomes directly to production and provided an incentive to increase output. Between 1952 and 1957 grain output increased nationally by 19%.[18]

Rural communes were established in 1958, as a logical extension of previous reforms. Within the commune the land, buildings and all other means of production are owned by the members. This is very different from 'state ownership', where property is owned nationally and the administration is highly centralised. Ownership is distributed in three levels but the land is owned at the smallest level—that of the production team.

A production team consists of a number of families and there may be seven or eight teams in a village. The team is the basic accounting unit of the commune and it owns land, animals and equipment. In the Chiliying Commune in Honan, for example, Number 29 Production Team consists of 36 households. It owns 310 mu (just over 20 ha) of land, 18 draught animals, a thresher, a grain mill and various other items of equipment. Members of the team decide for themselves how they will distribute their income. A village corresponds approximately to a Production Brigade. The brigade owns more expensive items of equipment, such as tractors or installations for irrigation or drainage, which the teams are able to use.

The Chiliying Brigade, which is the largest in the commune of the same name, owns several tractors, a flour mill, brick and tile works, farm tool repair workshop and a pig breeding farm. Its tractors are used by the teams and the pig farm sells weaners to the teams at 25% below the price set by the state as a maximum. The commune itself has repair shops that service the commune's 56 tractors and other larger equipment. There is a phosphate fertiliser plant, a cotton spinning mill, large-scale drainage and irrigation works that serve the whole commune and high-voltage power lines and transformers.

The communes and the two levels of ownership and administration below them exert so large an influence in the countryside that they have become the effective government, and their activities extend far beyond those immediately concerned with agriculture. They administer industry, finance and trade, education and cultural activities, public health, law and security within their territory. The commune's Revolutionary Committee, the local government, is directly under the county government, but comparisons with western systems of government can be misleading. At Chiliying there are 17 middle schools, 38 primary schools, an agrotechnical college with more than 200 students opened in 1973 and the commune recruits and trains its own regiment of militia.

In all, Chiliying Commune owns 93 000 mu (6200 ha) of land, has 38 Production Brigades, 298 Production Teams, 9100 households and 53 200 people.[19]

Although it is the aim of the communes to mechanise farming as quickly as possible, farming traditions are strong and Chinese peasant farmers are renowned for the economy with which they use resources. Thus the use of artificial fertilisers and pesticides is viewed with caution and all wastes are recycled.

The achievements are dramatic to say the least. Quite apart from vast schemes for irrigation, for the terracing of slopes, afforestation and soil conservation, yields themselves have risen sharply. In 1948, the year before the revolution, the area that became Chiliying Commune grew 600 kg of food grains per ha (80 jin per mu), and 187·5 kg per ha of cotton (25 jin per mu). By 1973 foodgrain production had increased by more than 13 times, to 8·25 tonnes per ha (1100 jin per mu) and cotton production stood at about 1·2 tonnes per ha (155 jin per mu), more than six times more than in 1948.[19]

By comparison, in 1973/74 the average yields of the EEC Nine were, for wheat, 3·8 tonnes per ha, barley 3·9, oats 3·4, maize 5·5 and for rice 4·0.[20] This shows that even though production in China increased from a very low base level, yields now are very high indeed, by any standard. Productivity per worker is relatively low, since this is a function of the degree of mechanisation, but in a country with a very large rural population and rather little employment in factory industry this is not of paramount importance. The Chinese hope to achieve sufficient mechanisation to eliminate some of the heaviest work on the land and to release farmworkers for industry. It seems ironical, considering the plight of, say, India, that with a population of 800 million or more, China is short of labour and has no unemployment!

Even if land reform can be achieved, incomes raised and food production increased, we cannot be certain that those most in need of food will receive it. Nothing is simple and it cannot be said too often that a process of technological transfer requires even more fundamental social changes.

In her study of Asian conditions, Dr I. Palmer found that the status of women may have a direct and important relationship to the nutritional status of the whole family.[21] In some societies the men are always fed first. This means that women and children eat only after the most appetising and often the most nutritious items have gone. 'Even where social eating habits are not quite so extreme women tend to deny themselves food first if there is any shortage in the family, whereas it cannot be so easily assumed that their husbands will force them to eat more'. The result, obviously, is debilitating to pregnant and nursing mothers, and to children. In this situation the arrival into the household of more food may mean only that already adequately fed men eat still more.

There is some disagreement about the relationship between family nutrition and the educational level of women. Palmer found no clear correlation with the education of women but in some societies a much closer relationship to the education level of men. With better education, men often come to desire the promotion of the welfare of their wives and children, and both educational and nutritional standards were raised for all members of the family. Even then, religious and cultural attitudes may have a counterbalancing effect. In Palmer's words:

> 'Occasionally it is necessary to remember that reading, writing and arithmetic do not automatically endow a group with the capacity for compassion and democracy.'

In Mexico on the other hand, Prof. Joaquin Cravioto has found a clear relationship between infant malnutrition and the educational level of the mother. Malnutrition, he asserts, does not occur in a vacuum, and he prefers to talk of 'the ecology of hunger'. He conducted a long and detailed study in a Mexican village in the course of which he tried to find common factors in the environments of deprived children. He considered the heights of parents, their age and weights, personal cleanliness, literacy and educational level, the frequency with which they read newspapers and the size and composition of the families. He considered the source of the family income, the per capita income and the proportion of it that is spent on food, sanitary facilities and the frequency with which fathers listened to the radio.

The only positive correlation he could find was the frequency with which mothers listen to the radio. It seems a trivial finding after so much work but it may be significant if listening to the radio indicates a greater awareness of the world outside—a mind that is more receptive to information and ideas. It may be hopeful, too, in that such an awareness and receptivity on the part of the mother may be transferred to her children.[22]

There are some people who suggest that any relationship between the rich industrial west and the developing countries of Africa, Asia and Latin America must be damaging, that all aid should be ended and that foreigners should cease their interference with established cultural patterns. In a perfect, unsullied world this would be quite true. There can be no doubt whatever that the colonial powers disrupted the cultures of those they encountered wherever they went and that it was their exploitive behaviour and imposition—sometimes with the best of intentions—that led directly to the present plight of the world's poor. Unhappily it is far too late for the rich now to withdraw from the scene. The disruption has already occurred in all but a very few remote areas, and the rich cannot absolve themselves from their clear responsibility to provide all the assistance they can.

There has been talk of 'triage' as an approach to developmental problems. This concept is derived from one developed in order to allocate rationally inadequate medical resources following a thermonuclear attack. It holds that the injured be divided into three groups and allotted priorities for treatment. There are those who will die no matter what treatment they receive; those who will recover without treatment; and those who will die without treatment but who can be saved with it. Where medical services are unable to treat everyone, the third group must be treated first to save lives, the second group second to minimise their injuries, and the first group must be given the lowest priority.

It is held that a similar approach be taken to the provision of aid and that countries be divided into those that will 'collapse', economically or socially, no matter what help they receive; those who will develop without any aid at all; and those whose development depends upon help from outside.

The comparison is very superficial, smacks of 'eco-fascism' and in any case could not be implemented, for although it is possible to identify countries in both of the second two categories, it is not possible to identify a single country in the first.

If the arbitrary provision or witholding of aid is one extreme of a spectrum, at the other is an equally undesirable philosophy that would link aid with the imposition of a particular pattern of development designed to suit the economic or political convenience of the donor. The only strategy that in the end has any real chance of success is one that allows each country or region to become self-reliant in its own way. The churches are becoming increasingly aware of this need, perhaps more rapidly than some governments. The Ecumenical Institute of the World Council of Churches holds regular consultations on matters relating to development, and in April 1976 it devoted one of these week-long sessions to 'Self-Reliance and Solidarity in the Quest for International Justice'. Its definition of self-reliance may serve as a pattern to guide future efforts:

'Self-reliance is an approach, an attitude, a world view of human, community, national, global development. It has emerged among the peoples of the dominated non-European countries as a positive assertion that there is an alternative to their dependence, subordination and exploitation and that alternative is not mimetic copying through catching up with those who have dominated, exploited and disregarded them.

'The central principle of self-reliance is the right, the necessity, the freedom and the capacity of each people to define and to struggle to achieve their own goals of community, national and human development through institutions and programmes chosen by themselves.'[23]

REFERENCES

1. Roy, R. (1976). Myths about technological change, *New Scientist*, **70**(999), 281.
2. FAO (1975). Press release 75/97, 14 November. Rome.
3. Select Committee on Overseas Development (1976). First Report, 1975–76 Session: *The World Food Crisis and Third World Development: Implications for United Kingdom Policy*. HMSO, London.
4. *The Guardian*, 23 March, 1976. London.
5. Poleman, T. T. and Freebairn, D. K. (1973). *Food, Population and Employment: The Impact of the Green Revolution*. Praeger Publishers for the Cornell University Program on Science, Technology and Society, New York.

6. Munthe-Kaas, H. (1970). Green and red revolutions, *Far Eastern Economic Review*, March 19.
7. Ladejinsky, Wolf. (1969). *Punjab Field Trip*, New Delhi. Mimeo.
8. Indian Agricultural Research Institute (1968). *Five Years of Research on Dwarf Wheats*, New Delhi.
9. Billings, M. H. and Singh, A. (April 1969). Conventional energy as a constraint to the Green Revolution 1964–84: The Punjab case, New Delhi. Mimeo for US AID.
10. Indian Programme Evaluation Organisation Survey of 1967–68. Kharif crop. Quoted in New Cereal varieties: Rice and Wheat in India, paper for US AID, *Spring Review*, March 13–15.
11. Sen, S. R. (Chairman) (1969). *Modernizing Indian Agriculture*, Report on the Intensive Agricultural District Programme (1960–68), Vol. V. Expert Committee on Assessment and Evaluation. Ministry of Food, Agriculture, Community Development and Cooperatives. New Delhi.
12. Rao, V. K. R. V. (1974). *Growth with Justice in Asian Agriculture*. UNRISD, Geneva.
13. Palmer, I. (1975). *The New Rice in the Philippines*. UNRISD, Geneva.
14. Golay, F. H. (1963). *The Philippines: Public Policy and National Economic Development*. Cornell University Press, Ithaca, USA.
15. *FHDO Rural Change in a Philippine Setting: A General Report on the Five Year Project, a Study on Alternative Extension Approaches* (1971). University of the Philippines, College of Agriculture.
16. Fegan, B. (1972). Jobs and farms: the lessees' alternatives to peasantization, *Philippine Sociological Review*, **20**, 1–2, January–April.
17. FAO (1976). Press release 76/23. Rome.
18. Cheng Shih (1974). *A Glance at China's Economy*. Foreign Languages Press, Peking.
19. Chu Li and Tien Chieh-yun (1974). *Inside a People's Commune*. Foreign Languages Press, Peking.
20. MAFF (1974). *EEC Agricultural and Food Statistics*. Ministry of Agriculture, Fisheries and Food, London, June.
21. Palmer, I. (1972). *Food and the New Agricultural Technology*. UNRISD, Geneva.
22. Watts, G. (1976). The ecology of hunger, *New Scientist*, **69**(988), 388.
23. Ecumenical Institute (1976). Self-Reliance and Solidarity in the Quest for International Justice. Ecumenical Institute (World Council of Churches), Bossey, Switzerland.
24. West Pakistan (1959). *Report of the Land Reforms Commission for West Pakistan*. Lahore, January.
25. Huizer, G. (1972). *Agrarian Unrest and Peasant Organizations in the Philippines*. Occasional Papers. Institute of Social Studies, The Hague.
26. Lilia C. Panganiban, *Land Reform Administrative Procedures in the Philippines: A Critical Analysis*. Land Tenure Center, University of Wisconsin. Quoted in Castillo, G., *All in a Grain of Rice*, and in Palmer, I. (1974). *The New Rice in the Philippines*. UNRISD, Geneva.
27. Mangahas, M. and Librero, A. (1973). UNRISD Report, Part II, September.

Chapter 12

A NEW ECONOMIC ORDER?

It has come to be recognised fairly generally that a principal underlying cause of hunger is poverty. People are hungry mainly because they cannot afford to buy the goods they need. Farmers cannot afford to grow more food than they do because there is no obvious market for their produce and, in any case, all too often they lack the means with which to buy the equipment and materials they need. It is possible to recognise this rather obvious fact and yet fail to see how it can be overcome and the problem solved. It is easy, for example, to assume in an idealistic kind of way that if the rich were to part with a little of their wealth to the poor, then the poor would be less poor.

Many politicians might agree with such a statement phrased in this way, for the simple reason that the problems encountered by anyone attempting to devise a way to implement it are so formidable that before long they will give up in despair and the *status quo* will be preserved. In some ways this summarised the history of relationships between the rich and poor nations for most of this century.

The donating of wealth by the rich to the poor is called aid. Before it can be administered we must know in a little more detail who is to be the donor, what he is to donate, to whom he is to donate it and for what purpose. Immediately we have asked the questions it is likely that we have imposed a cultural bias to the replies we expect or will accept. Many people believe, for example, that it is desirable that some poor countries reduce the rate at which their populations are growing. Accordingly most liberal-minded people in the rich countries would support the funding of programmes whose aim is to popularise and so increase the use of contraceptive devices. In the world as a whole, however, abortion is used more commonly to regulate the size of families than any contraceptive technique. Would we support the funding of programmes to provide free abortion on demand throughout the Third World? Perhaps we would, but would we agree that abortion should be promoted, as the use of contraceptives is promoted?

If we would then perhaps the argument should be taken a stage further. Throughout history in some cultures infanticide has been used as a means of disposing of those babies that could not be supported by the resources available to the community into which they were born. Would we support research and development programmes into more efficient means of infanticide? If we would not then we must force ourselves to consider the degree to which our revulsion at infanticide is the product of attitudes evolved within our own culture, attitudes that may not be shared by others.

The example is extreme, of course, but it is not absurd. Most people find infanticide repugnant but in certain Asian societies it is almost as repugnant to kill animals that compete with man for food. There are people who believe it immoral to take life, who will do so only in order to ensure their own survival: they will eat, for example, and tolerate the inevitable deaths of insects and small creatures crushed by their feet as they walk. Rats have as much right to live as do humans, however, and the fact that they compete with us for food—they need to eat as does any other animal—does not provide a sufficient justification for killing them.

It may be that the very concepts of wealth and poverty are subject to similar cultural bias. We define 'wealth' and differentiate between 'developing', 'developed' and undeveloped' countries on the basis of per capita annual GDP. If the average GDP per head stands at a certain figure—measured, significantly, in US dollars—then the country is at a particular stage of development and the aim must be to raise the lower to match the higher. Thus we may be tempted to visualise an ideal world that has grown into a kind of United States of California. Is it laudable? Is it appropriate? Is it feasible? Who wants it? The story of the Green Revolution, of the transfer of technologies from culture to culture, smacks a little of this dream. Perhaps the entire world has fallen under the spell of the Hollywood dream factory?

If we agree that by any reasonable standard the quality of life for many millions of people is far too low and that an improvement in their level of material prosperity is vital, even then we may base the decisions we make upon assumptions that are biased. We may assume that because we can imagine a single, unified world, such a world exists. The fallacy was cited by the Brazilian economic geographer, Professor Josué de Castro, as a reason for the disappointments that seem to follow inevitably upon development aid programmes:

'A kind of "ethnocentrism" has led a majority of modern development theorists to base their ideas and their proposed systems on the concepts of the classical school of economists, who almost entirely failed to comprehend the problem of economic development in the dependent and backward regions of the world. These theorists ignore the fact that there is no such thing as an integrated world economy but only a Western economy full of contradictions, a socialist economy still in the stage of experiment and evolution, and a more or less primitive trading system in the rest of the world. Therefore, not much study has been devoted to the economic structures of this "rest of the world", a field that has been abandoned to the sociologists, or rather the "folklorists". One has tended to overlook the human beings who inhabit these regions, with their traditional cultures so far removed and different from Western forms of civilisation. It had been thought that, by injections of capital and the introduction of inventions and technological innovations, it would be possible to change the general picture of traditional, non-Western structures and promote balanced development throughout the world. This miracle has not happened, and the result has been a widespread atmosphere of disillusionment and pessimism, and a fatalistic acceptance of the backwardness of the Third World as a virtually insoluble problem.'[1]

Those words were written in the introduction to a book published in 1972 and although one can understand very easily de Castro's pessimism and bitterness, yet the world has changed rather rapidly since then and today his view may seem unduly gloomy. It is not that economists have altered their classical concepts, or that the rich have undergone a kind of humanist conversion, but that the developing countries themselves, or some of them, have acquired a new political power that they are determined to wield and a clear articulate voice with which to express their view of the world.

In a large part the problems of aid were inherent in the institutions that supplied finance, mainly governments. Aid took the form of 'gifts' in money or kind, or loans. The 'gifts' were often not gifts at all, since they consisted either of industrial plant, equipment or materials manufactured in the donor country, or of money tied to specific projects and conditions. Goods that were donated were in fact bought by governments (the public sector) from their own industries (private sector) and so formed a means of channelling fairly modest sums of money from the public to the private sector of the donor economy. Of course, the recipient was intended to benefit—even politicians are not so cynical as that—but very often the major beneficiary was the economy of the donor, which was stimulated a little.

Much the same was true of monetary gifts, since in most cases a condition of the gift was that it should be spent on goods—often specified—to be purchased from the donor. Again money was shunted from the public to the private sector of the donor economy. In neither case did any capital leave the donor. Loans were subject to normal interest charges, so that after a period of several years they had to be serviced. Generally they matured after 15 years. There was a gift element in many such loans, in that interest rates were often much lower than the usual commercial rates: typically 3% rather than 10%. A period, often of 5 years, after the making of the loan before repayments of interest or capital must begin also constitutes a gift. Even so, by the end of 1969 the total outstanding external debt of, or guaranteed by, the governments of developing countries was about $60 000 million (a World Bank figure). Had all the development aid been supplied free from interest, that debt would have stood at about $10 000 million. The very substantial difference between the two figures represents interest.

So one effect of this kind of assistance is to place on to the recipient a burden of debt that cannot be repaid unless the developmental experiment is successful. If economic targets are missed, by even small margins, the debt is likely to accumulate. If capital were to be diverted from investment within the developing country in order to service the debt, then development itself would be inhibited and there would be a spiralling situation of a restricted development and growing external debt that would depress the economy.

Meanwhile the cost of such aid to the donor was not very high. Admittedly the capital sum earned no income for the grace period of about 5 years, but thereafter its real cost to the donor can be measured as the difference between the rates of interest charged and the economic growth rate of the donor's economy. Of course, there were periods during which the economies of individual industrial countries grew at 5% or more, but in many countries, averaged over one or two decades, the return on capital was sufficiently large for it to be regarded more as an investment—albeit a not especially profitable one—than as a gift. During this period the citizens of the developed donor countries may have been misled by their governments into believing that they were contributing much more to the development of the poor countries than in fact was the case.

Could the aid have been provided on easier terms? Professor A. Angelopoulos, the Greek economist, believes it could, and points out that shortly after the end of World War II, the USA loaned $3750 million to Britain with a maturity of fifty years, an interest rate of 2% and the provision that in certain circumstances payment of interest could be suspended or annulled.[1]

A situation was developing by the early 1970s in which countries that had received substantial amounts of aid were not just worse off than before but were virtually bankrupt, saddled with obligations to repay far more than they had ever received but with economies that were not generating wealth at anything like the required rate. Prof. Angelopoulos warns that unless measures are taken to relieve the burden, the outcome may be drastic:

> 'In the fifth century BC, when the people of Athens were heavily indebted, the famous philosopher Solon was called upon to act as a mediator. To cope with the dangerous situation Solon introduced the "sisachty", namely, the cancellation by law of all outstanding debts. If creditors wish to escape so radical a measure as the "sisachty", their only course is to give timely consideration to the easing of the burden of old debt.'[1]

The early 1970s were years of monetary crisis throughout the world. One major currency after another found itself in difficulties. One of the solutions proposed was the revaluation of gold and Prof. Angelopolous believed such a revaluation could have been used to benefit the poor countries. Briefly the argument is that currencies are valued in relation to one another, to the major currencies of the US dollar, the pound, and to the value of gold. Thus gold is, in effect, a kind of reserve currency and a number of industrial countries hold large stocks of it. Yet traditionally the price of gold was regarded as immutable. For many years it stood at $35 per oz. a price that was absurdly low in comparison with many other metals. If gold were to be regarded as a metal as well as a currency, its value would rise and countries holding gold would suddenly be wealthier. This would strengthen their national currencies even though these were not valued against gold directly. A share of this added wealth could be given to developing countries.

In fact the price of gold did increase when, in 1971, the US Treasury raised the value to $38 per oz. In February 1973 the US dollar was devalued and this raised the price of gold to $42·2 per oz. in the USA, but in London the price rose to $95 per oz. The monetary crisis continued and France announced that from January 1975 it would value its gold reserves at market-related prices. However, the US Treasury auctioned part of its holdings, which depressed the price, as did an agreement that the International Monetary Fund should sell part of its holdings, using the difference between the official price and the actual selling price to establish a fund for aid.

So while the position of gold remains unresolved it appears more likely that it will be allowed to float until it reaches a value based on demand and supply for it as a currency than that it will be revalued arbitrarily to something closer to its commercial value as a metal—used in jewellery, watchmaking and dentistry—although the idea that the profits from an increase in its value should be shared with developing countries is widely accepted in principle. It is naive to attribute the instability of currencies wholly or even largely to disparities between their values and the official price for gold. The problems of the industrial nations cannot be resolved so easily as that.

The institution most concerned with development is the World Bank. Its official title is the International Bank for Reconstruction and Development and it was conceived at the United Nations Monetary and Financial Conference held at Bretton Woods, New Hampshire, in July 1944, and was born on 27 December, 1945. It opened its doors in June 1946, and it now has 117 member countries. As set out in its articles of agreement, the purposes of the Bank are to : assist in the reconstruction and development of member countries by facilitating the investment of capital and promoting the long-range growth of international trade and the improvement of standards of living; promote private foreign investment by guarantees of, and participation in, loans and other investments made by private investors; make loans for productive purposes out of its own resources or funds borrowed by it when private capital is not available on reasonable terms. There are regional development banks for Africa, Asia and Latin America, which work in association with the World Bank, as do the International Finance Corporation (IFC) and the International Development Association (IDA) which is an inter-governmental organisation that makes loans on highly concessionary terms to the poorer members of the 'World Bank Group'—the countries assisted by the World Bank. In 1974 the World Bank and the IDA between them lent about $4300 million.

Monetary reform and the stability of currencies are promoted by the International Monetary Fund (IMF) also founded as a result of the Bretton Woods Conference.

The Organisation for Economic Co-operation and Development (OECD) which represents the rich countries, maintains the Development Assistance Committee, to coordinate their aid policies, and the European Economic Community also tries to make a coherent Community approach to aid.

Aid alone is not enough and as suggested earlier the very concept of aid is likely to carry a heavy cultural bias. It represents, in the cruellest light, the imposition by the rich industrial nations of patterns of development devised by them, not by the recipients. Assistance must be tied to projects that will secure economic advances that can be easily understood by western investors. Loans must be repaid with interest into an essentially industrial banking system whose foundations were laid in Europe. Perhaps this is inevitable, perhaps it is right and just, but if the charge of economic and cultural imperialism is to be answered, conventional forms of aid must be questioned frequently.

After all, the colonial record of the European powers was not a happy one. It is not simply that political domination offended the pride of peoples previously accustomed to governing themselves, though that is bad enough. Actual harm was done, usually with the best of intentions. We saw in the last chapter how colonial powers disrupted traditional societies but economies were disrupted as well. In India the British constructed vast systems for irrigation but only to increase the production of cash crops, often at the expense of the food crops that had been grown on the land now irrigated. Soil erosion was exacerbated by the building of railways, seldom with any means of regulating drainage from their embankments, while fuel for trains and ties for the rails were provided by serious deforestation. This upset drainage patterns still further and led to the use of cattle dung as a fuel for domestic cooking. Cattle dung had been returned to the soil, where it provided nutrients and sustained structure. So once again, food-producing capacity was reduced.

By the late nineteenth century, when the first phase of the European industrial revolution was well advanced, competition between industrial countries led to a scramble for raw materials and markets in Africa and Asia, combined with protection of home industries against competition. Indians were allowed to grow cotton but it had to be spun and woven in England. It is why the Ghandian symbol of the spinning-wheel became such a potent political force. Yet, while taking positive steps to frustrate any kind of economic development based on indigenous industries that might compete with those back home, the British had the effrontery to describe those peoples they had forced into economic subservience as 'the white man's burden'.[2]

Independence often brought too little real improvement socially and politically. Certainly former colonial peoples found themselves free to form their own institutions of government and administration, but in most cases the foundations for them had been laid down by the colonial powers. One elite was exchanged for another. The provision of aid also favoured elitism, an elite of technocrats, experts and advisers.

The realisation that aid in conventional forms could not lead to true independence encouraged developing countries, one after another, to consider the problems facing them at a much deeper level. Today the demands made by the poor have a psychological component at least as strong as the obvious economic one. In his address to the 44th Couchiching Conference, held at Geneva Park, Lake Couchiching, Ontario, Canada, in August 1975, the deputy administrator of the UN Development Programme, I. G. Patel, said:

'On a psychological plane, however, there is yet another and perhaps even more powerful factor which often pulls in a different direction—towards independence rather than interdependence. I am referring to the fact that most of the developing countries have such bitter memories of colonial exploitation or racial and other forms of discrimination that deep underneath the desire for economic progress lies the psychological need to put the hurt and the humiliation behind them once and for all. What the developing countries really want on a psychological plane is to regain their sense of dignity and self-respect, which they enjoyed for long centuries and which they lost only during the brief period of Western domination—a domination based essentially on industrial or technological revolution which is hardly two centuries old.

'While the developing countries proclaim the rhetoric of one world and advocate the language of international co-operation, they want to develop primarily on their own steam and would not accept a position of prolonged dependence on others no matter what the cost in economic terms. The fact that for the smaller and poorer among the developing countries international co-operation or interdependence is a stark economic necessity rather than an ideological nicety does not in any way reduce their sense of discomfort at having to demand things from a position of weakness.'[3]

This alters the picture of the world rather dramatically. Even if it could be achieved, developing countries do not want to be like California. Patel suggests that a per capita income of, say, \$400–\$500 per annum would achieve a decent minimum standard of living for everyone, provide security against internal strife, and allow an adequate degree of strength and resilience to cope with natural disasters without undue recourse to outside help. When the Chinese city of Tangshan was devastated by earthquake in the summer of 1976, outside aid was refused. The Chinese were able to deal with the situation themselves but their attitude in doing so caused some surprise and even mild criticism in the west.

Patel reinforces his argument by describing the attitude of developing countries to ideas of redistributing wealth or population. If their interest were primarily to achieve economic parity with the west in the shortest time possible, then they surely would urge that workers be allowed to move freely from areas of high unemployment to areas where they can find work. This would increase drastically the rate of immigration in the developed countries. They do not ask for this and never have. All they seek is that those of their citizens who have migrated be treated as the equals of the host population and not discriminated against on grounds of colour, race, religion or nationality. Nor do they seek any large-scale redistribution of wealth. They suggest that the rich donate 0·7 % of the GNP each year. Since tax levels in industrial countries are often higher than 30 % of incomes, this too, is a very modest demand. True, they wish for peace and improved relations among all nations, but this is no more than self-interest, since tension among nations can only make their own developmental tasks more difficult.

It is in this context that we must view some of the unusual developments of the 1970s. The sudden raising of oil prices by the OPEC states and the similar price rises for North African phosphates are unusual, because this kind of producer cartelisation can be applied to comparatively few commodities—and it is not certain that it has been applied to phosphates or, if it has been, that the cartel can be sustained. Producers of other commodities, such as copper and bauxite, have tried but with much less success, since their command of world markets was too insecure, alternative sources for the commodity or alternative commodities being more readily available to the consumer. All the same, such attempts represent positive assertions of independence, and the struggle for control of the phosphate reserves in the Spanish Sahara is part of the same story.

For countries that possess natural resources that they can control, the inevitable next stage is to extend that control from extraction to processing. Togo, for example, which in an article in *The Times* on 13 January, 1976 described its phosphate reserves as 'God's Gift to Togo', plans to increase its annual production from the 1·1 million tons of 1975 (2·5 million tons were produced in 1974, the year in which the mines were nationalised) to 3 million tons and to treat 1 million tons on site at Kpeme, to produce phosphoric acid and its derivatives. No doubt the eventual aim will be to treat most, if not all, the crude rock phosphate in Togo. The Caribbean states that produce bauxite aim, similarly, to process the ore themselves and to sell it as aluminium. This is obvious sense—an urgent insistence on the right to free themselves from economic domination by securing for their own peoples the whole of the profit from the resources in their territories, rather than the minor part of it represented by the mining profits. The future of copper and bauxite cartels was discussed again at the 1976 meeting in Colombo of non-aligned countries.

The demand for the right to control the whole of the processing of raw materials, so as to retain within the country that possesses the resource the whole of the income from its exploitation, is becoming more urgent almost daily. In places it has led to tension and sometimes to violence. The Caribbean bauxite producers have dealt firmly with the foreign-owned companies operating in their territory and Morocco is determined to gain full control over phosphate reserves in the Spanish Sahara. Early in 1976, Moroccans made a kind of ritual invasion of the Spanish Sahara and guerilla forces of the Polisario Front have been fighting for the country's independence from Spain. In the previously mentioned newspaper article about Togan phosphates, a footnote is appended:

'From 1976 onwards it would be sensible to include SAHARAN phosphate tonnage in the Moroccan figures; with a strong market their overall tonnage production could reach 30 million tons as we reach 3 million.'

Conflicts are generated within and between developing countries as well as between developing and developed ones. The Biafran war was concerned in no small part with control of the income from Nigeria's oil industry—in much the same way as, within a developed nation, demands for Scottish independence have been influenced by the frustration generated by the fact that oil exploration and exploitation in the North Sea has been outside the control of the Scottish people and the profits from that industry will accrue outside Scotland while environmental, social and economic problems that it creates will be left for the Scots to resolve themselves.

Less than a year after Papua-New Guinea became independent, Bougainville tried to secede, calling itself the Republic of the North Solomons. Bougainville possesses what may be the world's largest deposits of copper and the islanders believe that the profits from copper extraction go mainly to the central government in Port Moresby. There have been demonstrations and clashes with the authorities ever since the Bougainville mines were opened in 1968, but by February 1976 rioting was becoming more serious and the new government seemed unable to control it.

The first part of the development problem may be seen, then, as the need for developing countries to secure a real economic independence to accompany and complement their political independence. They must be able to realise the profits generated by resources within their territories.

Having achieved this, however, they must be able to sell their produce in world markets. In the case of essential supplies for industrial economies—oil, copper, phosphates—this is not too difficult. The industrial economies must have the materials, they cannot be obtained from other sources in the quantities required and so some kind of agreement must be reached. Those developing countries whose resources are not essential for the survival of the rich or must be sold in competition with similar commodities produced by the rich themselves, may find life more difficult.

American food aid was first supplied on the condition that recipient countries did not try to sell their own food surpluses in competition with American food to other countries, and this kind of protection of domestic industries has characterised trade relations for years. GATT, the General Agreement on Tariffs and Trade, exists to facilitate world trade by lowering barriers. It has made considerable progress but much remains to be done. The rich are very unwilling to make concessions and such economic groupings as the EEC often begin with a frankly protectionist attitude to imports from third countries that has to be modified little by little to accommodate some of the needs of those outsiders with little bargaining power.

Often, developing countries whose economies are over-dependent on a limited range of products are very vulnerable to price fluctuations. The fall in sugar prices in 1976 caused great difficulties among Third World producers of sugar cane, and the simultaneous fall in prices for bauxite did considerable damage to, for example, the Jamaican economy. The increase in world oil prices in the early 1970s caused many problems. In 1975, for example, the UNDP had to step in to assist a group of Latin American banana-exporting countries to face what they called the most acute crisis in the history of the banana market, caused by a simultaneous and sustained drop in banana prices and increase in oil prices. Between 1950 and 1972 the price of bananas in real terms fell by 44 % in the USA, by 59 % in the Federal Republic of Germany, by 32 % in France and by 50 % in Belgium. When increases in production costs are taken into account, real purchasing power of earnings from banana exports fell by 61 %.

This is serious, not to say devastating, because of the position bananas occupy in the economies of the countries that produce them. In 1973, 47 % of Panama's export earnings, nearly 34 % of Honduras' and 27 % of Costa Rica's, came from the sale of bananas. All three countries had large trade deficits. Clearly they need to charge more for their bananas, but they have no control over prices because about 99 % of their exports are carried in foreign ships and three US transnational corporations (Standard Fruit, United Fruit and Del Monte) have a virtual monopoly of marketing. Latin American countries are exporting an increasing share of the world's bananas: 66 % in 1967 and 79 % in 1972. Banana growing provides employment for about half the agricultural labour force in Honduras, Panama and Costa Rica. Yet the producers receive only 12 % of the final retail price of the crop. The USA is their biggest market—it takes 56 % of Central America's bananas and 21 % of South

America's—with the EEC and Japan taking most of the remainder. Attempts to form a banana cartel have not been very successful, although in 1974 a Union of Banana Exporting Countries was formed. So far all it has been able to achieve is a very modest export tax.

The situation is fairly typical of that in which many primary producers find themselves, though not all of them are in such extreme difficulty. GATT has examined those primary products that account for 50% or more of individual developing countries' exports and has compared incomes with the import bills of those countries. They found[4] that sugar producers have a positive trade balance but that producers of copper, rubber, coffee, tea, jute, tobacco, copra, iron ore, cotton, palm oil, lead, groundnuts, tin, groundnut oil, beef, cocoa, rice and lumber show deficits in imports of manufactured goods, steel, fertiliser, fuel or grains. Usually the deficit relates to more than one imported commodity, in many cases to all of them, and although the position shows slight improvements, it has deteriorated since the 1969–71 base years, especially with regard to fertiliser and fuel.

It is not surprising, then, to find that national external debts are mounting. Between 1968 and 1973, in southern Europe, they increased by 96·9%, in Asia by 108·9%, in Latin America by 109·6% and in Africa by 115·1%.[5] Yet the primary producers are selling into the wealthiest markets they can find. Three-quarters of their exports go to developed countries. Today, trade among developed countries accounts for 65·1% of total world trade, trade among developing countries for only 4·2% and 30·6% represents trade between rich and poor.

It is against a background of statistics such as these—for they have been tending in this direction for many years—that relationships between rich and poor have deteriorated steadily, so that the old east–west confrontation has been replaced by a north–south confrontation, whose main fora have been the successive meetings of the United Nations Conference on Trade and Development (UNCTAD), although the ill-feeling generated at three UNCTAD sessions has spilled over into all other major UN conferences.

In 1974 the General Assembly of the UN adopted a Charter of Economic Rights and Duties of States, proposed originally by President Luis Echeverria of Mexico and worked out by a 40-nation group under the auspices of UNCTAD. At the Sixth Special Session of the General Assembly, at which the charter was adopted, the voting was 120 in favour, 6 against and 10 abstentions. The countries opposing the charter were Belgium, Denmark, the Federal Republic of Germany, Luxembourg, the USA and the UK.

The charter aims to establish norms to govern international economic relations and postulates, among other things, the right of every state to exercise full permanent sovereignty over its wealth and natural resources and to regulate and exercise authority over foreign investments within its national jurisdiction. Special attention is to be given to those countries defined as 'least developed' on the grounds that per capita annual income amounts to less than \$100, manufacturing accounts for less than 10% of GNP and literacy among 15-year-olds is less than 20%. These countries are, in Africa, Botswana, Burundi, Chad, Dahomey, Ethiopia, Guinea, Lesotho, Mali, Malawi, Niger, Rwanda, Somalia, Sudan, Uganda, Tanzania and Upper Volta; in Asia, Afghanistan, Bhutan, Laos, Maldives, Nepal and Yemen; in Latin America, Haiti; and in Oceania, Western Samoa.

The Sixth Special Session also launched emergency relief operations for the countries most severely affected by rises in the prices of imported food and fuel. These countries were Afghanistan, Bangladesh, Burma, Burundi, Cape Verde Islands, Cambodia, Central African Republic, Chad, Dahomey, Democratic Republic of Yemen, Egypt, El Salvador, Ethiopia, Ghana, Guinea, Guyana, Haiti, Honduras, India, Ivory Coast, Kenya, Laos, Lesotho, Madagascar, Mali, Mauritania, Mozambique, Niger, Pakistan, Republic of Cameroon, Rwanda, Senegal, Sierra Leone, Somalia, Sri Lanka, Sudan, Tanzania, Uganda, Upper Volta, Western Samoa and Yemen. Attention is also to be given to those developing countries that are landlocked and so face special problems in exporting their products.

After the Sixth Special Session things began to move, if not directly toward immediate solutions at least toward a more reasonable discussion of the problems. The OECD prepared for a 27-nation Ministerial Conference held in December 1975, by trying to harmonise the position of the developed countries in the continuing north–south dialogue. In May the OECD had made a Declaration on Relations with Developing Countries and by January 1976 it was able to summarise the proposals made by some of the members of its Development Assistance Committee (DAC). For the most part these were no more than attempts by rich countries to assess their own positions and attitudes, but in some cases the amount of aid to developing countries was increased (The Netherlands, Norway, Sweden) or the terms on which it was given were improved (Canada, Germany, The Netherlands).

The new UN charter had been called the 'New Economic Order', an eye-catching and headline-catching title that might remind cynics of the Green Revolution that preceded it. The cynics might also observe that it was the pressure exerted by OPEC and other producer-cartels that led to this change of heart, not altruism on the part of the rich. Indeed the real purpose of the north–south dialogue, which reached a minor climax in December 1975, was to rationalise relations between producing and consuming countries of particular key commodities. The rich were having their arms twisted. At this stage the world was dividing itself roughly into four groups. Developing countries with no natural resources that could be exploited easily for profit looked for help to those that had, especially to the OPEC countries. Among the developed countries, there were those, like the USA, which favoured a continuation of aid policies and encouragement for the investment of private capital in developing countries and those, like the EEC, which favoured improving the terms of trade between rich and poor.

In January 1976 the IMF held a meeting of finance ministers in Kingston, Jamaica to consider ways in which the rules of the fund could be changed in order to benefit the poor. One of the proposals was to return one-sixth of the IMF'S gold reserves to those countries that originally subscribed them, at the official price of \$42·2 per oz., and to pay a further one-sixth into a trust fund, the proceeds from which would go to the least developed countries. Divisions were deep, however, between some politicians in the USA, supported by others in Holland, who felt that gold should not be allowed to acquire more importance as a currency, and between rich and poor, since the poor argued that the revenue from the trust fund would amount to less than was being given to the rich.

In all this the EEC was emerging as more responsible and generous than most blocs of rich countries. The Lomé Convention, successor to the Yaoundé Convention, signed in February 1975, was beginning to appear even more advanced in its thinking than had been imagined at the time it was signed. It is a five-year agreement between the Community and 46 developing countries (the Yaoundé Convention affected 19), including 17 of the least developed, and it allows them access to European markets. For 12 basic primary products: groundnuts, cocoa, coffee, cotton, coconuts, palm oil, leather and hides, wood, bananas, tea, sisal and iron ore, it includes a system for stabilising export revenue (STABEX) by insuring against bad years. Since 1971 the Community had accepted the principle of abolishing customs duties for 99·2% of finished or semi-finished products imported from developing countries. Not all the EEC's achievements were so creditable and in 1976 it allocated only 0·8% of its budget (the official UN target is 1% of GNP) for aid, compared to 4% in 1975.

The Sixth Special Session of the UN General Assembly, the first in UN history to be devoted entirely to economic matters, discussed Raw Materials and Development. The Seventh Special Session, held in September 1975, discussed 'major themes of the development process' and the structure and suitability of the existing UN system for dealing with this new phase of international relationships. While all of the UN's 138 members are free to adopt any position they wish, in practice consultation among like-minded delegations has led to the emergence of four main groups and in some organisations, such as UNCTAD, they work together quite formally, as Group A, the Afro-Asian countries, Group B, the developed market economy nations, Group C, the Latin Americans, and Group D, the Socialist countries of Eastern Europe. In other organisations the names of the groups are slightly different.

In recent years, however, a much larger group has been emerging, called the 'Group of 77' (although its actual membership may be closer to 100). It includes all the developing countries and it is able to present a co-ordinated position on most issues concerning economics and development. The membership of the Group of 77 is similar to that of the Non-Aligned Nations, which meets outside the UN.

The division between two fundamentally different approaches to development was becoming formalised, too, along ideological lines. The approaches were summed up by Professor Brian Johnson, of the University of Sussex, UK, who is an economist and who has spent many years studying the development process:

'The conflict between *dirigisme* and the play of free market forces has long been evident inside many nations attempting to achieve a better balance between their own rich and poor citizens. Now the same conflict is evident on the international stage and was . . . the ideological thread running through the Seventh Special Session. There are many other ways of describing the polarisation of views about achieving development. One could be labelled 'growth', the other 'distribution'. In fact, they correspond to the now familiar divide between the traditional economist's view of the possibilities of a finite world and that of the ecological school.'[6]

The traditional economic view holds that technology is a resource of no known limits, whose capabilities increase in proportion to the investment made in them. Thus if we wish to turn stones into bread, we will be able to do so if we are prepared to invest enough and work hard enough.

'Investment in technology, then, so long as it is sufficient, will be able to banish limits beyond all practical horizons of concern. On this analysis, the accumulation and re-investment of profits or surplus, whether from the state or the private sector, must take precedence over their distribution. Either inducements or official decisions to accumulate society's surplus will, of course, fuel faster economic growth, which, like a powerful automobile, generates the reserves of power that are required to pull both rich and poor societies out of dangerous situations.'

This, says Prof. Johnson, is the position of the USA, and especially of Dr Kissinger.

The alternative, 'socio-environmental' view is very different.

'The essential difference between the "resource fund" as opposed to the "technological optimist" view is that it concentrates on two aspects of development which are either largely, or entirely, ignored in straightforward neo-classical economic analysis. The first, the admission of the importance of "externalities" (or the social, health and aesthetic side effects of development), suggests that, for instance, the risks of disruption attending endless expansion of energy production or of raw material mining will far exceed the possible advantages of further conventional economic growth. The second aspect is the problem of achieving full human participation in development.

'These two concerns are inseparable because the social, environmental and employment factors of capital investment, designed to raise productivity, tend to grow with every increase in technological impact and in the investment required to provide each worker place. In other words, the high technology path to development will increasingly inflict its adverse effects on that part of the population which is least consulted as to its desirability and which is most likely to be excluded from its benefits. By contrast, development strategies that emphasise distribution as more important than growth tend, in most cases, to call for smaller-scale, more decentralised, and more labour-intensive techniques.'

This argument acquires a more overtly political dimension when it is related to resource consumption. There are those on the one hand who argue that the rich should not attempt to restrain their rates of consumption. Their waste heaps can be mined at some future date should raw materials become sufficiently scarce, and any reduction of raw material imports from developing countries would merely deal another blow, and perhaps a lethal one, to their economies. Opposing this view are those who hold that the higher the technology, the more elitist it will be and the more exploitive the social order it will encourage. The argument is supported by the reality that about 10% of the population of the world consumes more than half its annual production of raw materials. So the case for reducing consumption among the rich is gaining ground.

In 1974 a Ford Foundation study showed that Americans could achieve a comfortable way of life while consuming far less energy that the public utilities and oil companies had forecast. The Japanese environmental agency invented an 'Index of Public Benefit'. A study conducted in The Netherlands suggested that the ratio of per capita income between rich and poor should be reduced from its present 13:1 to 3:1 over a 40-year period—provided certain rates of increase in agricultural production and reductions in rates of population growth can be achieved. The most radical proposals, however, came from two Swedish officials, both members of the Swedish Cabinet Office's Secretariat for Future Studies, Göran Bäckstrand and Lars Ingelstam. They proposed:[6]

'A consumption ceiling (rationing?) should be placed on meat and oil.

'People, on average, should have to occupy one-fifth less living space than they do now.

'Consumer goods must become more durable (manufacturers should be responsible for the durability and recycling of their own goods).

'Some basic commodities, such as working clothes, shoes and bicycles, should be publicly produced.

'The privately owned car should be abolished.'

Predictably the recommendations caused a storm and were denounced by Sweden's transport minister before he had even read them.

In the EEC a group of non-governmental environmental organisations, the European Environmental Bureau, submitted to the Belgian Prime Minister, Mr Leo Tindemans, its recommendations for the future environmental policies of the Community as a background paper to his report on European Union, submitted to member governments in January 1976. Pollution was not mentioned but the environmentalists had a great deal to say about economic policies and about relations between the EEC and developing countries. While reducing consumption within the Community and assuring a more harmonious development of all the geographical regions in Europe, they would like to see an extension of the Lomé approach to price stabilisation. While achieving what they call 'mature growth' in Europe, they wish to see this extended to developing countries to ensure that they are not forced to adopt western technologies unsuited to their real needs. If implemented, their proposals would lead in time to much greater equality between what are now developed and developing economies.

UNCTAD IV met in Nairobi, Kenya, in May 1976. This was the crucial meeting where rich and poor countries confronted one another yet again. The UN Centre for Economic and Social Information (CESI) collaborated with UNCTAD to outline the main areas that would be discussed: commodities, manufactures, GATT, the flow of resources, technology transfer, inter-Third World trade, co-operation with the Council for Mutual Economic Assistance (CMEA) of Eastern Europe, debt and repayment and the needs of the disadvantaged.

Excluding petroleum, the export of raw materials (commodities) accounts for 75% of the total foreign exchange earnings of developing countries, and very wide fluctuations in world commodity prices have caused great instability and uncertainty in the countries that export them. Zambia, for example, depends on the export of copper for more than 90% of its foreign exchange, but the world price for copper has moved from a peak of £1268 a ton in 1972–74 to £512 a ton in January 1975. To deal with this situation, UNCTAD proposed an integrated programme for commodities with five key elements:

The establishment of a common fund for the financing of international stocks of commodities.

The setting up of international stocks for a number of commodities, including coffee, cocoa, tea, sugar, cotton, jute, hard fibres, rubber and copper.

The improvement of facilities for the compensatory financing of fluctuations in the export earnings of individual developing countries.

Multilateral trade commitments by governments on individual commodities.

The removal of trade barriers and other impediments to the expansion of commodity processing in developing countries.

'In essence, the main thrust of the Programme envisages the setting up of international stockpiles. Using money from a central fund, commodities would be bought up and stockpiled when prices are low, and sold off during periods of high prices. This would have the effect of dampening excessive price fluctuations. For commodities not amenable to a stockpiling approach, measures in the area of compensatory financing—along the line of, but more comprehensive than, the IMF compensatory financing scheme and the Common Market arrangements established at Lomé—are envisaged. In addition, UNCTAD is seeking ways of making it easier for developing countries to export not only raw materials but also manufactured goods. Linked to this is the need for building up the industrial capacity of developing countries which, in the initial stages, would concentrate on the processing and semi-manufacturing of raw materials.'[7]

On manufacturing, UNCTAD planned to use the Lima Declaration of 1975 as the starting point for a systematic programme. This Declaration, passed by members of the UN Industrial Development Association (IDA), called for industrialisation on such a scale as to give the developing countries one-quarter of the world's total manufacturing output by the end of the century. UNCTAD economists calculated that this would require an annual rate of growth of industrial output of 10 %, combined with a 12 % growth in industrial exports by developing countries. This is higher than the rate of growth advocated by the IDA (7 %) but UNCTAD calculated that it would achieve the 20-fold increase in manufacturing industry that is required.

Clearly it would be difficult to find markets for such a large volume of manufactured goods within traditional industrialised societies, and so UNCTAD favours the development of 'common markets' within the Third World, offering shelter and mutual aid that will lead to greater self-reliance. It is suggested, too, that GATT rules be waived in order to permit developing countries to subsidise their exports without running the risk of retaliation by the imposition of import duties by importing countries.

The theoretical commitment of GATT to the welfare of developing economies is enshrined in the 1973 Tokyo Declaration, which says that negotiations shall 'secure additional benefits for the international trade of developing countries so as to achieve a substantial increase in their foreign exchange earnings, the diversification of their exports, the acceleration of the rate of growth of trade . . . through . . . a substantial improvement in the conditions of access for the products of interest to the developing countries, and wherever appropriate, measures designed to attain stable, equitable remunerative prices for primary products'.

Unhappily, widespread recession in the industrial world caused developed countries to become more inward-looking, so that the Tokyo Declaration came to be little more than a pious expression of goodwill. Further, the main GATT objective of trying to liberalise trade by reducing or even removing tariffs altogether tends to erode the privileges granted to developing countries under the Generalised System of Preferences (GSP), which gives tariff concessions to developing countries. Obviously these are an advantage only so long as the tariffs remain in operation against developed countries. So UNCTAD prepared for a vigorous defence of GSP principles and demands for their extension to all agricultural and industrial products of interest to developing countries, and their strengthening by increasing the preferential margins.

The developing countries—the Group of 77—wished to see the modification of the 'rules of origin'. These are very complicated and are intended to guarantee that goods are granted GSP advantages only if they originate from an approved source. The rules could be made much simpler if all developing countries were granted the preferences. The original GSP was intended only as a temporary measure, to last for 10 years. The developing countries wished it to be extended.

The dangers of the economic recession remain, and developing countries feared 'backsliding' by industrial countries seeking to protect their own economies. Against this threat they asked for the adoption of a principle of 'compensation for market disruption': cash payment, import concessions or assistance to develop new industry. They asked, too, that developing countries be allowed to compete on a more equal footing with industries in developed countries for government contracts in those countries; that products from developing countries be identified clearly so there will be less chance of them missing preferential treatment; and the immediate implementation of concessions made to developing countries under Multilateral Trade Negotiations, rather than the usual long wait for ratification.

The 'flow of resources' means economic resources—aid. The rise in oil prices and the subsequent recession in industrial countries led to a fall in the amount of aid they received, but in fact aid had been declining for some time. During a 15-year period when the GNP of the DAC countries was growing by 3·5% a year, aid fell from 0·52% of GNP to 0·33%. As the industrial economies grew, none of the increase in their wealth was transferred to developing countries. This has affected the poorest countries most severely, for they have been able to develop their economies only very slowly. Those countries that are a little better off have been able to generate capital for investment and their growth rate has been double that of the poorest countries. The gap has been filled partly by the OPEC countries, whose aid commitments increased five-fold between 1973 and 1974, and amounted to 1·9% of their GNP.

UNCTAD believed new sources had to be trapped and were looking especially at:

'The developed countries reaching the development aid target of 0·7% of GNP—at the Seventh Special Session of the United Nations General Assembly on Economic Co-operation and Development, the developed countries confirmed "their continued commitment" to the "official development assistance target of 0·7% of gross national product", with those countries that have not reached that goal undertaking "their best efforts to reach these targets in the remaining part of this decade". OECD estimates that six countries have multi-year plans to "bring aid appropriations either above 1% of GNP (The Netherlands, Norway and Sweden) or to 0·7% (Belgium, Denmark and New Zealand). A number of countries also appear likely to reach the 0·7% target by the end of the decade.

'A "development tax" placed on the income of the developed countries, above the regular aid allotments.

'Giving more aid in the form of grants or very concessional loans.

'Establishing a "link" between the creation of Special Drawing Rights (SDRs) and development financing.

'The monies received from the sale of the IMF gold.

'The possible internationalisation of the resources of the seabed and ocean floor, and making the royalties from exploiting them available for development financing.

'The greater use of multilateral lending facilities such as development banks to make private credit available to those developing countries that do not have easy access to them.'[7]

As we have seen elsewhere, the transfer of technologies from developed to developing countries is fraught with difficulty. It is found, for example, that no matter how many scientists and technologists developing countries train, unless they can offer them immediate employment they drift to where they can find work. So developing countries suffer a perpetual 'brain drain'. The new technologies they can use tend to be devised in the industrial countries and so those developing countries wishing to import them must pay for licences and patents. By the end of the 1960s it is estimated that these charges amounted to $1·5 thousand million, that during the 1970s they were likely to increase six-fold and that they are equivalent to about 56% of the direct private investment going into developing countries during the 1960s, and about 5% of their export earnings. UNCTAD considered a range of proposals for improving the ways in which technologies are transferred, including a code of conduct and, possibly, reform of the international patents system.

Already there is a considerable amount of co-operation economically among developing countries, especially in the service industries. There is room for expansion, however, especially in research and development, industrial production, natural resource management and such infrastructure items as power generation, communications and the management of water basins.

Trade among countries with different economic systems has been expanding for several years and the socialist countries of Eastern Europe are now able to offer assistance to developing countries in a number of fields. Members of CMEA are now giving direct economic aid to developing countries in a number of forms and CMEA has formed multilateral partnerships with a number of developing countries including Yugoslavia, Iraq, Mexico, Colombia, Iran and Yemen. UNCTAD sought to encourage this trend because it believes there are opportunities that remain untapped.

So far as the repayment of debts is concerned, it was the view of UNCTAD that all too often the attitude adopted was based on the behaviour of creditors toward debtors in a conventional commercial relationship. When developing countries fall behind in their repayments meetings of creditors are called and schemes are devised to enable the debtor to resume payments as soon as possible. The aim is only to pay off debts and the development needs of the debtor are not considered. Thus the schemes that are devised may be economically damaging to the long-term prospects of the developing country concerned.

It was UNCTAD's hope that more flexible systems might be developed. In some cases the repayment periods might be extended, some loans to very poor countries might be converted into grants, minor debts might be excluded from discussion at meetings of creditors, the long-term creditworthiness of the country might be taken into account, and solutions might be worked out more quickly.

The Seventh Special Session had agreed to provide 1 thousand million Special Drawing Rights for agricultural development. Drawing rights from the World Bank are related to the moneys deposited, as with any other bank. Traditionally, therefore, the bank would appear to favour the major contributors to its funds. This anomaly is overcome by the provision of Special Drawing Rights to countries, by negotiation, which entitle them to drawing facilities that are not related to deposits they have made.

UNCTAD was important. The new power of the OPEC countries and of other countries or groups of countries to disrupt western economies meant that for the first time the rich really had to bargain rather than dictate. At the same time the populations of the poor countries were growing more radical politically, both in their attitude to power structures within their own countries and in their view of the world outside.

Dr Kissinger and the then US Ambassador to the UN, Daniel Moynihan, deplored this 'radicalisation', but, in the words of an article that appeared in *The Times*, '. . . sadly, the western nations have remained insensitive to the political and economic aspirations of the developing countries. Instead, the western world in general, and the United States in particular, has been prepared to countenance any dubious practice, from discriminatory use of aid to outright manipulation of political institutions. What has it mattered if a land reform programme in Latin America has been set back by many years, or a health programme has been suspended, so long as a regime sympathetic to the west is installed in a country which is deemed to be vital to western interests?'[8]

The article's author suspects that the lesson of the defeats suffered by the USA in the early 1970s is being learned only slowly, and he quotes Dr Kissinger's remark to the Senate Finance Committee on America's international economic policy:

'The success of our efforts in North–South diplomacy depends also on more sympathetic efforts by us to ensure that each developing country understands that our bilateral relations include that country's behaviour towards us in international meetings, in particular, its votes there on issues of the highest importance to us.'

This is an open threat of blackmail: aid becomes dependent on political support for the donor.

The UNCTAD idea of stockpiling key commodities to dampen down price fluctuations was rejected by the USA, Britain and France. Britain also rejected the idea of rescheduling debts. Dr Kissinger introduced the US proposed solution, in the form of a new international institution, to be called the International Resources Bank, that would mobilise private capital for development projects, would participate in negotiations between investors and developers, and would ensure that investments were safeguarded. He conceded that if other arrangements to finance the purchasing of buffer stocks failed, the bank might help, and he agreed that softer terms must be agreed for aid to the poorest countries. Predictably the prospect of still more private capital being invested by the rich, with a new international institution to ensure the safety of the investment, did not appeal to developing countries, and by the end of the conference the divisions between rich and poor were as wide as ever. The rich had been unwilling to make substantial concessions.

There was some agreement, however, at least on compromises. More talks were to be held on the possibility of creating a common fund to finance the purchase of buffer stocks of certain commodities, and there was to be a programme of negotiations, tied to a time-table, on particular commodities of interest to developing countries. There was little enough agreement among the rich, even on proposals to hold more talks, and nothing was done to alleviate the debt burden of developing countries or to produce an enforceable code of conduct covering the transfer of technology, although some months later OECD produced a somewhat bland code of conduct for multinational corporations that required them, basically, to observe the laws of the countries within which they operate and to refrain from political interference with the internal affairs of those countries.

In August 1976 the Non-Aligned Countries met in Colombo. Mrs Bandaranaike, Prime Minister of Sri Lanka and host to the conference, suggested that developing countries form a Third World Bank, which would issue a new reserve currency to free its subscribers from the traditional reserve currencies and so create a new centre of economic power within the Third World. Exports of primary commodities should be priced in relation to the prices charged by the developed countries for their exports. However, there was no more agreement among the developing countries than is found anywhere else. They were divided deeply between the communist and pro-western groups, so that it was difficult to agree even on simple terminology. Words like 'independence' and 'imperialism' have widely different meanings within different economic and political systems.

It seems, then, that it will be a long time before the Group of 77 are able to devise a comprehensive strategy to secure their own development. It may be even longer before the rich show any real willingness to make substantial concessions that would free the poor from a trading and monetary tradition that binds them inevitably into subservience. The gap between rich and poor continues to widen.

Yet the future may not be so grim as it seems. As suggested earlier, the very words we use—'rich', 'poor', 'developing', 'developed'—may be derived from concepts formulated within western cultures. A person who possesses a motor car is richer that one who does not, a person who takes holidays abroad is richer than one who takes no holidays at all. This may be true but the gap between rich and poor may be narrowed in ways other than providing motor cars and foreign holidays for everyone. Is a person whose working conditions and general lifestyle are so satisfactory that it becomes quite unnecessary to take holidays richer or poorer? What is the economic position of the person whose work is integrated so closely into the way he lives that the very idea of a holiday becomes incomprehensible, as though one could take a holiday from life itself? I own a car but would I be better or worse off if I lived in a society where I was required to move less because work, friends, family and areas of natural or urban amenity were much closer, and if I had access to a cheap and efficient public transport system?

It may be, then, that developing countries, working together though not on so grand a scale as the Non-Aligned Nations might envisage, at least at present, may develop in their own ways, basing that development on roots derived from their own cultures, not on alien cultures imposed from outside by military, political or economic force. Indeed there is much evidence, especially from Africa and Asia, that this is happening.

It does not absolve the rich countries from their responsibilities to assist wherever they can and in ways appropriate to the actual needs and wishes of others: to give help when it is requested and in the form in which it is requested. The real debt that the rich owe to the poor is the one described by Mr Patel: we owe the people of Latin America, Africa and Asia their dignity.

For the immediate future, prospects are a little brighter for primary producers. The FAO's annual *Commodity Review and Outlook* 1975–76, published in late August 1976, predicted a rise in the value of agricultural exports. The volume of trade declined slightly in 1975, compared to the 1974 level, because of rather lower prices. The outlook was for an increase in production and supplies, a recovery in demand and, with some exceptions, in prices, and some rebuilding of stocks. While the volume of international trade may show little change, despite the decline anticipated in world grain exports, its value could rise to 'new records'. The revived demand was expected to be most rapid for raw materials, such as rubber, cotton and hides and skins, as well as for such foods as meat, dairy products, bananas and sugar, and a return to the more intensive rearing of livestock was expected to lead to higher prices for feedgrains, oilcakes and meals, probably assisted by the substantially reduced harvests in Europe caused by the 1976 drought. In its forecast, published in December, OECD also predicted higher prices for primary products.

In the final chapter we must speculate about the alternatives open to us and the implication of choices that we must make or that, in some cases such as in our relationship with developing countries, we may have made already.

REFERENCES

1. De Castro, J. (1972). Introduction to Angelopolous, A., *The Third World and the Rich Countries: Prospects for the Year* 2000. Praeger, New York.
2. Whitcombe, G. (1972). *Agrarian Conditions in Northern India: The United Provinces under British Rule* 1860–1900. University of California.
3. Patel, I. G. (1975). What do the developing countries really want?, *Development Forum*. UN CESI, Geneva, September–October.
4. *International Trade* 1974–75. GATT.
5. FAO (1976). *Ceres*. Rome. January–February. Based on World Bank figures.
6. Johnson, B. (1975). When is enough really enough?, *Development Forum*. UN CESI. Geneva, November.
7. UN CESI/UNCTAD (1976). Supplement to *Development Forum*. Geneva, April.
8. Westlake, M. (1976). Should there be 'strings' to Third World aid?, *The Times*, 18 February, 1976. London.

Chapter 13

SCENARIOS FOR TOMORROW

The only thing we can say with confidence about the future is that we do not know what it holds. We cannot, for the world is far too complex a set of systems, with far too many independent variables, most of which we cannot control and large numbers whose workings and effects we do not understand or even observe. We cannot know what will happen to the climates of particular regions or to their soils under particular combinations of weather and culture. We cannot say whether a country whose outlook is bleak may suddenly find ways to exploit a resource for which other countries begin to exert an unanticipated demand. We cannot say whether the reverse may not happen to countries whose present wealth is derived from a particular kind of activity.

Will the present industrial countries that have few remaining mineral and fuel resources decline? What would happen, say, to the OPEC nations were a cheaper alternative to oil to be developed in response—the kind of response that might not surprise economists—to rising oil prices and doubts about the security of supplies? There is no aspect of the future that can be predicted without running a risk so large as to amount to virtual certainty that the prediction will be changed drastically by events that are not, and cannot be, foreseen. So there is no way we can know what will happen to rates of population growth or agricultural output, to commodity prices or development, to wealth or to poverty.

The formal study of 'futures' does not aim to predict. In this it is popularly misunderstood. Even so well-publicised a study as the Club of Rome's *Limits to Growth* made no predictions as such. Its aim and the aim of all studies of this kind is to consider the possible implications of certain policies or courses of action. They say that if we do this, then that may be the eventual outcome. This is not a prediction, so much as a warning. Yet it is inevitable, perhaps, that they should be regarded as predictions by the public.

There is an important exception to the general rule: the self-fulfilling prophecy. This is the prediction that stimulates a reaction that causes the very circumstance that was predicted. Everyone must be familiar with the contrived food shortage. An announcement is made of the possibility of a shortage of a particular commodity, accompanied by a request to the public not to hoard. At once consumers rush to the shops to buy up stocks of the threatened item, so that when the shortage comes they will not suffer. The sudden rush on stocks causes rapid depletion, there is a delay before new stocks can be moved from warehouses into shops, a panic begins, the new stocks are bought up more quickly than before, everyone hoards— because hoarding is a natural thing to do— and there really is a shortage. So the prophecy has fulfilled itself.

It is very dangerous to suggest that a situation is hopeless if it is not. Forecasts of inevitable doom, which became fashionable in the late 1960s and early 1970s, based sometimes on mistaken interpretations of speculative studies that began by simple extrapolations of past trends, served to alert the public and governments to the existence of problems whose solutions required changes more radical than most of those being proposed at the time. Taken a very short step further, however, they could have suggested—and sometimes did—that industrial societies were doomed to a collapse that was unavoidable, that the 'world food problem' was insoluble, that the rate of population growth could be arrested only by catastrophe.

It is the use of the word 'inevitable' that converts a warning into a prophecy that could fulfil itself. No one denies that there are problems connected with sustaining industrial societies in a world of diminishing resources, that there are difficulties, both acute and chronic, in ensuring adequate supplies of acceptable foods to all the people in the world, or that it is desirable to adjust the size of populations to those that can be supported by the resources available to them and that it is better to do so voluntarily, by deliberate choice, than by waiting for wars or natural calamities to intervene. Stated in this form, the problems can be examined, discussed and solutions to them can be sought. Possibly solutions will not be found but at least the search will be urgent. If we allow ourselves to be persuaded that solutions are theoretically impossible, that the search for them is akin to the search for the perpetual-motion machine, then we may relax. Nothing can be done, so nothing needs to be done. The rich can remain rich, societies that consume more than their fair share of the world's resources need take no steps to curb their appetites or to use resources more carefully.

If no solutions are sought, far less applied, it is at least possible that some or all of the dire predictions may come true. If a man is starving and I have food, I may share that food with him or I may eat it all myself. If I am told that a little food now will save his life and give him sufficient strength to try to grow food for himself, then I may decide to share my food with him, although to do so will leave me hungry. If I am told that by sharing my food with him the best I can hope to do is to postpone his death for a few hours, so prolonging his agony, then I may be tempted to withhold food. The prophecy of his death will come true.

The fallacy in this doom-laden approach to the future is illustrated very clearly by the 'triage' argument we considered earlier. The strategy, you will remember, was to divide the injured into three categories following a major catastrophe, and to treat first those who will recover only if treated, second those who will recover anyway but whose recovery can be accelerated, and last of all those for whom there is no hope. This, it is suggested, can be interpreted in such a way as to make it applicable to aid to developing countries.

Even at the most superficial level, no analogy exists. No one suggests applying medical triage until such a situation is reached that it becomes unavoidable. The catastrophe must have happened. It is difficult to see what event or events could affect the world economy in this kind of way. The problems we face arise from a set of relationships that is very complex and that changes with time. It is quite different.

We find ourselves trying to compare an acute emergency with a chronic condition. Here we do have parallels from medicine, for we know the medical equivalent of triage in a situation of chronic shortage. Such shortages are common in the British health service and they lead to a reordering of priorities on more obviously humane grounds. The first priority is the emergency, especially the emergency that endangers life. The second priority is given to illnesses that threaten life, but over a longer period. This includes terminal cases, which are treated with care if only to reduce pain and discomfort and enable the dying person to retain to the last some human dignity. The final category is that of complaints that do not and will not threaten life. The categories bear some similarity with those of the triage, with the important exception of the dying, who move up.

Our knowledge of human physiology is sufficient for doctors to be able to say, in most cases, whether a life is threatened, whether death is inevitable. We may expect such prognostic problems to be much reduced following a catastrophe. Can we say the same of countries and economic systems? In the mid-1970s, the economic position of Britain was parlous to say the least. Is it better to assume that recovery is impossible and leave people to make their own arrangements if they can, or should we assume that recovery is possible and attempt to achieve it?

Until we can predict human behaviour, individually and collectively, with absolute infallibility, we will be able neither to predict the future nor to apply any system of priorities in the allocation of aid based on such predictions. Although we cannot predict the future, we can at least speculate about it by considering some of the alternatives that appear open to us.

Perhaps, then, we should begin by looking at what has been said on the subject already. No reputable scientist will utter prophecies, so a glance through a tiny fraction of the existing literature furnishes us with no more than speculations about what may be possible, and warnings of what may happen should a deteriorating situation continue to deteriorate. Some of the sources quoted are from writers whose concern is the world situation. Others are concerned mainly, or exclusively even, with Britain. Since Britain imports half of its food, this distinction is more theoretical than real.

If there are changes in world food supplies, Britain cannot avoid being affected.

In 1955 Sir George Thomson, winner of the 1937 Nobel Prize for physics, envisaged a world fed largely on food synthesised in factories. Part of this food would be fed directly to humans, part to animals. In this world, he suggested, large parts of England might be allowed to revert to nature or be made into parkland, in which animals would wander freely, their natural diet augmented by synthetic supplements delivered automatically at distribution centres.[1] A pleasant world, this, in which factors other than food supply regulate human numbers. Advanced technologies will supply all conceivable wants and the cultures of the world will unify. There will be large seasonal migrations of people who will pass the winter in one place, the summer in another, in a perpetual holiday.

Is this realistic? It seems improbable, at least. The unification of cultures is being resisted strenuously everywhere, since in practice it means the imposition of one culture upon all others. Economic disparities are increasing and the abandonment of agriculture is a possibility so remote as to be quite out of sight. In the case of the English parklands, one wonders how they might be managed, for left untended much of lowland Britain would revert to impenetrable scrub, rather than the eighteenth century idyll of gentle grassland, trees, lakes and streams, which are maintained, where they exist, by careful and usually labour-intensive management. As a matter of fact, I was once asked to consider the implications of a British decision to phase out agriculture in favour of higher investment in manufacturing industry. I found it would be extremely difficult to prevent agriculture reviving as a main holiday attraction!

Sir George Thomson is a physicist not an agronomist or geographer. Georg Borgstrom is Professor of Food Science and Geography at the University of Michigan and his two books, *The Hungry Planet* and *Too Many; A Study of the Earth's Biological Limitations*, placed him firmly in the 'doom' camp when first they appeared. This was not altogether fair, for Prof. Borgstrom acknowledges freely that major advances have been made. His concern is for the relationship between population growth and food supply and it provides a cold counterblast to Thomson's euphoric vision. We threaten to deprive ourselves of a future, Borgstrom says, by refusing to recognise our predicament. We try to talk ourselves out of reality, believing our civilisation will achieve immortality as our science and technology succeed in perpetuating our way of life. He points out that if the food produced in the world today were shared equally, the result would be general malnutrition.

'If the minimum requirements of the entire present population were to be met, food production would have to be doubled immediately. Does anyone really believe that the magic required to meet such enormous needs is feasible? . . . It has taken the energetic West five centuries to treble its wheat production. In this century, with all the aid of modern science and technology, the increase in this progressive part of the world has been a modest 60%.'[2] Yet Borgstrom remains guardedly optimistic. He believes, or he did in 1965 when this passage was written (and probably later, for the book was revised and updated in 1967 and 1970), that provided the peoples of the industrial societies in particular can be educated to the problems we face, then they will modify their behaviour—in particular the rate at which they reproduce and consume resources—in time to save mankind and, possibly, civilisation. The risk, then, is Malthusian, and compounded by the refusal of those whose wealth is measured in terms of rates of consumption of non-renewable resources to recognise it.

Sir Joseph Hutchinson has defined over-population as the increase of population to a point at which it cannot be supported by the resources of the land available to it.[3] In 1966 and again in 1967, Sir Joseph presided over a series of lectures at the University of Cambridge, in what he called the 'food supply decade'. In his conclusion to the published lectures he emphasised the need to build up stocks of food adequate for emergencies, while reminding his readers that this need for security against climatic risk is 'as old as Joseph and Pharaoh'. In general, though, he is optimistic. While population growth at the rate current in the mid-1960s cannot be supported for very long, agricultural production can be persuaded to increase.

'... despite the constraints and rigidities of the current agricultural system ... there are opportunities now within our reach to increase the world's food supply very substantially. There can be no disagreement with the view that our first obligation is to provide the food and other biological resources for all those already born, or whose arrival we can foresee. In the longer term, however, it should be accepted that agricultural production cannot be multiplied indefinitely. It is not more than common prudence to plan for the stabilisation of human populations before the point is reached that food production can no longer keep pace with human multiplication, and readjustment by catastrophe becomes inevitable.'[4]

In September 1969 the Institute of Biology held a symposium in London to discuss 'The Optimum Population for Britain'. A vote was taken at the meeting on the proposition that 'The optimum population for Britain has already been exceeded'. Ninety percent of the professional scientists present voted in favour. The reason, probably, was mainly ethical. Even if it were possible to sustain a world population, or a British population, many times larger than that alive at present, what purpose would this serve? If Britain succeeded in doubling its food output in order to attain a high level of self-sufficiency, would this be regarded as an excuse to permit a further doubling of the population? In the words of L. R. Taylor, the convenor of the symposium, 'The irony of a country that operates Oxfam on 50% imported food cannot be entirely explained away by economic ratiocination'.[5]

It is notoriously difficult to estimate how much food might be produced within a particular area. As we have seen in this book, many factors are involved quite apart from agricultural skills and availability of natural resources. Professor G. W. Cooke, in discussing the carrying capacity of the land[6] quotes Clark,[7] who estimated that in Asia, 680 m^2 of land would be sufficient to provide one person with shelter, 'wood' (bamboo) and food at a dietary level equal to that prevailing in Japan. This would allow a population density, in Asia, of more than 1400 persons per km^2. This is approximately four times the carrying capacity of cultivated land in Asia in the late 1960s. In the view of British biologists, then, the solution to problems of hunger present no technical difficulties and the size of human populations will be regulated by other factors long before the theoretical limit of food production is reached.

Professor Paul Ehrlich has campaigned vigorously to bring the attention of the public and of governments to bear on the complex of problems caused by the interaction of population growth, resource depletion and environmental degradation. His view, that population growth will not continue much longer at its present rate, has been repeated often and over the years he has not deviated from it, although the solutions he has proposed have become more detailed and more subtle. He summed up his position in May 1976, in an article he wrote with John P. Holdren for *Environmental Conservation*, and which *The Ecologist* reprinted as a guest editorial:

'... believing that there will be 8 thousand million people in the year 2010 is somewhat akin to believing in Santa Claus. We will indeed be fortunate if the world can support 4 thousand millions in the year 2010, and the population size may well be much less than that—as a result of a continuing sequence of disasters and a general deterioration of the carrying capacity of the planet. If by some combination of unlikely events there are 8 thousand million people alive in AD 2010, it will be a fairly sure bet that their very presence will be mortgaging the future of all humanity—dramatically degrading the environment and reducing future carrying capacities.'[8]

In 1972 he argued[9] that considering its present technologies and patterns of behaviour, the world is over-populated now; that the number of persons and the rate at which populations are growing inhibit the solution of human problems; that the limits of food production by conventional means are very close and yet roughly half the human population is undernourished or malnourished; that attempts to increase agricultural production can only tend to accelerate the deterioration of the environment and this, in turn, will reduce the long-term capacity of the environment to sustain agriculture; that rapid population growth increases the risk of major pandemics and wars; that the solution to the complex of problems must be sought in changing human attitudes. Population control, he emphasises, is not itself a panacea, and he insists that no solution is possible that does not include, indeed start from, such economic and political reforms as would share access to the world's resources more equitably. The gap between rich and poor must be reduced. Ehrlich places such reform much higher in his list of priorities than do most writers in developed countries.

Nigel Hey, an American science writer and member of Science Book Associates, which describes itself as 'an organisation of writers and technical people active in many areas of science and technology' and much of whose work involves the preparation of audio-visual material and industrial training manuals, has also considered the problem.[10] He asks questions that reflect the guilt of the rich facing the poverty of others:

'Is the prosperity of the West truly of our own making—or are we actually mining the resources of weaker nations in order to enjoy it?... What will happen to the prosperous nations when the smaller, now-impoverished countries decide that their food resources must be harvested for their own people? No one can continue to ignore the global world [*sic*] problem without ignoring his own future welfare and that of his children.'

Hey is optimistic, though, about the possibilities of increasing food production by advances in crop plant breeding and management, improved soil husbandry, better management of water resources, increased high-energy inputs in those areas of the world where they would have the greatest effect, better crop protection and the reduction of post-harvest losses, and by improving methods of fishing and aquaculture.

If Ehrlich regards the reform of economic systems as vital, Lester R. Brown goes even further:

'The need to stabilise population sooner rather than later must not be viewed in isolation, but as part of a broader effort to create a workable world order. Such an effort must not only strive to slow population growth as rapidly as possible, but it must also seek to arrest the pursuit of superaffluence.... If the developed countries continue the pursuit of superaffluence as they have so successfully over the past quarter century, then the world will be threatened as surely as if its population had multiplied several times.... A workable world order will not likely evolve without a more equitable sharing of the world's resources among countries. It is no longer possible to separate efforts to stabilise population from the way in which resources are shared.... Widening gaps in consumption among national populations in a world of shrinking geographic distances is a formula for disaster.'[11]

Brown is an authority on the world food situation and is well aware of the dangers inherent in transposing agricultural technologies from North America and Europe into the tropics and sub-tropics. Nevertheless he believes it is in the developing countries that the greatest potential for expansion exists and that this should be encouraged and exploited:

'Concentrating international assistance efforts on the expansion of food production in the poor countries could reduce upward pressure on world food prices, create additional employment in countries where continuously rising unemployment poses a serious threat to political stability, raise income, and improve nutrition for the poorest section of humanity. Because this would help satisfy basic social needs, it would also help create the motivation for smaller families, which is a prerequisite to a substantial reduction in birth rates.'[11]

Dr Keith C. Barrons, an agricultural scientist, urges readers of his popular outline of the world food problem to 'take part in foreign aid decisions', but he emphasises the need to bring each region of the earth as close to self-sufficiency in food as is possible, backing this with food reserves for emergencies. His final word is for farmers:

'Finally a word to farmers or others who have land under their stewardship. Take it as a sacred trust. You didn't make the land. It is only yours to use for a short span of time but long enough to undo thousands of years of natural soil building processes. If you keep your soil in place and practise all we have learned about fertility improvement, you can then pass it on to its next custodian with the satisfaction of having exercised good stewardship and with the knowledge that it can be more productive of food than when you took it over. Thus you will have made a valuable contribution to the food supply of future generations.'[12]

Jonathan Power and Anne-Marie Holenstein, writing in the aftermath of the 1974 FAO World Food Conference, were cynical about the willingness of the rich nations to contribute significantly to any long-term solution. In their view the only course that remains is for developing countries to choose their own developmental models and to pursue them. There are many models from which to choose, but all of them are based in the countryside, on rural communities, on agriculture. Perhaps more than other writers they show the way in which the problems of agricultural production, food supply and overall economic development are interrelated.[13]

In 1972, I, too, considered the future of world food supplies, and my conclusion then was distinctly gloomy. I argued that by the late 1970s or early 1980s the pressure of rising populations in developing countries would reduce food exports from those countries and lead to a move away from cash-cropping to provide land for food production. This would make the developed countries more dependent on home production and this, in turn, would reduce food surpluses. By the mid or late 1980s declining petroleum reserves would require widespread modifications of agriculture, especially in those countries that rely on high-energy technologies. The outcome could be increasing strife in developing countries and a deepening gulf between rich and poor accompanied, quite possibly, by wars to secure control of natural resources.[14]

The most famous attempt to evaluate future possibilities was published in 1972 as *The Limits to Growth.*[15] This study was based on a model of the world built by a large computer. It began by recording the actual historical progress of five variables—population, resources, pollution, industrial output per capita and food per capita—from 1900 to 1970. Then the model was allowed to run into the future. It predicted collapse in a short time because of the exhaustion of resources. When these were doubled, the increased pollution caused by increased industrial activity reduced food production and increased the death rate. When resources are regarded as limitless—assuming unlimited energy to permit cheap extraction and processing of the very poorest mineral ores—it was again pollution that caused collapse. When pollution controls were introduced, effectively eliminating pollution, the limit of arable land was reached. To overcome this limitation the area of agricultural land was doubled.

Although each unit of industrial production caused practically no pollution, total industrial output was so high that it was pollution that caused collapse. The modellers then tested the effect of 'perfect' birth control, but practised voluntarily, as an alternative to increasing food production. The food crisis was postponed by only a decade or two. So food output was allowed to increase again and this time the combination of dwindling resources—although they are assumed to be limitless, as resources are utilised more difficult sources have to be tapped and so the cost of extraction rises until it represents an unacceptably high proportion of total investment—and increasing population caused collapse yet again. It was not until population and industrial activity were both stabilised that 'overshoot and collapse' were avoided.

There have been many criticisms of *The Limits to Growth*, but what is significant in the present context is that the failure of food supply was a factor precipitating the population collapse in a minority of the models. Even when no increase in levels of output was assumed, the food supply was sufficient to sustain a much larger population than exists at present. It was economic and social collapse, with rising pollution, that raised the death rate.

So we see that over a comparatively short period, opinions about the future of world food supplies have ranged from one extreme to the other, from Sir George Thomson's vision of a world of plenty, peace, leisure and universal wealth, to my own 1972 fears of catastrophic failures before the end of the century. We have seen *The Limits to Growth* warnings of imminent population collapse and many more warnings of the dangers ahead unless we mend our ways and learn to live within the limits imposed by nature. Most writers have been guardedly optimistic. The problem can be solved if sufficient determination exists to solve it.

We do not need to predict the future, however. It is possible to speculate about the kind of world that may result if we make certain assumptions about what will happen. With regard to food supplies per capita—the food:population ratio—we can allow that the situation will remain as it is now, that it will improve slightly, improve a great deal, deteriorate slightly, or deteriorate a great deal. With regard to relationships between rich and poor countries, we may assume that the rich countries may become more inward-looking and protectionist, that developing countries may achieve greater economic independence, that the gap between rich and poor widens still further, or that there are catastrophes. It then becomes possible to link some of these alternatives so that we can test their plausibility.

Let us imagine that their own internal economic problems, coupled with and partly caused by rising world prices for oil and other key commodities, causes the developed countries to become much more inward-looking. Developing countries might then decide they had no choice but to devise strategies that take no account of the industrialised countries. They might look toward OPEC for economic leadership and toward such countries as China and Tanzania for developmental models designed to exploit to the full the resources available to them. This approach could be highly successful. It would be likely to increase the feelings of local and regional identity and pride, cement bonds within the developing world and make real strides toward better standards of living. Rising prosperity might induce a sharp fall in the rate of population growth in those countries where such a fall would be most advantageous. If it were coupled with increased agricultural production, this would be likely to increase the per capita food supply. Countries might then begin to specialise, the grain producers supplying feedgrains as well as food for human consumption to their wealthier trading partners.

Food surpluses might be available for export outside the developing countries. In any case the increased production would reduce pressure on world markets and so prices would fall. This would benefit the poor in the short run, but in the longer run it would have a depressive effect on the major food exporters, principally in North America, Australasia and Western Europe. In those regions production might be cut back again, as it was during the 1960s and early 1970s, to support prices.

Trade between the major blocs—what today we call 'developed' and 'developing', but those terms might cease to be appropriate—would be rather one-way. The industrial economies would become dependent on imported supplies of oil and other commodities, but the developing countries would be aiming to supply their own industrial needs from home production or from production within their own trading community. Effectively, then, wealth would drain from countries that today are rich into countries that today are poor.

The model sounds attractive and its plausibility is improved by the fact that it requires no feelings of goodwill to be exchanged between north and south!

It assumes, however, that food output increases in the south. Of course, it may not. If the response of a majority of developing countries to their economic rejection by Europe and America is to become more conservative in their domestic policies, in a desperate attempt to sustain high standards of living for their own elites, then for want of essential reforms in land tenure and management—especially of marginal lands whose productivity is low and whose soils are fragile, but whose area is vast—agriculture may stagnate or develop too slowly. This would lead to increased tension internally and externally, as countries that were hard pressed began to look enviously at the resources of their neighbours. The formation of trading communities would be inhibited, there might be increasing violence. It is not too cynical to suppose that such discord might be exploited by the rich countries as a means of securing supplies of commodities and a new era of imperialism could result.

The increase in agricultural production might be inhibited less by inflexible political systems than by adverse climatic changes. This could stimulate greater international co-operation as national governments came to recognise that the welfare of their own people could be ensured best by an admission that in the new situation available food should be shared. It is also possible, however, that countries would feel impelled to grab what they could regardless of the consequences.

If the ratio of food output to population remains much as it is at present, the world will remain dependent for its food security on surpluses produced mainly in North America. It is far from certain, however, that North America will be able to continue to supply this security. Its own arable land is now in full use. It is possible, of course, that American agriculture might achieve substantial increases in average yields. Technically no doubt this is possible. In practice, however, two factors militate against it.

The first is the cost of such increases. Presumably they would be achieved by some increase in intensiveness, requiring larger inputs of energy-intensive materials, especially fertiliser, to feed new crop varieties more responsive to nutrient. Much research effort is devoted to the development of such varieties. We should not be misled by the fact that breeders are seeking to incorporate into cereals genetic factors that make the plant photosynthesise at a higher rate. Photosynthesis is the mechanism whereby carbon is incorporated into plant tissues but plants maintain a fairly constant ratio of carbon to nitrogen. One of the theories underlying the use of fertiliser is that by increasing the nitrogen content of plant tissues, the plant itself will respond by incorporating more carbon by photosynthesis, so growing to a larger size. The search for more efficient photosynthesis merely reverses this approach. If more carbon is incorporated, then the plant will demand larger quantities of nitrogen—in agricultural parlance it will become more 'hungry'. So larger fertiliser applications will be needed.

The obvious solution to this problem is to find other, cheaper ways to supply nitrogen. This, too, may be possible. It may even be possible to breed a legume-like cereal. Unfortunately nitrogen is only one of a number of nutrients required by plants and the provision of one will require larger quantities of the others to maintain a balance. So phosphate demand will increase. In North America this may present little difficulty, since North America has large reserves of phosphates and is not dependent on North African imports. Nor does potassium (potash) present any real difficulty, since this is, or could be, mined in large quantities in Europe. It is possible, however, that shortages of sulphur and the trace elements could present problems.

All of this will increase the cost of producing the larger crop. At present farmers do not receive prices that encourage them to expand and we must remember that at present if we ask them to grow more food we must do so in a context of current varieties and current technologies. The new varieties do not actually exist as yet. Nitrogen fertiliser must be manufactured industrially and then purchased, and it is expensive. Expansion must be preceded by higher prices to provide the initial profit for reinvestment, and it must be accompanied by a high level of market security.

We must suppose, then, that before we can grow more food, food prices rise. If food prices rise, to whom will the food be sold? At present, efforts are being made internationally to provide funds to buy in surplus food in order to accumulate reserve stocks. If and when such reserves are created, they will be used to provide emergency relief and to dampen down violent price fluctuations. It is not certain that they can be acquired at all, however, even if the developed nations are willing to share the cost.

There remains a doubt about the ability of American agriculture to increase its output even when the economic constraints have been removed. The doubt arises from uncertainties about the future climate in the northern hemisphere. We need suppose no major climatic change in order to observe that the history of the climate of the arable areas of North America has often been much less favourable for agriculture than it has been for the past 30 years or so. It is far from impossible that the recent period has been unusual and that the climate may revert to its more normal, harsher, pattern, with more frequent droughts.

The likelihood is that production will continue to match demand about as closely as it does at present, provided rising prosperity in developing countries does not exert sudden violent demand pressures. Since this situation is one in which famine tends to be exported by the rich, who can buy such food as they need to make good their own harvest failures, and imported by the poor who cannot, those countries that are poor and need to import food will be able to do so only with help from outside. This help will aim to increase their own internal agricultural productivity. In other words, life will go on as it has done in the past two decades and if the experiences of that period can be used as a guide there will be little overall improvement.

It is very probable, however, that demand for food will increase dramatically. As we saw earlier, as per capita incomes rise, elasticities of demand for food are such that a threshold is reached beyond which there is an increase in the consumption of meat. This imposes strains on the grain markets, several times greater than would be exerted were consumers taking their additional food in the form of grains which they ate directly. This threshold was reached in Japan in the late 1960s, in the USSR in the early 1970s and in the oil-rich states in the mid-1970s. Behind them are several developing countries very close to a level of prosperity high enough to stimulate food demand strongly.

The immediate effect will be to raise grain prices. In a free market this should stimulate production and so, after a year or two, bring prices down again to their previous level, but leaving cereal growers more affluent. In the real world, however, it is less than certain that cereal production can be increased sufficiently to satisfy the new, higher demand. If it cannot be increased as a matter of deliberate policy, supported and encouraged by governments with an outlet guaranteed and demand high, there is no reason to suppose it can be increased by ordinary market pressures either.

In this case, prices will fluctuate wildly and the whole of the world trade in all food commodities could become caught in great cyclical swings. If feedgrain importers respond to sharp price rises by restricting their imports, prices will fall, so orders will be placed again. Chaos could ensue and its victims, as always, will be found in those poor countries that need to import grains for human consumption. Farmers will suffer, too, since it would be almost impossible for them to plan ahead in so unstable a situation, and in Britain we have the example of the chronically depressed agriculture in the late nineteenth and early twentieth centuries, resulting from just such market chaos, to provide a warning of the consequences. Thus we may expect the major agricultural producing nations to adopt more overtly protectionist policies while at the same time they try to negotiate some mechanism for damping down the price swings.

The gap between rich and poor will grow wider, perhaps much wider. It is possible that the rich countries whose *per capita* GNP has only recently brought them into the 'developed' category will provide substantial aid for the very poor, paying for this out of their increased revenue from the resources they control. Again wealth will move from rich to poor, via the newly rich. In a real sense, of course, the world in general will be poorer, since a higher proportion of all incomes will be spent on food.

If population continues to increase at more or less its present rate, while pressure on food supplies grows as a result of rising prosperity in certain areas against the rather slower increases in food output, the situation will become very critical indeed. Those wealthy enough to buy the food they need will continue to do so, but at generally higher prices. So they will be relatively poorer. In those countries adapting for the first time to a meat diet, food will be costly, but this may make meat-eating even more of a mark of social status than it is at present and so may encourage those who can do so simply to pay the price. Among the very poor, hunger will be general and mortality may rise sharply to reflect this.

This would be a truly Malthusian situation, in which population had increased in size until it pressed sufficiently hard against a constraint imposed by the limits of a resource for it to be curbed. It supposes no fundamental change in political and economic relationships between rich and poor countries. This is not necessarily ill-will on the part of the rich, so much as a degree of conceptual rigidity that prevents them from imagining an economic relationship in other than commercial terms, based on the buying and selling of commodities and manufactured goods in a framework laid down according to market principles, with minor modifications.

It is quite unrealistic to think of 'world famine', if by that we mean famine affecting the entire world or even a large part of it. A world famine would require simultaneous harvest failures in all the major producing areas, probably for several successive years. North America would have to find it difficult or impossible to feed its own population, far less to export food, and so would Europe and Australasia. Further, productivity would need to be depressed so severely that even the strongest economic incentive to expansion proved insufficient. Such circumstances are not impossible: if the northern hemisphere found itself experiencing a full ice age it might well happen. Yet it is improbable.

The true famine, if it happens, will be felt in the poorest countries and among the poorest strata of society in those countries that are only a little more prosperous. It will harm the weak, those who lack economic, political or military power.

It may require, too, that the major food exporters, principally the USA, impose a 'rationing' system on their customers. In the past year or two there has been a good deal of speculation on this subject. The argument runs that if the USA is unable to produce sufficient surpluses to meet all the demands for food, then some way will need to be found of allocating priorities. Inevitably certain customers will be favoured more highly than others. Thus, it is argued, the export of food will become an instrument of foreign policy and food will flow preferentially toward countries deemed to be 'friendly'. In the case of the USSR and China this might reflect the state of detente existing at a particular time. In the case of developing countries it might be measured in terms of voting in the United Nations, where the Group of 77 and its equivalents have often been severely critical of US actions.

The fear is understandable and it can be supported by a number of statements made inside the USA itself, not least by the CIA. Yet it overlooks the political power of the American farmer, who does not react very sympathetically to costly errors made by his politicians in pursuit of political rather than economic objectives. Thus although there are Americans who would not be averse to the use of food surpluses as diplomatic weapons, the wielding of those weapons may be more difficult than it seems. At least one attempt was made and the results were described by Professor B. Johnson:

'In July 1974 the US decided to halt grain exports to the Soviet Union pending their coming to terms over SALT. Moscow, which badly needed the grain, nevertheless reversed the US decision by October without any significant concession. Though undoubtedly inconvenienced, the Russians simply turned to the same transnational corporations which had been setting up the American deal, and imported many millions of tons of assorted grains from other countries. Moscow was inconvenienced, but it was not held to ransom. Instead it was the US which took the brunt of the embargo. The prairie farmers, who had previously been called on by the government to get all possible acreage into production, and who often had gone into debt to so so, suddenly were filling the elevators with unwanted grain. By October, US market prices had dropped from \$4·70 to \$3·80 a bushel. That controversial embargo resulted in new farm lobby demands for unrestricted access to world markets, which is why Congress has so taken against the stockpiling of food for political aid. On top of which the aid climate is such in the United States, that . . . seven-eighths of the wheat exported from the United States is now sold, less than 15 % being shipped as 'aid', and the drop in the aid share has been 40 % in the last two years. So with the potential combination of a credit to Bangladesh from the Soviet Union, Iran or Kuwait and the support of US Congress, the chances of running a lordly lifeboat policy with food now seem pretty slim.'[16]

Indeed it is not difficult to see that were the USA to make a prolonged serious attempt to use food for political ends, so that world markets had to be distorted deliberately, chaos would follow. Since most exported food is sold, it would require sellers to refuse to accept some customers but to accept others at, if not the same price, at least a price reached by a similar commercial route. What then does the seller do if his first customer should return and offer a higher price? How is the seller to know the source of the money he is offered or, indeed, the final destination of his produce? If he sells to a lower bidder, what is there to prevent that buyer from reselling at a higher price, so the American seller ends by subsidising a middleman? Would it be necessary to bring all exporters into the plot in order to prevent US policy from being reversed unwittingly in, say, Australia? In the end how will politicians reconcile the fact that American produce is sold by private corporations, not by government agents?

If private companies, and especially transnational ones, are seen to behave with political bias they will attract considerable international criticism and complaint which may be backed by positive action to curb their activities. Indeed a major criticism of them already is that their purely commercial activities can distort national economies, making it difficult for legitimate governments to pursue legitimate internal economic policies. If suddenly they were to behave in an overtly political fashion, as instruments of US foreign policy, they might suffer damaging retaliation from their own customers.

It is suggested by some that American food aid is similar politically to Arab oil. In some senses this may be so, and should the major exporters wish to form a cartel on the lines of OPEC, probably they could do so. However, the aim of a producer cartel is mainly to raise the price of its commodity in world markets. This has to be effected indiscriminately. If, then, the seller wishes to favour a particular customer, he may make an *ex gratia* payment to that customer, or extend credit, or take one of any number of steps short of lowering the price of that which he is selling. True, OPEC did impose a selective embargo on oil supplies to countries they regarded as 'unfriendly', but this was imposed without warning to take advantage of surprise, it was sustained for only a limited period because it was bound to be circumvented if the affected customers were given enough time to make alternative arrangements, and it was intended to cause real, if temporary, damage.

This is very different from what is suggested for US food, which would be a sustained embargo of certain countries, while for others prices would be determined in the normal way, and intended not to cause harm so much as to avoid giving assistance. Before anyone embarks on such a course they might study the relative success of the attempt by the United Nations to sever all trade links with the illegal regime in Southern Rhodesia, enforced by a blockade of the sea ports by which goods might enter or leave. It is more difficult than it seems to isolate any country economically.

Nor can food be compared to armaments, whose sale is controlled strictly by governments and yet whose manufacture is a major industry. Almost all armament manufacture (the exception being sporting weapons and, in some countries, small arms that are sold directly to the public) is undertaken against government contracts. While the government may not be the seller of weapons, it is a party to such sales and it provides the base market upon which an export business can be built. Were a manufacturer to attempt to trade freely overseas in armaments, not only would he contravene certain laws but he would risk losing the government licences that permit him to operate his factories legally, and the government contracts that guarantee a large part of his income. He is in a very different position from a farmer!

It is fairly certain, then, that in the years to come world trade and aid policies will become increasingly matters of achieving purely economic objectives, rather than of imposing political systems or furthering foreign policies. As we saw in Chapter 12, developing countries today are much more interested in improving their trading positions than in persuading the rich to provide them with charitable handouts.

If this trend continues, if the newly rich countries continue to accept a major part of the responsibility for helping the very poor, and if the world climate and technological improvements permit food production to increase sufficiently to meet effective demand, then we may experience the best possible outcome.

Initially world food markets are likely to be unstable because of the lack of reserves to buffer prices, combined with the dietary changes that produce sudden fluctuations in demand for grain. However, improvements in trading relations favouring the poor countries will permit a general rise in their prosperity, assisted by various forms of economic and technical aid from countries whose wealth is founded on reserves of commodities vital to the economies of the industrial nations. Thus the newly rich nations will form a bridge between the traditionally rich and the very poor. The improvement in living standards among the poorest peoples will lead to increased demand for food, but it will also enable those countries to develop their own agriculture to meet at least the bulk of this demand. So they will become more genuinely independent and the world's dependence on North American food surpluses will be reduced. These surpluses can then be diverted into reserves to provide greater stability between good and bad years.

It is inevitable, certainly in this model, that the balance of economic power will become redistributed. The industrial nations will become relatively less wealthy. This need imply no inevitable drop in their actual living standards but it will mean a substantial narrowing of the gap between their level of affluence and that of the populations of the poorest countries. The economic influence of countries with valuable resources will probably stabilise, leaving them in a very strong position which they may continue to hold even after the resources on which they depend have been largely depleted. The rise in prosperity throughout the developing countries will lead to reductions, perhaps quite rapid and dramatic reductions, in birth rates, so bringing about a levelling off in the graph of rising population. In some countries populations may actually decline. This may happen, for example, in parts of Western Europe that are in any case rather overcrowded. Falling birth rates will alarm governments, who will take postively pro-natalist attitudes, but there is no reason to suppose they will be any more successful in increasing their population as a result of direct policies than other countries have been in reducing them.

Portugal, for example, has sought to increase the size of its population for many years with no real success. The country lacks a labour force sufficiently large to permit effective industrialisation that would make the country more prosperous. Yet its workers continue to migrate into other areas of Europe where work is easier to find. Ireland has a similar problem (although in recent years the rate of emigration has fallen sharply) and so do some Eastern European countries. In the end, then, the world will adjust to economic and political changes, but at a much higher global average per capita income, and the problems of 'structural famine'—the famine that is exported from one region to another—will be solved.

Already the 'Three Worlds' have divided themselves into four, and we are assuming that this division will continue. Our optimistic model assumes, further, that what we may call the Third World (the resource-rich countries) align themselves with the Fourth World (the very poor). So far they have shown every sign of doing so, but they may not continue in the same direction. They derive their income from sales to the industrial nations and since in a seller's market they have considerable influence over the prices they charge, it is in the interests of the industrial nations to woo them. The industrial nations seek, and will continue to seek, both to negotiate prices favourable to themselves and also to attract back the money they have paid in the form of investment in their industries. So the Third World nations may find themselves drawn more and more into the orbit of the industrial nations of the First and Second Worlds. As they themselves acquire a more secure industrial base to their own economies, the similarities among the first Three Worlds may come to exceed the differences and the Three Worlds may find themselves far removed from the Fourth.

The gap between rich and poor would continue to widen and at an even more rapid pace. Most trade would take place among the nations of the first Three Worlds with both commodities and money, and the Fourth World would be largely excluded. In this situation it is possible that the transference of famine to them would be more pronounced that it is today and all their efforts at development would be frustrated. They would lack capital for investment, so productivity would be low and unemployment high. Workers with skills would tend to emigrate to regions of higher employment, so the Fourth World would suffer an accelerated 'brain drain'. Such a drain is already a serious problem in some developing countries.

Life for most of the peoples of these countries could become very wretched, but even then the prognosis is not necessarily one of utter hopelessness. Largely excluded from the economy of the rich, the countries of the Fourth World could develop trading links among themselves and so achieve a different kind of development—different but in human terms no less real—based on the exploitation of those human and other resources that they do have. New measures of prosperity might have to be found for them, for in conventional terms of per capita GNP their low incomes might come to belie their true standard of living. Probably they would need to achieve a degree of economic isolation to protect their emerging manufacturing industries, and the movement of skilled workers outside the bloc might need to be curtailed. There is some evidence today that suggests this kind of development may occur. Development would be much slower than it need be otherwise, it might experience acute difficulties involving great suffering, but it might succeed in the end.

Two high risk scenarios remain. In one, the alignment of the Third and Fourth Worlds poses a perceived threat to the economies of the First and Second. In the case of the OPEC oil embargo this almost happened and there was talk of a war, initiated by the west, to secure control over Middle Eastern oilfields. For various reasons it did not happen—that time. There can be no certainty that at some future date, threatened with the failure of supply of an essential commodity, a desperate government might not launch a Suez-type attack that could not be checked in time to prevent it from triggering a major, probably nuclear, war in Europe, North America or the USSR.

It is unlikely that food itself could be the resource to create the initial conflict, since world trade in food is controlled by the countries that are capable of going to war. Certain resources required for the production of food could be the subject of an attack, however. The most obvious candidate is North African phosphate. If the phosphate producers were to ration production, as OPEC did with oil, and if they were to direct their supplies mainly to developing countries financed by, say, OPEC, then Europe could find itself deprived. It is just possible that the USA or the USSR, the two major world producers of phosphate, could step in to make good deficiencies, but this is far from certain since traditionally the whole of their production has been consumed in North America and in Eastern Europe respectively, and since both producers would be concerned mainly to maintain their own agricultural output. Faced with absolute shortage, then, and with their food production threatened, it is not impossible that a European government might invade or sanction an invasion by a country with a more overt political difference.

The other high risk scenario assumes climatic deterioration. As we have seen, the world's dependence on North American food surpluses is also a dependence on the climate of that continent, as well as on the climates of the world in general. There is an opinion held by a number of climatologists that the weather patterns experienced in North America over the last 30 years or so may not be maintained, that they have been unusually favourable to agriculture. Should the weather deteriorate, reducing production; real shortages of food could occur. If such a climatic deterioration were reproduced in Europe and the USSR, the result could be catastrophic. Food prices would soar, there might well be acute shortages of staple foods in the Soviet Union and in parts of Europe, both Eastern and Western, and the poorest countries would find themselves priced out of the markets in which they had hoped to buy commodities that would have averted severe hunger. Tensions within poor countries would increase, as such food as was available found its way into the cupboards of the rich and as merchants profited from black markets.

It is not a pleasant prospect but it is far from impossible. It is the scenario that corresponds most closely to 'world starvation'. Its worst effects might be averted by strict food rationing in North America and Europe, so reducing waste and maximising the food available for export. The effects would be reduced still further by enforcing—and it might require enforcement—a change in diets among the citizens of Western Europe, North America, Australasia and among the most affluent sections of societies elsewhere.

It is possible to eat more economically in terms of food resources. If grain that is fit for human consumption but that is fed to livestock were diverted back to human needs, diets would become much duller for some people, but larger numbers could be kept alive. To do this would require the rich to accept voluntarily a degree of self-restraint they have never shown in the past. The acceptance would need to be voluntary in some countries, since although governments can enforce measures upon their own people, they depend on those people for their mandate to govern at all, so that if the measure that is legislated is not accepted, the government itself may be replaced. Thus the rich could continue to buy all the food they wished, more or less, though they would pay much more for it.

To choose not to do so, to choose to use scarce resources more thriftily, would demonstrate a commitment to the welfare of others, members of different societies, different cultures, speaking diffferent languages, wearing different clothes, worshipping different gods, and bearing skins of different colours, peoples living thousands of miles away, that may seem incredible. Would you make real sacrifices in your standard of living to help someone you have never seen, will never see, with whom you could not converse without an interpreter and whom even then you might not understand since your views of the world would be so different? Would you do it to help someone who hates you, and who will continue to hate you no matter what you do, since he blames you for his plight?

The world food situation is serious but there is no reason to accept as inevitable the most gloomy prognosis we can find. Things can improve but if they are to do so, then everyone in developing and developed countries alike must become more aware of the nature of the problem. It is not simply that the world is incapable of producing sufficient food to satisfy the needs of a growing population. It is that resources of all kinds are monopolised by the rich. The rich are not necessarily wicked but they inhabit a world governed by rules that repress the poor. It is not just that the rich do too little to help the poor; they prevent the poor from helping themselves.

In the end, if everyone is to be fed, we—the rich—must accept the right of others to share what we have. Possibly we will have to accept levels of consumption rather lower than those we enjoy today. This need not be onerous and, so far as food is concerned, there is every reason to believe that economies would bring benefits in the form of improved health. Most important of all, from a philosophical point of view, we must accept the right of people to be different, indeed we must rejoice in the differences. We must abandon our assumption that our own way of life, our own values, are universally held, or could be, or should be. We must find pleasure in watching others discover ways of their own, without inferring from their chosen paths a criticism of our own.

Internationally the first need is to improve economic relationships between rich and poor and to reform monetary systems so as to permit developing countries to develop. This is far more important than direct aid. It means that we should allow imports of manufactured goods from developing countries in preference to ones from developed countries. It means that when I, as a consumer, face a choice between an article made in Europe and one made in Africa or Asia or Latin America, I should buy the one from the developing country.

Adequate food reserves need to be accumulated. Ironically one way to assist in this is for consumers to favour products from the Third World. Anything that promotes their general economic development will help to expand their agricultural production, so relieving pressure on world supplies, so allowing the existence of short term surpluses.

As Paul Ehrlich once said that there is no natural law that says everything will come right in the end. It may not. Yet we possess the information that allows us to diagnose the malaise accurately and we possess such technologies as we need to heal it. So we must conclude that if we want to allow every person in the world a decent standard of living, free from hunger and desperate poverty, then we are able to do so.

I do not believe the survival of mankind is threatened, although major thermonuclear war might well destroy utterly civilisation as we know it. I believe even more is at stake: our humanity. The challenge of the last years of the twentieth century is for human beings to realise a moral potential I am sure they possess. Human history records countless instances of acts performed out of love of human beings for other human beings, acts of altruism. We need to infuse such a spirit into a large majority of people and, through them, into their governments. We need confidence, the confidence to know not simply that remedies can be found but that mankind is worth saving. Much that has been written about the human predicament in recent years suggests doubt. Today the need is for sufficient courage to relax and trust one another.

If we succeed, we will add a new dimension to history and quite possibly raise civilisation to new heights. If we fail, then we record for those who follow, in a record that may survive long after man himself has become extinct, that we found it impossible to live together, that each of us was prepared to sacrifice the entire human race provided we could remain not alive—no one asks so much sacrifice as that—but vain and profligate.

We cannot judge ourselves, but across the centuries there will come others, and they will judge.

REFERENCES

1. Thomson, Sir George (1955). *The Foreseeable Future.* Cambridge University Press, London.
2. Borgstrom, G. (1965). *The Hungry Planet.* Collier-Macmillan, New York.
3. Hutchinson, J. (1966). Land and human populations, *Adv. Sci.*, **23,** 241–54.
4. Hutchinson, J. (ed.) (1968). *Population and Food Supply.* Cambridge University Press, London.
5. Taylor, L. R. (ed.) (1970). Introduction to *The Optimum Population for Britain.* Academic Press, London.
6. Cooke, G. W. (1970). The carrying capacity of the land in the year 2000, in Taylor, op. cit.
7. Clark, C. (1968). *Population Growth and Land Use*, pp. 123–57. Macmillan, London.
8. Ehrlich, P. R. and Holdren, J. P. (1976). Eight thousand million by the year 2010, *The Ecologist*, **6**(4), 121. Wadebridge, Cornwall, UK. Reprinted from *Environmental Conservation*, **2**(4). Geneva.
9. Ehrlich, P. R. and Ehrlich, A. H. (1972). *Population, Resources, Environment*, pp. 441–2. W. H. Freeman, San Francisco.
10. Hey, N. (1971). *How Will We Feed The Hungry Billions?* Julian Messner, New York.
11. Brown, L. R. (1974). *In the Human Interest.* W. W. Norton, New York.
12. Barrons, K. C. (1975). *The Food in Your Future*, p. 173. Van Nostrand Reinhold, New York.
13. Power, J. and Holenstein, A.-M. (1976). *World of Hunger.* Maurice Temple-Smith, London.
14. Allaby, M. (1972). *Who Will Eat?* pp. 245–6. Tom Stacey, London.
15. Meadows, D. H., Meadows, D. L., Randers, J. and Behrens, W. W. (1972). *The Limits to Growth.* Earth Island, London.
16. Johnson, B. (1976). 'Eco-fascists or nuclear ostriches?', *The Ecologist*, **6**(6), 201.

BIBLIOGRAPHY

AAAS (1967). *Agriculture and the Quality of Our Environment*. American Association for the Advancement of Science, Washington.

AAC (1970). *Modern Farming and the Soil*. Agricultural Advisory Council, HMSO, London.

ADAS (1976). *Wildlife Conservation in Semi-Natural Habitats on Farms*. Agricultural Development and Advisory Service, HMSO, London.

Allaby, M. and Allen, F. (1974). *Robots Behind the Plow*. Rodale Press, Emmaus, Penn., USA.

Angelopoulos, A. (1972). *The Third World and the Rich Countries: Prospects for the Year* 2000. Praeger, New York.

Aspen Institute for Humanistic Studies (1975). *Global Justice and Development*. Overseas Development Council, Washington.

Barker, T. C., McKenzie, J. C. and Yudkin, J. (1966). *Our Changing Fare: Two Hundred Years of British Food Habits*. Macgibbon and Kee, London.

Baron, S. (1972). *The Desert Locust*. Eyre-Methuen, London.

Bellerby, J. R. (ed.) (1970). *Factory Farming*. British Association for the Advancement of Science, London.

Bender, B. (1975). *Farming in Prehistory*. John Baker, London.

Borgstrom, G. (1969). *Too Many: A Study of the Earth's Biological Limitations*. Collier-Macmillan, New York.

Brothwell, D. and Brothwell, P. (1969). *Food in Antiquity*. Thames and Hudson, London.

Burnett, J. (1966). *Plenty and Want*. Nelson, London.

Coe, M. D. (1964). The chinampas of Mexico, *Scientific American*. W. H. Freeman, San Francisco, July.

Collis, J. S. (1973). *The Worm Forgives the Plough*. Chas. Knight, London.

Dimbleby, G. W. (1965). The origin and use of heath soils, *J. Soil Ass.*, **13**(6) and **13**(7). Haughley, Suffolk, UK.

Donaldson, J. G. F. and Barber, D. (1969). *Farming in Britain Today*. Pelican, Harmondsworth, UK.

Evans, G. E. (1956). *Ask the Fellows Who Cut the Hay*. Faber, London.

Evans, G. E. (1960). *The Horse in the Furrow*. Faber, London.

Ewer, R. F. (1963). The contribution made by studies of the associated mammalian faunas, *S.A. J. of Sci.*, **59**.

Eyre, S. R. (ed.) (1971). *World Vegetation Types*. Macmillan, London.

FAO (1970). *Agricultural Development: A Review of FAO's Field Activities*. Food and Agriculture Organisation of the UN, Rome.

FAO Periodical: *Ceres*. Rome.

Foth, H. D. and Turk, L. M. (1972). *Fundamentals of Soil Science*. Wiley, London.

Green, M. B. (1976). *Pesticides, Boon or Bane?* Elek, London.

Greene, D. L. (1970). Environmental influences on Pleistocene hominid dental evolution. *Bioscience*, **20**.

Harlan, J. R. (1970). Evolution of cultivated plants, in Frankel, O. H. and Bennett, E. (eds). *Genetic Resources in Plants: Their Exploration and Conservation*. IBP Handbook No. 11, London.

Hester, J. J. (1970). Ecology of the North American Paleo-Indian, *Bioscience*, **20**.

Hickling, C. F. (1968). *The Farming of Fish*. Pergamon, Oxford.

Hicks, Sir C. S. (1975). *Man and Natural Resources*. Croom Helm, London.

Hicks, U. K. (1974). *The Large City: A World Problem*. Macmillan, London.

Howe, J. W. (1975). *The US and World Development: Agenda for Action*. Overseas Development Council/Praeger, New York.

Hudson, K. (1972). *Patriotism with Profit*. Evelyn, London.

Hudson, N. (1971). *Soil Conservation*. Batsford, London.

Hunt, C. B. (1972). *Geology of Soils*. W. H. Freeman, San Francisco.

Hutchinson, J. (1966). Land and human populations, *Adv. Sci.* **23**.

IAEA (1972). *The Sterile-Insect Technique and its Field Applications*. FAO/IAEA, Vienna.

IAEA (1972). *Polyploidy and Induced Mutations on Plant Breeding*. FAO/IAEA, Vienna.

IAEA (1973). *Induced Mutations for Disease Resistance in Crop Plants*. FAO/IAEA, Vienna.

Lockeretz, W., Klepper, R., Gertler, M., Fast, S. and O'Leary, D. (1975). *Energy in Corn Belt Crop Production*. CBNS.

McNamara, R. (1973). *One Hundred Countries, Two Billion People*. Praeger, New York.

MAFF (1968). *A Century of Agricultural Statistics: Great Britain* 1866–1966. Ministry of Agriculture, Fisheries and Food, HMSO, London.

MAFF Annual: *Annual Review of Agriculture*. HMSO, London.

Manley, G. (1952). *Climate and the British Scene*. Fontana, London.

Mellanby, K. (1967). *Pesticides and Pollution*. Collins, London.

Mellanby, K. (1975). *Can Britain Feed Itself?* Merlin, London.

Mumford, L. (1961). *The City in History*. Penguin, Harmondsworth, UK.

Owen, M. (1973). Resources under pressure—water, in *Intensive Agriculture and the Environment*. CICRA Symposium. An Foras Talúntais, Dublin.

Partridge, M. (1973). *Farm Tools Through the Ages*. Osprey, Reading, UK.

Piotrow, P. T. (1973). *World Population Crisis: the United States Response*. Praeger, New York.

Pollard, E., Hooper, M. D. and Moore, N. W. (1974). *Hedges*. Collins, London.

Smagorinsky, J. (1963). General circulation experiments with the primitive equations, 1: The Basic Experiment, *Mon. Wea. Rev.*, **91**(3).

Steffan, R. (1971). *Introduction to Organic Farming Methods and Organic Markets*. Rodale Press, Emmaus, USA.

UNRISD (1971). *A Study of the Social and Economic Implications of the Large-Scale Introduction of High-Yielding Varieties of Food-grain: A Selection of Readings*. United Nations Research Institute for Social Development, Geneva.

Waller, R. (1973). *Be Human or Die*. Chas. Knight, London.

Wareing, P. F. and Cooper, J. P. (eds.) (1971). *Potential Crop Production.* Heinemann Educational Books, London.

Zohary, D. (1970). Centers of diversity and centers of origin, in Frankel, O. H. and Bennett, E. (eds). *Genetic Resources in Plants: Their Exploration and Conservation.* IBP Handbook No. 11, London.

INDEX